THIS BOOK IS NO LONGER PROPERTY OF
THE UNIVERSITY OF CHICAGO LIBRARY

Anecdotal Modernity

Buchreihe der ANGLIA/
ANGLIA Book Series

Edited by
Lucia Kornexl, Ursula Lenker, Martin Middeke,
Gabriele Rippl, Daniel Stein

Advisory Board
Laurel Brinton, Philip Durkin, Olga Fischer, Susan Irvine,
Andrew James Johnston, Christopher A. Jones, Terttu Nevalainen,
Derek Attridge, Elisabeth Bronfen, Ursula K. Heise, Verena Lobsien,
Laura Marcus, J. Hillis Miller, Martin Puchner

Volume 68

Anecdotal Modernity

Making and Unmaking History

Edited by
James Dorson, Florian Sedlmeier,
MaryAnn Snyder-Körber, and Birte Wege

DE GRUYTER

For an overview of all books published in this series, please see
http://www.degruyter.com/view/serial/36292

ISBN 978-3-11-062953-8
e-ISBN (PDF) 978-3-11-066849-0
e-ISBN (EPUB) 978-3-11-066573-4
ISSN 0340-5435

Bibliographic information published by the Deutsche Nationalbibliothek
The Deutsche Nationalbibliothek lists this publication in the Deutsche Nationalbibliografie;
detailed bibliographic data are available on the Internet at http://dnb.dnb.de.

© 2020 Walter de Gruyter GmbH, Berlin/Boston
Printing and binding: CPI books GmbH, Leck

www.degruyter.com

For Ulla Haselstein

Acknowledgements

The contributions to this book grew out of a conference held in 2018 at the John F. Kennedy Institute for North American Studies in Berlin with the title "Exemplary Singularity: Fault Lines of the Anecdotal." We would like to thank everyone involved in organizing the conference without which this volume would never have seen the light of day, including the indispensable administrative coordination by Roswitha Seidel and Catya de Laczkovich, the dedicated support from our student assistants Ronja Nayeri and Solveig Raschpichler, and the program and poster design by Hannah Nelson-Teutsch. We would also like to thank the German Research Foundation (Deutsche Forschungsgemeinschaft) and the Graduate School of North American Studies at Freie Universität Berlin for generously funding the conference.

The long journey from conference to finished manuscript would not have been possible without the laudable efforts of our translator, Michael Thomas Taylor, who made this book a bridge between different languages and disciplines. For copyediting we owe our deep gratitude to Ronja Nayeri, Solveig Raschpichler, Stefan Iacob, and especially Cynthia Schmitt, who was with this project from start to finish, and whose diligence and perseverance went beyond all expectations.

It is more difficult to pinpoint intellectual debts. We are grateful for the contributors to this volume for their willingness to bring the insights of specific disciplines into a larger interdisciplinary conversation. However, if there is any one person who has provided the intellectual stimulus and guidance over the years without which this book would be unthinkable, it is our mentor, colleague, and friend Ulla Haselstein. Thank you!

James Dorson, Florian Sedlmeier, MaryAnn Snyder-Körber, and Birte Wege
Berlin and Würzburg, 2020

Table of Contents

Florian Sedlmeier and MaryAnn Snyder-Körber
Introduction —— 1

TRUTH

Gerhard Regn
The Heathen in Heaven: Anecdote and Truth in Dante's *Commedia*
    Translated by Michael Thomas Taylor —— 33

Verena Olejniczak Lobsien
Anecdotal Ambiguity: Andrew Marvell —— 53

Helmbrecht Breinig
A Hideous and Intolerable … Anecdote? *Moby-Dick* and Questions of Truth Seen from the Human and the Non-Human Side —— 69

EVENT

Bettine Menke
Heinrich von Kleist's "Anecdote from the Last War": W-hole, the Joke an Anecdote (Nearly) Made
    Translated by Michael Thomas Taylor —— 85

Inka Mülder-Bach
Individual Case, Example, Exception: The Range of the Anecdotal in Fontane
    Translated by Michael Thomas Taylor —— 111

Andreas Mahler
Once is Nothing at All is Once: Traces of Eventfulness in Joyce and Beckett —— 131

Gabriele Schwab
The Politics of Splitting: Gertrude Stein's "Reflection on the Atomic Bomb" —— 145

STORY

Heinz Ickstadt
Plot and Anecdote in Henry James and Julian Barnes —— 157

Thomas Claviez
The Relevance of the Irrelevant: Wisdom and/of Contingency —— 169

Winfried Siemerling
Accumulated Time, the Anecdote, and the Vertical Imagination —— 181

RUMOR

Ralph J. Poole
The Fun of Deep Gossip: Lord Cornbury as Queen in Drag —— 199

Hendrik Birus
An Anecdote Peddler from the Age of Goethe
    Translated by Michael Thomas Taylor —— 217

Frank Kelleter
Anecdotal Manifestations of the Evangelical Here and Now: Four Conversions in Jonathan Edwards's Northampton —— 229

DETAIL

Friedrich Teja Bach
The Cage of the Image and the Trace of the Snail: On the Language of Pictorial Detail
    Translated by Michael Thomas Taylor —— 245

Susanne von Falkenhausen
Anecdote vs. History: Jeff Wall's *Dead Troops Talk*
    Translated by Michael Thomas Taylor —— 253

Christof Decker
A Unique Universalism: Ben Shahn and the Rhetoric of Visual Anecdotes —— 264

Andrew S. Gross
Wallace Stevens: Anecdote and Lyric —— 279

CODA

Anselm Haverkamp
Philosophy and Anecdote: Hegel's "Lehrer Löffler" —— 295

Barbara Vinken
"Fleurs de Paris" —— 299

List of Contributors —— 303

Florian Sedlmeier and MaryAnn Snyder-Körber
Introduction

Abstract: The introduction argues for the centrality of the anecdote to modernity. Anecdotal forms do not only circulate widely throughout the communication channels and discourse networks characteristic of the modern. In this circulation, anecdotes work to forge connections, create contexts, and account for world conditions in new forms of writing and particularly historiography. The introductory chapter further outlines key elements of the anecdote as a form and narrative mode through a close reading of Dorothy Parker's *nomen est omen* poem "Anecdote" (1926). A discussion of the new historicism foregrounds the anecdote's potential to both "make" and "unmake" historical constructions, to bolster as much as to destabilize established power. *Anecdotal Modernity: The Making and Unmaking of History* explores these dynamics in case studies covering examples from the threshold of the early modern period to the present, brought together through their focus on "Truth," "Event," "Story," "Rumor," and "Detail."

Keywords: Dorothy Parker, Hannah Arendt, Minor Forms, Networked Modernity, New Historicism.

1 Anecdotal Modernity

The anecdote is endemic to modernity

Modernity, in this assertion, is understood in terms of the interconnections created by technologies of travel and communication that coincide with the rise of global trade, colonialism, and imperialism first formed in the so-called "age of exploration." New relations of time, space, possibility, and ultimately also authority took shape through these developments. It is not just that a "new world" was discovered or that the limits of the "known" world were extended. The horizons of the "knowable" were expanded.

How to tell the story of that kind of change? While the story of modernization has most commonly been framed in terms of disruptions that "melt" formerly solid orders of life and "disembed" human subjects,[1] more recent

---

[1] On "melting" of formerly solid orders, see Berman (1988), varying Engels and Marx (1955: 13). On "disembedded" human subjects, see Giddens (1990: 21–28).

https://doi.org/10.1515/9783110668490-003

global historical approaches highlight the creation of new integrative connections.[2] In these readings, telegraphy, printing, and other forms of mechanical (and eventually digital) reproduction such as photography and film converge with routes of travel, capitalist exchange, and spheres of influence. Together, these institutions and forces do not so much "disembed" as "re-embed" subjects in new structures of space and time as well as in increasingly convergent patterns of social organization and bodily comportment down to ideas, images, and aspirations. Modernity, from this vantage point, is less a chronological category or a conceptual construction imposed on experience to transform contingency into causal order. Rather, it results from the lateral connections created by the medial "networking [of] the world" (Mattelart 2000) and "*cultures of circulation*" that do not merely "*transmit*" knowledge, as anthropologists Benjamin Lee and Edward LiPuma underscore (2002: 192; original italics). Circulation and exchange are rather "constitutive acts in themselves," shaping the modern world into a recognizable landscape (ibid.).[3] Global historian Sebastian Conrad speaks more specifically of the "repetition in movement" that characterizes circulation (2016: 101). Through this mechanism, exchange can be transformed into the "sustained and potentially patterned" connection (ibid.) that fellow historian Carol Gluck calls the "grammar of modernity" (2011: 676). These structures might bring forth different articulations in varying locations and time frames. They contain multiple and/or entangled modernities.[4] The underlying grid nonetheless persists, not least because these "grammatical" connections are perpetually self-constituting and strengthening. "Modernity is not optional," Gluck notes, "sad but true" (2011: 676).

Thus, to grasp modernity and its re-embedding of the subject in new frameworks, we have to look more closely at circulation and pose slightly different questions. Namely, what powers, feeds, and keeps the machineries of circulation moving? Alternatively phrased and focused, what circulates most widely and is repeated most frequently? Those questions direct us to different perspectives than either the older modernization theories with their sweeping pronouncements or newer global histories focused on material and technological transfers have attuned us to. For what circulates most widely and intensively has to be the latest hearsay, bits of rumor, "have you heard?" stories, and the witty report on "you-know-who" passed on with a raised eyebrow as well as narratives related and responded to with straight-faced pragmatism. These can be snippets lifted

---

[2] Cf. Bayly (2004); Conrad (2016); Osterhammel (2014).
[3] See also Lee and LiPuma (2004: 1–32).
[4] Cf. Eisenstadt (2017: 1–28); Therborn (2003).

from front-page headlines or back-page miscellanies as well as thumbnail sketches that succinctly sum up what we need to know about a particular person, place, or event. A medially updated version of this list would necessarily include the latest tweet, viral meme, and news flash. Epic forms are understood to restore a sense of totality in states of "transcendental homelessness" (Lukács 1971: 61). Similarly, "grand narratives" and "strong theories" hold the promise of wholly deciphered coherence.[5] All certainly travel across the communication networks constitutive of modernity.[6] However, none do so with the speed nor with the ease of the short narrative, (purportedly) drawn from life, and "told as being in itself interesting or striking" (*OED* s.v. "anecdote, n." 2019): in sum, the anecdote. If modernity rests on circulation, the anecdote may be a prime narrative form of modernity.

This volume hones in on the anecdote as the briefest of narrative forms, but one with exponential potential for convergence with other medial forms and practices as well as for wide and frequent circulation on its own. In its focus on a specific event, the anecdote has "an essentially dramatic structure" (Gossman 2003: 145). Attention is thus directed toward a singular action. Yet in being purportedly taken from life, as opposed to being invented by the dramatist's pen, awareness is equally attuned to the textures, colorings, and other singularities captured in the encounter. And that attention is not fleeting. Anecdotes possess a "touch of the real," as a key account phrases it (Gallagher and Greenblatt 2000: 20–38). While short forms might seem inevitably ephemeral, drifting out of memory and/or literally into the recycling bin with yesterday's paper, the connection to "the real" adds weight and significance beyond a single news cycle.

Ultimately, however, it might be the frequent "oddness" of anecdotes that secures their longevity (Wood 2019: 6).[7] The specifics are evocative and the situation is dramatic, but what does their convergence in a single narrative signify? In raising but not definitively answering this question, anecdotes engage reflection as they resist summation and abstraction. Such affordances secure the short and enigmatic narrative pride of place within projects that are keen on thinking through the materially and narratively specific and rethinking it: from the use of anecdotes as a field for thought experiments in philosophy and Enlightenment pedagogies to the more contemporary nonconceptualism of the German

---

5 Cf. Lyotard (1984: 31–37); Sedgwick (2003: 123–152).
6 Cf. Said (1982).
7 Cf. also Fleming (2011: "Kannitverstan").

philosopher Hans Blumenberg in which the drive of curiosity (not the stasis of conclusions) is key.[8]

This interest in the specific unto the idiosyncratic further combines with the modest scale of such stories to connect the evocativeness of the anecdote very strongly with the detail. A feature of the visual as well as the narrative arts, the detail is able to seize attention, drawing the eye away from overall composition and intention. Such tendencies do not render the detail or its narrative counterpart, the microstory, wholly destructive, however. Just as details can be compounded into larger pictures, anecdotal narratives can certainly be expanded and worked into more extended narratives. Indeed, the slightness and enigmatic oddity of the anecdote invite, even provoke, such expansion, as when minute observation serves as the "germ" from which a longer narration such as the novel develops (James 1984: 1071). Vividness sparks interest, while dramatic situation draws us in to generate the engagement that marketing and new media scholars describe as "sticky" and understand as the essential correlate of "spreadability": the intensive and extensive dispersal of content without which products, but also ideas and narratives "die" in the attention-driven circuitries of networked modernity.[9] Just as significantly, compact anecdotal materials compel collection. From the late eighteenth century on, miscellanies, almanacs, anthologies, calendars, and compendiums become a prominent means for bringing together small stories.[10] The consequences of such collections potentially exceed the sum of compiled parts. Sticking, spreading, amassing, anecdotes become the building blocks of histories that do not merely list events. They rather create context and account for the world as it is experienced and perceived. In this process, a new kind of authority is created: history not merely as a record or narrative, but also as world and knowledge production.

Thus, the boldest arguments to be made in connection with the anecdote go beyond the observation that the short, striking narrative is to be found everywhere in modernity: from the whispered rumors and smudgy newsprint pages that make up the devalued low-cultural reaches to the elevated heights of literature and scholarly practice. First, more than simply being present, the form appears to both feed and forge the historical conditions of modernity as well as the discourses of history that strive to render these conditions decipherable. A second claim is arguably more daring: the anecdote is able to accomplish the

---

8 Cf. Fleming (2012: 25); Zill (2014).
9 Cf. Jenkins et al. (2013: 3–4 and generally 1–46); Gladwell (2000: 89–132).
10 Cf. Fenves (2001: 155) and in overview Hilzinger (1997: 22–50).

work of "re-embedding" the modern subject in new contexts of connections and understanding not in spite of, but precisely due to being thoroughly and ineluctably minor.

In the remainder of this introduction, we aim to add weight to these assertions. First, we flesh out the formal characteristics of the anecdote as a distinct narrative mode by way of a self-proclaimed poetic "Anecdote." Second, we hone in on mobilizations of the anecdote within analytical practices intent on intervening in the epistemological conditions and narrative assessments of modernity. Specifically, we examine the new historicism as an exemplary project of making and unmaking history through anecdotal modes. After considering what the anecdote is and what the anecdotal mode enables analytically, we conclude with the contributions to this volume and their illumination of key elements of the anecdote from the fourteenth century to the present.

2 Modes of the Minor, or: Towards an Anatomy of Anecdote

As we are speaking of the anecdote, however, we necessarily have to start out small. Minor denotes lesser. More precisely, it means "the lesser (in any sense) of two things [...]; relatively small or (now) esp. unimportant; not regarded as being among the most notable of a specified group of persons or things; of little significance or consequence" (*OED* s.v. "minor adj. and n." 2019). The anecdote is minor in its material realization. Simply put, it is short, as the twentieth-century wit Dorothy Parker illustrates with an economy that can only be described as congenially anecdotal. Her *nomen est omen* poem "Anecdote" (1926) exemplifies the form in four compact lines:

> So silent I when Love was by
> He yawned, and turned away;
> But Sorrow clings to my apron-strings,
> I have so much to say. (2006: 88)

The composition comes in at just under twenty-five words (the use of the compound "apron-strings" brings the official word count down to twenty-four) and 109 characters total. Parker's quatrain would thus have been affordable as a telegraph as well as highly suitable for newspaper reprinting. It could neatly fill in typesetting gaps and solidify well into a boilerplate block.¹¹ Today, the poem would fit easily within the 280-character constraint of a tweet. Such formal brevity is apparent before counting or even reading begins. A written anecdote rarely exceeds a page and can, thus, be recognized by the scanning eye alone.

A reading of those scant lines of Parker's poem reveals an alignment of "relatively small" form with "unimportant" substance. "Anecdote" not only fills (and leaves open) printable space, it also reflects on its own minor form. Minor denotes a specific narrowness of focus in line with the "lesser than" quality of the anecdote; attention is directed towards the detail, the small rather than the grand gesture. Accordingly, the "drama" upon which Parker's "Anecdote" turns is the linkage of the two slight movements outlined in the second line: the yawn of the male beloved, followed by the turning of his body away from the poem's implicitly female speaker. By word-count measure, the five-word line is the shortest in the poem. Structurally, "He yawned, and turned away" is certainly the least poetically "showy" segment of the poem's four lines. It is clearly mimicking everyday speech. There, the formulation would hardly register. In the poem, however, the sketch of two small movements in the most compact and quotidian language possible creates a spare, yet somehow impactful image. What precisely is the reader being prompted to picture? Each action is simple, ordinary, trivial even. What the gestures outline together, though, is not insignificant: the word sequence follows a line of action, drawing out an arc of disdainful detachment.

For all its dramatic structuring and, on occasion, dramatic effects, the anecdote hardly rises to the level of genre. As Parker's poem ably demonstrates, this is not because anecdotes lack recognizable and repeatable characteristics. They are excluded from genre orderings because they are, quite simply, ignored. As accounts allegedly drawn from life, focused on details, and rendered in seemingly unstudied and even "chatty" language (Fleming 2011: "The Perfect Story" 73), anecdotes operate below the kind of cultural gatekeeping radar focused on the purity of form. Anecdotes can certainly be artfully shaped, but in those cases, the artistic achievement proceeds from the premise that anecdotal materials have been reshaped.¹² Anecdotes overall are not aligned with art,

---

11 Parker would have been well aware of this through her longstanding involvement in the magazine world, where she had to compose captions and such filler features often enough. For more, see biographical accounts (Dean 2018: 1–30; Meade 1989: 35–66).
12 In addition to Parker's "Anecdote," further examples that illustrate this include the early twentieth-century journalist Félix Fénéon's reshaping of miscellaneous news items into the tautly ironic *faits divers* or "novels in three lines," a form revived in new medial contexts by Teju Cole's twitter series *Small Fates* (2011–2013). It also includes Heinrich von Kleist's finely

but rather with colloquial, low, and oral-cultural forms such as gossip that are hardly assessed in terms of formal accomplishment. If anecdotes engage critical attention at all, it is for what they pragmatically do rather than how they might aesthetically please.

In keeping with this understanding of the anecdotal, Parker's "Anecdote" does not collect characteristics alone; it exemplifies the anecdotal by unfolding line-by-line, underscoring the minor in the sense of lesser-than in the process. Thus, the smallness of the yawn and the shrug in the short, but central second line is set off by the aggrandizing tendencies of the lines that precede and follow. All attention is directed, paradoxically enough, at the insignificant. At this point the poem deploys its perhaps most impactful, certainly most consistent compositional strategy: literalization. Parker lyrically reflects on the anecdote by crafting an anecdote – one which renders interpersonal minidrama literally minor in length, while spelling out grandness and idealization of romantic sentiments through the capitalization of "Love" and "Sorrow." The resulting contrast highlights the insignificance of yawning and bodily shifting. It is, after all, first in relation to that which is larger, more valued, or otherwise deemed "major" that the "minor" takes shape as a distinct category. The contrast gives those minor gestures significance within the anecdotal minidrama. The yawn and turn of line two reject the "Love" of the introductory line and create the "Sorrow" that follows; the movements are slight, but, in a continuation of the poem's literalizing conceit, they are evidently slighting in their consequences.

The real drama of "Anecdote," however, lies not in the petty insult presented as the superficial occasion for anecdotal narration, but rather in the deeper anecdotal structure that the incident is used to demonstrate. From this perspective, the slight and slighting gestures are not merely set off from the noble sentiments that are the proper weighty subjects of lyric poetry. The anecdotal incident is rather presented as an action: an action that breaks from (and potentially breaks up) grander discourse. Striking in the first line of Parker's poem is both the loftiness of "Love" and the stilted semantic inversion of "So silent I when [...]." Equally striking in the second line, mannerism and abstraction are interrupted by the particular and prosaic. Not only are shrugging, yawning, and taking loved ones for granted highly ordinary; these actions are rendered in direct, informal, and seemingly pragmatic language. When the description departs from grammatical diction in the second line, it does not take the form of the artful inversion prominent in the first. "He yawned, and

---

calibrated experiments in Berlin's first daily newspaper, *Berliner Abendblätter*, published every day except Sunday from October 1810 through March 1811.

turned away" instead progresses prose-like from subject to predicate only to be spliced at the midpoint with a comma that effectively elides. The subject is dropped in the resulting clause, creating a run-on sentence: the epitome of faulty, but familiarly colloquial expression.

"Sorrow" does return as a grandiloquent, duly capitalized sentiment in the third line. But the poem does not fully recover its grandness or, more specifically, complete itself in the full, balanced closure hinted at in its highlighted vocabulary. "Love" and "Sorrow" are connected not only through their abstraction-signaling capitalization, but also through the repetition of rounded vowels. Sounded out, the "o" series of "Love" and "Sorrow" creates a progression of incrementally longer vowel sounds that are suggestive of the full circle which the letter "o" graphically visualizes and which the lyric should ideally be moving towards as a closed formal composition. "Anecdote" does not achieve that ideal. On the contrary, the prosaic interruption of yawn, shrug, and comma splice resets the original poetic pattern into a more conventional sentence structure in which the capitalized, but vague histrionics of "Sorrow" deflates into the mundane specificity of "apron-strings."

That the language at this point approaches a cliché, in connecting the female position with "apron-strings," does not necessarily contradict the anecdote's close affiliation with the singular, specific, and realistic. The evocative details found in anecdotes seize attention and activate the imagination. In the case of the transformation of slight/slighting action into an event in "Anecdote," the poem sketches a simple, but striking picture of rejection that can certainly be retained in memory. To imprint that image and pass it on to others, however, arguably requires further props for memory. And what is the commonplace but a vast repository of the familiar, easily recognized as well as readily recalled and repeatable?

In this way, conventionality works together with vivid specificities and brevity to render the anecdote not just detachable from greater history or wider flows of discourse, but durable in that detachment. The anecdote can be varied in retelling. Yet brevity, focus, and a degree of anchoring in the commonplace maintain a core consistency within those variations. The anecdote thereby attains what English Studies scholar Annabell Patterson describes as "portability": "that is to say, [the anecdote is] relocatable from one chronicle to another, from a chronological to an achronological spot, from one style or even one ideological perspective to another" (1997: 165).[13] While Patterson's reference is

---

[13] See also the discussion of "nomadism" as a comparable concept in Fleming (2011: "A Perfect Story" 75).

specifically to the chronicle as a prominent mode of sixteenth-century historiography, her account – of how the short narrative modes we have come to designate as anecdotes are able to travel not in parts, but in more or less consistent wholes across a range of medial and discursive boundaries – applies equally to other periods and systems of text production and dissemination.

Print culture scholars such as Will Slauter and, most extensively, Robert Darnton have demonstrated the importance of anecdotal forms for the "communication systems" of the Enlightenment (Darnton 2010: 258). Short, shocking narratives have always fomented scandalmongering in oral exchanges: from village gossip to office scuttlebutt. In the seventeenth and eighteenth centuries, however, slanderous short narratives filled broadsides, pamphlets, and booklet-length libels as well as publishing modes recognizable to the present day such as gazettes, magazines, and newspapers; they thereby fueled political discussions of the day and ultimately shaped political realities as discontent heated up into revolution.[14] Less violently, but in the longer view no less dramatically, the oft-evoked "flood" of the popular printed word in the nineteenth century (for example, James 2004: 652) was a result of the latest news being concentrated into compact, reprintable paragraphs (Slauter 2012). Yet more pages were produced by the fixing of the not-so-new-news in boilerplate blocks. From this perspective, the condensed anecdotal item was not just a supplement that publishers could use to fill in gaps during typesetting. To a considerable extent, newspapers were literally composed of anecdotal materials fixed into typesetting building blocks.[15] Most certainly, the portable anecdote is key to our current digital publics in which linked, liked, and relocated microcontents create the connections and disconnects of Web 2.0.

Such close generative affiliations between the anecdote and print publics (later digital publics) provide the strongest argument for this volume's identification of the anecdote as a fundamental feature of a post-Gutenberg modernity. But of course, the anecdote has a deeper history. Although gossiping and spreading rumors are likely anthropological constants, the rediscovery in the Vatican library of the *Anecdota* manuscript – attributed to the sixth-century historian Procopius – established "anecdote" as a firm term for the telling of stories and crafting of histories in the early seventeenth century.[16] The first print edition

---

14 Cf. Darnton (2010; 2013); Slauter (2019).
15 On reprinting as the foundation of the print public sphere in the nineteenth century, see Law and Morita (2012) as well as more generally McGill (2003).
16 Earlier references in the *Suda*, a proto-encyclopedia of the tenth century, suggest that the manuscript and its stories of perversion and intrigue at the Byzantine court under Justinian had certainly circulated in the interim centuries. Cf. Gossman (2003: 151); Patterson (1997: 161).

was published in 1623 as *Arcana Historia* under the editorship of the papal librarian. Subsequent translations vary in their terminology between "Secret History" and "Anecdote," with the title of the H. B. Dewing-translated Loeb Classical Library edition *The Anecdota or Secret History* (1935) combining both terms. Within the classical canon we find numerous examples of short, self-contained narratives that can be described in contemporary terms as anecdotes. Plutarch, for instance, uses brief and striking stories to give the reader access to the *Lives* of his biographical subjects.[17] In *The Laughter of the Thracian Woman* (1987), Blumenberg traces the travels and transformations of a single anecdote. It is the story of the stargazing philosopher Thales of Miletus whose accidental plunge into a wall provokes laughter from a maidservant, the Thracian woman of the title. Blumenberg's study moves from the fables of Aesop (c. sixth and seventh centuries B.C.; collected by Babrius and Phaedrus: c. first century) through the *Theaetetus* dialogues of Plato (c. 369 B.C.) to the recourses of Friedrich Nietzsche and Martin Heidegger. This effort is less interested in illustrating the longevity of a single anecdote than in demonstrating the productivity of the collision between philosophical abstraction and the pragmatically laughing lifeworld figured in anecdotes. The anecdote, in this reading, is not just a metaphor for the challenges of theory, but a motor for its self-reflection and production.

In all these instances, the minor qualities of the anecdote secure the short narrative's integration and functionalization into more expansive modes of discourse such as biography, philosophy, and theory. "Portability" favors narrative circulation long before Gutenberg. Oral culture requires no printing press. Yet the brevity, clarity, and repeatable simplicity most particularly afford mechanical reproduction and successor technologies. These do not just integrate or reference short narratives, they quite literally build with them: a procedure that newspapers illustrate in their paragraph-by-paragraph construction as much as in the dismantling of each day's issue back into portable paragraphs.[18]

Tracing these dynamics not only offers insight into the "re-embedding" work of modern circulation. Our attention is guided to the paradoxes attached to the anecdotal and to two of them in particular: its status as an ultimately not so secret "secret history" and its "undercover authority." Regarding the former, it should be noted that anecdote translates to "unpublished" or, yet more directly in the original Greek, to "not yet given out" (*OED* s.v. "anecdote, n." 2019). However, each example has in fact been "given out" in some form, whether it is

---

17 Cf. Stadter (2014).
18 Cf. Slauter (2012).

Parker's auto-analytical verse, the biographical anecdotes that make up the parallel Greek and Roman lives penned by Plutarch, or the "base deeds" catalogued by Procopius in his name-giving history (1935: 7). What does hold is that each circulates at the minimal threshold of the public: as whispered rumors, in a handful of print lines, as part of a larger text, or as a "quiet manuscript" whose contents are passed on from hand to hand. In the case of print, dissemination potential is exponential relative to scale; the most minimally published text is able to circulate most widely and intensively.

As far as the second paradox is concerned, what the anecdote lacks in conventional authority (traveling, as it does, without byline or official sanction) it gains in the credibility granted to it precisely because of this distance from established power. This is the paradox of authority that is not institutional and open, but undercover and collective. In the case of the politically charged anecdote in particular, it is the perspective of officially silent, but ever-watchful insiders that informs the narrative. As much as Procopius supposedly finds himself "stammering" and "shrinking" at the task of documentation before him (and the retribution that may well follow), he nonetheless counts on the "support of witnesses": "For the men of the present day, being witnesses possessing full knowledge of the events in question, will be competent guarantors" (1935: 5). In this scenario, the author speaks not merely for himself, but for a community that both shares and supports his perspective. Anonymity does not weaken, but rather strengthens the veracity claim central to the anecdote as a narrative "drawn from life." The anecdote thereby establishes itself not just as a truth-telling form, but yet more specifically as a telling-truth-to-power medium. Assessed from this angle, the *Anecdota* is not merely a supplement or complement to the official and honorific accounts of empire building through war and public works. Secret history instead supersedes the others to become the touchstone for truth, for "the way it really is/was."

These dynamics raise the stakes, but also the potential emotional charge of the anecdote. The oftentimes scandalous contents titillate, particularly in their libelous variations. The truth-telling small story, however, piques curiosity as well as conviction about other and larger stories. Telling truth to power raises the specter of consequences for those in power as well as the teller of the collective tale. The greater the fear aroused of the possible consequences of revelation, the more shockingly true the account must be. The *frisson* of first encounter further fires an interest in wanting to know more. The anecdote thus builds up affect both in the short and the long term, without offering resolution, conclusion, or any other form of release. Herein it differs radically from other short forms such as the fable, saying, or aphorism. While the latter hone their materials into moral conclusions and concise *bon mots*, the anecdote remains open. Its details, drama, and narrative execution are not directly translated into significance. The anecdote leaves that task to us.

Given this openness, it is not surprising that in tracing the circulation of anecdotes we encounter not only a surprising range of contexts in which a single story might appear, thus bearing out once again the particular "portability" of short forms.[19] Equally striking are the numerous and often contradictory interpretations and functionalizations of anecdotes in the course of their travels. In this regard, the story of Polly Baker, an eighteenth-century New England woman who supposedly evaded punishment for the crime of unwed motherhood by evoking the higher law of *"Encrease and Multiply"* (qtd. in Wood 2019: 1), offers an exemplary case in point. As James Robert Wood demonstrates, the anecdote travels not only through the popular and elevated press, preoccupying the likes of Denis Diderot, Thomas Jefferson, and Benjamin Franklin (who likely invented the story as a hoax in his printer days to fill in columns on slow news days). It is in turns used for purposes of historiography, in progressive calls for free love, and is of course included in more than one "racy periodical" (2019: 3).

It would thus seem that anecdotes merely give the appearance of being containable on a single page or within a few brief lines. In instigating movement – of emotions, actions, interpretations, and the further traveling of the anecdote itself – the material form might better be understood as a prompt. In Parker's "Anecdote," "I have so much to say" is the conclusion of the poem only in the sense of being the last sequence of printed words in the quatrain. The spare formulation does not just stand in for, but directly states that there are many more observations, analyses and stories to be told. Gesturing towards narrative, but withholding narration stimulates interest and imagination, while retaining the enigmatic openness of the anecdote. Rather than wrapping up, the final line prepares for continuation. The direction of response thereby shifts from the question of "what does this mean?" to a stance between incitement and querying that the anecdote itself seems to set up.

The further words that "Anecdote" implies, but does not quite yet speak out, thus, might well be imperative: "do something with me." While more than one cultural practice and disciplinary formation has answered that call, the late twentieth-century effort to launch a "new historicism" stands out for the thoroughness of its reply.

---

[19] On the portability of forms generally, see Levine (2015: 5–11).

3 What Can an Anecdote Do?

No other theoretical project in the contemporary humanities has placed greater emphasis on (and held higher hopes for) the analytical potential of the anecdote than new historicism. The aims of the formation's key texts are invariably sweeping. In *Shakespearian Negotiations: The Circulation of Social Energy in Renaissance England* (1988), Stephen Greenblatt sets out to trace the "social energies" that emerged from and simultaneously shaped an entire epoch. His account of the formation of the modern subject in *Renaissance Self Fashioning: From More to Shakespeare* (1980) is hardly less ambitious. Moreover, in each of these instances, and in any number of other studies written in proximity to the journal *Representations* (1983–) or published in the monograph series *The New Historicism: Studies in Cultural Poetics* (1988–1997), the overarching goal was nothing less than the fundamental renovation of traditional historiographical practices, textual hermeneutics and, not least, common understandings of what constitutes a "text" at all. What was once defined in terms of words printed on a page was now to encompass all cultural production.

Challenging common ideas of what "texts" are and how one should analyze them was by no means a project unique to new historicism. Similar calls to rethink the objects and approaches of humanities inquiry echoed through broad swathes of the academy in the later twentieth century.[20] What is arguably distinctive about the new historicists is their approach to such challenges. How to begin the project of making multiple disciplinary worlds anew, and all at once? The answer is: with the anecdote. As Christopher Coates notes, "[a]ll but four of the combined eleven chapters" of *Renaissance Self Fashioning* and *Shakespearian Negotiations* open with a quote, short narrative, or "exhumed textual artefact" (1993: 276). This is significant because these two studies are touchstones for more than the career of their author. According to Coates (ibid.) and other observers of the formation,[21] they set up a blueprint for new historical analysis. As curious as each opening gambit in Greenblatt's pattern-making new historical projects are individually – one chapter opens with a laconic log entry recounting the burning of an east African village (1980: 21–22), another with a second-hand account of early modern gender-bending in the Alpine provinces (1987: 66–67) – all these recovered texts and tales ultimately correspond to the commonly agreed-upon contours of the anecdotal. The archival finds are brief or are compressed. Each opening narrative is self-contained

---

20 See, for example, Fish (1980).
21 See, for example, Vickers (1993: 214–217); Porter (1988: 776–778).

and distinct enough to register as an "artefact" while honing in on single events, further highlighted by vivid details and/or unexpected conjunctions. This is the "closest a narrative can get to a thing," observes Helen Deutsch of the use of anecdotes in such contexts; they serve as "stones critics kick to prove the reality and solidity of the historical materials that they analyze" (2009: 31). At the same time, the beginnings are open enough for the critics to do something with them. And the aim for Greenblatt and associated colleagues was to do something new both with and through these materials. Most importantly, the productivity of the anecdote for new historical inquiry extends beyond the opening and runs deeper than mere gambit.

The anecdotal mode works its way into the language of new historicism itself, becoming its key narrative as well as genealogical principle. In other words, the anecdotal informs both *how* new historicists analyze and *where* they position their project. This double operation of practicing and positioning new historicism is nowhere more clearly foregrounded than in Catherine Gallagher und Greenblatt's *Practicing New Historicism* (2000), making this late contribution to new historicist scholarship particularly instructive for our purposes here. Greenblatt and Gallagher exemplify the anecdotal argumentative modes of new historicism in the volume's six chapters. The first two, titled "The Touch of the Real" and "Counterhistory and Anecdote," specifically focus on the anecdote and bring together a spectrum of philosophical antecedents and theoretical allies. The jointly authored collection thereby offers examples of "what anecdotes can do?" specifically, in new historicism, as well as generally, in a longer modern tradition.

All of this makes *Practicing New Historicism* a multipurpose, but also somewhat paradoxical and at times anachronistic endeavor. Writing at the millennium, Gallagher and Greenblatt look back at the consolidation of what they assert "is not a coherent, close-knit school" (2000: 2). They refute some of the charges made against the formation as "a new interpretive practice" (1), a reference back to the days when new historicism was evoked with manifesto flourish as an insurrectionary "spectre" supposedly "haunting criticism" (Pechter 1987: 292), although by the 1990s at the latest it had certainly established itself as a standard academic practice. Yet more interesting than the slight disingenuity of disarming dated criticism is the drive to expand the retrospective beyond recollections of new historicist formation proper. Greenblatt and Gallagher work to forge a longer-standing "tradition of the new" or doing history "otherwise" that new historicism actualizes.

They begin with a return to hermeneutics in conjunction with cultural historicism, best exemplified, in their view, by the Enlightenment polymaths Giambattista Vico and Johann Gottfried Herder. Breaking with abstract universals and embracing cultural difference, Herder in particular, they argue, lays the groundwork for conceiving understanding as "an encounter with the singular, the specific, and the individual" (2000: 6). Gallagher and Greenblatt position this notion as an influence for the contributors of *Representations* – to the point of "the refusal of universal aesthetic norms, and the resistance to formulating an overarching theoretical program" (ibid.). But the rejection of a general aesthetic doctrine does not mean a rejection of aesthetics. To the contrary: culture comes to stand for the totality of phenomena and objects of a specific historical moment and geographical space. With this further argumentative move, aesthetic vocabulary is extended into the everyday and the commonplace which are, in turn, saturated with democratizing and participatory potential. Gallagher and Greenblatt trace back their notion of a "poetics of culture" to this version of Herder, arguing that his "brilliant vision of the mutual embeddedness of art and history underlies our fascination with the possibility of treating all of the written and visual traces of a particular culture as a mutually intelligible network of signs" (7). While there is an ostensible rejection of grand theory in the new historical embrace of the material and specific, the claim remains no less grandiose. At the intersection of history and the arts, collected anecdotes and pointed details, whether a potato or a mousetrap, structurally account for an entire culture – down to its material manifestations and sensual nuances, even if this culture remains textually mediated and necessarily uneven, punctuated by contradictions and ruptures.

The reference to Herder secures new historicism's continuation of a revisionist Enlightenment project and its ostensible political liberalism. The crossing of Clifford Geertz and Erich Auerbach in the "Touch of the Real" chapter, meanwhile, brings the project back more concretely to the anecdote as a technique of writing and connects itself with close, engaged, and, at certain junctures, redemptive analytical practices. Reading *The Interpretation of Cultures* (1973), Greenblatt, this chapter's principal author, notes that Geertz's claim to a better empiricism via the practice of "thick description" relies on "a little story – that is, an anecdote" (2000: 21) recorded in the cultural anthropologist's field journal. In its link to descriptiveness and narration, the anecdote comes to exemplify the "lived life, at once raw and subtle, coarse and complex" that new historicist literary critics aim to retrieve in "unfamiliar cultural texts" (28). The positioning of "human creativity, including narrative and linguistic creativity" as "a widespread, indeed democratic, possession" shows that Enlightenment humanism remains alive in this version of new historicism (30). It is here that Greenblatt locates a double function of the anecdote in new historicism: "to show in compressed form the ways in which elements of lived experience enter into literature" and "to show in compressed form the ways in which poetry, drama, and prose fiction play themselves out in the everyday world" (30). The underlying operation is indeed a classic hermeneutic one: the anecdote serves as a condensation that demands an attention to detail. It harbors more than its surface suggests, and every detail leads to the next and to the next until the whole completes itself. This tendency marks the difference between the ethnologically as well as literarily shaped new historicism, on the one hand, and the roughly contemporaneous practice of microhistory, on the other, which largely remains in the materially specific, lower ranges of a history "from below."[22]

While the impulse to move from the strikingly specific to the symptomatically representable has been criticized as a problematic analytical feint,[23] it is important to note that for new historicists it is a different kind of whole that is at stake than in more traditional arguments regarding representative, i.e. typical or classical literature. As much as Greenblatt in particular works with the canon, a non-canonical or canon-revisionist gesture is key to new historicism's self-understanding, to the extent that "the literary and the nonliterary" are conceived as "each other's thick description" (2000: 31). The anecdote figures prominently in the resulting destabilization and expansion of the category of the literary. "The turn to the historical anecdote," we read in the discussion of Auerbach, "promised both an escape from conventional canonicity and a revival of the canon, both a transgression against the domestic and a safe return to it" (47). But Auerbach, himself very much invested in the canon, provides new historicists with a critical practice anchored in the narrative, rhetorical, and stylistic production of "a quasi-magical effect: the conjuring of a complex, dynamic, historically specific spirit of representation out of a few paragraphs" (37). The "few paragraphs" that make an anecdote are a metaphorical condensation of what new historicists themselves metaphorically describe as the energy, magic, or "spirit" of a historical moment.

In its relation to detail and description, the anecdote, once placed in the context of the novel, may be a narrative digression that is constitutive of what Auerbach in *Mimesis: The Representation of Reality in Western Literature* (1946) calls "atmospheric realism" and "atmospheric Historism" (2003: 471; qtd. in Gallagher and Greenblatt 2000: 39, 40), by which he means the French realism of the nineteenth century. These sprawling novels can be considered assemblages of anecdotes and details that deliver an inherently fragmented account of social life-worlds and their respective historical moments. For

---

22 Cf. Ginzburg (1993).
23 Cf. Drakakis and Fludernik (2014: 498–499).

Greenblatt, Auerbach takes his own "anecdotal technique of *Mimesis*" from nineteenth-century novelists such as Honoré de Balzac and their "conviction that tiny details can be made to represent the nature of larger and larger wholes" (2000: 40). By consequence, new historicists emulate the same "anecdotal technique," to the effect that their texts imitate the strategies of literary texts. Here the ostensible aestheticization of new historicism comes full force, while the recourse to Auerbach adds pathos to the project of conjuring increasingly larger wholes. As is well known, Auerbach's reconstruction of Western literary tradition by way of the detail and the power of his own memory was not a dry academic exercise in 1940s Istanbul. In the midst of world war and genocide, he was writing to save humanist tradition from totalitarian annihilation.

We may dismiss some of the insinuated genealogies and certainly the more grandiose claims made by Gallagher and Greenblatt. How could you possibly bring the poetics of an entire culture to life in something as small as an anecdote? Does this not put too much historical stress on the minute and the minor, both of which may after all be nothing more than unreliable evidence or trivial hearsay? But such dismissal, in turn, might run the risk of assuming a stable historical record, couched in scientific, data-based neutrality that erases the specifics of human existence. The longer tradition of assessing and intervening in the constitution of history through anecdotal modes offers seemingly divergent, but actually convergent answers to this question. The anecdote is both capable of shoring up an authoritarian history, and of disrupting it. In both cases, the minor narrative shows itself able to exert major influence.

Hannah Arendt, one of the chief political theorists and philosophers of totalitarianism and authoritarian rule, makes a case for the anecdote as the better, the actual evidence before the law. In an introductory essay written for the English translation of journalist Bernd Naumann's documentation of the controversial Auschwitz trial in Frankfurt (1963–1965), she contends, against Naumann's hopes, that "the unprecedented crime of our century" cannot ascertain a general truth because it escapes the "categories and paragraphs" of legal proceduralism (1966: xxix). Instead, readers of Naumann's documentation "will find *moments of truth*" (ibid.; original italics). Such instances, which "arise unexpectedly like oases out of the desert," as Arendt writes, would be "the only means of articulating this chaos of viciousness and evil" (ibid.). "They are anecdotes," Arendt writes, "and they tell in utter brevity what it was all about" (ibid.).

She lists several of these anecdotes. As accounts of everyday hypocrisy, suffering, and violence, they bring to the fore the dehumanizing cruelty of systematic mass murder implemented by a totalitarian regime. Anecdotes, for Arendt, render palpable the historical record's cold, hard facts. They make the historical truth that postwar German institutions sought to unmake, or at least to euphemize. If the circulation of anecdotes may point to gossip, fake news, and rumors, their form and dissemination can also serve as a corrective to official consensus. The political aesthetic of the anecdote can speak truth to the fictions of power, to vary a now common phrase. What is more, the anecdotal "little story" can unmask the modalities of power itself. This becomes evident when Arendt recounts the following anecdote: "There is the son of an SS man on duty who comes to the camp to visit his father. But a child is a child, and the rule of this particular place is that all children must die" (1966: xxx). Because of that rule, "he must wear a sign around his neck, 'so they wouldn't grab him, and into the gas oven with him'" (ibid.). The fact that Arendt cites the anecdote without proceeding to an analytical reading is part of the point. In the narrative, totalitarian power becomes its own anecdotal evidence, exposing its haphazard fictions of genealogy and racial purity that here need signs (otherwise reserved for Jews, Roma, Sinti and others marked with single and double triangle badges in the concentration camp system) to secure their own survival, symbolically and quite literally.

Arendt's conception of the anecdote dovetails with the reflections of new historicist Joel Fineman. In his touchstone essay "The History of the Anecdote: Fiction and Fiction" (1989), Fineman thinks "of the anecdote, given its formal if not its actual brevity, as a *historeme*, i.e. as the smallest minimal unit of the historiographic fact" (1989: 57). The description recalls the common early modern and Enlightenment identification of anecdotes as "historiettes" (Stefanovska 2009: 16–18) and also partly resonates with the reflections of the German romantic writer Novalis (Friedrich von Hardenberg) on how such tiny narrative parts connect to larger wholes. In "Logological Fragments" (1798), Novalis suggests not only that the anecdote is "a historical element – a historical molecule or epigram," but also that history consists of "a series of anecdotes that have been welded together or have flowed into each other as a continuum" (1997: 69). We may say that Novalis's additive continuum of serial anecdotes strikes a different chord from Arendt's critique of the Auschwitz trial. There, the anecdotes of the lived lives of both victims and perpetrators, which tell of survival and death, evoke a testimonial plasticity against the protocols of a bureaucratic machinery that aim to contain the horror (and arguably continue the horror of human erasure) by reducing holocaust to abstract, anonymous numbers.

Arendt's understanding of anecdotes as political correctives to the historical record, or as actual manifestations of a more fundamental and less manipulated version of that record, resonates with a wide range of projects that have mobilized the anecdote for political ends. The digital activisms of #MeToo and #SayHerName, as recent examples, use social media platforms to encourage the posting and circulation of personally focused, essentially anecdotal accounts of sexual harassment, discrimination, and the intersections of racial with gender prejudices impacting black women in particular. These anecdotal accounts can be collected through the hashtag for a powerful cumulative effect: a procedure that recalls the nineteenth-century abolitionist practice of collecting brief individual accounts into omnibus collections documenting *American Slavery as It Is* (1839), aptly subtitled *Testimony of a Thousand Witnesses* (Weld 2011).[24]

There are also important connections to be made between these projects, Arendt's insights, and other theoretical reflections, including Fineman's further specifications of the anecdote as "the literary form or genre that uniquely refers to the real" and "lets history happen by introducing an opening into the teleological [...] narration of beginning, middle, and end (1989: 57, 61) that have "emplotted" and dominated our understandings of history since the nineteenth century.[25] The idea of the anecdote as providing an opening that can be leveraged into insight, and potentially also intervention, connects psychoanalysis and ethnology, the theories of poststructuralism and deconstruction, and the political projects of feminism and postcolonial studies. Multiple strands come together in feminist psychoanalytic critic Jane Gallop's call for an "anecdotal theory." Gallop's anecdotal theory draws on the theorizing potentials immanent "in narrative forms, in the stories we create, in riddles and proverbs, in the play with language" that African American studies scholar Barbara Christian identifies as the practices of a collective subject position: "black, women, third world" (1987: 52; partially qtd. in Gallop 2002: 2). Connections can also be made to earlier anecdotal histories, those written before and/or pushing against the grand emplotted histories of the nineteenth-century historical imagination: most prominently Procopius's *Anecdota* from which not only the term "anecdote," but the playbook for "secret history," as an account of dirty secrets undercutting noble pretensions and established power, was derived and extensively utilized from the seventeenth century on.[26]

The antiauthoritian potential of the anecdotal should not, however, obscure the fact that little stories can also consolidate power. They do so, paradoxically enough, by rendering rulers fallible, which is to say, human, relatable, and approachable. Or, as Walter Benjamin proposes in an initial note for his *Arcades Project* (1927–1940): the anecdote approaches us. He writes: "The anecdote brings things nearer to us spatially, lets them enter our life. It presents the

---

[24] See also Drew (2008).
[25] Cf. White (2014: 7–8).
[26] For an initial impression of secret history text production, see Woertendyke (2009: 259–262).

rigorous antithesis to the kind of history that demands 'empathy,' which makes everything abstract" (2002: 545). For Benjamin, the anecdote is "[t]he true method of making things present to us: to present them in our space (not ourselves in theirs). Only anecdotes move us in this direction" (ibid.). The potential of the biographical anecdote to not only characterize a person succinctly, but to further create the impression of a powerful proximity across otherwise unbridgeable social divisions explains the liberal use of anecdotes in political histories of the eighteenth century. In this time period, especially toward the century's end, absolutist power was not absolutely secure. The functionalization of the anecdote, but also the proliferation of the personal, particular, and trivial prompted unease and even a certain disgust at rising "anecdotomanie" (Darnton 2013: 255). In the course of his career, Voltaire found himself on both sides of the debates on the anecdote. In the early 1730s he critiqued the overreliance on details in historiography, decrying works "crowded with trifling incidents," overburdened with "infinite numbers of useless facts," and "interlarded" with falsehoods (1762: 57). In his own *The Age of Louis XIV* (1751), Voltaire devotes four full chapters to anecdotes, but not without adding a print warning in the margin: "be wary of anecdotes" ("il faut se défier des anecdotes," 1785: 80).[27] As literary historian Lionel Gossman has pointed out, however, it is not necessarily subversion that is being anticipated by such a note. The anecdotes so liberally used in historical writings of the period did not usually introduce doubt or set up a puzzle. Overwhelmingly, these historical anecdotes corroborated by "exemplifying and confirming a general rule or trend or epitomizing a larger general situation" (2003: 155); they were, in a word, conservative.

Once more, the anecdote proves difficult to pin down. What remains as constants beyond brevity, vividness, microdrama, and generally minor status are arguably two features: first, the anecdote's propensity to circulation and, second, its connection to the sociality of modern life in the form of "gossip, rumor, and what the French called 'public noises' (*bruits publics*)" of speech and print (2013: 263), as Darnton phrases it. Crucially, he adds, while "anecdotes were defined as hidden truths, they were often understood to be half truths" (ibid.). What is more, "they sometimes presented themselves in this way," effectively staging "a rhetorical game" in gossipy gazettes and other vehicles of the eighteenth-century public sphere that is the focus of his research into print cultures and rumor machineries of modernity (ibid.).[28] The point can arguably be

---

27 While eliminated in many later printing editions, the marginal warning is still reproduced in the 1785 printing. Cf. Voltaire (1785:80).
28 Cf. also Darnton (2010: 269–299).

extended to other time periods and media contexts. Anecdotes can speak truth to political power or can bolster power, but they seem to always already problematize, at times openly, the very notion of truth. Almost by consequence, they cannot be separated from diversion and entertainment value, attested to in their affiliation with humorous forms and modes ranging from joke to satire. They alert us to the inextricability of politics and amusement along with further paradoxes: oscillations between the singular and the exemplary, the accessible and the inscrutable, the didactic and destructive, the ephemeral and memorable, the anonymous and highly specific.

The delineated trajectory – from secret to official histories and finally public noises – should remind us that while the anecdote is endemic to modernity, both in the sense of being everywhere present and shaping the seeming fragmentations of this period into connection, it further allows for tracing transitions from the premodern to modernity, including continuities as well as ruptures. With respect to modes of communicative representation, it is situated at the intersection of oral storytelling and printed story, of articulation and writing. In regards to modes of political representation, the anecdote traverses the shift from aristocratic rule to democratic governance. Both political systems may be focused on the production of character and personality. Democracy, though, allows for the possibility of a redistribution of attention from a "History of the Great Men" who are, with Thomas Carlyle, (still) thought to make History writ large, to the stories of ordinary people, who become the concern of the historical novel circa 1800, onto the histories – made, unmade, and remade – in the centuries to come.

4 The Design of this Volume

A sweeping history of modernity could be told by way of the anecdote. The anecdotal also holds clear promise for illuminating modernity's present phase given the importance of short forms for the news and social media that algorithmically create our contemporary approximation of a public square. This, however, is not the focus of this volume. Nor do we follow the lead of many recent projects that, often taking the ubiquity and undeniable influence of microforms in the current moment as their starting point, set out to map the wide field of minor writing forms.[29] Finally, we do not hone in on particular authorial or historical constellations of anecdote production.[30]

---

[29] Cf. Gamper and Mayer (2017); Dumitrescu and Holsinger (2019).

Instead, in this volume, we approach the anecdote anecdotally, assembling instances in which the anecdote has been mobilized in the literatures and arts of Western Europe and North America. Organized in five sections, concise case studies explore different aspects of the anecdote: specifically, the relation of anecdotal narratives to *Truth*, the centrality of *Event* and *Story* as well as the proximity of the anecdote to *Rumor* and the intermedial category of the *Detail*. Implicitly or explicitly, the contributions all proceed from an understanding of the anecdotal as interconnected with the modern. Yet in their focus on specific functions and changing effects, they demonstrate the anecdote's particularly flexible productivity.

Truth

> If Suetonius could be confronted with the valets-de-chambre of the twelve Caesars, think you that they would in every instance corroborate his testimony? And in case of dispute, who would not back the valets-de-chambre against the historian? (Voltaire 1901: "Anecdotes" 176)

Our exploration of the anecdote begins at the cusp of the historical period commonly designated as modern, moving from the late middle ages towards the early modern period. It does so with not one, but two interlinked questions that themselves foreground transition and transformation: "How can a heathen, the Roman Emperor Trajan, enter Christianity's heaven?" And, "How are anecdotes made?" While new historicism relies on the anecdote to develop new analytical perspectives, the approach largely ignores the dimension of production, as Gerhard Regn rightly observes in his contribution. His essay "The Heathen in Heaven: Anecdote and Truth in Dante's *Commedia*" addresses this lack by attentively tracing the poet's transformation of anecdotes concerning Trajan into a vision of the heathen in heaven. That inclusion is by no means to be understood as questioning Christian frameworks. Rather, these frameworks are powerfully affirmed: not least by the poem's shaping of anecdotal materials into a theologically and aesthetically confirming ultimate truth. In "Anecdotal Ambiguity: Andrew Marvell," Verena Lobsien tracks a quite different case of transformation. Here, Marvell converts a chance incident, a 1654 coach accident that sent then-Lord Protector Oliver Cromwell tumbling, into a central section of the encomium "The First Anniversary of the Government und His Highness the Lord Protector" (composed 1654/1655). Far from elevating Cromwell into the

---

30 Cf. Lorenz und Nehrlich (2019).

realms of higher and binding truth, Marvell's poem brings the anecdote together with allegory to amplify ambiguity. It is first in Hermann Melville and Helmbrecht Breinig's reading of "A Hideous and Intolerable ... Anecdote: *Moby-Dick* and Questions of Truth Seen from the Human and Non-Human Side" that a counternarrative in the sense championed by the new historicists develops: not affirming dominant frameworks, nor engendering skepticism, but opening up insight into alternative viewpoints, which are, in Melville's famous novel, those of the whales. This shift is not achieved by the anecdote per se, but is built up on the awareness of the anecdote's limits as an epistemological tool.

Event

> [The anecdote] emerges in vivid contact with an audience, for whom the narrator effectively presents an experienced or heard event. ([Die Anekdote] entsteht in lebendigem Kontakt mit einem Publikum, dem der Erzähler ein miterlebtes oder gehörtes Ereignis wirkungsvoll darstellt. [Hein 1991: 15; our translation])

The contributions in this section explore the anecdote in its various links to notions of the event. In her essay, "Heinrich von Kleist's 'Anecdote from the Last War': W-hole, the Joke an Anecdote Nearly Made," Bettine Menke reads Kleist's anecdote as a reflection on the event of writing, where the relation between nonalphabetic elements of script and the telling of a joke is exposed. This reflection, Menke shows, is inextricable from a consideration of two different media of the anecdote: rumor and the newspaper *Berliner Abendblätter*. The underlying conception of the anecdote as an event that is contingent upon media resurfaces in Inka Mülder-Bach's contribution "Individual Case, Example, Exception: The Range of the Anecdotal in Fontane," which reads the anecdotal in Theodor Fontane's work as a question of genre. Fontane's childhood autobiography, she argues, conceives anecdotes as media of memory that accommodate the singular and the incommensurable. In contradistinction, Mülder-Bach contends, his novel *The Stechlin* (1898) conceives of its countless anecdotes and small stories as symptoms of the epistemological and political crises of modernity. In his essay "Once is Nothing at All is Once: Traces of Eventfulness in Joyce and Beckett" Andreas Mahler, too, situates the anecdote in a media-induced shift from eventful mimetic narrating to performative text presentation. His readings of James Joyce and Samuel Beckett trace this shift to show how the meaning of the anecdotal eventfulness of stories changes: from Joyce's delight in the anecdote's encyclopedic potential to Beckett's skepticism of the anecdote as a trigger for a ceaseless torrent of texts. The presentational in its relation to the representational also informs Gabriele Schwab's contribution "The Politics of Splitting: Gertrude Stein's 'Reflection on the Atomic Bomb'." Stein, Schwab argues, deliberately reframes the Bomb as a rhetorical, non-referential event of language. As such, it becomes an anecdote that is symptomatic of various modernist anxieties, ranging from emotional detachment to a schizophrenic, nuclear subjectivity, but it also denies the politics of fear associated with the threat of the nuclear age.

Story

> What above all comes back to me with this reminiscence is the sense of the inveterate minuteness, on such happy occasions, of the precious particle – reduced, that is, to its mere fruitful essence. Such is the interesting truth about the stray suggestion, the wandering word, the vague echo, at touch of which the novelist's imagination winces as at the prick of some sharp point: its virtue is all in its needle-like quality, the power to penetrate as finely as possible. (James 1934: 119)

This section consists of three essays that explore the relationship between anecdote and story. Heinz Ickstadt's essay, "Plot and Anecdote in Henry James and Julian Barnes," focuses on two different ways the anecdote was made use of in early modernist and postmodernist storytelling. By comparing the role of the anecdote for Henry James, where an anecdote is often taken as the "germ" for the plot, with how the anecdote functions in Julian Barnes's *The Noise of Time* (2016), Ickstadt argues that in the latter novel the anecdote no longer works organically within the composition of the novel, as it does in James, but has now become an element in a story of repressive plotting and aesthetic withdrawal. Thomas Claviez's essay, "The Relevance of the Irrelevant: Wisdom and/of Contingency," also draws out the way the anecdote lends itself to a postmodernist view of narrative contingency. Instead of reading a postmodernist text, however, Claviez turns to Walter Benjamin's famous essay "The Storyteller" (1936) as his entry point for exploring how the anecdote foregrounds the contingent character of storytelling. Winfried Siemerling's essay, "Accumulated Time, the Anecdote, and the Vertical Imagination," continues this line of investigation by relating the anecdotal to the field of black Atlantic critical memory culture. Through readings of literary texts by Sylvia Hamilton, Austin Clarke, and Dionne Brand, Siemerling shows how uses of the anecdote here support forms of critical witnessing that invite further contextualization and narrative completion from potentially disruptive perspectives.

Rumor

> Facts are anecdotes, but anecdotes are not always facts. (Disraeli 1793: 30–31)

The relationship between anecdote and factual evidence is a complicated one, as the three contributions in this section demonstrate in unique ways. At the center of Ralph J. Poole's essay, "The Fun of Deep Gossip: Lord Cornbury as Queen in Drag," is a persistent, centuries-old rumor: that the "worst British governor" of the colonial period, Viscount Cornbury, made a habit of appearing in public in women's clothing. Beginning with an eighteenth-century portrait which may or may not depict Cornbury, cousin to Queen Anne, in drag, Poole traces the varied debate about the truth of this anecdote and the concomitant impact of deep gossip all the way to our century. In Hendrik Birus's essay, rumor and anecdote are likewise focused on a single figure. In "An Anecdote Peddler from the Age of Goethe," the author revisits Karl August Böttiger's conversations with Goethe. Rather than being the mere "malicious gossip" motivated by animosity they might be taken for, Birus argues, Böttiger's anecdotes, which continue to be highly relevant for Goethe-scholars to this day, worked to counteract both the latter's dominance even beyond Weimar, and the self-idealization of his circle. Frank Kelleter's contribution, "Anecdotal Manifestations of the Evangelical Here and Now: Four Conversions in Jonathan Edwards's Northampton," rounds off the section on Rumor. The focus here is no longer on an individual, however, but a genre. Kelleter discusses anecdotal storytelling by means of four conversion accounts from the Great Awakening. The ideological and soteriological work of these and other evangelical anecdotes, he argues, depends primarily on their communicative velocity.

Detail

> Mechlin. – The Cathedral.
> The Last Supper by Rubens. [...] Under the table is a dog gnawing a bone, a circumstance mean in itself, and certainly unworth such a subject [...] Besides the impropriety one does not see how the dog came by his bone [...], but the word SUPPER was excuse enough for Rubens, who was always glad of an opportunity of introducing animals into his pictures. (Reynolds 1797: 17)

Details are by definition small, but in their potential for harnessing and even hijacking attention they are quite powerful. In literary description, but perhaps even more directly in visual representations they can draw the eye away from what would seem to be the proper subject of the image. The result is not simply distraction, but a reconfiguration of the entire composition. This potential is often, and in new historicism insistently, ascribed to the anecdotal. But is the detail in visual forms analogous to the narrative modes of anecdote? Can we speak of visual anecdotes at all? These questions are central to three of the four analyses in the penultimate section of the volume. Friedrich Teja Bach explores the affinities between anecdote and detail in "The Cage of the Image and the Trace of the Snail: On the Language of Pictorial Detail," ultimately demonstrating how the motif of the snail in renaissance painting, particularly in the *Annunciation* (1470–1472) of Francesco del Cossa, both reconfigures and consolidates the central message of the composition. Susanne von Falkenhausen yet more insistently tests the possibilities of anecdote for image study in "Anecdote vs. History: Jeff Wall's *Dead Troops Talk*" by using the term anecdote, which designates a format outside of art history proper, to analyze visual art works that place themselves within different traditions of narrative and emphatically non-narrative painting: history painting as medially re-envisioned by the contemporary photographer Jeff Wall, the large-scale abstract canvases produced by Jackson Pollock at the midcentury, and the small-scale genre compositions of the nineteenth-century French painter Ernest Meissonier. In "A Unique Universalism: Ben Shahn and the Rhetoric of Anecdotes," Christof Decker does not test, but rather demonstrates the transformation of a traumatic event into both narrative and visual anecdote. In the work of the twentieth-century US-American artist Ben Shahn, Decker draws out the development of a specifically anecdotal style in American visual modernism that combined word, image, and the human particular. Finally, Andrew S. Gross's "Wallace Stevens: Anecdote and Lyric" tells the story of a found object, a jar or glass container for preserving foods, that is transformed through poetic act and curatorial care into a self-immanence that can be described as anecdotal, offered as being "in itself interesting or striking" (*OED* s.v. "anecdote, n." 2019) as well as leaving "so much to say" (Parker 2006: 88).

Coda

In the spirit of the anecdotal, the two final essays in the coda are not closing statements as much as pointed accounts of two exemplarily singular events in cultural history. While Anselm Haverkamp's "Philosophy and Anecdote: Hegel's 'Lehrer Löffler'" takes up the anecdote of how Hegel's introduction as a young student to Shakespeare's works provided the impetus for his theory of history, Barbara Vinken in "Fleurs de Paris" turns to the anecdotes of the Eiffel Tower told first by Maupassant and then by Roland Barthes as exemplary moments in the shifting cultural history of Paris. Taken together, these two anecdotal accounts of the anecdote provide a fitting last word by encapsulating its generative power to continually shape and reshape not only the history of ideas, but history itself.

Works Cited

"anecdote, n." 2019. *OED = The Oxford English Dictionary*. 2000–. 3rd ed. online. Oxford: Oxford University Press. <www.oed.com/view/Entry/7367> [accessed February 25, 2020].
Arendt, Hannah. 1966. "Introduction." In: Bernd Naumann. *Auschwitz: A Report on the Proceedings against Robert Karl Ludwig Mulka and Others Before the Court at Frankfurt.* Trans. Jean Steinberg. New York: Praeger. xi–xxx.
Auerbach, Erich. 2003 [1946]. *Mimesis: The Representation of Reality in Western Literature.* Trans. Willard R. Trask. Princeton: Princeton University Press.
Babrius and Phaedrus. 1963 [c. 1st century]. *Fables.* Trans. Ben Edwin Perry. Cambridge: Harvard University Press.
Bayly, C.A. 2004. *The Birth of the Modern World, 1780–1914: Global Connections and Comparisons.* Malden: Blackwell.
Bell, Bill. 2012. "Signs Taken for Wonders: An Anecdote Taken from History." *New Literary History* 43.2: 309–329.
Benjamin, Walter. 2002 [1982]. *The Arcades Project.* Trans. Howard Eiland and Kevin McLaughlin. Cambridge: Harvard University Press.
Berman, Marshall. 1988. *All That is Solid Melts Into Air: The Experience of Modernity.* New York: Penguin.
Blumenberg, Hans. 2015 [1987]. *The Laughter of the Thracian Woman: A Protohistory of Theory.* Trans. Spencer Hawkins. New York: Bloomsbury.
Carlyle, Thomas. 1919 [1840–1841]. *On Heroes, Hero-Worship, and the Heroic in History.* Ed. Annie Russell Marble. New York: Macmillan.
Christian, Barbara. 1987. "The Race for Theory." *Cultural Critique* 6: 51–63.
Coates, Christopher. 1993. "What *Was* the New Historicism?" *The Centennial Review* 37.2: 267–280.
Cole, Teju (@tejucole). 2011–2013. *Small Fates.* Twitter.com.
Conrad, Sebastian. 2016 [2013]. *What is Global History?* Princeton: Princeton University Press.
Darnton, Robert. 2013. "Blogging, Now and Then (250 Years Ago)." *European Romantic Review* 24.3: 255–270.
Darnton, Robert. 2010. *The Devil in the Holy Water or the Art of Slander from Louis XIV to Napoleon.* Philadelphia: University of Pennsylvania Press.
Dean, Michelle. 2019. *Sharp: The Women Who Made an Art of Having an Opinion.* New York: Grove Press.
Disraeli, Isaac. 1793. *A dissertation on anecdotes; by the author of* Curiosities of Literature. London: Kearley and Murray.
Drew, Benjamin. 2008 [1856]. *The Refugee: Narratives of Fugitive Slaves in Canada.* Toronto: Dundurn Press.

Drakakis, John and Monika Fludernik. 2014. "Introduction: Beyond New Historicism?" *Poetics Today* 35.4: 495–513.
Dumitrescu, Irina and Bruce Holsinger. 2019. *In Brief.* Special Issue of *New Literary History* 50.3.
Eisenstadt, Schmuel N. 2017 [2002]. "Multiple Modernities." In: Schmuel N. Eisenstadt (ed.). *Multiple Modernities.* London: Routledge. 1–30.
Engels, Friedrich and Karl Marx. 1955 [1848]. *The Communist Manifesto with Selections from The Eighteenth Brumaire of Louis Bonaparte and Capital.* Trans. Samuel Moore. New York: Appleton-Century-Crofts.
Fénéon, Félix. 2007. *Novels in Three Lines.* Trans. Luc Sante. New York: New York Review of Books.
Fenves, Peter. 2001. *Arresting Language: From Leibniz to Benjamin.* Stanford: Stanford University Press.
Fineman, Joel. 1989. "The History of the Anecdote: Fiction and Fiction." In: H. Aram Veeser (ed.). *The New Historicism.* London: Routledge. 49–76.
Fish, Stanley. 1980. *Is There A Text in This Class? The Authority of Interpretive Communities.* Cambridge: Harvard University Press.
Fleming, Paul. 2012. "On the Edge of Non-Contingency: Anecdotes and the Lifeworld." *Telos* 158: 21–35.
Fleming, Paul. 2011. "'Kannitverstan': The Contingent Understanding of Anecdotes." *Oxford German Studies* 40.1: 72–81.
Fleming, Paul. 2011. "The perfect story: Anecdote and exemplarity in Linnaeus and Blumenberg." *Thesis Eleven* 104.1: 72–86.
Gallagher, Catherine and Stephen Greenblatt. 2000. *Practicing New Historicism.* Chicago: Chicago University Press.
Gallop, Jane. 2002. *Anecdotal Theory.* Durham: Duke University Press.
Gamper, Michael and Ruth Mayer (eds.). 2017. *Kurz & Knapp. Zur Mediengeschichte kleiner Formen vom 17. Jahrhundert bis zur Gegenwart.* Bielefeld: Transcript.
Giddens, Anthony. 1990. *The Consequences of Modernity.* Cambridge: Polity.
Ginzburg, Carlo. 1993. "Microhistory: Two or Three Things That I Know About it." Trans. John and Anne C. Tedeschi. *Critical Inquiry* 20.1: 10–35.
Gladwell, Malcolm. 2000. *The Tipping Point: How Little Things Can Make a Big Difference.* New York: Little, Brown and Company.
Gluck, Carol. 2011. "The End of Elsewhere: Writing Modernity Now." *The American Historical Review* 116.3: 676–687.
Gossman, Lionel. 2003. "Anecdote and History." *History and Theory* 42.2: 43–168.
Greenblatt, Stephen. 1988. *Shakespearian Negotiations: The Circulation of Social Energy in Renaissance England.* Oxford: Clarendon Press.
Greenblatt, Stephen. 1980. *Renaissance Self-Fashioning: From More to Shakespeare.* Chicago: Chicago University Press.
Hein, Jürgen. 1991. "Die Anekdote." In: Otto Knörich (ed.). *Formen der Literatur in Einzeldarstellungen.* Stuttgart: Kröner. 14–20.
Hilzinger, Sonja. 1997. *Anekdotisches Erzählen im Zeitalter der Aufklärung. Zum Struktur- und Funktionswandel der Gattung Anekdote in Historiographie, Publizistik und Literatur des 18. Jahrhunderts.* Stuttgart: Metzler.

James, Henry. 1934. *The Art of the Novel: Critical Prefaces by Henry James*. Ed. Richard P. Blackmur. New York: Scribner's.

James, Henry. 1984 [1898]. "The Question of the Opportunities." In: *Literary Criticism*. New York: Library of America. 651–657.

Jenkins, Henry, Sam Ford, and Joshua Green. 2013. *Spreadable Media: Creating Value and Meaning in a Networked Culture*. New York: New York University Press.

Law, Graham and Norimasa Morita. 2011. "Internationalizing the Popular Print Marketplace." In: Christine Bold (ed.). *US Popular Print Culture, 1860–1920*. Oxford: Oxford University Press. 211–229.

Lee, Benjamin and Edward LiPuma. 2004. *Financial Derivatives and the Globalization of Risk*. Durham: Duke University Press.

Lee, Benjamin and Edward LiPuma. 2002. "Cultures of Circulation: The Imagination of Modernity." *Public Cultures* 14.1: 191–213.

Lehman, Robert S. 2016. *Impossible Modernism: T. S. Eliot, Walter Benjamin, and the Critique of Historical Reason*. Stanford: Stanford University Press.

Levine, Caroline. 2015. *Forms: Whole, Rhythm, Hierarchy, Network*. Princeton: Princeton University Press.

Lorenz, Matthias N. and Thomas Nehrlich (eds.). 2019. "Internationale Tagung im Kleist-Museum. Kleists Anekdoten – Zur Größe der Kleinen Formen." *Kleist Jarbuch 2019*. Stuttgart: Metzler. 231–362.

Lukács, Georg. 1971 [1920]. *The Theory of the Novel: A Historico-Philosophical Essay on the Forms of Great Epic Literature*. Trans. Anna Rostock. Cambridge: MIT Press.

Lyotard, Jean-François. 1984 [1979]. *The Postmodern Condition: A Report on Knowledge*. Trans. Geoff Bennington and Brian Massumi. Minneapolis: University of Minnesota Press.

Mattelart, Armand. 2000 [1996]. *Networking the World, 1794–2000*. Trans. Liz Carey-Libbrecht and James A. Cohen. Minneapolis: University of Minnesota Press.

McGill, Meredith L. 2003. *American Literature and the Culture of Reprinting, 1834–1853*. Philadelphia: University of Pennsylvania Press.

Meade, Marion. 1989. *Dorothy Parker: What Fresh Hell Is This?* New York: Penguin.

"minor, adj. and n." 2019. *OED = The Oxford English Dictionary*. 2000–. 3rd ed. online. Oxford: Oxford University Press. <www.oed.com/view/Entry/118931> [accessed February 25, 2020].

Novalis (Friedrich von Hardenberg). 1997. *Philosophical Writings*. Trans. Margaret Mahoney Stoljar. Albany: State University of New York Press.

Osterhammel, Jürgen. 2014 [2009]. *The Transformation of the World: A Global History of the Nineteenth Century*. Trans. Patrick Camiller. Princeton: Princeton University Press.

Parker, Dorothy. 2006 [1926]. "Anecdote." In: Marion Meade (ed.). *The Portable Dorothy Parker*. New York: Penguin. 88.

Patterson, Annabel. "Foul, His Wife, the Mayor, and Foul's Mare: The Power of Anecdote in Tudor Historiography." In: Ronald R. Kelly and David Harris Sacks (eds.). *The Historical Imagination in Early Modern Britain: History, Rhetoric, and Fiction, 1500–1800*. Cambridge: Cambridge University Press.

Pechter, Edward. 1987. "The New Historicism and Its Discontents: Politicizing Renaissance Drama." *PMLA* 102.3: 292–303.

Plato. 1921 [c. 369 B.C.]. *Theaetetus. Sophist.* Trans. Harold North Fowler. Cambridge: Harvard University Press.
Porter, Carolyn. 1988. "Are We Being Historical Yet?" *The South Atlantic Quarterly* 87.4: 743–786.
Procopius. 1940 [c. 550]. *On Buildings.* Trans. H. B. Dewing. Cambridge: Harvard University Press.
Procopius. 1935 [c. 550]. *Anecdota or Secret History.* Trans. H. B. Dewing. Cambridge: Harvard University Press.
Procopius. 1914–1928 [c. 550]. *History of the Wars.* 5 vols. Trans. H. B. Dewing. Cambridge: Harvard University Press.
Reynolds, Joshua. 1797 [1781]. *A Journey to Flanders and Holland.* In: *The Works of Sir Joshua Reynolds.* Vol. 2. London: Cadell and Davies. 1–125.
Said, Edward W. 1982. "Travelling Theory." *Raritan: A Quarterly Review* 1.3: 41–67.
Sedgwick, Eve Kosofsky. 2003. *Touching Feeling: Affect, Pedagogy, Performativity.* Durham: Duke University Press.
Slauter Will. 2019. *Who Owns the News? A History of Copyright.* Stanford: Stanford University Press.
Slauter, Will. 2012. "The Paragraph as Information Technology: How News Travelled in the Eighteenth-Century Atlantic World." *Annales HSS* 67.2: 253–278.
Stadter, Philip A. 2014. "Plutarch's Compositional Technique: The Anecdote Collections and the Parallel Lives." *Greek, Roman, and Byzantine Studies* 54: 665–686.
Stevanovska, Malina. 2009. "Exemplary or Singular? The Anecdote in Historical Narrative." *SubStance* 118.38: 16–30.
Therborn, Göran. 2003. "Entangled Modernities." *European Journal of Social Thought* 6.3: 293–305.
Voltaire (François-Marie Arouet). 1901 [1764]. "Anecdotes." In: *A Philosophical Dictionary.* Part I, A- Calends. *The Works of Voltaire.* Vol. 3. Trans. William F. Fleming. New York: Dumont. 176–202.
Voltaire (François-Marie Arouet). 1901 [1751]. *The Age of Louis XIV. The Works of Voltaire.* Vol. 12. Trans. William F. Fleming. New York: Dumont. 176–202.
Voltaire (François-Marie Arouet). 1785 [1764]. *Le siècle de Louis XIV.* In: *Oeuvres complètes de Voltaire.* Vol. 12. Kehl: de l'imprimerie de la société littéraire-typographique.
Weld, Theodore Dwight. 2011 [1839]. *Slavery As It Is: Testimony of a Thousand Witnesses.* Chapel Hill: University of North Carolina Press.
White, Hayden. 2014 [1973]. *Metahistory: The Historical Imagination in 19th-Century Europe.* 40th Anniversary Edition. Baltimore: John Hopkins University Press.
Woertendyke, Gretchen. 2009. "Romance to Novel: A Secret History." *Narrative* 17.3: 255–273.
Wood, James Robert. 2019. *Anecdotes of Enlightenment: Human Nature from Locke to Wordsworth.* Charlottesville: University of Virginia Press.
Zill, Rüdiger. 2014. "Anekdote." In: Robert Buch and Daniel Weidner (eds.). *Blumenberg lesen. Ein Glossar.* Frankfurt am Main: Suhrkamp. 26–42.

TRUTH

Gerhard Regn
The Heathen in Heaven: Anecdote and Truth in Dante's *Commedia*

Translated by Michael Thomas Taylor

Abstract: The contribution directs its attention to a blind spot in new historical treatments of the anecdote. While new historicism deploys the anecdotal to spark new perspectives on textual traditions and to enliven the historical past, the approach largely ignores the dimension of production in its analyses. This essay, in contrast, foregrounds the question of production in its reading of Dante Alighieri's *Commedia*. Focusing on the poet's fashioning of anecdotes concerning the Roman Emperor Trajan into visions of "the heathen in heaven," the essay ultimately argues that the "little story" of Trajan functions as a *mise en abyme* of the larger work of the *Commedia*.

Keywords: Auerbach, Dante, Mimesis, New Historicism.

1

In *Practicing New Historicism* (2000), Catherine Gallagher and Stephen Greenblatt emphatically affirm the programmatic role that the anecdote plays for the new historicist project. In their view, it is above all the focus on the anecdotal that allows new historicist scholars to best pursue their "commitment to particularity" (19), as the authors write. It is in this way that they see a "circulation of social energy" (Greenblatt 1988: 1–10) being set into motion. New historicist cultural poetics believes it can thereby create the fiction of a reality effect in order to revive a dead past. Greenblatt's *Shakespearian Negotiations: The Circulation of Social Energy in Renaissance England* (1988) famously begins with the dictum: "I began with the desire to speak with the dead" (1).

Gallagher and Greenblatt consider two different, but nevertheless complementary, varieties of the anecdote as relevant within the literary-critical field of application of new historicism.[1] The first defines anecdotes as "little stories"

---

[1] Greenblatt expressed his theoretical reflections on the role of the anecdote for literary critical practice in Chapter 1, "The Touch of the Real" (Gallagher and Greenblatt 2000: 20–48), whereas the definitive formulation of this idea is a joint work of the two authors.

https://doi.org/10.1515/9783110668490-004

(2000: 21), which are mostly "marginal, odd, fragmentary, unexpected and crude," i.e., "unfamiliar cultural texts" providing access to historical reality, and which allow new historicists to interact "in interesting ways with the intimately familiar works of the literary canon" (28) in order to gain surprisingly new insights into "great" literature – something that at first seems to share nothing in common with anecdotes, beyond contemporaneity. Finally, the field notes of ethnology are an important reference text for the anecdotal "little stories" of new historicism.[2] This is possible because these little stories disrupt the well-rehearsed semantics of the "great" literary narratives that, as a rule, conditioned the reception of canonized works. A well-known example of this procedure can be found in the chapter of *Shakespearean Negotiations* entitled "Fiction and Friction," where Greenblatt draws from a cross-gender anecdote from the 1580s related by Montaigne, in order to produce an innovative reading of Shakespeare's comedy *Twelfth Night*, which was written soon thereafter (but not performed until 1601 or 1602) (1988: 66–93). The second variety does not consist in bringing together anecdote and literary text, but aims rather to "anecdotalize" canonical works themselves. This happens when the literary critic chisels out a small fragment from these works – a little story or even merely the description of a trivial concrete detail – that appears rather marginal in relation to the overarching narrative, but that precisely for that very reason is intended to enable a new way of approaching the reality into which the work is embedded and to which it refers: "a new access to the real" (47). The source of inspiration for this kind of anecdote is a classic work of literary criticism, written between 1942 and 1945, namely Erich Auerbach's *Mimesis: The Representation of Reality in Western Literature* (1946).[3] Unlike Auerbach, however, new historicists such as Gallagher and Greenblatt firmly distance themselves from a holistic hermeneutic that manifestly abstracts from the anecdotal text fragment to the work as an ultimately organically conceived whole. Instead, by means of an anecdotal presentation, they aim to "enliven" a reality that is no longer present and has become foreign in order to charge it with (social) energy.[4] The two versions of the anecdotal not only complement each other;[5] they also have in common

---

[2] See Geertz (1973).
[3] See Gallagher and Greenblatt (2000: 35).
[4] One important source of inspiration for this innovative method is traditional rhetoric, which fuses *enérgeia* (dynamization) and *enárgeia* (particularization), in order to allow these absences to appear vividly before the eyes.
[5] This complementarity is justified, however, with recourse to Auerbach: "The fact that Auerbach did not feel obliged to read every moment of his text, that he could concentrate on an anecdote and pressure it to reveal a whole system, in principle liberated the critic to look

that both are conditioned by the perspective of their reception: literary critics either fish their anecdotes out of the flotsam of past culture, thus assigning them an anecdotal status, or else split the works with which they deal into anecdotal fragments.

What is left out of the new historical treatment of the anecdotal is the perspective of production, that is, the question of how authors, especially those belonging to the literary canon, handled anecdotes. I would like to take up this question in the following by examining Dante Alighieri's *Commedia* (probably begun between 1304 and 1307 and completed in the last years of the poet's life before he died in 1321). Dante's poem about the afterlife recommends itself for such an analysis not only because Auerbach grants this text a privileged role in *Mimesis* among the other works the book discusses,[6] but also because the *Commedia* is conceived as the story of the multiple episodic encounters of the wanderer "Dante"[7] together with the souls of the three kingdoms in the next world. Moreover, Auerbach assigned a counter-discursive function to these episodes that is very much in line with the new historicists' conception of anecdotes, in the sense that these episodes potentially raise objections to the overarching cultural discourse, namely the *grand récit* of late medieval theology.[8] Since this interpretation of Dante by Auerbach was criticized quite early on,[9] while also becoming highly influential, it is time again to put it to the test. To this end, I will select an episode in which the anecdotal is not merely brought to bear in the broadly defined understanding postulated by the new historicists. According to Gallagher and Greenblatt, an anecdote does not require much: a brief (mostly narrative) piece of text that, by focusing on what is singular, strange, or surprising, revitalizes a cultural world that has become alien (including its canonical "high" literature). Yet much more is at stake. The

---

for fragments scattered across a period's whole textual production" (Gallagher and Greenblatt 2000: 46). The fragmentation of the literary work thus promotes the fragmentation of the embedding culture and vice versa.

6 Auerbach's reflections on realism emerged from his engagement with Dante, first in *Dante: Poet of the Secular World* (1929) and then in "Figura" (1938).

7 The *Commedia* is a first-person narrative: the experiencing "I" is the autobiographically stylized *persona* "Dante" (marked in the following always with quotation marks), whose journey into the afterlife is recounted by the narrating "I" (closely linked with the author Dante) in the book that is the *Commedia*.

8 The best-known examples are the wanderer's encounters with Francesca da Rimini (*Inferno:* V) and Count Ugolino (ibid.: XXXIII), in which Dante uses the mimesis of reality to positively steer the reader's sympathies, which appears as an objection to God's judgment.

9 See Friedrich (1942).

anecdote concerns an example that can also be reconciled, in a much more specific way, with the consensus definition of this genre in literary studies.[10]

2

Our anecdote begins with an encounter of the wanderer through the afterlife and the Roman Emperor Trajan who, despite having died as a heathen, finds his place in Christian paradise, where "Dante" meets him in the heaven of Jupiter, the sphere of the just rulers (*Paradiso* XX: 43–48).[11] The anecdotal aspect here is not so much the encounter itself but rather the narrative that is recounted on this occasion, leading to an explanation of why this heathen has made it to heaven despite the apparent contradiction with Christian dogma. The story is told by a mighty eagle who speaks as a divine allegory of justice, and whose figure is made up of the righteous who have entered into salvation and been transfigured into luminous flames ("the flames from which I take my form" ["i fuochi ond'io figura fommi"] [*Paradiso* XX: 34]). The focus is on the bird's head, which the wanderer sees in profile, with a constellation of the most righteous forming the bird's eye, and the psalmist David as its pupil ("He that blazes as the pupil with a central spark / was the one who sang the praises of the Holy Ghost" ["Colui che luce in mezzo a la pupilla, / fu il cantor de lo Spirito Santo"] [*Paradiso* XX: 37–38]); and in the lights that form the arch of the eyebrow, the prophet Ezekiel, Emperor Constantine, the Sicilian King William the Good, and the Virgilian hero Ripheus also appear, together with Trajan. The special importance that Dante attached to this anecdote is made clear by the fact he tells it twice, which is quite unusual for the *Commedia*, for even before the anecdote about Trajan is recited to the wanderer in paradise in an abbreviated form, it is brought to his attention in Purgatory, and in far greater detail (*Purgatorio* X: 73–93).

The tenth song of *Purgatorio* depicts "Dante's" ascent through the first circle of the Mountain of Purgatory, where the souls of the proud have to carry stone loads on their backs as penance – which, according to the law of *contrappasso*,

---

10 See Rohmer (1992: 566–579).
11 As is well known, the *Commedia* – set in the year 1300 and divided into three *cantiche* – tells the story of "Dante's" journey through the afterlife, passing through hell, purgatory, and paradise.

weighs down upon them deeply.¹² Even before the wanderer meets the sinners, he notices that the cliff at the edge of the path is decorated with a series of marble reliefs. These depict scenes of humility, counterimages to pride that serve to admonish the *superbi* who pass by; the cultural points of reference for Dante's readers are not so much the well-known examples of epic *ekphrasis* from the literature of antiquity as the works of Christian sculpture that adorned church portals, pulpits, or baptismal fonts for the purpose of edification.¹³ The theme of the first relief is the Annunciation of Mary, that of the second is the dance of David in front of the Ark of the Covenant, and that of the third is the story of Trajan and the widow. This story tells how the powerful ruler of the Imperium Romanum suspended the start of an important military campaign to give a nameless woman from the common people satisfaction for the death of her son, which was caused by his soldiers as they rode out;¹⁴ later adaptations of the anecdote further explain that the child was trampled by one of the horses.¹⁵

Research repeatedly categorizes this little story as belonging to the genre of the anecdote,¹⁶ and for good reason. According to the common definition of the genre, anecdotes are characterized in particular by the fact that the events they recount vividly depict the salient character traits of historical personalities of public interest (Rohmer 1992: 567); moreover, these events are not the focus of grand history writing because they are situated either in the private sphere or at the margins of representative publicity. This is why anecdotes often refer to things that are not historically proven or for which there is insufficient historical evidence, despite the fact that they always claim to be true. The tradition of the story about Trajan makes this quite clear. The event upon which the story

---

12 The Mountain of Purgatory has a three-part structure: Ante-Purgatory is in the lowest level, the seven circles containing the penitents are in the central and principle level, and Earthly Paradise is at the highest level.
13 See Gmelin (1955: 177).
14 Dante most probably knew the story about Trajan in the version passed down in the *Speculum historiale* by Vincent of Beauvais (mid-thirteenth century). An Italian version of this text is found in the *Fiori e vita di filosofi ed altri savi ed imperadori*, which was translated into Italian during the time of Dante's youth. There, it is hinted that the soldiers on horseback are responsible for the death of the widow's little son: "A widow asked him that justice be done to those who had caused the death of her dear son" ("una femina vedova [...] richeselo che li facesse diritto di coloro che le avevano morto un suo figliuolo") (Anon. 1959: 527). [Unless otherwise indicated, all translations from the Italian are by Michael Thomas Taylor in consultation with the author.] The anecdote was widely known in the middle ages. On the tradition of the Trajan anecdote, see Boni (1906: 3–39); Paris (1878: 261–298).
15 See Boesch (1951: 218–221).
16 See Chiavacci Leonardi (qtd. in Dante 1991–1997 II: 304n76); Szenec (1957: 106).

focuses is, of course, not a topic of "official" historiography. Rather, as a disturbance of great history, it is relegated to the periphery. The widow stops an important campaign of the emperor, which we may assume to be one of the Dacian Wars (Rohmer 1992: 567).[17] It is therefore not surprising, for instance, that Cassius Dio, the Roman historiographer of *Roman History* (written over twenty years at the turn of the first to the second century A.D.), does not mention our anecdote in his description of Trajan's campaigns (including those against the Dacians) (Cassius Dio 1925: 361–423). Elsewhere, however, in the Hadrian chapter of his work of history, Cassius Dio makes a remark in a single, concise sentence that aims to demonstrate Hadrian's accessibility to his subjects from among the common people: a woman appeals to the emperor with an unspecified request, and the emperor tries to fob her off with the remark that he has no time; this prompts the woman to reply that someone who behaves this way is not worthy of being emperor, whereupon Hadrian listens to her; the subject of justice is not mentioned in the story (436). This brief note, which is devoid of any narrative particularization (and thus at best represents an anecdote *in nuce*), was probably transferred thereafter to Trajan, becoming the starting point of our anecdote.[18] From today's perspective, the Trajan episode is thus historiographically unfounded. But this was unproblematic from a medieval perspective, insofar as it was common practice at the time for authors of historiographical works or the like (such as the *Lives* of famous figures) to attribute the status of testimony to their own text qua unspoken self-authorization.[19]

As already hinted at above, the anecdote of Trajan and the widow circulated widely in the Middle Ages – though, of course, it receives a very specific twist in Dante's retelling. What is unique is, first, the decision to tell the story as the *ekphrasis* of a bas-relief, and moreover of a quite unusual kind. The sculpture is not only of the highest perfection but also of a kind unknown to the viewer "Dante" in his earthly world, and which he therefore considers to be completely new: "this speech made visible, / new to us because it is not found on earth"

---

[17] The conquest of Dacia was already regarded by ancient historiographers as one of Trajan's outstanding achievements; see, in particular, the Trajan chapter in the *Roman History* written by Cassius Dio (1925: 361–423).
[18] In Cassius Dio's account, the Hadrian chapter follows directly after the Trajan chapter, which may have facilitated this transfer. The transfer from Hadrian to Trajan is probably connected with the fact that the former, unlike the latter, was not regarded as a morally exemplary ruler figure.
[19] This applies, in our case, to the *Vitae* of Trajan as well as to the correlative *Vitae* of Gregorius. Only in the *Legenda aurea* (c. 1264) by Jacobus de Voragine is the question of sources addressed.

("visibile parlare, / novello a noi perché qui non si trova" [*Purgatorio* X: 95–96]). The sculpture depicts how the widow, visibly filled with pain, grabs the reins of the emperor, who is on horseback, to stop him and present her concern. The sculpture itself is so successful that the viewer becomes aware of the developing dialogue in all its details – with twelve verses, the conversation is the longest part of the anecdote – even without hearing it acoustically; it is observable speech. Dante makes it unmistakably clear that it is not simply the wanderer's prior knowledge of our little stories that enables him to extrapolate from the depicted scene what was spoken in it;[20] rather, the dialogue is heard with a spiritual ear, directly and precisely as the first-person narrator tells it to the reader of the *Commedia*. This is important because the function of the anecdote as a bearer of truth beyond any doubt depends on it. The guarantor of truth is ultimately the one who created this astonishing "speech made visible" (*Purgatorio* X: 94–95). Who is this artist? None other than God: "He in whose sight nothing can be new / wrought this speech made visible" ("Colui che mai non vide cosa nova / produsse esto visibile parlare" [ibid.]).

The scene of dialogue in which Trajan's nature manifests itself is developed from a particular situation that the divine sculptor has captured in a *tableau vivant*. This shows the plaintive widow stopping the emperor on horseback, surrounded by his entourage, which carries the army's banners, upon which eagles are depicted on a gold ground, fluttering in the wind. New historicist practitioners of cultural poetics might note with approval that Dante here is optimally accounting for the "commitment to particularity" (Gallagher and Greenblatt 2000: 19) they consider so important, because focusing on the particular serves to evoke a larger historical connection to reality. The decisive detail is the banners which, with their eagle on a gold ground, refer to the flags that were the emblems of troops loyal to the emperor in Dante's time;[21] the standards of the Roman troops were known to be of a completely different kind, namely not made of cloth but of a metal which often had a shimmer of gold. This is important because Dante wants to present Trajan less as a figure from antiquity than as one of medieval Christianity. More precisely, he is intended to appear as the figure of the good emperor who embodies, for the author of the *Commedia* (as well as for Dante as a theorist of the medieval emperorship, which is the role he takes in his *Monarchia*, completed around 1312, at the same time that

---

20 The fact that our author does indeed bring such prior knowledge into play is shown by the prelude to the *ekphrasis*: "Depicted there was the glorious act / of the Roman prince" ("Quiv' era storiata l'alta gloria / del roman principato" [*Purgatorio* X: 73–4]). But this is irrelevant; instead, what matters is that "Dante" can actually hear the dialogue with his spiritual ear.
21 See Chiavacci Leonardi (qtd. in Dante 1991–1997 II: 305n80).

Dante was working on his *Paradiso*), hope for a restitution of the divinely ordained political order, the deplorable loss of which is one of the great themes of Dante's epic poem. This basic theme of the *Commedia* is expressed most pointedly in the grandiose apocalyptic vision in the chants of the Earthly Paradise, where the imminent arrival of the political savior figure of "a Five Hundred Ten and Five" ("un cinquecento diece e cinque" [*Purgatorio* XXXIII: 43]), which is to be considered imperial and connected with the imperial eagle, is announced as an antitype to the world-destroying six hundred sixty-six of the Revelation of John (Revelation 13.18).[22] As one sees, it is the seemingly insignificant detail of the banners fluttering in the wind over the troops that evokes the medieval imperial ideology and culture so important to Dante.

As expected, the tradition of our story about Trajan focuses on the ruler's sense of justice. A paradigmatic example is the story as found in the anonymous *Fiori e vita di filosofi ed altri savi ed imperadori* (late thirteenth century) of the Italian translation of the *Speculum historiale* (mid-thirteenth century) by Vincent of Beauvais, to which Dante refers directly or indirectly, and whose beginning makes unmistakably clear its central topic, namely the justice of the emperor: "Trajan was a very just emperor" ("Traiano fu imperadore molto iusto" [Anon. 1959: 527]).[23] Of course, Dante also gives the justice motif a sharp contour. Indeed, this is the topic around which the entire dialogue between the ruler and the widow revolves: the woman demands legal satisfaction for the serious harm inflicted on her by the emperor's troops, and Trajan grants it to her, despite the fact that thus a matter of the utmost importance for the empire – the forthcoming campaign – has to be stopped. The version of the anecdote given by the *Purgatorio* therefore ends with a formal declaration by Trajan that, before going to war, he wanted to fulfill his duty to the widow because justice demanded it: "I

---

22 The immediate context makes it clear that this is a figure of an imperial nature or with an imperial function: the announced "five hundred ten and five" will, as one reads in *Purgatorio*, put an end to the absence of the imperial eagle of Italy: "The eagle [...] shall not remain without heir forever" ("Non sarà tutto tempo sanza reda / l'agugalia" [XXXIII: 37–38]); for Dante, the political calamity consists essentially in the fact that since the time of Frederick II the emperors of the Roman Empire no longer resided in Italy, "the garden of the empire" ("'l giardin de lo imperio" [*Purgatorio* VI: 105]).

23 As mentioned above, the *Fiori* is an Italian translation of the *Speculum Historiale*. We do not know whether Dante read the episode about Trajan in the Latin or the Italian version. What we can conclude from Dante's treatment of the subject, however, is that he was also familiar with yet other versions of the story of Trajan and the widow. Among the vernacular texts, the *Novellino* is of particular importance, where the Trajan anecdote begins with the focus on the motif of justice: "The Emperor Trajan was a very just ruler" ("Lo 'mperadore Traiano fue molto giustissimo signore" [Anon. 1959: 118]).

must discharge / my debt to you before I go to war / Justice wills it" ("ei convene / ch'i' solva il mio dovere anzi ch'i' mova: / giustizia vuole" [*Purgatorio* X: 91–93]). Hence, at the end of his Trajan narrative, Dante thematizes, to great effect, the central motif of justice that is mentioned at the very outset in the *Fiori*.

The significance Dante attributes to Trajan's justice is, of course, also and not least of all evident from the fact that our author takes up the episode again in *Paradiso*, where Trajan finds his eternal place in the Jupiter sphere of the just rulers. The necessary though not-yet sufficient condition for Trajan to do so is for the emperor to have fulfilled the mission on earth that is the task of a truly godly ruler, namely, to create an order based on an earthly justice that reflects, and thus anticipates, divine justice. The description of the sphere of Jupiter (*Paradiso* XVIII–XX), which extends over three songs, clearly foregrounds this message from the very beginning. It describes how the blessed souls, appearing as stars arranged by the divine *artifex*, form an eagle's head emerging from a whole series of previously existing but constantly changing figurations. The first of these writes the decisive divine message in the firmament in golden letters, at the very outset in the eighteenth canto. The message reads "DILIGITE IUSTITIAM ... QUI IUDICATIS TERRAM" (*Paradiso* XVIII: 91–93) – those who judge others on earth must unconditionally respect and love justice. Here, the divine calligrapher quotes his own words – namely, the beginning of the *Liber Sapientiae* of the Old Testament, whereby the last letter of the quotation, the "M" majuscule of *TERRAM* as the sign of the divinely ordained monarchy,[24] finally transforms into the figure of the imperial eagle, which, unlike in the relief of *Purgatorio* depicting Trajan, no longer merely appears on a golden ground but is itself made of gold.[25] When the wanderer finally sees Trajan transformed into a source of light in the last of the three songs dedicated to the sphere of Jupiter (which is also the occasion for him to be reminded of our anecdote),[26] he knows that he is looking at the Roman Emperor as a divinely transfigured representation of the righteous ruler. The

---

[24] Latin: *monarchia*, which is also the title of the work in which Dante seeks to establish the Roman Emperor's immediacy to God.

[25] Or more precisely: in which he seems to be doing so. The "M" that transforms into an eagle is a golden letter only because it is formed from the shining golden lights of the blessed. The change from the golden background of the banners to the golden appearance of the eagle is a figure of enhancement that reflects the difference in rank between purgatory and paradise. On the letter "M" in the songs of the Jupiter sphere, see Malato (1970: 665–666).

[26] In its repetition, the anecdote is condensed to a minimum: Trajan is "the one who [...] / consoled the widow when she lost her son" ["colui che [...] / la vedovella consolò del figlio" [*Paradiso* XX: 44–45]).

anecdote of Trajan and the widow thus serves to profile the theme of justice by means of a singular event. In this respect, Dante is writing within the mainstream of texts that have told the Trajan story before him. Unlike most of his immediate predecessors, especially the authors of the *Fiori*, the *Novellino* (1280–1300), or the *Legenda aurea* (c. 1264), Dante does not restrict himself in representing this little story to profiling the central theme of justice. Rather, he supplements this with additional themes in such a way that the ethics of the anecdote are given a far more Christian twist than is the case in the *Fiori*, the *Novellino*, and the *Legenda aurea*. The fact that Dante thus builds much more closely on those older texts that first began circulating the Trajan story in a form available to us (i.e., the *Vitae* of Gregorius written by Paulus Diaconus from the eighth century and Iohannes Diaconus from the ninth century)[27] is worth mentioning in passing.

The first of the themes hinted at above is the *pietà*. I already mentioned that in the *Purgatorio*, Dante does not open the story of Trajan, as his immediate Italian predecessors did, by naming the theme of justice; rather, he explicitly refers to it only at the end of the tale. This observation, however, must be supplemented by noting that "justice" is merely the penultimate and not the last word of the anecdote. For the final statement of Trajan's "speech made visible" ("visibile parlare" [*Purgatorio* X: 95]) reads, in its entirety: "Justice wills it and compassion bids me stay" ("Giustizia vuole e pietà mi ritiene" [ibid.: 93]). When Trajan, who is after all a figure from antiquity, speaks of his *pietà*, then this is not the Roman-pagan *pietas* (in the sense of reverential-affectionate attachment to deities, fatherland, family, or the like),[28] but the Christian notion of mercy that Thomas Aquinas, whom Dante regards as one of his most important authorities in theological matters, in his *Summa Theologica* (1265–1273) called the greatest of all virtues (II II: q 30 a 4). The common Latin term for this is *misericordia*. Dante focuses on this aspect by interweaving multiple textual elements, each of which, at first glance, seems to be rather incidental. First, he stresses the widow as deserving of mercy. She is, in her position as widow, vulnerable and stands at the lower end of the social hierarchy.[29] Dante succeeds

---

27 The Trajan anecdotes contained in the *Vitae* of Gregorius written by the two clerics are printed in the *Patrologia latina* (1844–1865): *PL* 75, columns 56–57 (Paulus Diaconus) and *PL* 75, columns 104–105 (Iohannes Diaconus).
28 The standard example is Vergil's *Aeneas*, whose *pietas* was topical and first given prominence in the *exordium* of the *Aeneid* (c. 29–19 B.C. I: 9–10); see Moseley (1925: 387–400).
29 Cf. Chiavacci Leonardi: "in antiquity, the widow had the lowest position in the social hierarchy because she had no protector" ("la vedova era in antico all'ultimo grado della scala sociale perché protetta da nessuno" [qtd. in Dante 1991–1997: 304n77]).

in expressing this quite complex state of affairs by means of a minute stylistic detail, for unlike the other versions of the anecdote, he does not speak of a "vedova" (in the Latin versions: *vidua*), but chooses instead the diminutive form, i.e., "vedovella" ("poor widow" [*Purgatorio* X: 77]). The diminutive suggests to the readers that they should imagine a woman who has not only lost the breadwinner of her family, and who is therefore on her own, but also a woman who is among the least powerful members of society. The connotations evoked by the diminutive are continued by Dante, who then immediately calls the widow "miserella" ("that unhappy creature") [82]). In light of Christian ethics, this second diminutive articulates the truly important point in terms of a theological concept, namely the pity deserved by the widow from the common people who lost her dear son through the fault of the imperial troops.[30] This, in turn, is named by a third diminutive in the original, "figliuol" (translated as: "My lord, avenge my murdered son for me" [84]), which functions primarily to engender affective sympathy: the intention is for the reader (like the emperor) to have an emotional reaction to the fact that it was a small child who was killed, prompting support for the widow's cause. This purpose is also furthered by the concise visual representation of the mother's suffering, which the relief shows in a dolorous pose full of pain: "weeping, / revealed in her state of grief" ("di lagrime atteggiata e di dolore" [78]). The description of the scene evidently serves to make clear that the emperor is confronted with a case in which not only his justice but also Christian mercy – *misericordia* – is called for. Only when this justice is granted out of sincerely felt compassion can it be the full expression of an exemplary Christian ethos.

The necessary complement of justice is thus compassion, to which, of course, another Christian virtue is added, quasi as the complement of the complement: namely, humility. Like mercy, humility is also one of the moral virtues securing the Christian specificity of post-pagan ethics. Given the overwhelming abundance of relevant passages from the New Testament or patristic texts, it is unnecessary to provide individual citations.[31] It should only be pointed out that humility is so important because it marks the counter-pole to the original sin of *superbia* through which all evil came into the world, and which, in the opinion of Thomas Aquinas, is therefore also the origin of all other sins. In Dante's *Purgatorio*, the *superbia* is accordingly assigned to the lowest among the seven circles of penance of the Mountain of Purgatory, the highest point

---

30 Dante does not explicitly mention this point; rather, it must be inferred from the representation of the event – the crush of the cavalry as it rides out.
31 See McInerney (2016).

of which, by contrast, is the Earthly Paradise, as the threshold of the transition to the spheres of the Christian heaven.

The virtue of *umiltà*, unlike *giustizia* and *pietà*, is no longer explicitly named within our anecdote, nor does it need to be, because the framework within which it is embedded ensures the necessary clarity. The story of Trajan and the widow is one of the three bas-reliefs that the divine sculptor carved into the sides of the Mountain of Purgatory in the lowest terrace of pride, so that the *superbi* who repent there may be shown vivid "images of such humility" ("imagini di tante umilitadi" [*Purgatorio* X: 98]), i.e., images of exceedingly great humility, as a corrective to their sinfulness. This makes it clear that Trajan is not only an example of justice and compassion, but also of humility. Dante thus uses the anecdote to illustrate the outstanding characteristics of a historical personality in a way typical of this genre. The constellation of the three virtues of justice, compassion, and humility – in the *Commedia*, the triad always has theological connotations – depicts Trajan as a Roman emperor who exercises his office in a manner pleasing to God, mainly because the virtues mentioned are also constitutive attributes of the Christian God. This, in turn, means that the Roman Emperor rules over his subjects as the true God rules over his creatures: the monarch, who according to Dante's doctrine of rulership is endowed with power directly from God, is thus an *imago Dei*. This was true of the pagan emperors of the Roman Empire inasmuch as they fulfilled the ethical requirements of this investiture, though at best in a manner analogous to biblical typology: as figures of announcement fulfilled, in the era *sub gratia*, through the Christian emperors of the Holy Roman Empire. In Trajan's case, however, things are different. He fulfills the Christian ideas of virtue in such a perfect way that he was able, *ex post*, as it were, to become a Christian emperor despite having been a heathen. The coda of our anecdote tells how this was possible.

3

Trajan died in 117 as a heathen, unbaptized and not believing in Christ, which is why, according to dogma, his place after death was hell. Tradition holds that long after the death of the emperor, in the late sixth century, Pope Gregory the Great reflected upon the moral greatness of Trajan and pleaded for his salvation from the torment of hell. The bulk of sources indicate that God answered Gregory's intercession and wrought a miracle (Gregory was canonized not least of all because miracles were attributed to him).Dante omits the details of Gregor's actions, which are expanded upon in some variants of the story (Gregor strolls across the Trajan Forum and is reminded, probably by the monuments there, of the emperor and his merits; he weeps over the emperor's fate and prays for him in St. Peter's Cathedral; a divine voice finally announces the success of his intercession, etc.): in the *Purgatorio*, he only indicates in a half-sentence that Gregory's intercession was successful.³² According to Dante, the success is not merely that Trajan must no longer suffer the punishments of hell but that, as the return to the story of Trajan in *Paradiso* confirms, the emperor is indeed allowed to enter into heavenly salvation.³³ Dante explains this aspect in more detail in *Paradiso*: we learn there that God raised the deceased emperor from the dead, who then returned to earthly life for a short time – "back in his flesh for but a while" ("tornata ne la carne, in che fu poco" [XX: 113]) – converted to the Christian faith, and was so consumed with a great love of God – "to such fire / of the one true love" ("in tanto foco di vero amor" [XX: 115 – 116]) – that he became worthy of paradise. Unlike the anecdote about the emperor and the widow, Dante no longer describes Trajan's fate after death in the mode of *showing* that relies on dramatic "making-present," but in the mode of an argumentative-reflective *telling* that is seamlessly connected to the theological explanation of this singular event. Trajan's resurrection from the dead is but a marginal variant in the tradition of the Trajan story. Jacobus de Voragine points to as much, for instance, when he notes that "some have said" (1995: 179) Trajan was first called back to life and then entered into eternal salvation. The fact that the version Dante has chosen especially strains credulity is explicitly mentioned by our author.³⁴ His reasons for nevertheless choosing the variant in which Trajan is

---

32 Gregory, who came from a Roman patrician family, was canonized in 1297, only a few years before Dante began to compose the *Commedia* – the theme was thus topical. *Paradiso*, which speaks of "prayers / addressed to God" ("prieghi fatti a Dio" [XX: 110]), explains that this is an intercession in the strict theological sense. Trajan's "worth / urged Gregory on to his great victory" ("il cui valore / mosse Gregorio a la sua gran vittoria" [*Purgatorio* X: 74 – 75]): in speaking of Gregory's great victory, Dante means that the devout fervor of his intercession has led God, who is both omnipotent and merciful, to alter Trajan's infernal fate. In the case of Trajan, the Almighty God thus suspends the justice that results in hell; see *Inferno*: "Giustizia" – the inscription on the Gates of Hell reads – "mosse il mio alto fattore" ("JUSTICE MOVED MY MAKER ON HIGH" [III: 4]).
33 This version lists, with reference to Iohannes Diaconus, the *Legenda aurea*: "and often the Lord in his mercy grants [...] that Trajan's soul was not delivered from hell and given a place in heaven, but was simply freed from the tortures of hell. A soul (he says) can be in hell and yet, through God's mercy, not feel its pain" (Jacobus de Voragine 1995: 179).
34 "The first living soul [meaning Trajan who passed on to eternal life, G.R.] in the eyebrow and the fifth [this is a reference to Ripheus, the second pagan in paradise, G.R.] / make you wonder to find them adorning / the dwelling-place of angels" ("la prima vita del ciglio e la quinta / ti fa maravigliar, perché ne vedi / la region de li angeli dipinta" (*Paradiso* XX: 100 – 102). Here, Dante thematizes the astonishment caused by the unusual situation.

brought back from the dead are theological: he sees in this version the only possibility for paving the way to paradise for the heathen who did not die in the right faith, without violating the dogma that binds the salvation of the soul to faith in Christ.[35] Here, Dante can rely on Thomas Aquinas, who explicitly addresses the case of Trajan in his *Summa Theologica* (III, Suppl. q 71, a 5, ad 5), concluding, first, that the liberation of Trajan from the sufferings of hell was, on the basis of Gregor's intercessions, probable; and that second, the miracle of Trajan being raised from the dead could, in this context, be regarded as conforming to faith.

Dante recounts the miracle of resurrection in such a way that it appears theologically legitimized by the authority of the most important church teacher of his time. He can thus ensure that the message he wants to convey with the anecdote of Trajan and the widow gains a maximum of authoritativeness. The anecdotal narrative allows the powerful ruler of the Roman Empire to appear as a man who unites, in himself, the virtues of justice, mercy, and humility in such a way that, despite being a pagan, he embodies the ideal of the Christian ruler for whom the kingdom of heaven is opened up through the divine election of grace. Dante does not justify this election of grace through Augustine (God's will is unfathomable), but through Thomas Aquinas, because it has a meritocratic dimension: Trajan has, to a certain extent, earned this miracle. This aspect is eminently important because it indicates the ethical organizing principle of the entire *Commedia*. The (allegorically conceived) topographical structure of the afterlife vividly demonstrates that damnation, purification in purgatory, and heavenly salvation are all ranked according to the criteria of moral transgression and moral merit – in other words, not all torments of hell are the same, nor is all salvation equal.[36] Pagans who, like Aristotle, Plato, or Virgil, did not believe but lived well (that is, above all, wrote well morally) therefore end up in Dante's limbo, where their suffering does not consist in enduring

---

[35] The case of the second pagan in paradise, the Vergilian Ripheus, who also counts among the just souls in the heaven of Jupiter, is of a different nature. Through the grace of God, Ripheus accepted the Christian faith – which he could not have actually been aware of, having lived in pre-Christian antiquity – during his lifetime (cf. *Paradiso* XX: 118–129). The pre-Christian pagan Ripheus's election of grace, which is a case of implicit revelation, is given theological justification and can rely on Thomas Aquinas. The central sentence concerning the elect pagans reads: "though they did not believe in Him explicitly, they did, nevertheless, have implicit faith" ("Quia etsi non habuerunt fidem explicitam, habuerunt tamen fidem implicitam" [Thomas Aquinas II II: q 2 a 7 ob 3]). See also Chiavacci Leonardi (qtd. in Dante 1991–1997 II: 568n118–121).

[36] For the Blessed of Paradise, Dante explicates the argument regarding merit in *Paradiso* (IV: 34–39).

the torments of hell, but results solely from the condition of being far from God: this is not an invention of Dante, but theologically well founded. Iohannes Diaconus, for example, confirms this view in his discussion of the Trajan miracle.[37] Unlike John the Deacon, who could not yet have been familiar with the authority of Thomas Aquinas, Dante did not banish Trajan into limbo but placed him in the upper part of heaven – the heaven of Jupiter is the sixth of nine celestial spheres. As has already been noted, Dante wanted to make it clear that Trajan created, through his own moral perfection, the precondition for God himself to suspend divine law, a fact which is, in turn, brought to light by the anecdote about the widow.

The reference to John the Deacon focuses attention on the fact that story of Trajan gave rise to controversy during the middle ages. The *Legenda aurea*, which is to be situated both temporally and spatially in Dante's immediate milieu,[38] lists the most important variants of the Trajan narrative, including those Dante chose to include.[39] The range of options is an indication that Dante was under pressure to legitimate his version of the story, which he undoubtedly wanted to be understood as the only true version. His attempt to validate his version in an implicit reference to the authority of Thomas Aquinas is an attempt to claim theological legitimation, but Dante does not stop here. He supplements the theological argument with another argument, which he considers even more important: it focuses on the persuasiveness of his own "sacred poem," written together with heaven and earth as authors: "this sacred poem, / to which both Heaven and earth have set their hand" ("'l poema sacro / al quale ha posto mano e cielo e terra" [*Paradiso* XXV: 1–2]). Dante wants his *Commedia* to be evaluated as a written record of a visionary experience, the incommensurability of which the poet must, of course, compensate through the means of *poesis:* Dante thus stages himself in the double role of divine writer

---

[37] The relevant quote can be found above in note 26. The theological context is the discussion about *limbus patrum.*
[38] The *Legenda aurea* quickly attained wide circulation, and its author (the Archbishop of Genoa) was a well-known public figure – among other things, he served as a diplomat to the papal court of Boniface VIII in 1295. It is hard to imagine that Dante – who was, only a few years later, in 1301, also a member of a Florentine delegation to the court of Boniface VIII, did not know Jacobus de Voragine (and his work).
[39] The variants also touch upon the scene with the widow (for instance, indicating that the culprit in the death of the little boy was the emperor's son), but above all they concern Trajan's fate in the afterlife.

and earthly author.⁴⁰ The aim of the enterprise is to make credible the purported reality of the vision of the afterlife and the claim to truth associated with it.

The short story about Trajan functions as *mise en abyme* of the great *Commedia*. For the vision of Trajan's miraculous salvation that Gregorius reveals also certifies the ethical singularity to which Trajan's dealings with the widow bear witness, just as "Dante's" divinely inspired vision of the hereafter guarantees the truth of the events it beholds – which include, as one of many stories, the anecdote about Trajan and the widow and Trajan's admission into paradise. But that is not all, because the truth of the anecdote about Trajan is corroborated in another way. The story of the emperor and the widow reveals itself to the wanderer in the afterlife in the form of a work of art created by God. Thus there is no question that what the sculpture communicates can be anything but pure truth: "pure" also has a metaphysical dimension, for in taking shape in purgatory as a divine work of art, the anecdote about Trajan can appear as pure truth in the mode of beauty, entirely in accordance with medieval neoplatonism.⁴¹ Dante deploys a comparable procedure, moreover, when he again turns to the story of Trajan in *Paradiso:* here, God appears not only as a calligrapher who writes his message on the firmament in golden letters but also as a painter who, as the text expressly states, paints the supernaturally glorified appearance of Trajan on the sky in the Jupiter sphere.⁴²

Dante's version of the anecdote about Trajan, along with the surprising coda consisting of Gregorius's miracle, is a striking case of exemplary singularity. Admittedly, it in no way aims at subverting the culturally dominant Christian discourse by means of a counter-discourse. On the contrary, Dante is concerned precisely with the affirmation of what he considers to be a binding truth, whereby legitimation by undisputed theological authorities goes hand in hand with a claim, grounded in theological inspiration, that the poem is authorized by its own *poesis*. Counter-discursive functionalizations of the anecdote, in the narrower sense, and of the anecdotal, in a broader sense of the term, only

---

40 See Regn (2007). On Dante's handling of the discursive template of the vision, see Regn (2014); on the problem of fiction in the *Commedia*, see Regn (2009). The discussion about the inadequacy of the modern concept of fiction for the *Commedia* was initiated by Singleton (1957) and has been one of the core questions of Dante research since at least Hollander (1980).
41 In theological terms, the pure truth is beautiful because it is formed by divine *artifex* and thus no longer sullied with the stain of the fallen world, the *peccatum original*.
42 "The first living soul in the eyebrow [...] / make you wonder to find them adorning / the dwelling-place of angels" ("La prima vita del ciglio [...] / ti fa meravigliar, perché ne vedi / la region de li angeli dipinta" [*Paradiso* XX: 97–101]). In contrast to the quasi physically solid sculpture of the *Purgatorio*, we are now dealing with an image that has passed over into the immaterial, entirely in harmony with the nature of the third sphere of heaven.

become strikingly evident in Italy shortly after Dante. This happens most tellingly in Giovanni Boccaccio's *Decameron* (c. 1349–1353), where little stories of peculiar, singular, and therefore "unheard of" events undermine a modeling of the world in which Christian ethics are fundamentally important. This is apparent not least in the fact that Boccaccio conceived his collection of novellas as, among other things, a secular parody of Dante's "sacred poem."[43]

Works Cited

[Anon.] 1959 [13th c.]. *Fiori e vita di filosofi ed altri savi ed imperadori*. In: Cesare Segre and Mario Marti (eds.). *La Prosa del Duecento*. Milano: Ricciardi. 521–532.

[Anon.] 1959 [13th c.]. *Il Novellino*. In: Cesare Segre and Mario Marti (eds.). *La Prosa del Duecento*. Milano: Ricciardi. 793–882.

Auerbach, Erich. 2013 [1946]. *Mimesis – The Representation of Reality in Western Literature*. Trans. Willard R. Trask. Princeton: Princeton University Press.

Auerbach, Erich. 2007 [1929]. *Dante: Poet of the Secular World*. Trans. Ralph Manheim. New York: NYRB Classics.

Auerbach, Erich. 1984 [1938]. "Figura." In: *Theory and History of Literature*. Vol. 9: *Scenes from the Drama of European History*. Trans. Ralph Manheim. Minneapolis: University of Minnesota Press. 11–76.

Biblia Sacra iuxta vulgatam versionem. 1994. Eds. Roger Gryson and Robert Weber. 4th ed. Stuttgart: Deutsche Bibelgesellschaft.

Boccaccio, Giovanni. 1980. *Decameron*. Ed. Vittore Branca. Turin: Einaudi.

Boesch, Paul. 1951. "'Kaiser Trajan und die Witwe' auf schweizerischen Glasgemälden." *Zeitschrift für schweizerische Archäologie und Kunstgeschichte* 12: 218–221.

Boni, Giacomo. 1906. "Leggende." *Nuova Antologia*: 3–39.

Cassius Dio. 1925 [late 1st, early 2nd c.]. *Roman History*. Vol. 8. Trans. Earnest Cary. Cambridge: Harvard University Press.

Dante Alighieri. 2007 [early 14th c.]. *Paradiso*. Trans. Robert Hollander and Jean Hollander. New York: Anchor Books.

Dante Alighieri. 2003 [early 14th c.]. *Purgatorio*. Trans. Robert Hollander and Jean Hollander. New York: Anchor Books.

Dante Alighieri. 2002 [early 14th c.]. *The Inferno*. Trans. Robert Hollander and Jean Hollander. New York: Anchor Books.

---

[43] Parody in the formal medieval meaning of a "counter-song" – which incidentally does not diminish Boccaccio's great admiration for Dante. On the *Decameron* as counterpart to the *Commedia*, see most recently Regn (2018). In other words, only with Boccaccio is the *novella* no longer merely a generic concept but also an epistemological category. This is different prior to Boccaccio: in the *Novellino*, whose collection of anecdotal narratives had, at the time, already been labelled as *novelle* (Anon. 1959: 795), counter-discursiveness does not yet play a role, as the story of Trajan contained therein also proves.

Dante Alighieri. 1998. [early 14th c.]. *De Monarchia*. Ed. and trans. Richard Kay. Toronto: Pontifical Institute of Medieval Studies.
Dante Alighieri. 1991–1997 [early 14th c.]. *Commedia*. 3 vols. Ed. Anna Maria Chiavacci Leonardi. Milano: Mondadori.
Friedrich, Hugo. 1942. *Die Rechtsmetaphysik der Göttlichen Komödie: Francesca da Rimini*. Frankfurt am Main: Klostermann.
Gallagher, Catherine and Stephen Greenblatt. 2000. *Practicing New Historicism*. Chicago: University of Chicago Press.
Geertz, Clifford. 1973. *The Interpretation of Cultures*. New York: Basic Books.
Gmelin, Hermann (ed.). 1955. "Die Reliefbilder der Demut." In: *Dante/Die Göttliche Komödie. Kommentar 2. Der Läuterungsberg*. Stuttgart: Klett. 177–185.
Greenblatt, Stephen. 1988. *Shakespearian Negotiations: The Circulation of Social Energy in Renaissance England*. Berkeley: University of California Press.
Hollander, Robert. 1980. *Studies in Dante*. Ravenna: Longo.
Jacobus de Voragine. 1995 [c. 1264]. *The Golden Legend: Readings on the Saints*. Trans. William Granger Ryan. Vol. 1. Princeton: Princeton University Press.
Malato, Enrico. 1970. "Emme." In: Umberto Bosco (ed.). *Enciclopedia dantesca*. Vol. 2. Roma: Istituto dell'Enciclopedia Italiana. 665–666.
McInerney, Joseph J. 2016. *The Greatness of Humility: St. Augustine on Moral Excellence*. Eugene: Pickwick Publications.
Moseley, Nicholas. 1925. "Pius Aeneas." *The Classical Journal* 20.7: 387–400.
Paris, Gaston. 1878. "La légende de Trajan." *Bibliothèque de l'École des Hautes Études, Sciences historiques et philologiques* fasc. 35: 261–298.
Regn, Gerhard. 2018. "The *Incipit* of the *Decameron*: Textual Margins as an Index of Epochal Change." In: Igor Candido (ed.). *Petrarch and Boccaccio. The Unity of Knowledge in the Premodern World*. Berlin: De Gruyter. 176–193.
Regn, Gerhard. 2014. "Virgil's 'Perhaps:' Mythopoiesis and Cosmogony in Dante's *Commedia* (Remarks on *Inf.* 34, 106–26)." In: R. Howard Bloch, Alison Calhoun, Jacqueline Cerquiglini-Toulet, Joachim Küpper and Jeanette Patterson (eds.). *Rethinking the New Medievalism*. Baltimore: Johns Hopkins University Press. 51–68.
Regn, Gerhard. 2009. "Gott als Dichter. Die Wirklichkeit der Fiktion in Dantes *Paradiso*." In: Ursula Peters and Rainer Warning (eds.). *Fiktion und Fiktionalität in den Literaturen des Mittelalters*. München: Fink. 365–385.
Regn, Gerhard. 2007. "Double Authorship: Prophetic and Poetic Inspiration in Dante's *Paradise*." *Modern Language Notes* 122: 167–185.
Rohmer, Ernst. 1992. "Anekdote." In: Gert Ueding (ed.). *Historisches Wörterbuch der Rhetorik*. Vol. 1. Tübingen: Niemeyer. 566–579.
Schabert, Ina (ed.). 1972. *Shakespeare-Handbuch*. Stuttgart: Kröner.
Seznec, Jean. 1957. "Diderot and 'The Justice of Trajan.'" *Journal of the Warburg and Courtauld Institutes* 20.1–2: 106–111.
Shakespeare, William. 1998 [c. 1601]. *Twelfth Night, or What You Will*. Eds. Roger Warren and Stanley Wells. Oxford: Oxford University Press.
Singleton, Charles S. 1957. "The Irreducible Dove." *Comparative Literature* 9: 129–135.
St. Thomas Aquinas. 1947 [1265–1274]. *Summa Theologica*. Trans. by the Fathers of the English Dominican Province. New York: Brenziger Brothers, Inc. <https://www.sacred-texts.com/chr/aquinas/summa> [accessed December 30, 2019].

P. Vergilius Maro. 2019 [29–19 BC]. *Aeneis*. Ed. G. B. Conte. Berlin: De Gruyter.
Vincent of Beauvais. 1483 [mid-13th c.] *Speculum historiale*. Nürnberg: Anton Koberger. <http://digital.ub.uni-duesseldorf.de/ink/content/titleinfo/3133943> [accessed August 6, 2019].

Verena Olejniczak Lobsien
Anecdotal Ambiguity: Andrew Marvell

Abstract: In this essay, I question the anecdote's validity claims and try to demonstrate its poetic potential. Arguing that the anecdotal holds a close relationship to ambiguity with its structural resemblance to allegory, I attempt to show how it may come to serve and articulate an attitude of skeptical reserve in situations of political uncertainty. A close reading of Andrew Marvell's presentation of Cromwell's 1654 coach accident in his poem on the anniversary of the protectorate illustrates the poet's strategy of anecdotally transforming the spectacular event. By means of allegorizing its hero to an extent that renders him simultaneously admirable and menacing, the text effectively overcharges the accident with significance. Obscuring the figure at its center, it thus invites the reader to reserve judgment while enjoying its wealth of apocalyptic resonance and the ingenuity of its ambivalent invective.

Keywords: Allegory, Ambiguity, Andrew Marvell, Skepticism.

1 Ambiguity and the Anecdote

One of the characteristics of the anecdote is its ambiguity. It holds a profoundly equivocal relationship with truth. In a way, this appears obvious: if the exemplary is said to show itself in the singular instance, its general validity and paradigmatic power are called in doubt precisely by the uniqueness and unrepeatability of what it reports, perhaps even by its "unspeakable" nature, certainly by its quality of being literally "unedited," hence not meant to be published, according to the original definition of the anecdotal. The contingency of what is anecdotally told thus opens the door to skepticism. What could, under different circumstances, have happened differently or led to a different end, appears readable in radically different ways. Its truth is suspended; it becomes a matter of opinion or an object of interpretation. Its virtue as evidence is, as it were, placed in brackets, separated from the context that rendered it meaningful, a thing to be critically inspected, with assent withheld, judgment reserved, and belief indefinitely postponed.[1] It is rendered questionable, an object of doubt. The possibility that truth may shine forth in the singular is not excluded,

---

[1] The maneuver of skeptical *epoché*; cf. my study of early modern literary skepticism (Lobsien 1999).

https://doi.org/10.1515/9783110668490-005

but it remains debatable. Hence, ambiguity spreads its tapestry of possibilities and competing claims to validity at the very moment in which historiography seeks to make pointed use of the anecdotal in the service of demonstrating indisputable truth. The anecdote causes a skeptical fault line in the otherwise consistent narrative to open up. Ideological façades meant to be decorated by these miniature stories receive, by these very means, cracks through which hearsay filters together with potentially unwelcome interpretations – unforeseen, inadmissible, alternative readings of events that seem to be clearly significant. Historical truth thus becomes fissured, permeable, and multivocal; its firm outlines beginning to waver, its solidity to quake by virtue of the very modes through which these frameworks for truth are established, affirmed, and protested.

Ambiguity has a fundamental allegorical dimension. Its doubleness of meaning is structured like an extended, narrativized metaphor: in the rhetorician Quintilian's terms, a "continua metaphora" (*Institutio Oratoria* IX.ii.46).[2] The anecdote, too, may gain allegorical qualities. Where this happens, the fault lines it is capable of inscribing into events and interpretations become visible in a particularly suggestive manner. What appeared clear is again laid open to questioning. The seemingly univocal is rendered duplicitous. It is this connection between form and function of the anecdotal that I want to explore by looking at a rather special kind of politically engaged literature: the poetry of Andrew Marvell. Marvell was a writer in unstable times – years of severe social and political upheaval, troubled by interior insecurity and unclear scenarios of external threat; plagued by confessional dissent and religious disintegration, with memories of regicide and the experiences of civil war still fresh in people's minds: a period characterized by widespread uncertainty and, not least, all-embracing dissimulation. The anecdotal plays a central role not only in Marvell's prose writings, the polemical controversies fought out in a rhetoric both witty and toxic, for which he first became known and soon notorious among his contemporaries. It also figures strongly in his poetry, by which he is still familiar, published only after his death and canonical since its modernist rediscovery. It is here in the poems that the anecdote as a short form with its texturizing power comes into definition most clearly and unfolds its ambiguity-inducing potential most impressively. My example is taken from a relatively long poem (402 lines), focusing on a central passage from Marvell's encomium on the first anniversary of Oliver Cromwell's protectorate, "The First

---

[2] For an in-depth exploration of the structures and functions of allegory in literature and culture, see Haselstein (2016).

Anniversary of the Government under His Highness the Lord Protector" (composed 1654/1655).³

It is no coincidence that Marvell's poems yield some of the most telling examples in William Empson's famous book-length essay *Seven Types of Ambiguity* (1930). Marvell offers highly-charged puns as well as "confused" explications of complex ideas that appear to illustrate Empson's claims superbly; his all-pervasive irony has also become one of the commonplaces of later Marvell criticism.⁴ Empson himself gives only an untechnical and wide, itself ambiguous definition of ambiguity understood as co-presence of different meanings due to a verbal modulation that creates space for alternative responses to one and the same utterance.⁵ Thus, in Empson's understanding, too, the basic structure of ambiguity appears metaphorical. It is from this point of view that I want to describe Marvell's anecdotal strategies. Arguably, to say something while meaning something else, with something wholly different in mind from what is said, seems to describe a secretive, indeed a double agent's mentality – and in a quite literal sense Marvell appears to have been that, too. His habitual intransparency may be an attitude fostered by turbulent times, a way of adapting to inescapable pressure and facing conflicts not immediately resolvable. It does make itself felt in a kind of dazzling slipperiness in dealing with potentially explosive implications as well as in a consistent dissimulation of authorial voice.⁶ But the ambiguity of Marvell's poetry also contains strategies capable of showing how survival is possible in situations of radical disruption and uncertainty and how these may be turned to productive, certainly creative, uses.

---

3 All references in the following are to Smith's translation of *The Poems of Andrew Marvell* (2003), with line numbers noted in brackets after the quotation; here 287–298. For dating and biographical information I rely on Smith (2010).
4 See, above all, the classical study by Colie (1970). For Quintilian, in his *Institutio Oratoria* (c. 95), *dissimulatio* is closely related to irony (VIII.vi.54–59; IX.ii.44–48; cf. also VI.iii.84–87), while irony is regarded as constitutive of allegory.
5 "I [...] shall think relevant to my subject any verbal nuance, however slight, which gives room for alternative reactions to the same piece of language" (Empson 1973: 1). Empson seems to have in mind both a scaling of different kinds of ambiguity and a conscious opting for more than one meaning: "'Ambiguity' itself can mean an indecision as to what you mean, an intention to mean several things, a probability that one or other or both of two things has been meant, and the fact that a statement has several meanings" (5–6). Ambiguity in this sense is "the ambiguity of 'ambiguity'" (6), a self-reflexive indicator of varying interest as well as a phenomenon of literary effect, answering to textual claims of equivalence with respect to incompatible, opposite, logically irreconcilable or simply different things. For a discussion of Empson's concept of ambiguity, see also Lobsien (2016: 522–525).
6 Cf. Chapter 5.1 on "Dissimulating Dogma in Andrew Marvell's Writings" in Lobsien (2010: 237–254).

2 The Author as Chameleon[7]

Marvell's life and person change their appearance according to the background against which they are viewed.[8] As intellectual, writer, civil servant, politician, parliamentarian, the author appears, to say the least, elusive; a man of changing hues. Much in Marvell's life remains in the dark and is likely to continue so. Our knowledge is scanty especially with regard to the areas of his life that tend to draw psychological curiosity, such as his early childhood and upbringing, education, loves, and emotional attachments. And we may assume that he would have preferred it that way. He was an intensely private person, "naturally [...] inclined" to keep his thoughts to himself, as he wrote in a letter of 1675 to Mayor Shires (Marvell 1971: 166). His form of life appears to have been a product of choice and of a self-fashioning that consciously eschewed the confessional. If Marvell is a poet in hiding, a man who pursued "strategies of anonymity" (Smith 2010: 314),[9] he must have felt secrecy, concealment, and dissimulation in some areas to be necessary. To some extent, these may be seen as protective measures in a deeply troubled period of English history that was also a time of secret surveillance, of new liberties carefully watched and new compulsions to control, of anxiously observed pluralization and frightening radicalization in religion and politics. In 1650, around the middle of his life (1621–1678), Marvell took up employment as tutor in languages to Mary Fairfax, whose father, Thomas, third Lord Fairfax, had just resigned from supreme command of the republican forces in opposition to Cromwell's Scottish campaign and had retired to his country home, the family seat Nun Appleton in Yorkshire. After two years in the comparative tranquility of Appleton House, Marvell entered the Cromwell administration, on a recommendation by Milton, and was appointed Latin secretary to the head of the intelligence service, John Thurloe. After the Restoration and again in a relatively smooth transfer, he managed to continue in government service for a while, retaining his lodgings in Whitehall, before he was elected joint Member of Parliament for Hull in 1659. He retained his seat to his death. The Cromwell government as well as his constituents must have found Marvell sufficiently trustworthy and calculable to be chosen and re-elected for this kind of responsibility. Nearly everything beyond his public life, however, remains difficult to determine – discrete to a fault, the resulting impression of

---

[7] With a nod to Nigel Smith's aptly titled biography of Marvell (Smith 2010).
[8] For a more detailed version of the following biographical sketch, see also Lobsien 2019.
[9] Cf. Patterson (1978: 48).

the man is that of an iridescent play of colors upon an unknown or indifferent base, prone to changing from one moment to the next.

3 A Significant Accident

In a poem of 1654 (or 1655) Marvell celebrates an anniversary liable to call forth mixed responses in his contemporaries: "The First Anniversary of the Government under His Highness the Lord Protector." His poem, ostensibly in praise of Cromwell, circles around a highly topical question of political significance with far-reaching implications. Its considerable, indeed risky potential was brought to a head by a recent event, and it is this actuality which is touched on by the composition's central anecdote. What is at stake amounts to no less than the question of what Cromwell means – what he stands for after the first year of his reign and what is to be expected from him in the future. Marvell, faced with the "problem of assessment" (Patterson 1978: 48), tackles his inquiry into the Lord Protector's significance by striking a note that appears to be typical of his poetry: in swinging iambic pentameters he manages from the first to distance his epideictic text[10] from the tone of laudatory adulation demanded by the *genus demonstrativum* and to suspend his praise in an ambiguous balance somewhere between potentially comical and tragical modes. The opening lines offer a first example of this balancing act:

> Like the vain curlings of the wat'ry maze,
> Which in smooth streams a sinking weight does raise;
> So man, declining always, disappears
> In the weak circles of increasing years;
> And his short tumults of themselves compose,
> While flowing Time above his head does close.
>
> Cromwell alone with greater vigour runs,
> (Sun-like) the stages of succeeding suns:
> And still the day which he doth next restore,
> Is the just wonder of the day before.

---

[10] Annabel Patterson was the first to insist that we read Marvell's Protectorate poems with reference to the rules of rhetoric they strive to follow in accordance with their Ciceronian precepts: as "exercises in praise, remarkably original contributions to the epideictic mode," indeed as "Experiments in Praise" (1978: 51). It might be added that they are also a medium for undercover experiment with conflicting modes of thinking, antagonistic points of view, and irreconcilable evaluations – exercises in skepticism.

> Cromwell alone doth with new lustre spring,
> And shines the jewel of the yearly ring. (ll. 1–12)

This beginning sets the affective pattern the poem is to employ again and again through its long course. It starts with a mild shock effect that is immediately taken back or mitigated, but whose disturbing, if not threatening potential remains latent. Marvell first confronts us with an image of *vanitas*, of human life vanishing into insignificance like a plummet sinking to the depths, leaving mere surface ripples on a medium that will soon elide even those. In the context and by itself, this seems startlingly indecorous. For a second the possibility of Cromwell's failure and decline – in fact: his humanity – is entertained, only to be quickly overwritten by the equally alarming claim that he is somewhat more than human. Instead of diminishing yearly, Cromwell's vigor will be renewed and indeed heightened. He "alone" is exempt from the common lot of humankind, instead going from strength to strength. Unlike others (divinely? unnaturally?), he appears not to be subject to the passing of time. By means of a disquieting combination of the frisson of slight terror, on the one hand, with hyperbolic praise that seems to cast Cromwell as a super-man, elevating him to extraordinary, if not supernatural stature, on the other, Marvell the eulogist makes the Lord Protector enter the stage as an ambiguous figure against an ominous background. This is an atmosphere in which things may happen – and they do.

Almost in the exact middle of his text Marvell places the anecdote of an event that afforded rich material for contrary interpretations to critics as well as to partisans of the Protector: during the first year of his rule, Oliver Cromwell had received a present of horses from the Count of Oldenburgh. When, on September 29th, 1654, he drove a coach of six in Hyde Park, the noble animals bolted and the coach overturned. The charioteer was hurled to the ground, but suffered no major injuries apart from the indignity. For Cromwell's enemies and opponents, followers of the recently executed King as well as extremist Puritan groups (like the Fifth Monarchists, favorite objects of Marvell's invective here and elsewhere), this was grist to their mills – not only as a gossipy "scoop," but also as a highly significant event that seemed to clamor for a construction according to the respective outlook.[11] Here the hubris of an illegitimate ruler with its anticipated punishment seemed to be outlined in almost paradigmatic

---

11 Such as the robust mockery in one of the so-called *Rump-Songs*, "A Jolt on Michaelmas day 1654," whose anonymous author compares Cromwell to another charioteer, namely Phaeton, and sees him saved only to be spared for another fall – from the hangman's cart (1662: 363–366).

fashion. How could such a spectacular fall be read otherwise than as a bad omen to one riding so high?

Even for more moderate minds (or those with lesser grievances) it must have been difficult to resist the interpretation that would have urged itself on many, namely to view Cromwell's accident according to the topical pattern of *De casibus*. This teaches us to understand the fall of the high and mighty not as individual and singular occurrence, but as a "case" (*casuale*) engineered by fate, hence as example of a general rule. Cromwell's fall would have brought to mind not only Fortune's Wheel, but all kinds of related commonplaces referring to sudden reversals of fate, man-made or divinely ordained inversions of human order for better or worse: "Pride goes before a fall";[12] "He hath put down the mighty from their seats" (Luke 1.52); "Sceptre and Crown / Must tumble down."[13] In this light, the Lord Protector's accident must unfailingly have heralded his political downfall, the bolting horses emblematic of the forces he was trying to harness in an obviously futile attempt.

Cases of this type carry a truth claim; they are cases in point.[14] They also function allegorically, every occurrence illustrating and confirming the underlying rule. George Wither, an ardent Cromwellian, attempted to beat allegorical readings of this kind at their own game, but in effect only provoked them by his protestations. In his *VATICINIVM CAVSVALE* [sic], with the elaborate subtitle *A Rapture Occasioned By the late Miraculous Deliverance of His Highnesse the Lord Protector, From a Desperate Danger* (1655), he immediately admits that the coach accident can hardly fail to be understood as an omen and portent. But he also, in priestly pose, insists in his "Vaticinium" that the incident has to be read as a sign of grace – of Cromwell's election as well as God's providence. The Lord Protector's life is saved, he is delivered from mortal danger,[15] hence this can only be taken as a sign that he is "GOD's especial *Favourite*" (Wither 1655: 3; original italics). By no means must the event be viewed as an example that anticipates the fall of the mighty; at the most, an admonition to

---

12 Proverbs 16.18: "Pride goeth before destruction, and an haughty spirit before a fall" – proverbial, it seems, at a very early stage.
13 The well-known lines from the dirge "The Glory of Our Blood and State" in the Royalist poet James Shirley's 1659 dramatic entertainment *The Contention of Ajax and Ulysses*, which, according to Sir Paul Harvey, "is said to have terrified Oliver Cromwell" (1946: 721).
14 As *casus* or case history in the stricter sense the underlying narrative is, like the proverb, also a short form in its own right; cf. Jolles (1974). In a generic continuum of short forms, the anecdote would appear to occupy a position somewhere between proverbial saying and case history.
15 According to the generic pattern of *soteria*; cf. Patterson (2013: 139–140).

be mindful of the fallibility and perishable humanity that Cromwell shares with everyone else. Fundamentally, also because no real harm was caused, the incident can be seen as no less than an allegorical anticipation of the resurrection. For it had to be a miracle, didn't it, "That, from his *seat*, into GODS's [sic] *Armes* he fell? / And, that, *He* falling, fell not in such wise, / As they, who *Rise*, *to fall*; But, *Fell*, to *Rise?*" (2; original italics).

Compared to Wither's awkward and somewhat desperate gestures of defense, which continue to name and thus conjure up what they wish to reject, Marvell proceeds in a much more indirect, elegant, but at the same time ambiguous manner. His representation of the occurrence and his treatment of its official reading performs the artistic feat of reading differently by seeing otherwise. Marvell succeeds in rewriting the unedited and unscripted (or not yet finally scripted) episode with a difference, presenting its hero as an indubitably glorious victor, but at the same time as a figure capable of freezing the blood in one's veins. The poet's achievement, we might say, lies in transforming the anecdotal – hearsay, gossip, the unedited and unpublished – into an anecdote – a singular event crafted into concise singularity. The "trick" hinges on Marvell's allegorical management of ambiguity.

First of all, it seems remarkable that the accident as such receives no narrative treatment at all. On the contrary, the text unhesitatingly and with some abruptness refers to Cromwell's "sudden fall" (l. 175), as if it were self-evident – so present in everybody's mind that it needed no introduction. There is no word about how it could come to pass that the Protector's "crown of silver hairs" (l. 180) was thus ungently brought into contact with dirt and "dust" (ibid.). While common knowledge of the accident is presupposed, run-of-the-mill commonplace interpretations are averted. As part of this strategy its fortunate outcome is placed in a sequence of mortal dangers already and successfully overcome, i.e. a series of attacks on Cromwell's person ("poniarding conspiracies," [l. 171]) that he had survived unharmed. Thus, agency, and with it blame, are shifted away from Cromwell. The fall is, from the first, relativized and explained as a consequence of the sinful urge to freedom harbored by a contrary and unruly people. All of us, including the speaker, were infected by this dangerous spirit and are therefore guilty. We as Cromwell's ungrateful subjects are like his horses part of the "brutish" powers that attempted to overturn the chariot:

> How near they [i.e. "Our sins" (l. 174)] failed, and in thy sudden fall,
> At once assayed to overturn us all.
> Our brutish fury struggling to be free,
> Hurried thy horses while they hurried thee.

> When thou hadst almost quit thy mortal cares,
> And soiled in dust thy crown of silver hairs. (ll. 175–180)

At the same time, Marvell redefines the incident as a story of miraculous delivery: a repeated and repeatable event that indicates (as in Wither's poem) the providential election of the person saved. To his friends, this rescue by a hair's breadth provides reason for "joy" (l. 186) amidst modest tears.[16]

In addition, however, the accident is presented as a natural event *sui generis*. Marvell does not step on the scene as poet-prophet, as *vates* in possession of superior knowledge ready to be pronounced with unshakeable conviction, but instead describes in considerable detail the fearful excitement and terror of the horses. After their sudden obsession by "[o]ur brutish fury struggling to be free" (l. 177) has passed, they now stand, "wanting their noble guide" (l. 191), bewildered, guilty and transfixed by "leaden Sorrow" (l. 194); objects of pity rather than blame:

> But the poor beasts wanting their noble guide,
> (What could they more?) shrunk guiltily aside.
> First wingèd Fear transports them far away,
> And leaden Sorrow then their flight did stay.
> See how they each his tow'ring crest abate,
> And the green grass, and their known mangers hate,
> Nor through wide nostrils snuff the wanton air,
> Nor their round hoofs, or curlèd manes compare;
> With wand'ring eyes, and restless ears they stood,
> And with shrill neighings asked him of the wood. (ll. 191–200)

In their confusion and terrified perplexity the "poor beasts" (l. 191) turn to the god of the animal world, the Great Pan ("asked him of the wood" [l. 200]). The panic of the horses thus causes Cromwell to appear not so much as a fallen Phaeton, but as pastoral hero mourned by nature, subject of a pathetic fallacy of cosmic dimensions. Even if it is no more than a dubiously flattering suggestion

---

[16] This is, again, framed in a figure that complicates contradictory affects in an ambiguous manner. True, the fall itself is regarded as a lesson in humility and safeguard against hubris, to be reported accordingly. But the feelings it gives rise to are mixed, and rightfully so: "So shall the tears we on past grief employ, / Still as they trickle, glitter in our joy. / So with more modesty we may be true, / And speak as of the dead the praises due:" (ll. 185–188). Cromwell may be still among the living, yet an ominous note ("as of the dead") remains, as he is, for a second, imagined dead.

that he himself equals the natural deity, "Cromwell falling" is capable of throwing the whole world into panic, causing universal and apocalyptic dismay:

> Thou Cromwell falling, not a stupid tree,
> Or rock so savage, but it mourned for thee.
> And all about was heard a panic groan,
> As if that Nature's self were overthrown.
> It seemed the earth did from the centre tear;
> It seemed the sun was fall'n out of the sphere: (ll. 201–206)

But the poem fashions Cromwell not only as a personification of "Nature's self" (l. 204) who had let slip, for an unlucky moment, the reins which should have controlled the centrifugal forces. In Marvell's version he changes between the terrifying Great Pan himself and a ruler over nature as well as (political) culture – pilot of the ship of state in constant danger of being wrecked[17] and governor also of "Justice," "Reason," hope ("Courage"), and faith ("Religion").[18] Furthermore (and not without some poetic strain), he is compared to yet another divine figure, in this case biblical, namely the prophet Elijah. Cromwell's coach accident now is turned into a type of Elijah's ascension in a chariot of fire, leaving his mantle behind him:[19]

> But thee triumphant hence the fiery car,
> And fiery steeds had borne out of the war,
> From the low world, and thankless men above,
> Unto the kingdom blest of peace and love:
> We only mourned ourselves, in thine ascent,
> Whom thou hadst left beneath with mantle rent. (ll. 215–220)

The imagined ascent is phrased in a barely perceptible conditional mode ("had borne") that adds the slightest nuance of irreality to Elijah-Oliver's *raptus* to the heavens, triggering an unsettling oscillation between a wished-for transfiguration and a – perhaps equally desirable – leavetaking for good. It might have been a kind of liberation from the man who governed the Commonwealth with a strictness inconvenient to many – "the headstrong people's charioteer"

---

17 In another suggestive maritime image (as at the beginning of the poem) that conjures up the notion of sinking to the depths and death by water: "And then loud shrieks the vaulted marbles rent. / Such as the dying chorus sings by turns, / And to deaf seas, and ruthless tempests mourns, / When now they sink, and now the plund'ring streams / Break up each deck, and rip the oaken seams" (ll. 210–214).
18 Cf. ll. 207–208.
19 Cf. 2 Kings 2.11–13.

(l. 224). The accident might also have put an end to the authoritarian ruler, who (only a year ago) allegedly had needed considerable persuasion to exchange his retired life and privacy for the burdensome office of state.[20] This earlier assumption of office now appears in Marvell's text as the taking up of a heavy, oppressive, almost deadening burden, as a radical self-humiliation and stepping down that anticipates the fall in another mode. The seeming ascent to a high position of command really is a kind of condescension, the giving up and loss of a different kingship:

> For all delight of life thou then didst lose,
> When to command, thou didst thyself depose;
> Resigning up thy privacy so dear,
> To turn the headstrong people's charioteer; (ll. 221–224)

The motivation, however, for this voluntary self-abasement is bound to cause some uneasiness, if not anxiety. It is laid bare, startlingly, as the sheer urge for unlimited self-elevation:

> For to be Cromwell was a greater thing,
> Than ought below, or yet above a king:
> Therefore thou rather didst thyself depress,
> Yielding to rule, because it made thee less. (ll. 225–228)

Previously Cromwell had several times refused to be made king. Now Marvell makes explicit the reason for such modesty and apparent humility: this ruler refuses the crown not because absolute rule is considered problematic as such, but because the sovereignty he possesses already, as it were by nature, is immeasurably superior. To be Cromwell is best, there is no dignity higher than that. A greater hubris, of course, is hardly conceivable, either.

Marvell's allegorical reinterpretation of a significant accident as anecdote continues to extrapolate the meanings that radiate from this center. Outlining the Lord Protector's stature by means of ever more glaring hyperbole the poem magnifies him to a point at which he becomes downright threatening and potentially destructive. Cromwell is imagined not only as "Angelic Cromwell" (l. 126), but as frightful nemesis, striking terror into Europe's princes. The anniversary is, in fact, a small-scale apocalypse, with the Lord Protector

---

[20] Marvell had pondered this hesitation in another ambiguous meditation on Cromwell's intentions and political agenda in "An Horation Ode upon Cromwell's Return from Ireland" (1650). Cf. Marvell (2003: 267–280).

appearing as an eschatological, at the same time thoroughly ambivalent figure. Marvell's text places Cromwell wholly on the side of irresistible truth, about to burst forth with providential and fatal force, while his enemies are moved to the opposite side, aligned with a world of lies, hypocrisy, falseness, dissimulation. The paradox that emerges, however, is that Marvell's Cromwell is rendered increasingly duplicitous, the heavier the allegorical artillery mustered on behalf of his glorification.[21] While just about everybody else, in particular milleniaristic zealots like the Fifth Monarchists with their "lying prophecies" (l. 172), may have merited damnation as "race most hypocritically strict" (l. 317), Cromwell rises above the crowd like a harbinger of the Day of Doom. His coming to power certainly heralded a moment of long-awaited *kairos:*

> Hence oft I think, if in some happy hour
> High grace should meet in one with highest power,
> And then a seasonable people still
> Should bend to his, as he to heaven's will,
> What we might hope, what wonderful effect
> From such a wished conjuncture might reflect.
> [...]
> Foreshortened Time its useless course would stay,
> And soon precipitate the latest day.
> But a thick cloud about that morning lies,
> And intercepts the beams of mortal eyes,
> That 'tis the most which we determine can,
> If these the times, then this must be the man. (ll. 131–144)

Although the speaker hastens to disclaim privileged foreknowledge as to the exact date of the apocalypse, even at the earlier point in time that has now come around again, Cromwell begins to resemble the returning Christ at whose Second Coming truth will ultimately be revealed and the great "mysterious work" (l. 137) perfected. If millenarian diction seemed appropriate at Cromwell's coming into office, heralding him as "the approaching, not yet angry Son" (l. 106), at his first anniversary the comparison with the angel of the covenant appears even more apt. It is on this apocalyptic note, too, that the poem ends, resuming its initial watery image and stressing, in equal degree,

---

21 This ranges from the Great Pan through Elijah or Gideon, who refused to be Lord of Israel (ll. 249–256); to Noah and his "house" (ll. 283–292), who recultivated the land after the devastations of the (civil) "wars' flood" (l. 284), planting "the vine / Of liberty" (ll. 287–288) not for themselves but "for others" (l. 288; without missing an allusion to Noah's inebriated nakedness, which, of course, is said not to apply to Cromwell but to his enemies) and, with less elaboration, to Alexander the Great cutting the Gordian knot (l. 384).

its lethal and beneficent dimensions in its address to the "great prince" (l. 395): "And as the angel of our commonweal, / Troubling the waters, yearly mak'st them heal" (ll. 401–402).²²

It is at this nuclear point of Marvell's milleniaristic refashioning of Cromwell's career that the poem's ambiguity becomes most disquieting. For what exactly is it that will come into being at this "latest day" (l. 140)? What is it that is signified by this anniversary of Cromwell's coming into office and anticipated, perhaps "precipitate[d]" by it? What does it reveal? What does Cromwell represent? The stronger the metaphysical charge of these hyperboles, the denser the opacity surrounding the hero of these lines; the more does the ambition of the man of whom it is said, tautologically, that he wants to be only what he is,²³ verge on the truly ultramundane. As Cromwell comes to stand for nothing but himself, he is turned into the poem's blind spot. By clothing his figure in shining allegorical armor in its central anecdote, the poem also lays open the fatal weakness and exposes the menace that emanates from this armor's very strength. Instead of becoming evident, Cromwell's true worth is concealed, his meaning hidden ever more deeply. In Marvell's poem of praise he is a blank check offered to the imagination – enter any sum you like. His appearance of authenticity is the most inscrutable mask of all.

In essence, this keeping the center opaque, perhaps empty, is a skeptical maneuver. In this, Marvell follows a characteristic strategy, but he also writes "secret history"²⁴ – and he does so with a vengeance. By keeping open its options, showing arcane continuities beneath the apparent ruptures, uncovering possible hubris and incalculable ambition hidden in seeming humiliation and fall, damning by praise and rehabilitating the condemned, Marvell's poetry points a way towards dealing with radical uncertainty. Its secrecy offers a safe retreat from authorial liability. Its ambiguity bears witness to and to some extent

---

22 The allegorical address is densely charged with biblical and topical resonance, as Nigel Smith points out in his commentary (2003: 298). The main allusion is to the description of the pool of Bethesda in John 5.4: "For an angel went down at a certain season into the pool, and troubled the water: whosoever then first after the troubling of the water stepped in was made whole of whatsoever disease he had." But there are also echoes of the angel of the covenant (Genesis 15.18, 17.2–13; Malachi 3.1–5), itself a composite figure associated with the coming of Christ as well as, by way of Revelations 10: 1 (and Genesis 9.12–17), with the *parousia*. The lines create a sense of Cromwell not only preparing Christ's Second Coming as a forerunner and messenger, but in fact prefiguring it typologically.
23 In an unsettling parody of the self-presentation of the divine "I AM THAT I AM" (Exodus 3.14) that stresses the spiritual vanity implicit in the seeming modesty.
24 Thus Dr. Johnson's definition of "anecdote"; cf. Johnson (1755), alluding to the Latin title of Procopius's collection *Anecdota or Secret History* (c. 550).

advocates a mentality able to accommodate change. Inflating projections of political and metaphysical significance to the point of bursting, it effectively manages to suspend their claims to absolute validity. The multiple determination of allegory is its favorite medium, the anecdote its most prominent form.

Works Cited

[Anon.] 1662. *Rump: or An Exact Collection Of the Choycest Poems and Songs Relating to the Late Times. By the most Eminent Wits, from Anno 1639. to Anno 1661.* London: Henry Brome.
The Bible: Authorized King James Version with Apocrypha. 1997 [1611]. Eds. Robert Carroll and Stephen Pricket. Oxford: Oxford University Press.
Colie, Rosalie. 1970. *"My Ecchoing Song": Andrew Marvell's Poetry of Criticism.* Princeton: Princeton University Press.
Empson, William. 1973 [1930]. *Seven Types of Ambiguity.* 3rd ed. London: Chatto & Windus.
Harvey, Paul (ed.). 1946 [1932]. *The Oxford Companion to English Literature.* 3rd ed. Oxford: Clarendon Press.
Haselstein, Ulla (ed.). 2016. *Allegorie. DFG-Symposion 2014.* Berlin: De Gruyter.
Johnson, Samuel. 1968 [1755]. *A Dictionary of the English Language.* Hildesheim: Olms.
Jolles, André. 1974 [1930]. *Einfache Formen. Legende, Sage, Mythe, Rätsel, Spruch, Kasus, Memorabile, Märchen, Witz.* Tübingen: Niemeyer.
Lobsien, Eckhard. 2016. *Englische Poetik 1650 bis 1950. Feldstruktur und Transformation.* Würzburg: Königshausen & Neumann.
Lobsien, Verena Olejniczak. 2019. "Andrew Marvell, *Upon Appleton House* (1651)." In: Ingo Berensmeyer (ed.). *Handbook of English Renaissance Literature.* Berlin: De Gruyter, 573–593.
Lobsien, Verena Olejniczak. 2010. *Transparency and Dissimulation. Configurations of Neoplatonism in Early Modern English Literature.* Berlin: De Gruyter.
Lobsien, Verena Olejniczak. 1999. *Skeptische Phantasie. Eine andere Geschichte der frühneuzeitlichen Literatur.* München: Fink.
Marvell, Andrew. 2003. *The Poems of Andrew Marvell.* Ed. Nigel Smith. Harlow: Pearson Education.
Marvell, Andrew. 1971. *The Poems and Letters of Andrew Marvell.* Vol. 2: *Letters.* Ed. H. M. Margoliouth. 3rd ed. Oxford: Clarendon Press.
Patterson, Annabel. 2013. "'So with more modesty we may be true': Marvell's Poems on Cromwell." In: Thomas Healy (ed.). *Andrew Marvell.* London: Routledge. 130–150.
Patterson, Annabel. 1978. *Marvell and the Civic Crown.* Princeton: Princeton University Press.
Procopius. 1935 [c. 550]. *Anecdota or Secret History.* Trans. H. B. Dewing. Cambridge: Harvard University Press.
Quintilian. 1920–1922 [c. 95]. *The Institutio Oratoria of Quintilian.* 4 vols. Trans. H. E. Butler. Cambridge: Harvard University Press.
Smith, Nigel. 2010. *Andrew Marvell: The Chameleon.* New Haven: Yale University Press.

Wither, George. 1655. *VATICINIVM CAVSVALE. A Rapture Occasioned By the late Miraculous Deliverance of His Highnesse the Lord Protector, From a Desperate Danger.* London: T. Ratcliffe and E. Mottershed.

Helmbrecht Breinig
A Hideous and Intolerable ... Anecdote? *Moby-Dick* and Questions of Truth Seen from the Human and the Non-Human Side

Abstract: In *Moby-Dick*, a novel that is also a search for meaning, truth, and the nature of reality, Herman Melville makes use of multiple textual forms and genres, among them the anecdote. Indeed, since all human hunting stories are anecdotes, the novel as a whole might be seen as an anecdote of gigantic proportions. It contains a number of what zoologists call ethological anecdotes describing the observed behavior of non-human animals. Just as Melville through his narrator Ishmael rejects a purely allegoric or symbolic reading, he also points out the limitations of the anecdotal even in its transdifferent oscillation between fact and fiction. As he exemplifies by the inset "Town-Ho's Story," the anecdote's focus on external events makes it an epistemological tool only in the restricted sense of providing factual material while leaving its truth value undecided. When we turn to the question of truth seen from the hunted animals' side, we have only very limited insight. However, Melville presents the whales' point of view when he has Ishmael reflect on their gaze and the awareness reflected by it. He thus makes clear that what is needed in our interaction with other animals is empathy and trans-species compassion, the importance of which Jacques Derrida insists upon in his last books.

Keywords: Epistemological Uncertainty, Hermann Melville, *Moby-Dick*, Non-Human Animals.

In his *Paris Review* interview of 1994, Chinua Achebe quotes an African proverb:

> There is that great proverb – that until the lions have their own historians, the history of the hunt will always glorify the hunter. [...]. Once I realized that, I had to be a writer. I had to be that historian. It's not one man's job. It's not one person's job. But it is something we have to do, so that the story of the hunt will also reflect the agony, the travail – the bravery, even, of the lions.

All human hunting stories are anecdotes. They are structurally oral, they focus on the incidental and on the singular – be it the skill of the hunter or the prowess or cleverness of the hunted, but they may also contain aspects of the exemplary. Do hunting animals also tell hunting stories? Hardly, because the hunt is their normal way of life, their survival. But we cannot be sure about that. Do the

https://doi.org/10.1515/9783110668490-006

hunted ever tell the stories Achebe demands? We don't know, either, but it were well if they could and did, because this might save the lives of other members of their species. If Moby Dick's real-life models, like the whale who sank the whaling ship *Essex* in 1821, would have told their story to other whales, thereby encouraging them to resist, the so-called whale fishery might have come to a speedy end and petroleum might have entered the rank of the lubricant for industrialization a lot earlier.[1] Whales can communicate over long distances, and some species of the cetacean family even identify themselves by name, a name they have given themselves, as opposed to the human practice of naming (and thus claiming control over) other humans, mostly children, and of course other animals. If whales should name their pursuers, we would not be able to learn about that. Their naming act would be part of an attempt to turn tables, to gain control over humans – or would it? Recently, sperm whales and orcas have taken to stealing the catch of Alaskan fishermen, which seems to be a more plausible way of getting even (Schmundt 2017: 111).

Thus, we have two uncertainties to begin with: the seeming incomprehensibility of animal communication and the question of whether animals[2] tell stories or, more specifically, anecdotes.

One of the sentences in Ludwig Wittgenstein's *Philosophische Untersuchungen* (1953) quoted most often is the following: "If a lion could speak, we could not understand him" ("Wenn ein Löwe sprechen könnte, wir könnten ihn nicht verstehen" [1999: 568; my translation]). Would a lion who could speak still be a lion? Or else, isn't the assumption that other animals cannot speak just a piece of human arrogance, ignoring the myriad ways in which they do in fact communicate, albeit not in what we call language? Yes, the lion can "speak," and we cannot understand him. However, since Wittgenstein's time, ethologists, biologists, and linguists have made enormous progress in deciphering and, as it were, translating communication by non-human animals into messages that we can understand, although most of the work has still to be done.[3] Also, our understanding of such communication is inevitably anthropomorphic.

---

[1] Maybe they did, but their efforts were insufficient. It is possible that far more ships were lost by attacks from sperm whales than is documented. Cf. the television documentary *Der Aufstand der Wale* (2015).

[2] In this paper, the term always means non-human animals, *other* animals. It should also be understood that it is inacceptable to lump the millions of species of animals together under a term like "the animal." Thus, the generalizing plural "animals" should always be read as meaning a plurality of both species and individuals.

[3] Cf. Meijer (2018).

What is at issue here, among other things, is our ability to deal with the Other or even the alien. I will not enter the debate that Wittgenstein's sentence has elicited, a debate about the nature of language, of understanding, of humanness and lion-ness. A more urgent question for me is: can we share the Other's stories, the Other's anecdotes? Since many or perhaps most animals have a sense of the past, because they learn from past experiences in order to survive and since they communicate the lessons of the past to others, at least their offspring, they must have ways of narrating such experiences. Anybody who has watched their dog reenact hunting scenes in their dreams knows that components like time, event, and actants must make these dreams just as narrative as human dreams.[4] However, we can only guess at how these narrative elements are experienced, and without finding out much more about the content of animal communication we remain ignorant about the existence and purposes of anecdotes told by this or that species, including whales.

What we do have, however, is a variety of human anecdotes *about* animals, which usually escape the attention of literary scholars: zoological or ethological anecdotes. These are narrative renderings of observations by scientists or other knowledgeable persons, notably indigenous people or farmers, of the behavior of non-human animals in particular situations.[5] Such anecdotes are necessarily anthropomorphic, but the charge of anthropomorphism applies to a great deal of what ethologists do anyway when they observe other animals. What is at issue here is not so much what has been observed, but how to interpret it. I quote from Robert W. Mitchell's summarizing conclusion of his, Nicholas S. Thompson's, and H. Lyn Miles's important anthology *Anthropomorphism, Anecdotes, and Animals* (1997):

> In fact, anecdotes are one of our primary ways of interpreting human behavior, although with humans anecdotes are not used to discern whether or not humans have intentions or other psychological states, but rather what those intentions or psychological states might be [...]. In the study of animal behavior and psychology, anecdotes are narrative depictions of animal behavior interpreted psychologically [...]. Although the term "anecdotes" is often used in a dismissive sense, implying untrustworthy, casual observations, the anecdotes of current concern to scientists depict behavioral patterns detected repeatedly and independently by experienced and well-trained observers [...]. Note, however, that the existence of these [...] patterns is usually not what is being contested [...]; rather, what is contested is their causal (psychological) interpretation [...]. For their interpretation, anecdotes depend upon storytelling. Stories capture aspects of complex social

---

4 The narrative structure of (human) dreams is analyzed in Kilroe (2000).
5 Cf., for instance, Smuts (2001).

> interaction that cannot be otherwise adequately described at present. [...]. If stories are accepted as methodologically useful for understanding animal mentality, then researchers must not only examine the same behaviors from within a variety of different stories (i.e., from a variety of perspectives) to find maximum consistency [...] but must also imagine that animals may look at the world from a perspective very different from that of the "ordinary person" [...]. [H]ow far one can go in understanding alien experiences is uncertain [...]. (421–425)

In sum, anecdotes are epistemological tools, narrative explorations of the behavior of humans or other animals. Whereas ethological anecdotes try to highlight the exemplary, the patterns in animal behavior, and in this sense serve to deepen our knowledge, anecdotes about humans often focus on the singular, spectacular, or ludicrous and seem primarily intended to produce entertainment. And yet, such anecdotes, too, often serve to uncover typical ways of behavior, character traits, exemplary moments in history. Singularity and exemplarity also characterize whaling anecdotes.

In the "Introductory Remarks" of *The Natural History of the Sperm Whale* (1839), Thomas Beale, one of Hermann Melville's major sources, complains about the insufficient use of actual observations and the tendency to fabricate sensational and sensationally misleading stories:

> Since the year 1775, in which we date the origin of the sperm-whale fishery from this country, although many thousands of persons have been from time to time engaged in the pursuit, and must have possessed the best opportunities of observing the habits and manners of this immense animal, yet not one has stepped forward to vindicate its history from the absurd and fabulous accounts with which it has been loaded, and of which many instances will be found in the following pages. (2–3)

Beale contributed to distinguishing verifiable information about anatomy and habits of the whale from the use the animal had been put to in all kinds of entertaining or didactic fables and allegories, beginning with the biblical story of Jonah, whose literal believability was hotly discussed among theologians of Melville's time: were the whale's jaws and throat wide enough so that he could have swallowed Jonah whole and alive? (The answer is: no). The respective merits of fact-seeking anecdotal material and the allegorical treatment of such material turned out to be of significance even in the most important literary work about whaling, Melville's *Moby-Dick; or the Whale* (1851).

Another of Melville's sources, Owen Chase's *Narrative of the Most Extraordinary and Distressing Shipwreck of the Whale-Ship Essex, of Nantucket; Which Was Attacked and Finally Destroyed by a Large Spermaceti-Whale in the Pacific Ocean* (1821), is a hunting anecdote, although not a short one. Actually, it narrates not just one but two central *unerhörte Begebenheiten* ("unheard-of events" – Johann Wolfgang von Goethe's criterion for the novella [Eckermann 1836: 319]), that is, extreme cases of such unusual and interesting (or humorous) incidents as are usually seen as genre markers of the anecdote, namely the sinking of the ship and the survival of part of the crew by cannibalism. When Chase reports the whale's attack, he raises the question of what might have motivated the change from the common behavior of sperm whales – their peacefulness – to the singular – the destruction of the ship:

> [...] I [...] endeavoured to realize by what unaccountable destiny or design, (which I could not at first determine,) this sudden and most deadly attack had been made upon us: by an animal, too, never before suspected of premeditated violence, and proverbial for its insensibility and inoffensiveness. Every fact seemed to warrant me in concluding that it was anything but chance which directed his operations; he made two several attacks upon the ship [...] both of which [...] were calculated to do us the most injury [...]. His aspect was most horrible, and such as indicated resentment and fury. He came directly from the shoal which we had just before entered, and in which we had struck three of his companions, as if fired with revenge for their sufferings. [...] It is certainly [...] a hitherto unheard of circumstance, and constitutes, perhaps, the most extraordinary one in the annals of the fishery. (1821: 37–39)

Chase cannot help putting his account of this singular event into the context of a larger or higher meaning – "destiny or design" – although he leaves it to his readers to reflect upon this question. It is a question that turns out to be of central importance in *Moby-Dick*.

In Chapter 45, "The Affidavit," the novel's narrator Ishmael attempts to underline the factual plausibility of key elements of his story. Yes, individual whales can be recognized and have been met again by the same person; if they are sufficiently famous for their ferocity they will be identified by a name given by the sailors; yes, whales may kill their pursuers and have been known to sink whole ships. Ishmael complains:

> So ignorant are most landsmen of some of the plainest and most palpable wonders of the world, that without some hints touching the plain facts, historical and otherwise, of the fishery, they might scout at Moby Dick as a monstrous fable, or still worse and more detestable, a hideous and intolerable allegory. (Melville 1988: 205)

In this chapter, his method of demonstrating the plausibility of the existence of the white whale and of his narrative as a whole is to heap up anecdotal material concerning encounters with whales, the legendary fame of some of them, and their destructive power. Thus, his defense against two hostile approaches to his text, one calling it a fable, that is, a fantasy, an untruth, the other calling it an allegory, that is, for him, a figurative narrative symbolically demonstrating some abstract meaning, is to emphasize its basis in fact.[6]

However, reducing his narrative to its factuality, albeit an anecdotal factuality, would be just as bad for Ishmael as calling it a flight of imagination or an allegorical demonstration of certain fixed ideas. In Chapter 99, "The Doubloon," referring to the coin Ahab has nailed against the mainmast as a reward for the sailor who first descries Moby Dick, we find this passage:

> But one morning, turning to pass the doubloon, he [Ahab] seemed to be newly attracted by the strange figures and inscriptions stamped on it, as though now for the first time beginning to interpret for himself in some monomaniac way whatever significance might lurk in them. And some certain significance lurks in all things, else all things are little worth, and the round world itself but an empty cipher [...]. (430)

Factual knowledge is not enough; it must be connected to meaning. And yet this quote shows Ishmael's clever way of differentiating his own approach to truth and reality from Ahab's. If in the last sentence the emphasis is on *certain*, "some certain significance," if Ishmael is mentally following Ahab's train of thought, we have to read the sentence as a token of Ahab's paranoid fixation on the white whale as an agent or embodiment of evil. If the emphasis is on *some*, we are in the realm of Ishmael's growing conviction that no single certainty is to be had, that therefore epistemological uncertainty is the lot of humans and that doubt ought to be our way of dealing with truth, the real.

To achieve the necessary textual openness to get this insight across, anecdotes are an appropriate genre. Melville uses them besides many other techniques like symbolism, metaphors, linguistic ambiguity, and so forth. Genres are communicational contracts between authors/speakers and readers/listeners. One of the central genre distinctions in narrative texts is the criterion of fictionality. Novels and short stories are fictional, by definition. Historiographic or scientific texts, for instance those on whales and whaling, are not. According to Gottfried Gabriel's early and important study on semantic theory, *Fiktion und Wahrheit* (1975), fictional speech is that "non-asserting speech that does not claim to be referential or fulfilled" (28; my translation), "fulfilled" meaning that there would be at least one object for which the predicator is true. The text – and here Gabriel uses John R. Searle's speech act theory[7] – presents

---

6 The editors of the critical edition of *Moby-Dick* have pointed out that "Moby Dick," here, can refer only to the whale because, at the point of writing and typesetting this passage, the book did not yet bear its final title (Melville 1988: 811). However, considering the whale's role, any allegorical function that he possesses would cast its shadow over the novel in its entirety.
7 Cf. Searle (1975).

assertions that need not fulfill the conditions of the illocutionary speech act of asserting, such as that the assertion is true, that the speaker believes in its truth, that they will defend its truth, and that they are ready to accept such assertions that follow from their own assertion. That is, a fictional text has to be intended as such by the author and, hopefully, accepted as such by the reader, because, according to Searle, there is no inherent textual property that identifies a text as fiction.[8]

Now, an anecdote, according to Gabriel's more recent essay "Zur Lage der Anekdote" (2014), is non-fictional, or claims to be. It consists of what Searle would call representative illocutions such as "statements, assertions, descriptions, characterizations, identifications, explanations [...]" (1975: 325n5). But we all know that this claim is problematic, because many anecdotes do not fulfill the truth conditions of statements or assertions, but have been told with the purpose of entertaining, caricaturing a certain person, creating humorous points, and so forth. This suspension of the conditions of the communicational contract between author and reader concerning factually true assertions resembles the one pertaining to fictional texts, and here as there we as readers or listeners accept this suspension, perhaps with a smile. The anecdote thus oscillates between non-fiction and fiction, and the reader is confronted with a case of transdifference, the term referring to "phenomena of a co-presence of different or even oppositional properties, affiliations or elements of semantic and epistemological meaning construction, where this co-presence is regarded or experienced as cognitively or affectively dissonant, full of tension, and undissolvable" (Breinig and Lösch 2006: 105). The term is usually used in the context of ethnic, gender or other identity conflicts, but it has its usefulness also in the field of textual semantics. Thus, I would argue that our enjoyment of many anecdotes arises from such dissonance, such dividedness of our cognitive or affective response.

Moby-Dick contains large amounts of anecdotal material – not for entertainment but for exploring facets of factual truth or deeper meaning. Almost each of the nine "gams," the encounters with other whaling ships, presents such material. In one case, "The Town-Ho's Story," this material is developed into a full narrative text, which some critics have taken as a short story in its own right, but which I consider part of the overall exploratory structure of the novel, a novel containing, as is well-known, not only the main novelistic storyline but

---

[8] I will not consider here the famous debate between Searle and Jacques Derrida. Cf., for instance, Koblížek (2012).

dramatic scenes, personal essays, factographic descriptions, and other genres.[9] The story of the ship *Town-Ho* is transmitted to the men on board of the *Pequod* in two versions, a reduced one for the officers and the full narrative for the crew. In both instances the story concerns the appearance of Moby Dick as the agent executing "one of those so called judgments of God" (Melville 1988: 242). "[The] secret part of the story was [...] the private property of three confederate white seamen of that ship" (ibid.) who tell it to Tashtego, one of the *Pequod's* harpooners, with "injunctions of secrecy" (ibid.). However, Tashtego rambles in his sleep and reveals so much that other members of the crew ferret the rest out of him but consider it such sensitive material that they keep it among themselves. This chain of oral transmission makes the story truly anecdotal, *not edited* in the original Procopian sense of the anecdote, and creates suspense until Ishmael puts "the whole of this strange affair [...] on lasting record" (243). He thus turns it into a literary anecdote only to re-oralize it right away by presenting it in "the style in which I once narrated it at Lima, to a lounging circle of my Spanish friends, [...] upon the [...] piazza of the Golden Inn" (ibid.).

The story, as one will remember, involves a conflict between the sailor Steelkilt, "a tall and noble animal with a head like a Roman," and the mate Radney who is "ugly as a mule; yet as hardy, as stubborn, as malicious" (246). Steelkilt pokes fun at Radney who retaliates by ordering him to clean the deck, which is not a chore he ought to be assigned to. Steelkilt refuses and after an altercation breaks Radney's jaw. Having thus also broken the hierarchy on board, Steelkilt then leads a mutiny which ends in the main perpetrators being bound and flogged by the captain. Only Steelkilt is flogged by Radney, in spite of Steelkilt's threat to murder the mate if he dared whip him. Afterwards, Steelkilt makes preparations to kill Radney during the night, but, when at this point a sailor sights Moby Dick, they make chase and Radney is able to harpoon the whale who responds by knocking him into the water, grabbing him in his jaws, and going down into the deep, thus saving Steelkilt from committing murder. When the *Town-Ho* lands at an island for repairs, Steelkilt and most of the crew desert and make their escape by intimidating the captain.

The story has been read as the novel *Moby-Dick* in a nutshell, involving the basic conflict of good and evil. Steelkilt has been seen as a Christ figure and Radney as satanic, but other critics have pointed out that both characters and the question of guilt remain largely ambiguous and uncertain, and in this way

---

[9] The story was also published independently in *Harper's New Monthly Magazine* in October 1851, while the novel was going to press.

the narrative does resemble the novel as a whole.[10] However, Melville takes great pains to render this story as an anecdote representing both the potential and the limits of the anecdotal. Ishmael tells the story in an oral situation and quotes not only himself but the questions and interjections of his audience. He insists on the truth of the anecdote and supplements it by additional information concerning the areas and people both antagonists came from. That is, he fulfills the requirements listed by Searle for illocutionary speech acts, including his defense of his own veracity by swearing on a bible. But the playfulness of the narrative situation and of Ishmael's way of presenting the story cast doubt on its truth even within the fictional truth pattern of the novel (which, of course, is entirely fictitious). Ishmael, who at the time of his visit of Lima is a much younger and less mature storyteller, plays with his material but clearly indicates that the anecdotal aspects of the plot of *Moby-Dick* are insufficient for his overall purpose. When one of his Peruvian listeners asks, "Whom call you Moby Dick?" he answers, "A very white, and famous, and most deadly immortal monster, Don; – but that would be too long a story" (256) – indeed, a story we know as the novel *Moby-Dick*. This metafictional comment breaks the time-scheme of the younger and the older Ishmael as narrators. When pressed to tell more, Ishmael refuses and pretends to be feeling unwell – or is he indeed made dizzy by the blurring of reality levels? It is the very similarity of some aspects, agents, and plot elements between the anecdote and the novel that makes clear that to reduce the latter to its anecdotal core would be as intolerable as turning it into an allegory. The anecdotal transdifference of the narrative situation at the Golden Inn is dissolved by Ishmael's words: "So help me Heaven, and on my honor, the story I have told ye, gentlemen, is in substance and in its great items, true. I know it to be true; it happened on this ball; I trod the ship; I knew the crew; I have seen and talked with Steelkilt since the death of Radney" (259). The truth value of *Moby-Dick*, the novel, on the other hand, cannot be reduced to such emphasis on external events, but is to be seen in the immense richness of its potential meanings, the result of an ever expanding and evermore futile search by the narrator for the foundations of the world.

The question of truth seen from the human side thus finds two answers: the monosemous, insisting one of "crazy Ahab," for whom "all the subtle demonisms of life and thought; all evil, [...] were visibly personified, and made practically assailable in Moby Dick" (184), and the other, the polysemous, infinitely open, searching, and multi-facetted one of Ishmael. But how about truth seen from the non-human side? Is Melville also trying to be the historian of the

---

10 See, for instance, the discussion in Egan (1982) and Reddick (1996).

hunted, as in the passage by Achebe quoted in the beginning? When we turn to the third central figure of this novel, the sperm whale whom the sailors call Moby Dick, we are confronted with a blank embodied by the whiteness of the whale and by his enormous brow, where "this high and mighty god-like dignity inherent in the brow is so immensely amplified, that gazing on it, in that full front view, you feel the Deity and the dread powers more forcibly than beholding any other object in living nature. [...] I but put that brow before you. Read it if you can" (346–347).

Nobody can, of course. Melville's novel provides us with a host of information and anecdotes about whales, their species, appearance, anatomy, and other qualities. All we know beyond that, all the anecdotal information we have about the white whale is that he will react aggressively when attacked, and he carries the scars and harpoons of many attacks. He will also defend his companions against such attacks. Interpretations of this behavior range from Ahab's assumption of Moby Dick's fiendishness to Starbuck's view of the whale as a "dumb brute [...] that simply smote thee from blindest instinct" (163–164). But we have no utterance from the whale that we could comprehend. Remember: "If the lion could speak we wouldn't understand him" – not yet, at least. Whatever else the novel may be, in the context of "naturalcultural" studies, to use Donna Haraway's term (2008: 16), it can be called an ethological anecdote of an enormous scale that also contains a number of shorter ones. There is no reason why studying and interpreting thoughts and motivations of other humans should be categorically different from doing the same with other animals. In interpreting Ahab's behavior, Ishmael is doing what has been called "me-morphizing" (Rollin 1997: 130), that is, assuming that Ahab functions like other human beings in similar circumstances, thus applying the kind of human psychology he can command. In interpreting Moby Dick, he has no such psychological basis, although he narrates a certain consistency in the whale's acts as an agent under attack. But what we can learn from the novel is that whales can and do suffer – remember Shylock's "if you prick us do we not bleed?" (Shakespeare 2010: 74; III.1.67). The whale's eyes are comparatively small and they are separated by his enormous forehead, so that each of them perceives quite separate objects – William S. Merwin's great poem "Leviathan" (1956) contains this phrase: "with one eye he watches / Dark of night sinking last, with one eye day-rise [...]" (2013: 99). This dual perspective may be more comprehensive, but also more limited than the human one. In the whale's contest with his human pursuers, the power of the gaze rests largely with the latter, even though Radney frantically tries to escape from Moby Dick's gaze when he is thrown from his boat. There is one passage that describes the situation when the whaleboats of the *Pequod* find themselves in the middle of a large herd of whales quietly living their family life. And there, Ishmael observes whale mothers suckling their young:

> [A]s human infants while suckling will calmly and fixedly gaze away from the breast, as if leading two different lives at the time; and while yet drawing mortal nourishment, be still spiritually feasting upon some unearthly reminiscence; – even so did the young of these whales seem looking up towards us, but not at us, as if we were but a bit of Gulf-weed in their new-born sight. Floating on their sides, the mothers also seemed quietly eyeing us. (Melville 1988: 388)

The whales gaze from the harmony of their non-human yet, in this situation, so human-like world at their worst and only enemies whose nature they have not yet become aware of. If there might be a similarity between the human and the non-human, if there might even be a moment of shared narrative, this situation is immediately shattered by the violence and mercilessness of the hunt.[11]

The gaze does not only signify power, but also knowledge. As Jacques Derrida puts it:

> The ontology of the living being, of the living being in general, be that ontology regional or general, is a theoretical knowledge, with its *logos*, its logic, its rational and scientific order. And theoretical knowledge is, at least in its dominant figure, a seeing, a theatrical *theorein*, a gaze cast onto a visible object, a primarily *optical* experience that aims to touch with the eyes what falls under the hand, under the scalpel [...]. (2009: 277; original italics)

Derrida spent much of his final years on deconstructing our concepts of "the animal" (a collective singular he makes fun of), notably Martin Heidegger's dictum that the animal was "poor in world" ("weltarm," [2004: 263]).[12] He objects to the notion that "beasts in general (supposing any such thing to exist) [...] do not understand our language, do not respond or do not enter into any convention" (55–56). And, as a central point, Derrida agrees with Jeremy Bentham, who

> always seemed to me to be on the right track in saying – in opposition to this powerful tradition that restricts itself to power and non-power – that the question is not, "can the animal do this or that, speak, reason, die, etc.?" but "can the animal suffer?" is it vulnerable? And in the case of vulnerable suffering, of *pashkein*, of patience, passion and passivity, of the affectivity of suffering, power is a non-power; the power to suffer is in that case the first power as non–power, the first possibility as non-power that we share with the animal, whence compassion. It is from this compassion in impotence and not from power that we must start when we want to think the animal and its relation to man. (2011: 243–244; original italics)

---

11 See my discussion of this passage in Breinig (2016).
12 Cf. also Derrida (2008).

Melville's *Moby-Dick* goes beyond the mere hunting story and beyond an anecdotal accretion of factual observations by raising fundamental questions about the essential identity of the hunters and their prey, about power and compassion, about the nature of truth and the ways of approaching it, including the nature of narrative. That Melville has not left out "the agony, the travail – the bravery even" of the hunted makes his novel one of the most important fictions on the interaction of humans and other animals in world literature.

Works Cited

Achebe, Chinua. 1994. "Interview: The Art of Fiction No. 139." Interview by Jerome Brooks. *The Paris Review* 133; no pg. <www.theparisreview.org/interviews/1720/chinua-achebe-the-art-of-fiction-no-139-chinua-achebe> [accessed August 19, 2018].

Beale, Thomas. 1839. *The Natural History of the Sperm Whale*. London: John van Voorst.

Breinig, Helmbrecht. 2016. "Wa(h)lverwandtschaften: Zweifelhafte Beziehungen zwischen Menschen und anderen Tieren bei Herman Melville und W. S. Merwin." In: Sonja Glauch, Florian Kragl, and Uta Störmer–Caysa (eds.). *Der Philologische Zweifel: Ein Buch für Dietmar Peschel*. Wien: Fassbaender. 1–26.

Breinig, Helmbrecht and Klaus Lösch. 2006. "Transdifference." *Journal for the Study of British Cultures* 13.2: 105–122.

Chase, Owen. 1821. *Narrative of the Most Extraordinary and Distressing Shipwreck of the Whale-Ship Essex, of Nantucket; Which Was Attacked and Finally Destroyed by a Large Spermaceti-Whale in the Pacific Ocean [...]*. New York: W. B. Gilley.

Der Aufstand der Wale: Moby Dicks wahre Geschichte. 2015. ZDFmediathek. <https://www.zdf.de/dokumentation/terra-x/moby-dicks-wahre-geschichte-der-aufstand-der-wale-100.html> [accessed February 27, 2019].

Derrida, Jacques. 2011. *The Beast & the Sovereign*. Vol. 2. Eds. Michel Lisse, Marie-Louise Mallet, and Ginette Michaud. Trans. Geoffrey Bennington. Chicago: University of Chicago Press.

Derrida, Jacques. 2009. *The Beast & the Sovereign*. Vol. 1. Eds. Michel Lisse, Marie-Louise Mallet, and Ginette Michaud. Trans. Geoffrey Bennington. Chicago: University of Chicago Press.

Derrida, Jacques. 2008. *The Animal That Therefore I Am*. Ed. Marie-Louise Mallet. Trans. David Wills. New York: Fordham University Press.

Eckermann, Johann Peter. 1836. *Gespräche mit Goethe in den letzten Jahren seines Lebens, 1823–1832*. Vol. 1. Leipzig: Brockhaus.

Egan, Philip J. 1982. "Time and Ishmael's Character in 'The Town-Ho's Story' of *Moby-Dick*." *Studies in the Novel* 14: 337–347.

Gabriel, Gottfried. 2014. "Zur Lage der Anekdote." *Idee: Zeitschrift für Ideengeschichte* 8.3: 21–25.

Gabriel, Gottfried. 1975. *Fiktion und Wahrheit: Eine semantische Theorie der Literatur*. Stuttgart: frommann-holzboog.

Haraway, Donna J. 2008. *When Species Meet*. Minneapolis: University of Minnesota Press.

Heidegger, Martin. 2004. *Die Grundbegriffe der Metaphysik. Welt – Endlichkeit – Einsamkeit.* Ed. Friedrich W. von Herrmann. Frankfurt am Main: Klostermann.
Kilroe, Patricia. 2000. "The Dream as Text, The Dream as Narrative." *Dreaming* 10.3: 125–137.
Koblížek, Tomáš. 2012. "How to Make the Concepts Clear: Searle's Discussion with Derrida." *Organon F* 19: 161–169.
Meijer, Eva. 2018. *Die Sprachen der Tiere.* Berlin: Matthes & Seitz.
Melville, Herman. 1988 [1851]. *Moby-Dick; or, The Whale. The Writings of Herman Melville. The Northwestern-Newberry Edition.* Vol. 6. Eds. Harrison Hayford, Hershel Parker, and G. Thomas Tanselle. Evanston: Northwestern University Press.
Merwin, W. S. 2013. *The Collected Poems 1952–1993.* Ed. J. D. McClatchy. New York: The Library of America.
Mitchell, Robert W. 1997. "Anthropomorphism and Anecdotes: A Guide for the Perplexed." In: Robert W. Mitchell, Nicholas S. Thompson, and H. Lyn Miles (eds.). *Anthropomorphism, Anecdotes, and Animals.* Albany: State University of New York Press. 407–427.
Reddick, Marcia. 1996. "'Something, Somehow like Original Sin': Striking the Uneven Balance in 'The Town Ho's Story' and *Moby-Dick.*" *American Transcendental Quarterly* 10.2: 81–89.
Rollin, Bernard E. 1997. "Anecdote, Anthropomorphism, and Animal Behavior." In: Robert W. Mitchell, Nicholas S. Thompson, and H. Lyn Miles (eds.). *Anthropomorphism, Anecdotes, and Animals.* Albany: State University of New York Press. 125–133.
Shakespeare, William. 2010 [1600]. *The Merchant of Venice.* Ed. John Drakakis. London: Bloomsbury.
Schmundt, Hilmar. 2017. "Sushi für Moby." *Der Spiegel* 46: 111.
Searle, John R. 1975. "The Logical Status of Fictional Discourse." *New Literary History* 6.2: 319–332.
Smuts, Barbara. 2001. "Encounters with Animal Minds." *Journal of Consciousness Studies* 8.5–7: 293–309.
Wittgenstein, Ludwig. 1999 [1953]. *Philosophische Untersuchungen.* 12th ed. Frankfurt am Main: Suhrkamp.

EVENT

Bettine Menke
Heinrich von Kleist's "Anecdote from the Last War": W-hole, the Joke an Anecdote (Nearly) Made

Translated by Michael Thomas Taylor

Abstract: The challenged exemplarity of the singular, which anecdotes tend to tell, shapes Kleist's text – as the exceptionality of the singular, as an exposition of what refuses itself to or rather exceeds the figure, the legible image, any frame in which it might gain evidence. Kleist's text stages this problem in a scene of script in which nonalphabetic elements of script perforate (hole, *löchern*) the (intelligible) text and gain, in them, a phatic dimension. The scene also negotiates the crossing and dissociation of the anecdote and the joke (which is not even told here), especially with regard to their differing temporalities. The point (which the joke, here, does not have) is effective in its metonymic multiplicity instead of in itself. A short last section of this essay relates the status of the "anecdote" to its medium: to the rumor, and to its contemporary printed medium, the *Berliner Abendblätter*.

Keywords: Exemplum, Joke, Medium, Scripturality.

Kleist's "Anecdote from the Last War," which I will read here, appeared on October 20th, 1810, attributed to "x." in the daily newspaper *Berliner Abendblätter* published by Kleist (issue 18, 73–74).[1] The "Anecdote" tells of a "joke" ("Witz") made by a Prussian "Tambour" who "continued the war" against the Napoleonic army "on his own" after the defeat at Jena and was then "arrested by a troop of French gendarmes who had tracked him down, and was then taken into town and sentenced to death by firing squad." As a "(human) individual [Mensch] [who] as you will soon hear, has no peer in Greek and Roman history," the Tambour proves himself with this "most monstrous joke" that is his

---

[1] Here and in the following the page refers to the original, which is accessible as a facsimile in the reprint edited by Helmut Sembdner or in the BKA edition as a CD-ROM; otherwise, references are to the Brandenburger Kleist edition: BKA II/7 = BA I, 96. In the appendix to this article, Kleist's anecdote is reprinted together with a translation by Isabel Kranz and Bettine Menke. Most German texts have been translated by the translator; all translations into English are modified as necessary.

https://doi.org/10.1515/9783110668490-007

last wish. When asked, "what was it he wanted? He pulled down his pants and said: "sie mögten ihn in den .... schießen, damit das F... kein L... bekäme" ("would they please shoot him in the .... so that the s... wouldn't get a h... in it").[2] This – using indirect speech – is not the way to tell jokes, or to pass them on. The "most monstrous joke" that is announced is not so much told by the text as staged by giving its medium, script, a scene. Here, I begin by pursuing (1) the question of the exemplarity of the singular that anecdotes tend to recount, which the text frames in terms of exceptionality and theatricality by giving the anecdote a scene of script, to then (2) take up the medium of the "anecdote": the rumor, the (printed) leaves.

1

Kleist's "Anecdote from the Last War" announces a singular case. For the qualification – "This human individual, [who] as you will soon hear, has no peer in Greek and Roman history" – not only separates what is told from a tradition of examples, from the Greek and Roman canon. Rather, the "anecdote" also specifies a singular, exceptional case: "[den] ungeheuersten Witz, der vielleicht, so lange die Erde steht, über Menschenlippen gekommen ist" (the "most monstrous joke to have passed human lips since the beginning of time"). In this way, the question of exemplarity leads to the exception that is the example as such if we follow the etymology of *eximere*: as that which is excerpted, excised,[3] and *ex-cepted*, as that which is rare, astonishing, indeed even exceptional[4] – that is, at the same time, presented in such a way that the singular or exceptional case indicates, or, more precisely, constitutes, the class of cases to which it shows beside itself: para-digma, according to Aristotle's *Rhetoric*.[5] This is the

---

[2] Author's note (to the translation): single letters cannot be translated; only the potential reading of words opens the possibility of translating "F" and "L" as "s" and "h."
[3] Also: "what is taken from a set," the "sample of goods" (see Dicke 1997: 534–535); Willer, Ruchatz, and Pethes (2007: 14, 21–23, 32–34); Willer (2004: 53).
[4] On the notions of rare and extraordinary in Michel de Montaigne's *Essais*, see Lyons (1987: 138–140, 122–123, 130); Willer, Ruchatz, and Pethes (2007: 21–23, 31–33, 44–45).
[5] "It is reasoning [...] from part to part, like to like, when two things fall under the same genus but one is better known than the other" (Aristotle 2007: 43); regarding Aristotle, see Agamben (2009: 18–19); "it is the exhibition alone of the paradigmatic case that constitutes a rule" (ibid.: 21, cf. 18, 23). "What the example shows is its belonging to a class, but for this very reason the example steps out of its class in the very moment in which it exhibits and delimits it" (Agamben 1998: 22); it is para-deigma as "what is shown beside" (ibid.).

paradox of the example, the "exemplary exception" (Agamben 1998: 23).[6] Thus, exemplarity does not stand in opposition to singularity, but the supposed borderline splits the exemplary (in) itself, which must relate singularity and exemplarity "at this internal divide" (Lowrie and Lüdemann 2015: 1).

"In medieval Latin," John Lyons reminds us, "exemplum meant 'a clearing in the woods'" (1987: 3).[7] The organization of examples, the fact that "they are made," "cut out," and "frame[d]" (ibid.: 33, 31),[8] makes possible (in the first place) the relatedness of the singular case to those unknown masses of forest, marked only by the edge of the clearing, to which that which is singled out, made visible, would nevertheless have to point in some way, would have to chart.[9] Hence the anecdote would also, as an exemplary clearing, relate to the thicket of history,[10] as an unknown outside, inasmuch as the anecdote – which on the one hand, demarcates and excepts, and on the other hand, framed, self-contained from within – would constitute an "intelligible whole" that, at the same time, gives the narrative model for ungrasped otherness and history as a whole.[11] However, at the same time, it also ruptures (and denies) the order

---

[6] The example is excluded from the normal case, not because it does not belong to it, but "because it exhibits its own belonging" (Agamben 1998: 22); conversely, the exception is "included in the normal case precisely because it does not belong to it" (ibid.; see also Agamben 2009: 23); see also (with reference to "Kleist's rhetorical staging of the example") Giuriato (2007: 227–230); Willer (2004: 53); Willer, Ruchatz, and Pethes (2007: 10, 32–33, 40).
[7] See Wild (2002: 223, passim).
[8] See Willer, Ruchatz, and Pethes (2007: 21–23, 31–33).
[9] "[T]o give an example is a complex act which supposes that the term functioning as a paradigm is deactivated from its normal use, not in order to be moved into another context but, on the contrary, to present the canon – the rule – of that use, which cannot be shown in any other way" (Agamben 2009: 18). "The paradigmatic case becomes such by suspending and, at the same time, exposing its belonging to the group, so that it is never possible to separate its exemplarity from its singularity" (ibid.: 31).
[10] "Only the clearing gives form or boundary to the woods. Only the woods permits the existence of a clearing. Likewise, example depends on the larger mass of history and experience, yet without the 'clearings' provided by example that mass would be formless and difficult to integrate into any controlling systematic discourse. Most of all, the clearing, the *exemplum* posits an inside and an outside – in fact, the clearing creates an outside by its existence." (Lyons 1987: 3).
[11] Fineman describes the traditional view (of Thucydides): "he introduces, discovers, presupposes [...] regularizing, normativizing, essentializing laws of historical causation by reference to which it becomes possible to fit particular events into the intelligible whole of a sequential, framing narrative – a whole that then becomes a pattern in accord with which one can understand an altogether different set or sequence of historical events" (Fineman 1989: 52); "the identification of recurrent patterns" in order "to have a clear view both of the events which have

that generates meaning, that is also the order of its narrative form, in the sense articulated by Fineman: "the opening of history that is effected by the anecdote, the hole and rim [...] traced out by the anecdote," is operative against the narrative order of history – "as a totalizing whole" (Fineman 1989: 61).[12] Kleist's "Anecdote" does this, funnily enough, in literalizing performance.

Clearing, in German *Lichtung*, literally underlines the example's fictitious making-visible by singling out or exposing. This is conceived, on the one hand, as evidence of what is lucid or plausible, because it suspends its figuration and its medium, literally shining forth out of itself – as if it were present before one's eyes, becoming immediately intelligible;[13] and on the other hand, as a becoming-visible and being ex-posed in the sense of spectacularity (see Lyons 1987: 120, 124).[14] As a spectacle, the example aims at a fascinated seeing;[15] it is tied to isolation and exteriority (see ibid.: 121).[16] The interrelation of exception and exhibition had its paradigm in the older one of monsters, which exposed themselves as exceptions to the laws of nature, and thus to the laws themselves,[17] and which were put on display.[18] Kleist's phrase of the "ungeheuersten Witz" keeps this relationship, emphasized by its English translation as the "most monstrous joke." According to Grimm's *Deutsches Wörterbuch* the German word "ungeheuer," as well as the immense or terrific, connotes the *monstra*, abnormities, the "irregular formation" of a body that, "because of its

---

happened and of those which will someday, in all human probability, happen again in the same or a similar way" (ibid.).

12 "The anecdote produces [...] the occurrence of contingency, by establishing an event as an event within and yet without the framing context of historical successivity, i.e., it does so only in so far as its narration both comprises and refracts the narration it reports" (Fineman 1989: 61).

13 See Kemman (1996: 33); on *evidentia* and *exemplum*, it is implied that "you have only to look at this" (Lyons 1987: 29; see Wild 2002: 218; Willer, Ruchatz, and Pethes 2007: 8–10).

14 See Lyons (1987: 124); Willer, Ruchatz, and Pethes (2007: 44–45, 37–38 and passim).

15 How does the "example's power [...] to fascinate and astonish us" (Lyons 1987: 119) relate to its "power to persuade" – and of what? Fascination includes the danger of being arrested by a singular case.

16 See Agamben (1998: 22–23): the paradigm is produced by exposing, excepting, showing (alongside) and exhibiting, demonstrating, putting on display (see 2009: 22, 28).

17 The unity of nature was demonstrated precisely by its exceptions, by what was monstrous, or of a different nature (see Montaigne 1962: I.23, II.30, II.12; see also Moser 2000: 21–22); that which is unprecedented, for which there is no example, is understood as an "abnormality" "which as such still refers to the norm" (Szondi 1967: 21; see also Agamben 1998: 23).

18 What is left to the abnormity of nature, according to an example from Montaigne, is putting (in this exceptional case) himself on display to "earn [...] his living" (Montaigne 2003: 158 [Montaigne 1962: I.23]).

grotesque formation, sets one in astonishment, and in fear and fright"; that which is deformed and foreign, as "dreadful, gruesome," as well as "inhuman, abominable [...] ghastly, disgusting, disfiguring, as well as extraordinary, excessive, overwhelming."[19] What is *ungeheuer*/monstrous is what exceeds formation and finds no place in any "Gebilde" or form (see Hamacher 1986: 12).[20] It denies the anthropomorphism of form by disfiguring it.

All of these traces are drawn out by Kleist's "Anecdote." Presenting the exception as a clearing (*Lichtung*), the anecdote brings to the fore the theatricality, and thus the entanglement of site and seeing (see Wild 2002: 222); a comparison with what is presumably the pretext, "Sonderbarer Einfall im Augenblicke des Todes" [Strange invention at the moment of death], in which nothing of this is to be found, makes this especially clear (Bergk 1810: 246–247).[21] Kleist's text narrates happenings(s) that are not only subjected to a scene framing it violently, but that rather enacts a turning in the staging of the scene to take place. It is not that the clearing of the anecdote is (as it were) organized as a scene in this way; rather the scene is folded into what is told. The "square" ("Platz"), where the execution takes place, becomes a stage, becomes theatrical – as a space devoted to the spectacle, just as "expectation" prompts those who are to carry out the sentence to gather as spectators. They are made spectators of another spectacle (*Schauspiel*). Early modern rituals of punishment transformed the body of the delinquent, in order to set an example, into a spectacle with the force to attract an audience, in which the power of law was to manifest itself physically as horror (see Wild 2002: 221–223).[22] Here, by contrast, we encounter

---

19 "Ungeheuer" as adjective, adverb, and noun, Grimm's *Deutsches Wörterbuch* (1854–1984), vol. 24, columns 692–708: "ungeheuer, monstrum, *ein gegenstand, der wegen seiner grotesken ausbildung in erstaunen, auch in furcht und schrecken, bes. bei abergläubigen setzt; man versteht darunter jede regelwidrige bildung eines naturkörpers*"; "*schändlich, entsetzlich, gräszlich, schrecklich, unmenschlich, grauenvoll, abscheulich u. s. f.*"; "*als ausdruck der sog. intension für gewaltig, ungewöhnlich grosz (wichtig, bedeutungsvoll), auszerordentlich nach erscheinung, anzahl, wesen und wirkung, übermäszig, überwältigend u. dgl., bedeutungen.*"

20 Hamacher thus defines the "contingency and particularity of historical events" that "do not [allow] us to draw from them a universal knowledge" as "ein Ungeheures," "that finds no place in any aesthetic form" (Hamacher 1986: 12). He refers here to the aesthetic discourse around 1800 about "Bild," "bilden," and "Gebilde" in which the relationship between form, image, and imagination is crucial.

21 In an apologetic letter about this Tambour, dated October 23rd, 1810, Kleist refers to the "Beobachter an der Spree" from October 22nd, 1810 (see KSW II: 913); this "weekly paper [was] already delivered in Berlin before Sunday" and could have been able to serve as the basis for the text written by Kleist that was published on October 20th (Sembdner 1939: 87–88).

22 The "stage" (*Schaubühne*) of the excruciated bodies makes visible the power of law, the prevailing justice and power of the sovereign (Wild 2002: 222). The theater of executions became

the Tambour's setting of a scene, turning the situation in turning his body around. But the Tambour is not the master of the scene; he sets it, he stages it by entering it and becoming its figure (see Peters 1999/2000: 83), by physically exposing himself.[23] The staged speech makes a scene by turning around the arrangement of the scene of execution – by turning out the backside of the body (instead of the face), upon which the power of law is to manifest itself. What would thereby be displayed is what (to follow Mikhail Bakhtin, with Renate Lachmann) is disclaimed by the official canon of the closed shape of the self-contained anthropomorphic body: that other orifice of the body out of which the interior spills out to the exterior, giving birth to the grotesque body, doubled in itself, in its hybrid unshapelyness (see Bakhtin 1984: 359, 357–363/ Lachmann 1984: 37–39) – the other hole instead of the mouth, by which the regulated inclusion of the exterior into the interior would be organized in its appropriation (so that the interior would be closed in its inclusive totalizing), and through which the human voice passes, conveying an interior. One might ascribe meanings to this bodily exposure, since the Tambour's performance in front of the French soldiers literally continues his actions, after the "dispersal of the Prussian army," as an ambush from behind: following the tactics of the partisans invented in Spain to fight against the modern Napoleonic army.[24] But this exposition disfigures the body from its anthropomorphic shape, where it would be legible; it presents the monstrous self-excessive body.

---

visually convincing (as a visual insistence of the immediate example) by generating fear and terror. Christopher Wild argues that this is the "dark side of the culture of exemplarity" (ibid.: 223–224), which relies on "exemplary replication" according to "the logic of the citation" (ibid.: 218–219, 221–222). Rituals of punishment signify in the mode of a citation; they are a precise counterpart to martyrdom, which authenticates *imitatio* by means of the body (see ibid.: 226). "Counterexamples are meant to interrupt the chain of exemplary replication and prevent the spread of mimetic infection" (ibid.: 224). The complexity of their signification manifests itself in the fact that in the "plays of the injured body," rituals of punishment and scenes of crucifixion, the execution block and the altar, intersect (ibid.: 224–226).

23 On Kleist's anecdote "Der verlegene Magistrat" (The embarrassed magistrate) (*Berliner Abendblätter* 4, issue 16), in which a deserter "make[s] a sort of theatrical scene" in order to "evade punishment" (Peters 1999/2000: 80), a "theater outside the theater" (ibid.: 85). "In the over-affirmation of the rules for controlling the scene, as found in 'The embarrassed magistrate' and the 'Anecdote from the last war' (if one relates them to the adjacent discussion on theatrical aesthetics), Kleist allows the technique of setting a scene to emerge as such, namely, as the technique of 'historical' action in its impossibility" (ibid.: 86).

24 The reversal turns the situation provided with a framing violence, inasmuch as it aggressively makes ascriptions to those who are in charge of the situation, the French soldiers standing around; as an obscene request, it insinuates certain sexual preferences to the French.

Here, there is no vivid and clear scene (*anschauliche Szene*). In *this* clearing, no *evidentia*[25] (at which the examples are aiming) is gained, that is no "mimesis and truth" in an enlivened image (*enárgeia*). An image that is seemingly produced without any mediation as the "effect" of a force (*enérgeia*) (Wild 2002: 218);[26] one that – in making its figuration and its medium forgotten – would produce an event and appear as a *Schauspiel:* a spectacle (see ibid.: 228, 238). What happens here is exactly what evidential clarity does not allow for: exhibiting (itself) (*ostendit*), pure ostentation (see ibid.: 227).[27] Kleist's scene asserts the *Zur-Schau-Stellung*, the putting-on-display, the visual insistence as such of the theater: as a happening, the gesture of ostentation, not (actually) beyond the intelligible image[28] (as the scene in the eighteenth century is conceived) but before becoming an image. Before (and after) all possible legibilities, the exposition, by means of or as the exposed hole that denies the wholeness of shape, is excess – as would be laughter, which is missing here.[29]

Contrary to the superlative of "the most monstrous joke perhaps to have passed human lips since the beginning of time [solange die Erde steht]," the joke here comes from no human lips at all. On the one hand, the drummer's turning around replaces the face that figures speech with the other bodily opening on his backside, which does not give voice to an interior that may be accounted for, making it understandable. On the other hand, the text of the

---

25 On the complex relation of the corporeal *Schauspiel* and *evidentia*, see Wild (2002: 223, 226–228, 231–232); on the interrelation of *theatrum* and the *evidentia* of rhetoric, see Breuer (2001: 197, 214–225).

26 On the doubling in the (Lat.) term *evidentia* (Wild 2002: 226–228) as a translation of both the Greek paronyms *enérgeia*, the force (that brings about), and *enárgeia*, the image alive in all of its details, hypotyposis, that puts a scene or event before the (mind's) eyes (227); see Campe (1997); Wild (2002: 216–218, 231); Kemman (1996: 40). Thereby the "visual insistence of the theater" would be transformed into a vivid, clear (*anschaulich*) image, one seems to see what is represented (Wild 2002: 231–232, 238–239).

27 The *Schauspiel* of *evidentia* would be demonstrative of something *and* ostensive (Wild 2002: 223).

28 Wild argues that *evidentia* is conceptualized in such a way that the medium of representation is pushed to its limits (see Wild 2002: 230, 236–238). Lyons and Wild emphasize the excess that would (no longer be a living image but rather) be without form: *light* as such (see ibid.: 238–239); "divine poetry" would not be seen "any more than the splendor of a lightning flash," it does "not persuade our judgement" but "overwhelm[s] it" (Lyons 1987: 146, 144).

29 According to Renate Lachmann, laughing – as in the phrase "to crack up with laughter" (*Sich-Ausschütten-vor-Lachen*) – belongs to those corporal actions that "eccentrically turn the inside out" and thus manifest the other, the grotesque body (Lachmann 1987: 39); this is similar in the French *éclater de rire*; see (with reference to Freud's discussion of laughter) Felman (1989: 174/1983: 121).

anecdote that tells of the joke that the Tambour "made" (rendering his words in indirect speech) presents, instead of semantic units that might be spoken, that could be attributed to the mouth and the face, typographical marks in which the written (literally) insists, inasmuch as it never will pass any "human lips."

> zog er sich die Hosen ab und sprach: sie mögten ihn in den .... schießen, damit das F... kein L... bekäme.
>
> he pulled down his pants and said: would they please shoot him in the .... so that the s... wouldn't get a h... in it.

Any attempt to reproduce this vocally (or by speaking it) makes obvious that we are dealing here with effects of script.[30] "[S]igns prior to and beyond alphabets cannot be reproduced by the human voice," writes Friedrich Kittler (1990: 259). These marks of punctuation – that are, to quote Derrida, "operative [pauses] of alphabetic writing" (1982: 96)[31] – cannot be accounted metaphorically to any face that might be given to a presumed voice of the text, or that might figure the intelligibility of the utterance, and they are not to be transcended in understanding. By inserting breaks, this punctuation, accentuates the dissociability of the supposedly whole body of the word – at the threshold before it has become a word, and thereafter.

If one were to assume that the first omission is to be attributed to the decency of the narrator of the "Anecdote," the question would arise all the more insistently of why the other two words are both marked and withheld by marks of omission – *Auslassungpunkte* – are, as it were, cryptographically concealed and enigmaticizingly given to be read. For if we take the missing words to be "Fell" and "Loch" ("skin" and "hole"), there should have been no problem for these terms to appear in literary texts around 1810. The presumed pretext upon which the "Anecdote" is based also spelled out words like those conjectured here: "Nun so bitt' ich, [...] mich im Hintern schießen zu lassen, damit der Balg ganz bleibe" ("Now, if you please, shoot me in the ass, so that my hide stays whole" [Bergk 1810: 246–247]). If the text ought to be read in this way (inferring "Fell" and "Loch"), then these three or four points (which also had

---

30 One English translation is so presumptuous as to entirely eliminate this nonspeakability: "he pulled down his trousers and asked, could they please shoot him in the a[rse], so as not to tear a hole in his skin" (Miller 1982: 268).

31 Like "punctuation, figure, spacing," they belong to the "nonphonetic functions" of "alphabetical writing" (Derrida 1982: 96).

been used to mark an omission us such)³² here mark, respectively, the absence of one alphabetical letter and hence the empty places of letters that might take their place as substitutes.³³ In the first instance, one could read them as stepping in for "four letters,"³⁴ or "four-letter words";³⁵ or in place of the points, by substituting alphabetical characters one might read cryptographically deciphered words.³⁶ And one might take the ellipses as a possible strategy of the text to counter Prussian censorship under the conditions or regulations of which the *Berliner Abendblätter* were published³⁷ (as, for instance, Heine does in his "Die deutschen Censoren – – – – –" in playing on the anticipating of possible interventions of other censoring hands; see Heine 1995: 283).³⁸ As a double understanding of the text: (instead of) the punctuation, whose political meaning, its "good sense,"³⁹ would here be politically nasty, it would be insinuated (as Hermann in Kleist's play *Hermannsschlacht* seems to do) that the French

---

32 Philologists introduced punctuation marks like the asterisk to indicate something missing, in order to achieve "the most authentic and precise carrying on of the tradition of manuscripts as possible" (Klein and Grund 1997: 27–28), as an "invention to write the absence of the letter," by transforming words into "a set of discrete, countable elements" (Siegert 2003: 20, 18).
33 Thus the "empty place" is "marked" for which "each letter is always only a substitute" (Siegert 2003: 10).
34 The German "four letters" would result in a peculiarly underwhelming joke: "as a euphemism for the bum," and hence a euphemism for a euphemism (Grimms 1854–1984: vol. 26, column 261).
35 See the famous case of **** in Sterne's *Tristram Shandy* (1978: II, vi, 115, further II, vi, 116 and III, xxxi, 258); see Schulze (1980: 401, 404). On the "double meaning" of the obscene as that which is "unrepresented [...] as well as overexposed," see Stamer (2005: 132, 129).
36 Such a cryptography would, on the one hand, take the points as *signum omissionis*, as marks of a "case of something unsaid or unsayable," while, on the other hand, bringing them back to markings of the "empty place," "for which each letter is always only a substitute," with the functions of these markers as described by Siegert (2003: 10).
37 On the censorship regulations and authorities to which the *Berliner Abendblätter* was subject, see Moering (1972: 200–217); see also Peters (2003: 20–22, 35–36, 52); Peters (1997: 2–5); see also the censor's files relating to the *Berliner Abendblätter*, discussed in Barnert, Reuß and Staengle (1997: 30–31, 256–353); on the instances of political, literary, and general censorship, see no. 40, no. 41, no. 48, no. 55, no. 57, no. 60, no. 69, no. 71, no. 75, no. 60.
38 See additionally Heine (1995: 286). These are indices of a holding back that anticipates a reading of the instance of censorship that would inscribe itself in deletions, which does not so much, in erasing, prevent this future intervention as indicate its possibility. For this reason, marks of the censor's deletions – that is, the practice of typographically marking the gaps, in filling those the censoring deletions had left in a text that had already been set to print – was then itself forbidden (in 1823, and again in 1834); see Houben (1983: 204).
39 Even according to Freud, it is the plain "good" sense that decides about a joke, which will pass by the censor only by virtue of its façade of a sense it promises, which only as a "good" joke is joke at all (Freud 1982: 114, fn).

occupying forces would not even stop at expropriating the dead body, like that of an animal, or like that of the country, for economic uses.[40] Such a statement denouncing the occupiers, like any political pronouncement, would have been forbidden from appearing in the *Berliner Abendblätter* under Prussian censorship (Peters 2003: 35–36, 52). Yet the marking of omission in the anecdote, which indicates another, a double talk, at the same time disapproves such an understanding, however doubled it may be. The marks, which indicate the empty places of all sorts of substitutable letters, block, as placeholders in their place, any transition into letters, into semantic units of the word, of the sentence, into the meaning (into which the signs are supposed to make themselves transparent). Every respective substitution, every reading that they open in their place is (simultaneously) suspended by the points.[41] They mark latent possibilities of reading and hold them suspended in latency.

The semantic units such as the fictive human face that would have to figure the understandability of texts and make it plausible as a coherence of the inner and the outer are perforated by the visible, interruptively insistent remainders of writing: by points as small stains, dots on the paper that leave holes in the text. This also applies to the one who "made" the joke: if, according to the Tambour's last request, the deadly holes, the bullet holes, may only be produced where one hole already exists, waiting, as it were, for the violent impact of others, then this is contra-dicted by those holes in the text that leave behind these typographical points as a prick, speck, little hole.[42] The text executes, visibly multi-holed, exactly what the drummer wished to avoid. If the shots and bullet holes are anticipated here, on the paper, in black on white, then the hole has multiplied itself contrary to the request of the Tambour – in script, visibly, in further holes, like or as corporeal perforations.[43] Marks of script tease,[44] strike back against,

---

40 See Kleist, *Die Hermannsschlacht* (BKA I/7, vs. 1763–1813, 114–17). As (in talking to Thusnelda) Hermann insinuates the occupying forces might make use of expropriated body parts (of the German woman), that would also be the implicit accusation the Tambour makes against the French soldiers in wanting to keep his skin intact and thus usable for a drum, given that he can no longer expect to be able to "save" (in the familiar, metaphorical sense) "his skin."
41 This makes the French word "point de suspension" explicit as *signe du latent* (Rault 2015).
42 This is how Roland Barthes determines the *punctum* or the στίγμα (see 1980: 49). On the relation of punctum and stigma, and that of the "0" and the (nothingness of a) zero point in mathematical and operative functions in various discourses, see Schäffner (2004: 185, 187–191). The Latin "pungere" has a history as *diastizein:* puncturing, tattooing, branding (see Schnyder 2009: 74–75, 85–86).
43 This connection is inherent to *punctum* or στίγμα as a hole and "material prick," such as the corporeal stigma; see Schäffner (2004).

the drummer. The recoupling of the event of an utterance to its supposed intention is burst apart by/in the scriptural material. The suspension of auctorial disposition is characteristic of the trickster, which is how we might conceive of the Tambour;[45] here, too, it is questionable whether the intention of the text can be secured by its auctorial instance (marked as empty by an "x");[46] the anecdote is an-auctorial.[47]

The point on the paper on which the text is organized in writing functions like a hole in the surface that endows the paper with three-dimensionality: it gives the paper a hidden body.[48] Point and hole – these are tipping points between semioticity and materiality.[49] The punctuations that, on the one hand, are coded indices of the places of the letters[50] invoke, on the other hand, in a manner that cannot be limited, the hole in the real and thus the hole of the real[51] – as an impact into representation, a hole or stain in representation, that denies representation in referring it to its medium.

Point and hole make and discuss, as it were, "the anecdotal hole" that, according to Fineman (1989: 61), constitutes the anecdote as such.[52] It would

---

44 The French *raillerie*, a word for joke or mockery, would be translated here quite literally into the German *Stichelei*, meaning "pricking" or "piercing" as well as "teasing"; it has been demonstrated repeatedly that Kleist's texts often function via an open or hidden detour of French.
45 The *trickster*, first theorized in ethnology as a figure among North American peoples, is defined not only by his trickiness, but also by the fact that he himself can be deceived by his own tricks. In the trickster's act of speech, attributions and distinctions collapse (see Schüttpelz 2010: 212–214, 210). The *trickster* also emerges as "the effect of the operation of the aporetic anecdote on the writing of history" (Fineman 1989: 62).
46 Kleist's (presumed) handling of censorship in the *Berliner Abendblätter* leads to unresolvable questions of reading because considerations, repressions, conditions, experiences, contingencies, and dissimulations cannot be translated back into what is "actually meant" (see, especially, Peters 2003).
47 "Under no condition can *auctoritas* express itself anecdotally" (Fenves 2001: 152–153); see below in II.
48 The *sorts* of Artaud are perforated (loophole): "[...] where the drawing / point by point / is only the restitution of a drilling, / of the advance of a drill in the lower depths of a latent sempiternal body" (Derrida 1998: 115; see also Schäffner 2004: 192; Derrida 2006: 94).
49 J. Dünne writes of "the interface/hub [Schaltstelle] between materiality and semioticity" (2017: 240) with regard to *Auslassungspunkte* relating to Siegert's history of writing.
50 *Auslassungspunkte* were given the function of encoding traces, "real gaps," and "radical absence" in the real, of transferring them "into a set of discrete, countable elements" (Siegert 2003: 20, 18).
51 "The anecdote produces the effect of the real," Fineman writes (1989: 61), but this is incompatible with referentiality (see ibid.: 56); see Stefanovska 2009: 27.
52 "[T]he opening of history that is effected by the anecdote, the hole and rim [...] traced out by the anecdote within the totalizing whole of history" (Fineman 1989: 61). In the play of hole/

open itself here: literally, in the material of writing, in/as an intersectioning of a joke and an anecdote in the interior of Kleist's "Anecdote." I initially intended to address in my contribution. For jokes and anecdotes, which share a decontextualizing brevity, a pointedness, operate differently. This is shown by their different temporality, as Marianne Schuller has noted in arguing that the tense for telling anecdotes, the simple past, speaks of a completed past, occurrences that have come to a conclusion, thus buttressing the narrator's distancing from what is being told (see 1997: 6).[53] By contrast, Schuller continues, a joke is told in the present tense (see ibid.: 6–7) in order to now "let happen"[54] what is not understood at all, or only understood "too late."[55] Without being present, a joke is only "'there' quasi in action,"[56] or the "presence of the joke" (that is laughter) coincides with "absence" (of the instance of consciousness, of "us," the "we," who only belatedly will notice that "we" are already laughing) in which it occurs (to us) as an "ungewollter 'Einfall'" (Freud 1982: 157).[57] Not here; here, no joke is being told. Rather, scriptural remainders invade (*einfallen*):[58] punctuating, leaving holes or pricks, in the respective now of reading, to mark, as Samuel Weber claimed for the present tense of the joke, the "time" of the "utterance and inscription" – here and now and "yet again and again and everywhere where writing and reading take place" – with "an iterability that can never completely come to itself."[59] It would not yet be sufficient to grasp this as a dissociation and a crossing of anecdote and a joke in Kleist's

---

w-hole that Kleist's text is allowing, the groundlessness of "mere" wordplay may be made evident, which becomes ineluctable at the very least when dealing with Kleist's "Anecdote from the Last War" in English.

53 But Kleist's anecdote "describes, in itself, an 'in-between' which, as far as it is intertwined with the themes of death and life, concealed is present as a place of absence and difference" (Schuller 1997: 7).

54 Here, I am quoting phrases from Fineman (1989: 60–62, 56–57).

55 It is understood (a moment) "too late" when laughter has already set in (see Weber 1994: 89–91; Freud 1982: 142–146); whether a joke is happy or unhappy is determined by the laughter of the one who hears it (which excludes understanding) (see Kofman 1990/1986).

56 "To the extent that something presents itself that is eluded from our presence of mind [Geistesgegenwart]" that "can never be represented as such" (Schuller 1997: 6).

57 This is how Weber reads the temporality of the joke (see Weber 1994: 85–87; Freud 1982: 142–144, 157).

58 Author's note (to the translation): the German word "einfallen" means "occur to s.o." or "come to mind" as well as "invade," or "penetrate," as well as in the physical sense "collapse" or "break."

59 In such a way "that its time is here and now [...], the time [...] of an iterability that can never fully come to itself except *unterdes* [Weber is quoting Freud 1982: 143], *in the meantime*" when we are already laughing, in our "absence" (Weber 1994: 89; original italics).

"Anecdote"[60] – not sufficient as a conflict between whole (as the whole of a completed narration that contextualizes an event, integrates it and thus erases it) and hole (whose opening or interruption would let happen and would bring an event to the fore),[61] between narration that would close itself and narratively figure intelligibility, and the unintelligible "singularity of the event"[62] that has no presence, that is not the event of a joke that is not told. The event, the *punctum*, the "point of singularity"[63] is "effective" here in its visible multiplication – not it itself.[64] The point of the text, a word with which the joke is conceived as striking, as pointed or acuminated, penetrating, dazzling, and perplexing, the point with which the anecdote perforates and exceeds its form (as Fineman argues),[65] would here be repeated, iterated: displaced from itself, depotentiated – and hence effective thus: as punctuation, leaving holes, piercing, parasitic haunting

---

60 In the case of Kleist's "anecdote" "Der Branntweinsäufer und die Berliner Glocken" [The brandy drunk and the Berlin bells] "[t]he historically powerful event of the anecdote is due to the joke of the soldier who, in causing the seemingly stable structure of the Prussian army to contradict itself, thereby disintegrates it" (Breithaupt 2003: 338; see ibid.: 347). "The joke of the anecdote" of Kleist's "Der Branntweinsäufer und die Berliner Glocken" proceeds via a "doubling": "Whereas the drinker is first struck by the officers, later it is the bells that strike," and this, the impact of the words, as that which he hears their strikes: "Kümmel, Kümmel! Kümmel!" or "Anisette! Anisette! Anisette!" and more over, is what he follows: following the same "mechanism of strikes" intended to keep him from drinking, he again becomes a drunk: "The soldier of the anecdote is thus quite obedient, and follows orders as he hears them [gehörsam]" (ibid: 337).
61 Here, I am alluding to several of Fineman's phrases, for example: "the anecdote is the literary form that uniquely lets history happen by virtue of the way it introduces an opening into the teleological, and therefore timeless, narration [...] establishing an event as an event" (1989: 61).
62 This "conflict of understanding between the singular of the event [das Singuläre des Ereignisses] and the general of a knowledge that concerns the narrative construction of the story as history and in history" (Campe 2002: 429) has been read above all in Kleist's "Unwahrscheinliche Wahrhaftigkeiten" (translated by Carol Jacobs as "Improbable Veracities" [1979: 45–46]).
63 According to Barthes, "a point of singularity that punctures the surface of the reproduction – and even the production – of analogies, likenesses, and codes. It pierces, strikes me, wounds me, bruises me [...]" (Derrida 2001: 39).
64 "However lightning-like it may be, the *punctum* has, more or less potentially [plus ou moins virtuellement], a force of expansion [une force d'expansion]. This force is often metonymic" (Barthes 1980: 74; Barthes 2006: 45). The *punctum*, "this singular, which is never in one area, mobilizes everything everywhere; it makes itself into a plural." It does not fit in but "induces" metonymy, "and this is its force" (Derrida 2001: 57).
65 "[T]hat there is something about the anecdote that exceeds its literary status, and this excess is precisely that which gives the anecdote its pointed [...] access to the real" (Fineman 1989: 56).

(of the text),⁶⁶ as a perforation that divides the text and at the same time holds it together.

The story breaks off – with a coup, by a dash: "–". The narrative order that might provide the entirety of the anecdote and the context that might make the event readable cannot be relied upon here. Rather, at the moment any inner narrative closure of the "Anecdote from the Latest War" fails, the text continues: "– Wobei man noch die Shakespearesche Eigenschaft bemerken muß" ("– Whereas one must also notice the Shakespearean quality"). Now, one might recognize – in the quasi-philological note in the added sentence pointing out the "Shakespearean quality," "that the Tambour does not, with his joke or wit [der Tambour mit seinem Witz], leave his sphere as a drummer" – the paradigma-forming indication of a model (for the type of the "drummers"?); or the concept common to the eighteenth century of the ways of speaking of Shakespearean dramatis personae might provide a framing⁶⁷ in which the flagrant "monstrous joke" would be furnished with "a reassuring word" of readability, in a "gesture that closes the anecdotes,"⁶⁸ and would undergo a "motivating formation of coherence."⁶⁹ But the stroke of the dash – interrupting, bridging, and holding the distance – keeps the play open between the "anecdotal hole and whole" (following Fineman), between the setting of a frame and its suspending,⁷⁰ so that what is singular is admitted as amorphous,⁷¹ and the event in its

---

66 With Barthes in Derrida's reading: the punctum "is never inscribed in the homogenous objectivity of the framed space [the studium] but instead inhabits or, rather, haunts it" (Derrida 2001: 41). The *punctum* "induces" metonymy: "this is its *force*, or rather than its force (for it exerts no constraint, it remains entirely in reserve), its *dynamis* [...]" (ibid.: 57). It is thus not about Austin's *performative*, which must be completed and completely determined; about the relationship between the *performative* and the joke; see Felman (1989/1983).
67 On the epistemological framework of the narrated singular case, see Willer, Ruchatz, and Pethes (2007: 39–40); Lyons (1987: 3, 29–31); "particular events" are made significant by being contextualized, made "to fit [...] into the intelligible whole" (Fineman 1989: 52). However, as Paul de Man asks: "can any example ever truly fit a general proposition?" (1984: 276).
68 As it appears to happen at the end of Kleist's "Der Griffel Gottes," as Jacobs argues (1989: 178, 184, 189); see also Kleist's "Anecdote" about the Capuchin or narratives such as "Michael Kohlhaas" or "Verlobung in Santo Domingo" (Betrothal in Santo Domingo).
69 This is what Campe (2002: 423–424) argues regarding narration or the novel.
70 The "double intersection, the formal play of anecdotal hole and whole" introduces an event "as an event within and yet without the framing context of historical successivity, i.e., it does so only in so far as its narration both comprises and refracts the narration it reports" (Fineman 1989: 61). It plays on and over every narrative closure of holes ("plugged up") that might ever again enable this narration to "itself be opened up by a further anecdotal operation" (ibid.).
71 The aestheticization of history, which relies on the unity of happenings and knowledge, has therefore, since Aristotle, excluded chance and the amorphous, according to Hamacher (1986:

contingency.⁷² The stroke or dash marks the supplement. The "general of a knowledge" (Campe 2002: 429) would here be obtained only in a marked addendum appended by a dash as a sewing stitch, while indicating the rupture, the gap over which it passes, which it at the same time holds open. The supplementarity of the added sentence as an appendix designates the nonclosure, the lack within.

With the "sphere of the drummer," retrospectively, the identification of the "F..." as the skin [Fell] of the drummer (who cannot save his skin in the familiar figurative sense)⁷³ with the animal skin, from which the skin of a drum is made, somehow seems to be sustained.⁷⁴ But this "sphere" also indicates the sphere of the text, the scene of its scriptedness, because like drum skins, the pages to be written on were once made from animal skins. Thus, retroactively, the remainders of script that punctuate, haunt the text, chopping it, (may have) become the mute manifestations of the beater of the drum. In the word *Trommelfell*, the skin of the drum and the eardrum coincide, the eardrum, which must be set into oscillation by reverberations and echoes of sounds so that we hear.⁷⁵ The scene of writing, the scene of the script into which the written marks invade, break in, and on which they insist as remainders, by scattering themselves, accentuates script in its phatic function and makes space for the percussions, strikes, and vibrations.⁷⁶ As the written gains its phatic dimension from the punctuation, in which it would come to touch with the senseless noise, so the fleetingly falling *Abendblätter* refer, as Peter Fenves makes readable, the anecdote to the disarticulated swooshing, murmuring, or noise of its medium.

5–7, 12–15); Kleist's "Unwahrscheinliche Wahrhaftigkeiten" ("Improbably Veracities") does just the opposite.
72 "The anecdote produces [...] the occurrence of contingency" (Fineman 1989: 61), and in this way lets history happen (cf. ibid.: 60–62). Aristotle's *Poetics* opposes the general to the particular as an event (see Hamacher 1986); that should be differentiated according to the "categories of the singular and the contingent," as Campe writes (2002: 426–427).
73 It is funny when someone speaks of the "saving idea [Einfall]" of the tambour, who "instead of worrying about his life, worries about its proper execution" (Moering 1972: 200, 127).
74 One English translation goes so far as to inform us: "one must note the Shakespearean propriety of the drummer, who in making his joke remained true to his calling as a beater on skins," and it annotates this with "[f]or a drummer, the fewer holes in the skin of a drumhead the better" (Miller 1982: 268).
75 Is *this* the motivation for the initial announcement "as you will soon hear"?
76 In a way of writing (*écriture*) that does not allow words to communicate in an illusory way, the words are "lancés [...] des explosions, vibrations, des machineries" ("cast as [...] explosions, vibrations, devices"); "this *écriture* turns knowledge into a feast" (Barthes 1978: 20; Barthes 1979: 35; see also Felman 1989: 141).

2

It is this, the medium of the anecdote, that I will now refer to in coming to an end. For, as shown here by Kleist's "Anecdote from the Last War," anecdotes that (are to) make the singular into something exemplary by placing it into the framework of a narrative order (one in which it could be considered readable) that eventually turns against itself and exceeds and dislocates its very own linguistic formation do not allow for any claims about gaining knowledge – beyond the crossing out and perforation and besides the percussions. The anecdotes, however, are first and foremost constituted by the relation to their medium; for as something not publicly published (Greek: ἀνέκδοτα, anékdota), they were told and retold outside, besides the official historiography guaranteed by authorities; they were passed on elsewhere.[77] At the end of the eighteenth century and during the historicist nineteenth century, written anecdotes entered into countless collections[78] and were retold in writing, carried on – written out and off, transcribed – as also happened with the "Anecdote from the Last War." Their medium are the sheets of the *Berliner Abendblätter*, in which they appear as an-authorial, nonauthoritative and nonauthorizable texts[79] and, as anecdotes, confront (supposedly) "pure information."[80] "Instead of giving evidence [...] [anecdotes] pass along hearsay," Peter Fenves writes (2001: 152).[81] Rumor is

---

[77] The Greek concept of anecdote was a technical term from the history of editing that was used to denote "records of great political personalities that were (for whatever reasons) not published or intentionally not disclosed" (Hein 1991: 14). *An-ekdota* denotes what is not-edited, defined by the exclusion, the others, the remote counter- or marginal place of official historiography; see Schuller (1997: 7–8); Fenves (2001: 162, 172), and many others; on the relationship of anecdote and historiography in/from the early modern period on, see Stefanovska (2009: 16–22).

[78] "The time before the wars of liberation positively reveled in anecdotes," specifically, in written "anthologies of anecdotes that continued for volumes" (Reinhold Steig, *Heinrich von Kleists Berliner Kämpfe* [1901], qtd. in Moering 1972: 108); see, among other sources, the *Sammlung von Anekdoten und Charakterzügen* cited here as possible source texts for Kleist's anecdotes.

[79] "What the *an* of *anecdote* negates is authority. Under no condition can *auctoritas* express itself anecdotally" (Fenves 2001: 152–153; see also 161, 155).

[80] See Campe (2015: 12); or, as Peters argues, in "anecdotal forms," "miscellaneous events, daily occurrences, sometimes even police reports," Kleist examines the "different relationships of fictionality and reporting" (1999/2000: 76, 78).

[81] "To the extent that the subject matter of anecdotes is compromised by their unregulated circulation – for who knows any longer what they are about? – anecdotes fall into the indistinct 'categories' of gossip, hearsay, or chatter" (Fenves 2001: 155; see Stefanovska 2009: 17, 19, 21).

not only *what* the anecdote passes on, but as hearsay it is also its "medium"[82] (which it shares with the joke).[83] The rumor "always quotes those who are momentarily not present": "No one had ever been there," no one who cites it and passes it on is the author of what it says (Neubauer 1998: 46, 42–43). It withdraws the source, pushing it further and further back into the depths of time. Nor is the written/printed version of the anecdote in the daily papers ever secured by providing it with a place that allows it to be authorized; rather, as Fenves writes, it performs "the temporal displacement that published anecdotes already display" (2001: 162). Since the written "Anecdote from the Last War" makes it possible to be read or quoted, rewritten, elsewhere and at a different time,[84] it would be uncertain to what the "last war" – the shifter "last" – would refer; the referent of the temporal deixis of "last" would have become uncertain; the shifter would have torn itself away from what it pointed to just now or any time before;[85] and the referent would, again and again, displace itself – if not day for day, as the *Berliner Abendblätter* replace each other, then war for war. The anecdote, which does not locate in the historical sequence, is incompatible with official historiography.

The *Berliner Abendblätter* published by Kleist convey circulating rumors ("Gerüchte") (especially about the "Mordbrennerbande," or "murder and torch gang") and correct them (as it might seem) from time to time. Above all, however, they make it possible to read not only the message but also its medium: a delivery (*Zukommen*) "according to the structure of rumor" (Peters 2003: 160) that produces the message in the first place; and this is especially the case when apparently an information to correct a rumor is given.[86] When

---

82 *Fama* is "always at the same time current news and its medium, which is multi-eared and multi-tongued *hearsay*" (Neubauer 1998: 38, 61).
83 The joke is "passed from one person to another like the news of the latest victory" ["neueste Siegesnachricht"; Freud 1982: 19] (Freud 1989: 13; see Weber 1994: 89).
84 In the case of the Capuchin anecdote (Nov. 30, 1810, issue 53) both have been found, its textual source and its "adoption" "largely adopted word for word" in 1811 (Moering 1972: 129); see Reuß (1997b: BKA II/8, 384–392); Reuß (1997a: 3–9).
85 See Hegel (1970: 88). "Car si Jean-Louis sait parfaitement qui'il est et quel jour il écrit, son message, parvenue jusqu'à moi, est tout à fait incertain: *quel lundi? quel Jean-Louis?*" (Barthes 1975: 168) / "For if Jean-Louis knows perfectly well who he is and on what day he is writing, once his message is in my hands it is entirely uncertain: *which Monday? which Jean-Louis?*" (Barthes 2010: 165). What the "last war" would be, would be determined by the date of the respective *Abendblatt*, or by a recontextualization through the commentary of editions; the displacement, however, is inherent to the temporal deixis.
86 For example, in "Miszelle": "Ein franz. Courier, der vergangenen Donnerstag in Berlin angekommen, soll, dem Vernehmen nach, dem Gerücht, als ob die französischen Waffen in Portugal

news is passed on and delivered in this way, there is no certainty about the content of what is being passed on, or about the referent – and not even about the allegedly shrewd strategy of the alleged author in dealing with the censoring administration.[87]

The program of the *Abendblätter* is a temporal one; according to Sibylle Peters, it consists "above all in the frequency of its appearance" (2003: 156), its daily-ness. Since the *Abendblätter* are therefore subject to the time pressure of their respectively contingent press deadlines,[88] they also thereby volatalize themselves (day by day) incessantly. The *Berliner Abendblätter* stopped being published some day, but as ephemeral media of daily dissipation, they remain without unity and wholeness. Their continuation in writing day by day gives them over to the fleetingly carrying on (and away) along with the expiring, deteriorating leaves of the *Abendblätter*.[89] Words are quotable and quoted detached from their origin, written forth and rewritten, now and then again substituting, carried forth, thereby attributable to no mouth and no face that would take responsibility for them, flying like leaves: "feuilles volantes" (Lacan 1969: 37)[90] "loose sheets as/or leaves."[91] All issues of the *Abendblätter*, all sheets,

---

Nachtheile erlitten hätten, widersprochen, und im Gegentheil von Siegsnachrichten erzählt haben, die bei seinem Abgang aus Paris in dieser Stadt angekommen wären"; "A French courier who arrived in Berlin last Thursday is said [as was heard] to have contradicted the rumor that French forces in Portugal had suffered setbacks, and to have told instead of news of victory that had reached the city of Paris as he was leaving" (*Berliner Abendblätter*, vol. 31, Nov. 5, 1810, BA I, 160). Or by: "Nothing is more unfounded than the rumor that on the 1st to 3rd there was a general battle in which Massena was captured and 27,000 men were lost" (ibid.); this spreads precisely the rumor it claims to deny. Who is speaking when, in the *Abendblätter*, rumors are reported, identified as unfounded, rectified, etc.?

87 On the unresolvable "Verwirrspiel" between considering the censor and counterstrategies, see Peters (1997: 2–5; 2003: 126–128, 20–28, 34–38, 49–60), which also suspends the "all too simple model of communication underlying all censorship," that is "a bartering of sovereignty" (ibid.: 166, 20; see 133–135, 157–179).

88 The epitome for the contingency of the regulation of contingency is the press deadline as "itself a contingent connection of planned and contingent happening in the form of interruption" (Peters 2003: 65–66).

89 Fenves draws attention to the "widely circulating rumor" ranging from "inarticulate noises" to "the pages of the *Berliner Abendblätter*, as if these regularly appearing, rustling 'evening leaves' were a place of refuge for the purely sonorous" (2001: 162, 166–167, 172–173).

90 Lacan thereby objects to the proverbial "Scripta manent" (writings remain and persist), claiming this [manent] "true rather, of spoken words [*paroles*]," while "scripta" "volant": "[l]es écrits emportent au vent" ("[w]ritings scatter to the four winds"). "Et, s'ils n'étaient feuilles volantes, il n'y aurait pas de lettres volant" / "And were there no loose sheets/leaves, there would be no purloined letters" (Lacan 1969: 37; Lacan 2007: 19).

texts, and topics, refer and are referred to other circulating utterances, to coming or already blown-away (flying) emissions, sheets, leaves, shifting away, replacing and deferring each other.[92] The *Abendblätter* each respectively refuse and dissipate, in flying-away (already again) and in deferring (not yet), the final, always (only) retrospective, establishment of an instance of wholeness, a frame that would decide what belongs or does not, what is inside or outside, what is of significance or not, what is form or mere chance. Always already and always again, the framing of each text is suspended in/for every (merely) particular issue/*Blatt*, as it is by each following issue, or sheet, suspended to its medium, the rumor, as Ovid figures it, as an indeterminate murmuring of voices, as the noise of the distant sea.[93]

Works Cited

Agamben, Giorgio. 2009 [2008]. "What is a Paradigm?" In: Giorgio Agamben. *The Signature of All Things. On Method*. Trans. Luca D'Isanto with Kevin Attell. New York: Zone Books. 9–32.

Agamben, Giorgio. 1998 [1995]. *Homo Sacer: Sovereign Power and Bare Life*. Trans. Daniel Heller-Roazen. Stanford: Stanford University Press.

Aristotle. 2007 [4th c. BC]. *On Rhetoric: A Theory of Civic Discourse*. Trans. George A. Kennedy. New York: Oxford University Press.

Bakhtin, Michail. 1984. *Rabelais and his World*. Trans. Hélène Iswolsky. Bloomington: Indiana University Press.

Barnert, Arno, Roland Reuß, and Peter Staengle. 1997. "Polizei – Theater – Zensur. Quellen zu Heinrich von Kleists 'Berliner Abendblättern.'" *Brandenburger Kleist-Blätter* 11: 29–353.

Barthes, Roland. 2010 [1975]. *Roland Barthes by Roland Barthes*. Trans. Richard Howard. New York: Hill and Wang.

---

91 The phrase "fliegende Blätter" is common in German, as it is in French (see Lacan 1969: 37) and was formerly also used to denote the newspapers in circulation, referring mainly to the loose sheets (which are not bound as a book).

92 The "network of references" of the newspaper's issues or sheets "shifts in itself from day to day" (Peters 2003: 59); on the mediality of the newspaper, see Peters (2000: 143–147, 158–160).

93 This is how Ovid describes the house of *fama*: "tota fremit vocesque refert iteratque, quod audit. nulla quies intus nullaque silentia parte, nec tamen est clamor, sed parvae murmura vocis, qualia de pelagi, siquis procul audiat, undis esse solent" (Ovid 1996: 634; XII, l. 47–51). "The whole place resounds with confused noises, repeats all words and doubles what it hears. There is no quiet, no silence anywhere within. And yet there is no loud clamour, but only the subdued murmur of voices, like the murmur of the waves of the sea [...]" (Ovid 1984: 184; XII, l. 47–49).

Barthes, Roland. 2006 [1980]. *Camera Lucida: Reflections on Photography.* Trans. Richard Howard. New York: Hill and Wang.
Barthes, Roland. 1980. *La chambre clair. note sur la photographie.* Paris: Gallimard, Seuil.
Barthes, Roland. 1979. "Lecture: In Inauguration of the Chair of Literary Semiology, Collège de France, January 7, 1977." *Oxford Literary Review:* 4.1. 31–44.
Barthes, Roland. 1978. *Leçon: leçon inaugurale de la chaire de sémiologie littéraire du Collège de France, prononcée le 7 janvier 1977.* Paris: Édition du Seuil.
Barthes, Roland. 1975. *roland barthes par roland barthes.* Paris: Éditions du Seuil.
Bergk, Johann Adam. 1810. "Sonderbarer Einfall im Augenblick des Todes." In: *Sammlung von Anekdoten und Charakterzügen aus den beiden merkwürdigen Kriegen in Süd- und Nord-Deutschland in den Jahren 1805 bis 1809.* Vol. 7.3. Leipzig: Baumgärtner. Kleist BA (CD) Quellensammlung Q109601 A. 246–247.
Breithaupt, Fritz. 2003. "Kleists Anekdoten und die Möglichkeit von Geschichte." In: Wolfgang Wirth and Jörn Wegner (eds.). *Literarische Trans-Rationalität: für Gunter Martens.* Würzburg: Königshausen & Neumann. 335–352.
Breuer, Ingo. 2001. "'Schauplätze jämmerlicher Mordgeschichte.' Tradition der Novelle und Theatralität der Historia bei Heinrich von Kleist." *Kleist-Jahrbuch* 2001: 196–225.
Campe, Rüdiger. 2015. "Kleists Verfahren der Aktualität" (Ms.) (Vortrag für: *Gegenwartsbezug und Vergegenwärtigung. Zur 'Aktualität'und zur "Zeit rhetorischer Figuration" (Campe) vor und während der Verzeitlichung der Gegenwart*, Workshop of the DFG project "Aktualität – zur Geschichte literarischer Gegenwartsbezüge und zur Verzeitlichung der Gegenwart um 1800" in the context of the DFG Priority Programme "Ästhetische Eigenzeiten"; Bonn, May 28 and 29, 2015).
Campe, Rüdiger. 2002. "Kleists 'Unwahrscheinliche Wahrhaftigkeiten.'" In: Rüdiger Campe. *Spiel der Wahrscheinlichkeit. Literatur und Berechnung zwischen Pascal und Kleist.* Göttingen: Wallstein. 418–438.
Campe, Rüdiger. 1997. "Vor Augen stellen: Über den Rahmen rhetorischer Bildgebung." In: Gerhard Neumann (ed.). *Poststrukturalismus. Herausforderung an die Literaturwissenschaft. DFG-Symposion 1995.* Stuttgart: Metzler.
de Man, Paul. 1984. "Aesthetic Formalization: Kleist's *Über das Marionettentheater.*" In: Paul de Man. *The Rhetoric of Romanticism.* New York: Columbia University Press. 263–290.
Derrida, Jacques. 2006. "Das Schreibmaschinenband. Limited Ink II." In: Jacques Derrida. *Maschinen Papier. Das Schreibmaschinenband und andere Antworten.* Wien: Passagen-Verlag. 35–138.
Derrida, Jacques. 2001. "The Deaths of Roland Barthes." In: Jacques Derrida. *The Work of Mourning.* Eds. Pascale-Anne Brault and Michael Naas. Chicago: University of Chicago Press. 31–68.
Derrida, Jacques. 1998 [1986]. "To Unsense the Subjectile." In: Jacques Derrida and Paul Thévenin. *The Secret Art of Antonin Artaud.* Trans. Mary Ann Caws. Cambridge: MIT Press. 59–148.
Derrida, Jacques. 1982 [1972]. "The Pit and the Pyramid: Introduction to Hegel's Semiology." In: Jacques Derrida. *Margins of Philosophy.* Trans. Alan Bass. Chicago: University of Chicago Press. 69–108.
Dicke, Gerd. 1997. "Art. Exempel." In: Klaus Weimar, Harald Fricke, Klaus Grubmüller and Jan-Dirk Müller (eds.). *Reallexikon der deutschen Literaturwissenschaft.* Vol. 1. Berlin: De Gruyter. 534–537.

Dünne, Jörg. 2017. "Suspendierte Texte. Célines Auslassungspunkte." In: Helga Lutz, Nils Plath and Dietmar Schmidt (eds.). *Satzzeichen. Szenen der Schrift*. Berlin: Kadmos. 239–242.
Felman, Shoshana. 1989. *Le scandale du corps parlant. Don Juan avec Austin ou la séduction en deux langues*. Paris: Éditions du Seuil.
Felman, Shoshana. 1983. *The Literary Speech Act. Don Juan with J. L. Austin, or Seduction in Two Languages*. Trans. Catherine Porter. Ithaca: Cornell University Press.
Fenves, Peter. 2001. "Anecdote and Authority. Towards Kleist's Last Language." In: Peter Fenves. *Arresting Language. From Leibniz to Benjamin*. Stanford: Stanford University Press. 152–173.
Fineman, Joel. 1989. "The History of the Anecdote: Fiction and Fiction." In: Harold Aram Veeser (ed.). *The New Historicism*. New York: Routledge. 49–76.
Freud, Sigmund. 1989. *Jokes and Their Relation to the Unconscious*. Standard Edition. Trans. James Strachey. New York: Norton.
Freud, Sigmund. 1982 [1905]. *Der Witz und seine Beziehung zum Unbewußten*. In: Sigmund Freud. *Studienausgabe*. Vol. 4. *Psychologische Schriften*. Eds. Alexander Mitscherlich et al. Frankfurt am Main: Fischer. 9–219.
Giuriato, Davide. 2007. "Kleists Poetik der Ausnahme." In: Willer, Stefan, Jens Ruchatz, and Nicolas Pethes (eds.). *Das Beispiel. Epistemologie des Exemplarischen*. Berlin: Kadmos. 220–240.
Grimm, Jacob and Wilhelm. 1854–1984. *Deutsches Wörterbuch*. Repr. 1st ed. Leipzig: Hirzel.
Hamacher, Werner. 1986. "Über einige Unterschiede zwischen der Geschichte literarischer und der Geschichte phänomenaler Ereignisse." In: Albrecht Schöne (ed.). *Akten des VI Internationalen Germanisten Kongresses*. Vol. 2. Tübingen: Niemeyer. 5–11.
Hegel, Georg W. F. 1970 [1807]. *Phänomenologie des Geistes*. In: Georg W. F. Hegel. *Werke*. Eds. Eva Moldenhauer and Karl Markus Michel. Vol. 3. Frankfurt am Main: Suhrkamp.
Hein, Jürgen. 1991. "Die Anekdote." In: Otto Knörich (ed.). *Formen der Literatur*. Stuttgart: Kröner. 14–20.
Heine, Heinrich. 1995 [1827]. *Reisebilder. Zweiter Teil: Ideen. Das Buch Le Grand*. In: Heinrich Heine. *Sämtliche Schriften*. Ed. Klaus Briegleb. 3rd rev. ed. München: Hanser. 245–308.
Houben, Heinrich Hubert. 1983. "Bedenkliche Gedankenstriche." In: Burckhard Garbe (ed.). *Texte zur Geschichte der deutschen Interpunktion und ihrer Reform 1462–1983*. Hildesheim: Olms. (= Germanistische Linguistik, 4–6/1983). 202–209.
Jacobs, Carol. 1989. "The Style of Kleist." In: Carol Jacobs. *Uncontainable Romanticism. Shelley, Brontë, Kleist*. Baltimore: Johns Hopkins University Press. 171–196.
Kemman, Ansgar. 1996. "Art. Evidentia, Evidenz." In: *Historisches Wörterbuch der Rhetorik*. Vol. 3. Ed. Gert Ueding. Tübingen: Niemeyer. 33–47.
Kittler, Friedrich A. 1990 [1985]. *Discourse Networks 1800/1900*. Trans. Michael Metteer and Chris Cullens. Stanford: Stanford University Press.
Klein, Wolf Peter and Marthe Grund. 1997. "Die Geschichte der Auslassungspunkte. Zu Entstehung, Form und Funktion der deutschen Interpunktion." *Zeitschrift für germanische Linguistik* 25.1: 24–44.
Kleist, Heinrich von. 1997. *Sämtliche Werke. Brandenburger Ausgabe*. Vol. II/7 and II/8: *Berliner Abendblätter*. Ed. Roland Reuß and Peter Staengle. Basel: Stroemfeld/Roter Stern. (= BKA for *Brandenburger Ausgabe*) (= BA for *Berliner Abendblätter*)

Kleist, Heinrich von. 1997. "Anekdote aus dem letzten Kriege." In: *Sämtliche Werke. Brandenburger Ausgabe*. Vol. II/7. *Berliner Abendblätter* I. Ed. Roland Reuß and Peter Staengle. Basel: Stroemfeld/Roter Stern. 96.

Kleist, Heinrich von. 1997. "Der verlegene Magistrat." In: *Sämtliche Werke. Brandenburger Ausgabe*. Vol. II/7. *Berliner Abendblätter* I. Ed. Roland Reuß and Peter Staengle. Basel: Stroemfeld/Roter Stern. 22.

Kleist, Heinrich von. 1997. "Miscellen." In: *Sämtliche Werke. Brandenburger Ausgabe*. Vol. II/7. *Berliner Abendblätter* I. Ed. Roland Reuß and Peter Staengle. Basel: Stroemfeld/Roter Stern. 160–161.

Kleist, Heinrich von. 1997. "Unwahrscheinliche Wahrhaftigkeiten." In: *Sämtliche Werke. Brandenburger Ausgabe*. Vol. II/8. *Berliner Abendblätter* II. Ed. Roland Reuß and Peter Staengle. Basel: Stroemfeld/Roter Stern. 42–46.

Kleist, Heinrich von. 1997. *Die Hermannsschlacht*. In: *Sämtliche Werke. Brandenburger Ausgabe*. Vol. I/7. Ed. Roland Reuß and Peter Staengle. Basel: Stroemfeld/Roter Stern.

Kleist, Heinrich von. 1979. "Improbable Veracities." Trans. Carol Jacobs. *Diacritics* 9.4: 45–46.

Kleist, Heinrich von. 1965. *Sämtliche Werke und Briefe*. 2 Vols. Ed. Helmut Sembdner. München: Hanser. (= KSW)

Kofman, Sarah. 1990. *Die lachenden Dritten, Freud und der Witz*. München: Verlag Internationale Psychoanalyse.

Kofman, Sarah. 1986. *Pourquoi rit-on? Freud et le mot d'esprit*. Paris: Editions Galilée.

Lacan, Jacques. 2006 [1966]. *Écrits. The First Complete Edition in English*. Trans. Bruce Fink. New York: Norton.

Lacan, Jacques. 1969. "Le séminaire sur 'La Lettre volée.'" In: *Ècrits I*. Paris: Seuil/Points. 19–56.

Lachmann, Renate. 1987. "Vorwort". In: Michail Bachtin. *Rabelais und seine Welt: Volkskultur als Gegenkultur*. Trans. Gabriele Leupold. Ed. Renate Lachmann. Frankfurt am Main: Suhrkamp. 7–46.

Lowrie, Michèle and Susanne Lüdemann. 2015. "Introduction." In: Michèle Lowrie and Susanne Lüdemann (eds.). *Exemplarity and Singularity: Thinking through Particulars in Philosophy, Literature, and Law*. New York: Routledge. 1–15.

Lyons, John D. 1987. *Exemplum. The Rhetoric of Example in Early Modern France and Italy*. Princeton: Princeton University Press.

Miller, Philip B. (ed.). 1982. *An Abyss Deep Enough. Letters of Heinrich von Kleist with a Selection of Essays and Anecdotes*. New York: Dutton.

Montaigne, Michel de. 2003. *The Complete Essays*. Trans. M. A. Screech. London: Penguin.

Montaigne, Michel de. 1962. *Essais*. In: Michel de Montaigne. *Oeuvres completes*. Ed. A. Thibaudet and Maurice Rat. Paris: Pleïade.

Moering, Michael. 1972. *Witz und Ironie in der Prosa Heinrich von Kleists*. München: Fink.

Moser, Christian. 2000. "Angewandte Kontingenz. Fallgeschichten bei Kleist und Montaigne." *Kleist-Jahrbuch* 2000: 3–32.

Neubauer, Hans-Joachim. 1998. *Fama. Eine Geschichte des Gerüchts*. Berlin: Berlin Verlag.

Ovidius Naso, Publius. 1996. *Metamorphosen*. Lateinisch – deutsch. Ed. and trans. Erich Rösch. 14th ed. Zürich: Artemis & Winkler.

Ovidius Naso, Publius. 1984. *Metamorphoses*. Ed. and trans. Frank Justus Miller. Rev. 2nd ed. Cambridge: Harvard University Press.

Peters, Sibylle. 2003. *Heinrich von Kleist und der Gebrauch der Zeit. Von der MachArt der Berliner Abendblätter*. Würzburg: Königshausen & Neumann.
Peters, Sibylle. 2000. "Von der Klugheitslehre des Medialen. (Eine Paradoxe.) Ein Vorschlag zum Gebrauch der 'Berliner Abendblätter.'" *Kleist-Jahrbuch* 2000: 136–160.
Peters, Sibylle. 1999/2000. "Wie Geschichte geschehen lassen? Theatralität und Anekdotizität in den 'Berliner Abendblättern.'" *Kleist-Jahrbuch* 1999/2000: 67–86.
Peters, Sibylle. 1997. "Die 'Berliner Abendblätter' als Agencement: Vom Kalkulieren mit dem Zufall." In: Tagungsbeiträge *Von der Zeitschrift zum poetischen Text. Die "Berliner Abendblätter" Heinrich von Kleists* (Villa Vigoni) (Institut für Textkritik, Heidelberg 2005). <http://www.textkritik.de/vigoni/> [accessed February 20, 2019].
Rault, Julien. 2015. *Poétique du point de suspension. Essai sur le signe du latent*. Nantes: Éditions Cécile Defaut.
Reuß, Roland. 1997a. "Geflügelte Worte. Zwei Notizen zur Redaktion und Konstellation von Artikeln der 'Berliner Abendblätter.'" *Brandenburger Kleist-Blätter* 11: 3–11.
Reuß, Roland. 1997b. "Bemerkungen 'Zu dieser Ausgabe.'" In: *Sämtliche Werke. Brandenburger Ausgabe*. Vol. II/8. Berliner Abendblätter II. Ed. Roland Reuß and Peter Staengle. Basel: Stroemfeld/Roter Stern. 384–392.
Schäffner, Wolfgang. 2004. "Die Wunder des San Francesco d' Assisi und der Therese Neumann. Elemente einer Mediengeschichte des Stigmas." In: Bettine Menke and Barbara Vinken (eds.). *Stigmata. Poetiken der Körperinschrift*. München: Fink. 181–195.
Schnyder, Peter. 2009. "Das Komma. Vom geheimen Ursprung der Philosophie." In: Christine Abbt and Tim Kammasch (eds.). *Punkt, Punkt, Komma, Strich? Geste, Gestalt und Bedeutung philosophischer Zeichensetzung*. Bielefeld: transcript. 73–86.
Schuller, Marianne. 1997. "Eine Anekdote Kleists in der Zeitung." In: Tagungsbeiträge *Von der Zeitschrift zum poetischen Text. Die "Berliner Abendblätter" Heinrich von Kleists* (Villa Vigoni) (Institut für Textkritik, Heidelberg 2005) <http://www.textkritik.de/vigoni/> [accessed February 20, 2019].
Schulze, Martin. 1980. "Do you know the Meaning of****? Die markierte Aussparung als Indiz für die planvolle Komposition des *Tristram Shandy*." In: Gerd Rohmann (ed.). *Laurence Sterne*. Darmstadt: Wissenschaftliche Buchgesellschaft. 394–435.
Schüttpelz, Erhard. 2010. "Der Trickster." In: Eva Eßlinger et al. (eds.). *Die Figur des Dritten. Ein kulturwissenschaftliches Paradigma*. Frankfurt am Main: Suhrkamp. 208–224.
Sembdner, Helmut. 1939. *Die Berliner Abendblätter Heinrich von Kleists, ihre Quellen und ihre Redaktion*. Berlin: Weidmann.
Siegert, Bernhard. 2003. *[…] Auslassungspunkte, Vortrag an der Hochschule für Grafik und Buchkunst Leipzig*. Ed. Julia Blume and Günter Karl Bose. Leipzig: Institut für Buchkunst.
Stamer, Peter. 2005. "'[…]' im Δ der Auslassung." In: Krassimira Kruschkova (ed.). *Ob?scene. Zur Präsenz der Absenz im zeitgenössischen Tanz, Theater und Film* (= Maske und Kothurn. Heft 51/1). Wien: Böhlau. 129–142.
Stefanovska, Malina. 2009. "Exemplary or Singular? The Anecdote in Historical Narrative." *SubStance* 38.1: 16–30.
Sterne, Laurence. 1978 [1759–1767]. *The Life and Opinions of Tristram Shandy, Gentleman*. Eds. Melvyn and Joan New. Gainsville: University Press of Florida.
Szondi, Peter. 1967/1970. "Über philologische Erkenntnis." In: Peter Szondi. *Hölderlin-Studien. Mit einem Traktat über philologische Erkenntnis*. 2nd ed. Frankfurt am Main: Insel. 9–34.

Weber, Samuel. 1994. "Die Zeit des Lachens." *Fragmente* 46: 77–90.
Wild, Christopher J. 2002. "'Weder worte noch rutten.' Hypotypose: Zur Evidenz korporealer Inskription bei Andreas Gryphius." In: Bettine Menke and Barbara Vinken (eds.). *Stigmata. Poetiken der Körperinschrift*. Paderborn: Fink. 215–242.
Willer, Stefan, Jens Ruchatz and Nicolas Pethes. 2007. "Zur Systematik des Beispiels." In: Stefan Willer, Jens Ruchatz, and Nocolas Pethes (eds.). *Das Beispiel. Epistemologie des Exemplarischen*. Berlin: Kadmos. 7–59.
Willer, Stefan. 2004. "Was ist ein Beispiel? Versuch über das Exemplarische." In: Gisela Fehrmann, Erika Linz, Eckhard Schumacher, and Brigitte Weingart (eds.). *Originalkopie. Praktiken des Sekundären*. Köln: DuMont. 51–65.

Appendix

"Anekdote aus dem letzten Kriege"

Den ungeheuersten Witz, der vielleicht, so lange die Erde steht, über Menschenlippen gekommen ist, hat, im Lauf des letztverflossenen Krieges, ein Tambour gemacht; ein Tambour meines Wissens von dem damaligen Regiment von Puttkamer; ein Mensch, zu dem, wie man gleich hören wird, weder die griechische noch römische Geschichte ein Gegenstück liefert. Dieser hatte, nach Zersprengung der preußischen Armee bei Jena, ein Gewehr aufgetrieben, mit welchem er, auf seine eigne Hand, den Krieg fortsetzte; dergestalt, daß da er, auf der Landstraße, alles, was ihm an Franzosen in den Schuß kam, niederstreckte und ausplünderte, er von einem Haufen französischer Gensdarmen, die ihn aufspürten, ergriffen, nach der Stadt geschleppt, und, wie es ihm zukam, verurteilt ward, erschossen zu werden. Als er den Platz, wo die Exekution vor sich gehen sollte, betreten hatte, und wohl sah, daß alles, was er zu seiner Rechtfertigung vorbrachte, vergebens war, bat er sich von dem Obristen, der das Detaschement kommandierte, eine Gnade aus; und da der Obrist, inzwischen die Offiziere, die ihn umringten, in gespannter Erwartung zusammentraten, ihn fragte: was er wolle? zog er sich die Hosen ab und sprach: sie mögten ihn in den .... schießen, damit das F... kein L... bekäme. – Wobei man noch die Shakespearesche Eigenschaft bemerken muß, daß der Tambour mit seinem Witz, aus seiner Sphäre als Trommelschläger nicht herausging. (x.)
(*Berliner Abendblätter*, 20. Oktober 1810)

"Anecdote from the last war"

Perhaps the most monstrous joke to have passed human lips since the beginning of time was made by a Tambour during the last war; a drummer, who, as far as I know, belonged to the Puttkamer regiment at the time. This individual had, as you will soon hear, no peer in Greek and Roman history. After the dispersal of the Prussian army at Jena he had gotten hold of a rifle, with which he, on his own, had continued the war; thus, after having shot down and robbed every Frenchman who crossed his path, he was arrested by a troop of French gendarmes who had tracked him down, and was then taken into town and sentenced to death by firing squad, as befit his actions. When he stepped onto the square where the execution was to take place and realized that everything he had to say in his defense would be to no avail, he asked a final wish of the colonel commanding the unit; and when the colonel, while the officers who surrounded him gathered in eager anticipation, asked him: what was it he wanted? He pulled down his pants and said: would they please shoot him in the .... so that the s... wouldn't get a h... in it. – One must note the Shakespearean quality that with his joke the Tambour did not overstep his (professional) sphere of a beater on drums.
(Trans. Isabel Kranz, Bettine Menke)

Inka Mülder-Bach
Individual Case, Example, Exception: The Range of the Anecdotal in Fontane

Translated by Michael Thomas Taylor

Abstract: The essay explores Fontane's use of the anecdote and his reflection on the genre in two of his last works, the childhood autobiography *Meine Kinderjahre* and the novel *Der Stechlin*. In his autobiography Fontane highlights the anecdote as an indispensable medium of memory and as a narrative form of knowledge distinguished by its usefulness. Anecdotes not only school the reflective faculty of judgement and the ability to recognize the exemplary or general in a particular case, they facilitate a thinking of singularity and a recognition of the incommensurable. By contrast, the numerous stories told in the novel *Der Stechlin* are symptoms of a fundamental crisis of society. They also raise questions about the epistemology and politics of small narrative genres that are addressed in conversations about heroism and point to the limits of the anecdotal. On the one hand, in an age in which clichés have come to govern imagination and discourse, and standardized identities have become the norm, the notion of an original trait or characteristic *proprium* conveyed in anecdotal form becomes increasingly problematic. On the other hand, the gap between the individual and society, between the single case and the general rule seems to have become so insurmountable that individuality can manifest itself only in acts that except themselves from general rules and thus in stories that transcend the anecdotal logic of singularity and exemplarity in favor of the logic of exception.

Keywords: Exemplarity, Singularity, Exception, Heroism, (In)Authenticity

1

When Theodor Fontane was asked, on the occasion of his seventieth birthday in 1889, to write an autobiography, he observed that he of all people, a man who "never" aimed "for the great," but always for "the mid-sized" and "the small," had been "puffed up to a small-sized figure of greatness" (*Briefe*

1890–1898: 17–18).[1] Fontane does not seem to have felt entirely at ease in this role.[2] In any case, he took his time with the autobiography, and when he finally turned to writing it, on the advice of his doctor and in the midst of a depression accompanied by severe writing blocks, the "puffing up" had apparently continued to occupy him to such an extent that he addressed it in his text.

> Als mir es feststand, mein Leben zu beschreiben, stand es mir auch fest, daß ich bei meiner Vorliebe fürs Anekdotische und mehr noch für eine viel Raum in Anspruch nehmende Kleinmalerei mich auf einen bestimmten Abschnitt meines Lebens zu beschränken haben würde. (*Kinderjahre:* 9)

> When it became clear to me that I would describe my life, it also became clear to me that – given my predilection for the anecdotal and, even more so, for a kind of *Kleinmalerei* [painting a very detailed picture] that claims a great deal of space – I would have to limit myself to a certain chapter of my life.

Thus begins Fontane's autobiography *Meine Kinderjahre*, published in 1893, the preface of which already offers a sample of the author's predilection. In this preface, Fontane interweaves the poetics of his autobiographical narrative with the anecdote. He not only declares that his "predilection for the anecdotal" and for "Kleinmalerei" motivated his decision to limit himself to one chapter of his life. An apophthegmatic anecdote, told not without self-irony, also serves to justify his choice of his childhood years:

> Ein verstorbener Freund von mir (noch dazu Schulrat) pflegte jungverheirateten Damen seiner Bekanntschaft den Rat zu geben, Aufzeichnungen über das erste Lebensjahr ihrer Kinder zu machen, in diesem ersten Lebensjahre "stecke der ganze Mensch." (*Kinderjahre:* 9)

> A deceased friend of mine (a school inspector at that) used to advise newlywed ladies with whom he was acquainted to take notes about the first year of their children's life, since, as he claimed, this first year of life "contained the whole person."

The school inspector's advice clarifies the concept of what Fontane calls a "chapter." For a year of childhood that contains "the whole person" is not only part of a whole in a quantitative respect: it is its nucleus and can thus stand in for this whole. Moreover, the apophthegma thematizes the relationship between the particular and general. It deals with a particular communicative situation and leads to an oral dictum which aims to transcend the particular

---

[1] Unless otherwise indicated, all translations are by Michael Thomas Taylor.
[2] See Fontane's letter to his daughter of July 9th, 1893: "Operating with great figures while always keeping oneself, as a small-sized figure of greatness, in mind, always art, always literature, always a professor, always a celebrity – all of this is bad" (*Briefe 1890–1898:* 267).

situation in favor of a general statement.³ Given these conditions, Fontane can apply the apophthegma to his own undertaking: if his friend's dictum "can more or less claim general validity, then perhaps this childhood history of mine can pass for a life history, too" (ibid.). But Fontane also considers the "opposite case," in which the dictum cannot claim general validity, so that the "whole person" is not always contained within one's childhood years. In this case, there would still remain

> die Hoffnung, in diesen meinen Aufzeichnungen wenigstens etwas Zeitbildliches gegeben zu haben: das Bild einer kleinen Ostseestadt aus dem ersten Drittel des Jahrhunderts und in ihr die Schilderung einer noch ganz von Refugié-Traditionen erfüllten Französischen-Colonie-Familie, deren Träger und Repräsentanten meine beiden Eltern waren. (ibid.)

> the hope that in these notes of mine I have at least given something of a picture of those times: the picture of a small town by the Baltic Sea from the first third of the century and, as part of it, the description of a family belonging to the French colony and still entirely imbued with refugié traditions, the bearers and representatives of which were my two parents.

This picture of the age of his childhood, in turn, testifies to Fontane's predilection for anecdotes and *Kleinmalerei* not only to the extent that it represents a small, provincial town, but also because it is ruled by the twilight between factuality and fictionality that characterizes anecdotes. Just as the anecdote claims factuality without authenticating it,⁴ Fontane assures us that he has "sketched everything according to life" (ibid.). Yet he deliberately leaves open the status of what he has recounted. In the similarly autobiographical volume *Von Zwanzig zu Dreißig* (1898), he notes, in reference to "Frederician anecdotes": "the fakes are just as good as the real ones, and sometimes even a little bit better" (2007: 412). In his childhood history, he accordingly does not want to be confronted with the "question of authenticity" (*Kinderjahre*: 9). This is why, he explains, he added the subtitle "'autobiographical novel'" to *Meine Kinderjahre* (ibid.).

The small and the great, part and whole, the particular and the universal, singularity and exemplarity, individual case and general rule, the oral dictum and the written tradition, factuality and fiction: in the preface to his childhood autobiography, Fontane expounds the coordinates and conceptual pairs in which the anecdote continues to be situated and negotiated to this day. The

---

3 Cf. Niehaus (2013: 186–190).
4 Cf. also Moser-Rath (1977: 534–535); Schlaffer (1997: 87–88); Niehaus (2017: 183–184, 195–199).

connection between autobiographical writing and the anecdote that he establishes is, of course, not surprising in itself. Long before Procopius introduced the concept of *anekdota*, "biographical historiography [...] was marked by anecdotal features" (Moser-Rath 1977: 529). The most prominent example is Plutarch, who explicitly thematizes the "epistemological value of 'small' incidents" (Neureuter 1973: 460) in the preface to his biography of Alexander the Great. In the historical context of Fontane's autobiographical writing, however, reflections on the form of the anecdote have specific functions.[5] They serve to forge an alliance between the genres of the *Zeitroman* (which might be translated as a "novel of its times") and (childhood) autobiography,[6] the contours of which are defined by a double delimitation: on the one hand, against official historiography and on the other, against the narration of autobiography as *Bildungsgeschichte*.[7] Taking this constellation as my point of departure, I would first like to show how Fontane's childhood autobiography employs and stages the anecdote as a narrative form and form of knowledge. The second part of my essay will be devoted to the place and fate of anecdotes in Fontane's late novel *Der Stechlin* (1898).

2

The epoch covered in *Meine Kinderjahre* ranges from 1819 to 1832. During this period, political events and developments of far-reaching importance take place "out there in the world" (*Kinderjahre:* 109), which Fontane, of course, does not ignore. Quite the contrary: the memory of the Polish "insurrection" (111) in 1830/1831, for example, plays a prominent role and gives Fontane the opportunity to reflect on his own lifelong ambivalence towards struggles for freedom and revolutionary efforts. And yet, historical events enter into the text only to the extent that they entered into the child's horizon – and only in the way that they once made their entrance. Thus, the narrator recalls the events of the 1820s by describing the "peep-box images," in which the child encountered them in a "fairground show booth" (109), and in which they made an indelible impression on him. The memory of the July Revolution and the Polish uprising is associated with the child's first reading of newspapers, the circumstances and consequences of which are described in as much detail as the events themselves. History

---

5 For a foundational treatment of the anecdote in *Meine Kinderjahre*, see Lange (2000) and Lange (2008: 65–112); see also MhicFhionnbhairr (1985: 242–261); for an examination of Fontane's poetics of the anecdote in general, see also Wülfing (2010).
6 Cf. Niggl (1971: 266).
7 Cf. Lange (2000: 85); Lange (2008: 74).

thus dissolves into a multitude of stories, scenes, and images that are interwoven with Fontane's life.

Conversely, this life story is not told as a continuous history of development or *Bildung*. It is divided into two salient phases defined by a change in residence, and thus by topography. The chapter headings announce characterizations of the everyday life of a childhood collective: "How we lived in our house" (Chapters 9, 10), "What we experienced at home and in town" (Chapter 11), "How we went to school and learned" (Chapter 13), "How we were raised" (Chapter 14), "How we played outside" (Chapter 15). The composition of these chapters is marked by alternations between portraits of individual persons, depictions of places, summary descriptions of characteristic habits, and narrative accounts of individual incidents, with the narrator repeatedly yielding, in the interest of minor matters, to his tendency toward digressions that deviate from the main path. The result is an autobiographical picture of the times, a thick description composed of a multitude of small traits from different kinds of history: local history and social history, history of mentalities and history of culture. But the result is not an autobiographical *Bildungsroman* or the totality of a life history. Almost the opposite is true: if the *Kinderjahre* can stand as a synecdoche for the "whole person," then not least of all because it is these years of childhood in which the "patchwork" of incomplete, accidental, and unordered knowledge has been compiled, which in Fontane's own view characterizes his work "literally and to a particularly high degree during his entire life" (177).

By forging an alliance between the genre of autobiography and the *Zeitroman*, Fontane, the lover of anecdotes, seeks to trace the early formative influences of his narrative inclinations and to find the voices that resonate in the secondary orality of the anecdotes and conversations in his novels (see *Kinderjahre:* 82). Here, the father, a "conversationalist and storyteller" (18), who picked up a "wealth of anecdotes" about "all possible topics" from "newspapers and journals" (121), proves to be a key figure. With these anecdotes he not only stands out in sociable conversation but becomes the child's most important teacher. As Fontane sees it, he "actually owes all that is best, and in any case, all that is most useful" (121) of what he knows to his father's instructions in history and geography. In the description of this education, Fontane characterizes the anecdote as an indispensable "form of historical knowledge" and an irreplaceable medium through which this knowledge is "passed on" (Lange 2000: 80). Since he continues to work with this form in his retellings of his father's stories, as well as in the anecdotes he tells about his father and other figures from his childhood, the anecdotal knowledge of his autobiography is a self-reflexive one. What Fontane passes on through his anecdotal narrative style is not least of all a knowledge of the form of the anecdote itself.

As far as the subject matter is concerned, his father's instructions are devoted to topics which are selected "quite arbitrarily" (*Kinderjahre:* 118). But the lessons always lead to "historical anecdotes" (120), or they take these anecdotes as their starting point; and the father always avoids frontal teaching in favor of what he calls his "Socratic method" (92, 121, 125). The lessons proceed by means of questions and answers and in the manner of a dialogue, in which the father imparts something new by linking it with what is already known and solidifies this knowledge by having his student retell or repeat it. Thus, one of his favorite stories, the anecdote about the ritual call to commemorate Napoleon's "First Grenadier," La Tour d'Auvergne, is not only recounted, but restaged as a role play with his son (120–121).

The father is convinced that his anecdotes disseminate "useful knowledge" (95) and Fontane agrees with him without reservation. He lost "nothing" of what his father taught him, and "nothing was useless for him" (121). In his reflections on the imprint of his father's lessons, he focuses on three features of the anecdote. They are very close to the features that Walter Benjamin in his essay on "The Storyteller" (1936) distinguishes as specific qualities of small narrative genres.[8] For one thing, the anecdote has a memorializing function. Anecdotes are media of *memoria*; they serve to remember the past and to commemorate the dead. It is not for nothing that Fontane has his father say: "I cultivate what is historical" (*Kinderjahre:* 95). For the father tends to and builds upon the soil of cultural memory and thus the stock of collective experiences. His anecdotes preserve what is past so that it can be passed on. They imprint themselves into memory by dint of their brevity and narrative form; they are designed to be retold and circulated. This leads to a second aspect of the anecdote that Fontane illuminates, its communicative function. As its extensive literary tradition shows, the anecdote is often handed down in writing. But unlike the "files and government papers" (*Briefe 1879–1889:* 135) of official historiography, the anecdote is both an indispensable component of the culture of oral conversation and an elixir of entertainment and sociability – and not only to the extent that it contributes to distraction, but also because it provokes "astonishment and reflection" (Benjamin 2002: 148). This finally leads to the anecdote's epistemological function. Fontane describes the knowledge he owes to his father's teaching as "useful" because anecdotes have a practical benefit. The succinct detail of an event or the characteristic trait of a person might also pass on a knowledge of what has been "excluded from official historical consciousness" (Weber 1993: 199). But for Fontane, the practical benefit of the anecdote does not reside in

---

[8] Cf. Lange (2008: 85, 90–92, 102–103).

its informational content. Rather, what is essential is that by focusing on individual cases, the anecdote trains one to develop, independently and on one's own, criteria for judging human behavior in general, and the actions of historical actors in particular. It thereby not only schools the reflective faculty of judgment, which seeks the general from a given particular.[9] Rather, anecdotes facilitate a thinking of singularity and a recognition of the incommensurable. Regardless of whether the incident told by an anecdote is unique or exemplary, whether it stands alone or points as a particular case to a general truth, whether it punctures or fits into that whole of which it is a part,[10] there is always something in its narrative that transcends its reference, that resists conceptualization, that remains interesting for its own sake[11] and cannot be separated from the narrative form of its presentation.

This is the subject of the section of the *Kinderjahre* entitled "Grand Party" (Chapter 10). The chapter tells of a gentlemen's evening in the house of the narrator's parents,[12] which the narrator "still remembers particularly vividly, because even years later it was recalled frequently and with all kinds of details" (*Kinderjahre:* 92). On this evening, in the presence of little Theodor, his mother, and his aunt, the conversation of the assembled gentlemen once again turns to one of the anecdotes about Napoleon that belong to the hobbyhorses of Fontane's father, namely, the anecdote of how Henri Gratien Count Bertrand, Napoleon's confidante and most loyal companion, is said to have temporarily handed over his own wife to his emperor during Napoleon's exile on Saint Helena. One of the men confronts the father with the question of whether he would have "been willing to make a similar act of loyal sacrifice" (93). The anecdote is thus transformed into a *casus*, a case, demanding to be weighed and judged. The father's ingenious answer refuses any insight into himself, which is what his friends were after. Instead, it formulates a paradox in which the exemplary nature of the case is connected with its singularity. The father declares he would have decided to make a similar sacrifice "unconditionally" – but only "if" (that is, under the condition that) he "had been Bertrand" (ibid.). He furthermore points out that the decision probably lay with Madame Bertrand and that, in the "upper regions" (94) of great historical actors, whose secret stories these anecdotes divulge, other forces are at work and other standards apply than in ordinary life.

---

9 Cf. Gabriel (2014: 23–24).
10 Cf. Fineman (1989: 61).
11 Cf. Novalis (1968: 569).
12 On the "gentlemen's evening" as a "site of the anecdote" in Fontane, see Wülfing (2010: 60–61).

And with that, the men's interest in the incident is exhausted. But the evening is not over yet. After the gentlemen have broken up their gathering, Fontane's narrative turns to a dispute between his parents that gives exemplary evidence of their fundamentally different characters and hints at the breakdown of their marriage. While the father weighs Bertrand's behavior and declares it to be incommensurable, his mother weighs the father's behavior and, once again, judges it to be frivolous. The father defends his love of the anecdotal and prides himself on the fact that the gentlemen did not succeed in "embarrassing" him in front of his wife. To which she replies: "I'm afraid not. And that's the worst part of the matter" (95). As the narrator tells it, the mother thus has the last word. But the verdict on the "matter," the *causa* of the dispute, remains pending.

3

If Fontane's *Meine Kinderjahre*, an "autobiographical novel" and a picture of the times of his childhood, were instead one of his marriage novels, this anecdote could be imagined as one of its closing scenes. For, of course, it is not only in his (auto)biographical and historiographical writings that Fontane operates with the toolkit of small features and incidents. Rather, the anecdote also marks a central formal element of his novels. Fontane generally owes his plots to historical anecdotes, case histories, or criminal cases that came to his attention through memoirs or newspaper reports, or that were communicated to him in letters or conversations. *L'Adultera* (1882) is inspired by a contemporary scandal that Fontane was able to follow in the newspapers, and in which some of his acquaintances were also caught up; *Schach von Wuthenow* (1883) is based on a report by Mathilde von Rohrs from the *chronique scandaleuse*; *Effi Briest* (1895) goes back to the adulterous affair and duel connected to Elisabeth von Ardenne, which Fontane heard about from the wife of the owner of the *Vossische Zeitung*, and so on. This is in accord with Friedrich Spielhagen's realist slogan to "'find, not invent'" ("finden, nicht erfinden"), which, according to Fontane, "[holds] a truth that cannot be heeded enough" (*Von Zwanzig bis Dreißig:* 387). But the significance of the anecdote for his novels is not limited to materials and intrigues that allow him to connect with *realia*. Nor does it merge with the *Kleinmalerei* that Fontane himself frequently invoked, or with his predilection for supposedly "minor matters," however central the art of detail is for his narrative style and the texture of his novels. Rather, the anecdote functions as the starting point for a process of narration that intones the individual case in so many voices and views it from so many perspectives that it becomes questionable what the case was in the first place. The narrator is reluctant to comment on and illuminate the characters' inner lives; he cultivates an outside view. Accordingly, the fictitious conversations, carried out not least of all through the exchange of stories, become all the more important. While the anecdote is significant in Fontane's childhood autobiography primarily as a small form of historical-anthropological knowledge, and as a form of knowledge about small things, in these novelistic conversations it takes on further functions. It serves to characterize the figures, who present themselves through the mirror of the stories they tell. And at the same time, it is staged as a narrative medium for the production and circulation of the social imaginary.

In *Der Stechlin* the conversations take on an incomparable weight. Of Fontane's late novels, it is the only one that was begun after the remembering, repeating, and working through of his *Kinderjahre*. "Everything is conversation, dialogue, in which the characters present themselves and, with themselves, the story" (*Briefe 1890–1898:* 650): this is how Fontane outlines the narrative style he achieves in *Der Stechlin*. By shifting the story into conversation, this style picks up from the earlier novels while also marking a new compositional approach. After the test run of the *Poggenpuhls* (1896), Fontane attempted in *Der Stechlin* to write a "political novel" (562) and "Zeitroman" (650), whose plot is not only not inspired by an anecdote or a scandal, but which no longer has any plot at all. Instead of threading its own times onto the strand of a plot, the novel presents its age as an asynchronous, uncanny, and heterogeneous state that eludes conventional narrative integration. What takes its place and ensures the "connection between things" (*The Stechlin:* 218; trans. modified) is a texture whose smaller and larger patterns are composed of countless formal and thematic correspondences. Like the Stechlin-See (Stechlin Lake) – which, according to legend, maintains underground connections to the volcanic hotspots of the world and begins to stir when it bubbles and spews fire on Iceland or Java – this texture testifies to the state of contemporary globalization and the technologies for news communication and traffic it depends on, while weaving together *faits divers* from all parts of the world.

This mixture is brought into play through conversations held by the novel's characters. Fontane shapes these conversations into highly sensitive seismographs that register even the most imperceptible movements in the social fabric. It is here, in these conversations – the soliloquies and tête-à-têtes, the dialogues and discussions, the speeches and debates, the chit-chat and small talk, the gossip and chatter[13] – that unexpected vortices, whirlpools, and fountains show up,

---

13 On the diversity of forms of conversation and their "various levels of significance," see

which point to subterranean waves of excitation. The disposition that is capable of momentarily tilting the balance and disturbing the surface of the conversation at certain points is an "irritability" (104), an aggressivity and hypersensitiveness, that manifests itself in parapraxes as well as in the numerous stories with which, and about which, the characters talk, often enough violating social decorum. They tell of executions, martyrs' deaths, heroic deeds, and ghost ships; they tell of a rat hunt in the catacombs of Paris and the purgatory of a princess from Siam, whose bath of atonement in ox blood, ordered by priests, finds great acclaim among the noblemen of the Margraviate of Brandenburg as an example of a purification and restitution to be carried out by "extraordinary means" – "*Igni et ferro*" (166).

The narrative forms in which these stories circulate are just as diverse as the forms of conversation. With the main character, Count Dubslav of Stechlin, Fontane erects a monument to the *causeur*. As a conversationalist who prefers "a good idea […] to a good constitution" (32; trans. modified) and lets himself be persuaded by an anecdote about Bismarck to run for the delayed Reichstag elections, Dubslav has a passion for the historical anecdotes, which reduce the "distances" from the great protagonists of history "to familiar closeness" (Blumenberg 1998: 136), and identify them by means of a small, yet also salient and characteristic feature. An example of such a small feature can be found in the "brief little story" (*The Stechlin*: 246) about Wilhelm I that the court chaplain Frommel tells Dubslav while the old man rests after the exhausting festivities of Woldemar's and Armgard's wedding. Frommel himself claims to have experienced it firsthand. When the "good old Emperor" (ibid.; trans. modified) was forced, on a rainy day during a treatment in Gastein, to limit his walks to his rooms, under which, as he knew, a seriously ill person was lying, he dragged together runners and carpets, without any help from the staff. He did so, as he explained to the entering chaplain, so that the "sick man lying down there below me" did not "get the feeling that I'm more or less trampling on his head up here […]" (ibid.).

The first anecdote that Dubslav himself tells seems to be of a similar kind. But it has a different significance. Once again, the story concerns one of the great figures of Prussian history: this time, King Friedrich Wilhelm IV. During a hunting stay at Rheinsberg Palace, the king enjoyed the "blood and tongue sausage" of Countess La Roche-Aymon so much that she had a box full of sausages delivered to Potsdam every Christmas. Until, that is, one day the "good king" decided

---

Graevenitz (2014: 638–647); Neumann is particularly interested in dinner discussions (2011: 150–160).

"to even things up for all those good gifts" and sent the countess a "blood carniole" shaped like a "dainty little blood sausage" with "little golden knots" and with "diamonds" jewelled on these "little knots" to which he attached "a little note": "'One good sausage deserves another'" (31; trans. modified). It is impossible to miss the innocuousness of this anecdote and the irony of its fairytale tone. Indeed, years before, in the first volume of *Wanderungen durch die Mark Brandenburg* (1862), Fontane told the anecdote in a different version, at the end of which the "good king" is disenchanted.[14] Yet one need not know this to notice that the anecdote in *Der Stechlin* characterizes not the king but the narrator. For Dubslav presents it to a visitor as a "memento," and specifically, in place of a "photograph" (ibid.; trans. modified). This not only points to a competition between stories and photographs as media of memory. It also reverses the traditional memorial function of the anecdote: by handing over the sausage story not as a memory of the king, but of himself, Dubslav already anticipates his death at the very beginning of the novel. It has often been said that Dubslav "loses himself in anecdotes" (Müller-Seidel 1994: 435), but actually there can be no question of that, despite all the conversation. The *causeur* and *raconteur* is approaching his end: the first anecdote he tells in the novel will already have been his last.

Lying on his deathbed, Dubslav asks Lorenzen, the pastor in Stechlin who, despite holding Christian-social or even social-democratic convictions, is closest to Dubslav among all his neighbors, to tell him "something downright nice and cheerful" (*The Stechlin:* 287). Dubslav says he has always liked "miscellany" the best, but he would also be happy with "stories about robbers in their dens," "anecdotes from every corner of the world," or a story from the orbit of Friedrich II, for example, something like an old "anecdote about Zieten or Blücher" – all of which, of course, Dubslav is familiar with, but for which he would nevertheless be grateful, since they have a "cavalry-like freshness" to them, something "high-spirited" and "heroic" (ibid.; trans. modified). "Heroic" is the cue for Lorenzen's entry. He drags the dying man into a conversation that is by no means nice and cheerful. The attention of the characters is directed to the question of heroism, but their dialogue is ambiguous: while talking about heroism,

---

14 As discussed in the editor's notes in *Der Stechlin*, in the version from *Wanderungen* (Volume 1: *Die Grafschaft Ruppin*), the countess sends her sausage "gift" to the king every year for several years, receiving a different precious "return gift" each time. This exchange of gifts comes to an end when the countess learns from the newspaper that one of Potsdam's "royal master butchers" was "favored" for his sausage with the same present as she was (*Der Stechlin:* 459). A detailed comparison of the versions can be found in MhicFhionnbhairr (1985: 168–170).

Fontane has the men address, both casually and persistently, questions about the epistemology and politics of the anecdote.

In a previous chapter Lorenzen had already declared to Melusine: "The old-fashioned battles with all their battalions [...] they're disappearing from modern history. From real history, I mean, the kind that's worth reading about. [...] In their place it's inventors and discoverers" (228). And this is where he now begins:

> [Lorenzen, I.M.-B.] "*Mein* Heldentum – soll heißen, was ich für Heldentum halte –, das ist nicht auf dem Schlachtfelde zu Hause, das hat keine Zeugen oder doch immer nur solche, die mit zugrunde gehen. Alles vollzieht sich stumm, einsam, weltabgewandt. Wenigstens als Regel. Aber freilich, wenn die Welt dann ausnahmsweise davon hört, dann horch' ich mit auf, und mit gespitzterem Ohr, wie ein Kavalleriepferd, das die Trompete hört."
> [Dubslav, I.M.-B.] "Gut. Meinetwegen. Aber Beispiele." (*Der Stechlin:* 341)
>
> [Lorenzen, I.M.-B.]: "*My* kind of heroism – which is to say, what I consider to be heroism – isn't to be found on the battlefield; it has no witnesses, or else always only the sort who perish along with it. Everything takes place in silence, in isolation, out of sight of the world. At least as a rule. But then of course, when by way of exception the world does get to hear about it, well, I listen carefully too, I perk up my ears, so to speak, like a cavalry horse catching sound of a trumpet call."
> [Dubslav, I.M.-B.] "All right. Fair enough. But how about some examples." (*The Stechlin:* 288)

Lorenzen's words recall the etymological meaning of "anecdote" as something that has not been published. While this meaning was originally tied to the technology of publishing, the anecdote gradually came to be identified with a story that made public something nonofficial or private. In contrast, the nonpublic that Lorenzen refers to is the deadly sphere of existentially extreme situations that, as a rule, have no survivors. In response to Dubslav's request for examples that, as an exception, testify to this kind of heroism, Lorenzen first lists the types he has in mind: "fanatical inventors," "great climbers," and "finally [...] explorers of all four corners of the earth, including the ones who take part in expeditions to the North Pole" (288). When – prompted by the mention of "explorers to the North Pole" – the old man expects an anecdote about "that eternal Nansen fellow" or about "a polar bear" (288), Lorenzen replies by pointing to the character of the lonely spy Harvey Birch from James Fenimore Cooper's novel *The Spy* (1821) as a literary example of the heroism he has in mind. In a final step, he then segues from Nansen and Cooper to a North Pole adventurer from the New World, the American polar explorer Adolphus Washington Greely, who led an Arctic expedition in 1884.

What Fontane's pastor has learned about this expedition is the following: after only four of his original crew were left and the provisions had to be strictly rationed in order to reach a rescue station with these four men, Greely noticed that the crew member carrying the food was stealing from the rations.[15] "There was no possibility of ordinary punishment," Lorenzen says, and the men were too weak for a fight. Greely gathered the three others to stage a "court-martial scene," announced that the man carrying the food was to be shot "in the back," carried out the deed, reported himself to the authorities upon returning to New York, and, Lorenzen continues, was "found [...] not guilty" in a trial and "carried home in triumph" (289; trans. modified).

Dubslav thus gets a story, but it is very different from what he asked for. Not only does the anecdote offer nothing in the way of amusement. Rather, by choosing this story and by telling it the way he does, Lorenzen presents himself as a character who has not the slightest sense for the anecdotal. Instead of being set in the anecdotal nonpublic or private sphere, the Greely incident takes place in the deadly zones of ice beyond civilization; and instead of leading to a point made in language, it remains "silent" also insofar as it ends with the silent execution of "a man secretly condemned" (289; trans. modified). What is more, Lorenzen does not understand the crucial importance of *Kleinmalerei*. As he explains, he may "be wrong in specific details or in minor facts," but in his view this is irrelevant and does not change the fact that "in the main" his story is correct (ibid.). Above all, however, the Greely story transcends the notions of singularity and exemplarity in favor of the notion of exception. It is not for nothing that in Lorenzen's version of the story Greely explicitly tells the men that with their actions they have given up on being an "example" (290; trans. modified). For even though the story is presented by Lorenzen as an "example" of a heroism that has turned its back on the world and reaches the public only "as an exception," this example not only constitutes an exception, it also is concerned with one. Lorenzen thus transforms the example into a logic that, following Giorgio Agamben, has recently been repeatedly discussed, a logic that behaves both complementary and contrary to the logic of exemplarity.[16] Even in its Latin etymology, the *exemplum* is something "taken out" (*exemere*). But while the exceptional position of the *exemplum* consists of representing, in an exceptional way, as it were, the classes of elements or cases to which it

---

15 On the quite considerable differences between Greely's own report and the story that Fontane has Lorenzen tell, see MhicFhionnbhairr (1985: 178–182). Fontane's knowledge of the expedition was probably based on newspaper articles. He tried to find out more and contacted his friend Paul Meyer among others, but Meyer's information came too late to be considered (cf. *Briefe 1890–1898:* 688).
16 Cf. Agamben (1998: 20–29); Agamben (2009: 11–39); Willer, Ruchatz, and Pethes (2007: 21–31); Möller (2015: 96–110).

belongs, and from which it is taken out, in order to demonstrate this belonging,[17] for the exception the opposite holds true: it presupposes a rule to which it does not belong, from which it is excluded, and within which it is, for that very reason, also included.

There is a reason why Fontane addresses the narrative logic of exemplary and exceptional actions in the context of a conversation about heroism. For *Der Stechlin* is a "political novel" also inasmuch as it reflects on the political and social implications of narrative forms. As the head of the expedition, Lieutenant Greely had, according to Lorenzen, both "the role of leader and commander," as well as "the obligations of the judge" (290), thus uniting executive and judicial power. Greely exercised this double power by doing "something terrible," "something which, torn from its context, runs counter to every Divine commandment, to every law and our every precept of honor" (ibid.; trans. modified). The exception that Lorenzen's story recounts thus includes a decision about the state of exception, and this impresses the pastor all the more, since in Greely's case "the real thing, true courage" of the hero is accompanied by "[s]hame and disgrace" (ibid.). The dialogues between Dubslav and Lorenzen in one of the last chapters of the novel thus refers back to the first dinner conversation, in which Dubslav notes conversationally: "Heroism is a state of exception, and mostly the product of a desperate situation" (19; trans. modified). Only that for Lorenzen, the desperate state of exception becomes the condition of possibility of freedom, providing the platform that allows an individual to appear who, through "a decision entirely of his own accord" (288; trans. modified), carries out a heroic act that, in itself, violates all laws and commandments.

4

Whether Fontane imagined the bachelor and loner Lorenzen to be a reader of Søren Kierkegaard must remain an open question, if only for the reason that, so far, no final proof has come to light that Fontane himself read Kierkegaard.[18]

---

17 As Möller emphasizes contra Agamben, the Greek term *paradeigma*, whose determinations in Aristotle's *Rhetoric* Agamben takes as a guide for his own deliberations on the example, differs "quite clearly in its semantics from the Latin exemplum" (Möller 2015: 109n5). The Latin expression is already etymologically "suggestive of a synecdochic relationship" (Möller 2015: 96), while the *pará-deigma* does not function like a part to a whole, but juxtaposes equal parts.

18 However, there are numerous indications. See, among others, Kobel (1992); Kobel (1994); Fried (2008: 165–192); Mülder-Bach (2009: 629–632); Allen (2016).

The narration of the Greely story, however, suggests that both might be the case. In telling this tale, Lorenzen confronts the dying Dubslav with what Kierkegaard, in *Repetition* (1843), defines as the "legitimate exception": an exception that thinks "the universal with intense passion," that explains both "the universal and itself," indeed, that forces the universal to "acknowledge" its "partiality" for the legitimate exception (1983: 228; trans. modified). This legitimate exception could not be further from the above-mentioned anecdote about William I that the court preacher Frommel, Lorenzen's theological colleague, tells Dubslav on the evening of Woldemar's and Armgard's wedding. But it testifies to the persistence and virulence of a problem that also characterizes the anecdote, and whose trace can be followed, among other things, in the colloquial use of a linguistic particle that virtually acquires the character of a leitmotif in *Der Stechlin*.

In asking for an anecdote about Wilhelm I, Dubslav addresses Frommel with the words: "Anything you can tell me about him? Something of the sort by which one can actually ["recht eigentlich"] recognize him right off" (246; trans. modified).[19] "Actually" – "eigentlich": Dubslav has a predilection for the colloquial use of this expression, which he shares with numerous other figures of Fontane's, and this predilection is related to his inclination for the anecdote in a complicated way. It is precisely a characteristic *proprium* that is represented in the anecdotal narration of a single, remarkable incident: something *Eigenes* (particular, of one's own), something genuine or individual, in which something universal, general, or exemplary might in some circumstances possibly become apparent, something "eigentlich *Menschliches*," something "actually" or "really and truly *human*," as Willibald Schmidt puts it in Fontane's novel *Frau Jenny Treibel* (1892: 360). Yet the explicit affirmation of such *Eigentlichkeit* (actuality or authenticity) empties out what it affirms. It is the symptom of a depletion of what is one's own (*eigen*) or what one actually and truly (*eigentlich*) is that gives way to a language of clichés and prefabricated samples of identity. This depletion is what calls forth, in the first place, the emphatic and authenticating colloquial expressions of *Eigentlichkeit* that continually devalue what they demand or claim, culminating in a type of sentence familiar to every reader of

---

19 Translator's note: The German phrase "recht eigentlich" cannot be translated. In this phrase, "recht" means "quite" but also carries connotations of "correct," "right," "apt," or "appropriate." "Eigentlich" means "actually," or "in truth being the basis of a fact, actually, truly" (Duden: "einer Sache in Wahrheit zugrunde liegend; tatsächlich, wirklich" [s.v. "eigentlich" https://www.duden.de/node/135875/revision/135911; accessed December 7, 2019]) but the word also holds echoes of "eigen," as that which is inherently authentic, proper or inherent to, typical or unique of, a person or thing. "Recht eigentlich" denotes a peculiar trait or authentic feature – which, here, would allow the character to be recognized or known.

Fontane: "Every one of us is actually ["eigentlich"] a disabled veteran, when you come to think about it" (*The Stechlin:* 98); "actually ["eigentlich"] there really aren't anything but sub-humans any more" (245; trans. modified); "[a]ll collecting is in general ["überhaupt"] crazy" (303; trans. modified).[20] The meaning of these declarative sentences lies solely in what they disclose about their speaker in their respective context. Detached from this context and read as a predication of facts, they are meaningless. They make both blanket and empty statements about what is actually the case, or about all that is in general the case. Though they claim to predicate a characteristic *proprium*, they are a counter-pole to the anecdote. For the anecdote eschews the declarative form in favor of the narrative representation of a succinct detail. Even if this detail is exemplary, even if it enables one to "actually recognize" something general or essential, this generality can only be had in the form of a narrative, not as an abstract statement.

This presupposes that something of its own, something actual, genuine, or authentic, can still be identified. In Fontane's late work, however, this assumption has become problematic. About Dubslav we learn, right at the outset of the novel, that he is both an "archetype," the typical representative of "the nobility" from the Margraviate of Brandenburg, and "one of those refreshing originals in whom even weaknesses turn into advantages" (3; trans. modified). But it is precisely this synthesis of social typology and originality, which makes him an "exceptional case" (310; trans. modified). And because this is so, because stereotypes and standardized identities have become the norm, Lorenzen sympathizes with Lieutenant Greely and thus with an exceptional case of a different order. When he declares: "Genuine heroism [...] always stands in the service of an idea of one's own ["Eigenidee"], of one's very own decision ["eines allereigensten Entschlusses"]!" (288; trans. modified), then he is also driven by the question of authenticity and individual qualities ("Eigenheit"). But the gap between the particular and the universal, between the single case and the general rule, between the individual and society, between a "real" hero and "the

---

20 On this form of sentence, see Mecklenburg (2000: 95–96); Lange (2008: 99–102); Neumann (2011: 146). It is so characteristic that it is often quoted in titles, cf. Mecklenburg (2000); Neumann (2011: 161–174). The use of the particle "eigentlich," however, is not limited to this form of sentence, but goes far beyond it. This talk of "actuality," *Eigentlichkeit*, is, one could say, jargon; but it is precisely not to be confused with what Adorno called the "jargon of authenticity" (1973). Fontane's talk of what is "eigentlich" is colloquial; it does not pretend to be anything other than what it is, and at the same time, it is a symptom that draws attention to a fundamental "Uneigentlichkeit," or "inauthenticity." Fontane's intention, however, is not to denounce this "inauthenticity." He diagnoses it, makes it productive for his novels, and possibly even "cautiously and skeptically affirms it" (Neumann 2011: 146).

masses" (290), has, from Lorenzen's point of view, become so insurmountable that what is "one's very own" can only be proven through an act that excepts itself from general rules, even more: an act that is a crime according to the standards of civilization.

The novel, however, does not side with deeds; rather, it narrates conversations and speeches. In Fontane's world, language is the touchstone of individuality and authenticity, and Fontane's characters become recognizable in their act of speaking. What presents itself in these acts cannot be conveyed in any other way than through discourse. Lorenzen's eulogy at Dubslav's funeral is no exception to this rule. "He was really and truly ["recht eigentlich"] free," Fontane has his pastor say. "He held to good works and was really and truly ["recht eigentlich"] that which we should in general ["überhaupt"] call a Christian" (*The Stechlin:* 319–320; trans. modified). Faced with the impossible task of summarizing the "true nature" (ibid.: 319) of the protagonist in a few words, Lorenzen, too, resorts to those colloquial phrases of authentication that devalue what they aim to affirm. Who Dubslav "really and truly" was cannot be expressed in concepts or predicated in statements. At his funeral, whoever wishes to get to know him is referred back to the novel – from which the actual nature of the protagonist cannot be abstracted any more than something universal, general, or exemplary can be abstracted from the narration of the anecdote.

Works Cited

Adorno, Theodor W. 1973 [1964]. *The Jargon of Authenticity.* Trans. Knut Tarnowski and Frederic Will. Evanston: Northwestern University Press.
Agamben, Giorgio. 1998. *Homo Sacer: Sovereign Power and Bare Life.* Trans. Daniel Heller-Roazen. Stanford: Stanford University Press.
Agamben, Giorgio. 2009. *De signatura rerum: Zur Methode.* Trans. Anton Schütz. Frankfurt am Main: Suhrkamp.
Allen, Julie K. 2016. "Theodor Fontane: A Probable Pioneer in German Kierkegaard Reception." In: Jan Stewart (ed.). *Kierkegaard's Influence on Literature, Criticism and Art. Tome I. The Germanophone World.* London: Routledge. 61–78.
Benjamin, Walter. 2002 [1936]. "The Storyteller." In: *Selected Writings.* Vol. 3: *1935–1938.* Trans. Edmund Jephcott and Howard Eiland. Eds. Howard Eiland and Michael W. Jennings. Cambridge: Belknap Press. 143–167.
Blumenberg, Hans. 1998. *Gerade noch Klassiker: Glossen zu Fontane.* München: Hanser.
Fineman, Joel. 1989. "The History of the Anecdote: Fiction and Fiction." In: H. Aram Veeser (ed.). *The New Historicism.* New York: Routledge. 49–76.
Fontane, Theodor. 2007 [1894]. *Meine Kinderjahre.* In: Walter Keitel and Helmuth Nürnberger (eds.). Section III, volume 4, 2nd ed.: *Theodor Fontane. Werke, Schriften und Briefe.* München: Hanser. 7–177.

Fontane, Theodor. 2007 [1898]. *Von Zwanzig bis Dreißig.* In: Walter Keitel and Helmuth Nürnberger (eds.). Section III, volume 4, 2nd ed.: *Theodor Fontane. Werke, Schriften und Briefe.* München: Hanser. 179–539.
Fontane, Theodor. 1995 [1898]. *The Stechlin.* Trans. William L. Zwiebel. Columbia: Camden House.
Fontane, Theodor. 1994 [1898]. *Der Stechlin.* In: Walter Keitel and Helmuth Nürnberger (eds.). Section I, volume 5: *Theodor Fontane. Werke, Schriften und Briefe.* München: Hanser.
Fontane, Theodor. 1982. *Briefe 1890–1898.* In: Walter Keitel and Helmuth Nürnberger (eds.). Section IV, volume 4: *Theodor Fontane. Werke, Schriften und Briefe.* München: Hanser.
Fontane, Theodor. 1977. *Briefe 1879–1889.* In: Walter Keitel and Helmuth Nürnberger (eds.). Section IV, volume 3: *Theodor Fontane. Werke, Schriften und Briefe.* München: Hanser.
Fontane, Theodor. 1974 [1993]. *Frau Jenny Treibel oder "Wo sich Herz zum Herzen find't."* In: Walter Keitel and Helmuth Nürnberger (eds.). Section I, volume 4: *Theodor Fontane. Werke, Schriften und Briefe.* München: Hanser. 297–478.
Fried, Michael. 2008. *Menzels Realismus: Kunst und Verkörperung im Berlin des 19. Jahrhunderts.* München: Fink.
Gabriel, Gottfried. 2014. "Zur Lage der Anekdote." *Zeitschrift für Ideengeschichte* 8: 21–25.
Graevenitz, Gerhard von. 2014. *Theodor Fontane: Ängstliche Moderne.* Konstanz: Konstanz University Press.
Kierkegaard, Søren. 1983. *Kierkegaard's Writings. VI: Fear and Trembling/Repetition.* Ed. Edna H. Hong and Howard V. Hong. Princeton: Princeton University Press.
Kobel, Erwin. 1994. "Die Angst der Effi Briest: Zur möglichen Kierkegaard-Rezeption Fontanes." *Jahrbuch des Freien Deutschen Hochstifts*: 254–288.
Kobel, Erwin. 1992. "Theodor Fontane. Ein Kierkegaard-Leser?" *Jahrbuch der Deutschen Schillergesellschaft* 36: 255–287.
Lange, Katrin. 2000. "Merkwürdige Geschichten: Anekdoten in Fontanes Kindheitsautobiographie *Meine Kinderjahre,* Geschichten und Geschichte." In: Hanna Delf von Wolzogen with Helmuth Nürnberger (eds.). *Theodor Fontane: Am Ende des Jahrhunderts.* Vol. 3: *Geschichte. Vergessen. Großstadt. Moderne.* Würzburg: Königshausen & Neumann. 78–86.
Lange, Katrin. 2008. *Selbstfragmente: Autobiographien der Kindheit.* Würzburg: Königshausen & Neumann.
Mecklenburg, Norbert. 2002. "'Alle Portugiesen sind eigentlich Juden.' Zur Logik und Poetik der Präsentation von Fremden bei Fontane." In: Konrad Ehlig (ed.). *Fontane und die Fremde, Fontane und Europa.* Würzburg: Königshausen & Neumann. 88–102.
MhicFhionnbhairr, Andrea. 1985. *Anekdoten aus allen fünf Weltteilen: The Anecdote in Fontane's Fiction and Autobiography.* Bern: Peter Lang.
Möller, Melanie. 2015. "Exemplum and Exceptio: Building blocks for a rhetorical theory of the exceptional case." In: Michèle Lowrie und Susanne Lüdemann (eds.). *Between Exemplarity and Singularity: Literature, Philosophy, Law.* New York: Routledge. 96–110.
Moser-Rath, Elfriede. 1977. "Anekdote." In: Kurt Ranke and Rolf Wilhelm Brednich (eds.). *Enzyklopädie des Märchens. Handwörterbuch zur historischen und vergleichenden Erzählforschung.* Vol. 1. Berlin: De Gruyter. 528–541.
Mülder-Bach, Inka. 2009. "'Verjährung [...] ist etwas Prosaisches': *Effi Briest* und das Gespenst der Geschichte." *Deutsche Vierteljahrsschrift für Literaturwissenschaft und Geistesgeschichte* 83: 619–642.

Müller-Seidel, Walter. 1994. *Theodor Fontane: Soziale Romankunst in Deutschland*. 3rd ed. Stuttgart: Metzler.

Neumann, Gerhard. 2011. *Theodor Fontane: Romankunst als Gespräch*. Freiburg im Breisgau: Rombach.

Neureuter, Hans Peter. 1973. "Zur Theorie der Anekdote." *Jahrbuch des Freien Deutschen Hochstifts:* 458–480.

Niehaus, Michael. 2013. "Die sprechende und die stumme Anekdote." *Zeitschrift für deutsche Philologie* 132: 183–202.

Niggl, Günter. 1971. "Fontanes 'Meine Kinderjahre' und die Gattungstradition." In: Wolfgang Frühwald und Günter Niggl (eds.). *Sprache und Bekenntnis*. Berlin: Duncker und Humblot. 257–279.

Novalis. 1965. "Anekdoten." In: Paul Kluckhohn und Richard Samuel (eds.). *Novalis. Schriften: Die Werke Friedrich von Hardenbergs*. Vol. 2: *Das philosophische Werk I*. 2nd ed. Darmstadt: Wissenschaftliche Buchgesellschaft. 567–569.

Schlaffer, Heinz. 1997. "Anekdote." In: Klaus Weimar, Harald Fricke, Klaus Grubmüller und Jan-Dirk Müller (eds.). Vol. 1: *Reallexikon der deutschen Literaturwissenschaft*. Berlin: De Gruyter. 87–89.

Weber, Volker. 1993. *Anekdote: Die andere Geschichte. Erscheinungsformen der Anekdote in der deutschen Literatur, Geschichtsschreibung und Philosophie*. Tübingen: Stauffenberg.

Willer, Stefan, Jens Ruchatz und Nicolas Pethes. 2007. "Zur Systematik des Beispiels." In: Ruchatz, Jens, Stefan Willer, and Nicolas Pethes (eds.). *Das Beispiel: Epistemologie des Exemplarischen*. Berlin: Kadmos. 7–59.

Wülfing, Wulf. 2010. "'Immer das eigentlich Menschliche.' Zum Anekdotischen bei Theodor Fontane." In: Roland Berbig (ed.). *Fontane als Biograph*. Berlin: De Gruyter. 59–76.

Andreas Mahler
Once is Nothing at All is Once: Traces of Eventfulness in Joyce and Beckett

Abstract: The modernist epoch witnesses a marked shift in narratives from event-based, mimetic world-making to media-aware, performative text-making, from a representational telling of stories to the self-conscious presentational display of prose. In this process, the anecdotal element of the stories told, their eventfulness, is no longer the end and purpose of the narrative act but the beginning and trigger of a virtually endless textual production. The article traces this shift by, first, focusing on Joyce's use of the anecdote as a starting point for the deployment of his encyclopedic textual trajectory and, then, by proposing to see Beckett's prose-making as a counter-movement, negating, undermining, and hollowing out Joyce's cornucopian optimism. In other words, where Joyce discovers the faultline of the anecdotal and (self-lovingly) puts it to his use, Beckett exposes it and (critically) puts it on display.

Keywords: Event(fulness), Mimesis, Nothing(ness), Performance.

1

From an etymological point of view, the anecdote is, with Dr. Johnson, "something yet unpublished," a "secret history" (cf. Cuddon 1992: 42–43); it can laconically be defined as a "brief story with a point, attributed to a real person" ("[k]urze, pointierte Geschichte, die einer wirklichen Person nachgesagt wird" [Schlaffer 1997: 87; my translation]); for the new historicist, it is "the literary form or genre that uniquely refers to the real" (Fineman 1989: 56). In light of this, let me begin with anecdotes, a whole bunch of anecdotes. My first one leads me as far back as to pre-Iserian times to the University of Würzburg, Germany, in the 1950s.[1] Shortly after the war, students there, the legend goes, urged their professor to read on something more modern and more extravagant than Old English and the Anglo-Saxon period: Shakespeare, for example. Overwhelmed by the students' commitment and interest, the professor

---

[1] Before Wolfgang Iser went to Cologne to start his career as a reception theorist (and later on moved to the University of Konstanz and the world), he was for a brief period of time a professor of English at the University of Würzburg, Bavaria; I owe the anecdote to my academic teacher Wolfgang Weiß (and apologize if I should have remembered it wrongly).

enthusiastically took up their suggestion and began his new lecture with the words: "This semester's lecture is about William Shakespeare. A deep understanding of Shakespeare's works presupposes a profound knowledge in the history of the English language. I will begin with the shift from 'long ā' to 'long ō.'"[2]

Understandably, my topic here is not Old English. Less understandably, perhaps, I will begin with Old High German. This is my second anecdote. Most students of the history of the German language are familiar with a little dictionary by the name of *Taschenwörterbuch des althochdeutschen Sprachschatzes* (A pocket dictionary of Old High German), which was printed in its sixth edition in 2014 and is among students aptly known as "the Köbler." According to the Köbler, Old High German has a magic word which suits my interests in this article both perfectly and mysteriously: it is the word *īo* and, as the Köbler tells us, it stunningly means something like "once, always, never" (cf. Köbler 1994: s.v. *īo*; my translation).[3]

This is apt to explain my title. Because a word that means "once," "never," and "always" at the same time seems to be a good pathway to the topic of the anecdotal as well as to its faultlines: to its singularity, its typicality and exemplarity, but also to its eternal validity and sway.

2

This brings me to my third anecdote. In the year 1904, more precisely on June 10th, a certain James Joyce "was walking down Nassau Street in Dublin" when all of a sudden, as the biography reports, "he caught sight of a tall, good-looking young woman, auburn-haired, walking with a proud stride. When he spoke to her she answered pertly enough to allow the conversation to continue" (Ellmann 1982: 156; all quotes). As everyone knows, this woman was Nora Barnacle, and her telling name immediately invited comments from Joyce's friends (as well as from his father) as to her clinging nature: "you'll never ever get rid of her," they warned him. But getting rid of her was the last thing Joyce would have wanted to wish for: the girl from Galway, chambermaid at the, as Ellmann puts it, "slightly exalted rooming house" (ibid.) by the name of Finn's Hotel, became his great love and soon she became his wife, too. The brief encounter first triggered a brief correspondence, and only six days later,

---

[2] For a brief overview of Old English, with special regard to the central development of the long vowels, see Baugh and Cable (1978: 54–56).
[3] I am deeply indebted to Karin Donhauser for attracting my attention to this entry and its consequences.

on June 16th, there was a first date – with, as everyone knows, severe narrative consequences.

As the anecdote has it, one of their first outings together brought James and Nora to Howth Hill, situated towards the north-east of Dublin bay and well-known for its little panorama train as well as for its bonfires at midsummer – and not least for its notorious wild rhododendrons. Howth makes a frequent appearance in Joyce's work. Howth Castle is the seat of the earls of Howth, whose history can be traced back to Armorican Brittany. In Joyce's Dublin, the name "Howth" seems to stand for "holiday" and "desire," "dreams" and "projections," "license" and "lust," for biographical "truth" and literary "play."

Joyce mentions Howth Hill as early as in *Dubliners* (1914). For Eveline, it is a site of freedom and long past happiness: "Another day, when their mother was alive, they had all gone for a picnic to the Hill of Howth. She remembered her father putting on her mother's bonnet to make the children laugh" (*D* 31).[4] For Mrs Kearney in "A Mother," it is, in all its singularity and substitutability, one of the places to show off with:

> Every year in the month of July Mrs Kearney found occasion to say to some friend:
> —My good man is packing us off to Skerries for a few weeks.
> If it was not Skerries it was Howth or Greystones. (*D* 124)

There are similar references in *Stephen Hero* (1944) and *Portrait* (1916). In *Ulysses* (1922), Howth Hill time and again appears in Stephen's and Bloom's view; and in the Nausicaa chapter, it is the distant place of Gerty McDowell's wistful longings:

> The summer evening had begun to fold the world in its mysterious embrace. Far away in the west the sun was setting and the last glow of all too fleeting day lingered lovingly on sea and strand, on the proud promontory of dear old Howth guarding as ever the waters of the bay, on the weedgrown rocks along Sandymount shore and, last but not least, on the quiet church whence there streamed forth at times upon the stillness the voice of prayer to her who is in her pure radiance a beacon ever to the stormtossed heart of man, Mary, star of the sea. (*U* 13.1–8)

In *Ulysses*, however, Howth also figures as the place where Molly and Bloom meet and become intimate for the first time. The Penelope chapter shows this from Molly's perspective: "the sun shines for you he said the day we were

---

4 See Joyce (1993); all quotes from Joyce follow the usual abbreviations and conventions: *D*=*Dubliners* (page), *U*=*Ulysses* (chapter.line) and *FW*=*Finnegans Wake* (page.line). For useful annotations, not least with regard to the passages on Howth Hill, see Gifford (1982), Gifford and Seidman (1989), and McHugh (1980).

lying among the rhododendrons on Howth head in the grey tweed suit and his straw hat the day I got him to propose to me" (*U* 18.1571–1574). And Lestrygonians gives us the scene from Bloom's point of view:

> Glowing wine on his palate lingered swallowed. Crushing in the winepress grapes of Burgundy. Sun's heat it is. Seems to a secret touch telling me memory. Touched his sense moistened remembered. Hidden under wild ferns on Howth below us bay sleeping: sky. No sound. The sky. The bay purple by the Lion's head. Green by Drumleck. Yellowgreen towards Sutton. Fields of undersea, the lines faint brown in grass, buried cities. Pillowed on my coat she had her hair, earwigs in the heather scrub my hand under her nape, you'll toss me all. O wonder! Coolsoft with ointments her hand touched me, caressed: her eyes upon me did not turn away. Ravished over her I lay, full lips full open, kissed her mouth. Yum. Softly she gave me in my mouth the seedcake warm and chewed. Mawkish pulp her mouth had mumbled sweetsour of her spittle. Joy: I ate it: joy. Young life, her lips that gave me pouting. Soft warm sticky gumjelly lips. Flowers her eyes were, take me, willing eyes. Pebbles fell. She lay still. A goat. No-one. High on Ben Howth rhododendrons a nannygoat walking surefooted, dropping currants. Screened under ferns she laughed warmfolded. Wildly I lay on her, kissed her: eyes, her lips, her stretched neck beating, woman's breasts full in her blouse of nun's veiling, fat nipples upright. Hot I tongued her. She kissed me. I was kissed. All yielding she tossed my hair. Kissed, she kissed me. (*U* 8.897–916)

The passage is a remembrance of things past. It describes the first serious meeting between Bloom and Molly as an encounter enhanced by its surrounding nature, as a moment of intimacy and togetherness, with the rhododendrons seemingly giving their consent. This almost looks like one of Gerty McDowell's projections: "All quiet on Howth now. The distant hills seem. Where we. The rhododendrons. I am a fool perhaps. He gets the plums and I the plumstones. Where I come in. All that old hill has seen. Names change: that's all. Lovers: yum yum" (*U* 13.1097–1100). And it finds itself repeated once again a little later: "Howth settled for slumber tired of long days, of yumyum rhododendrons (he was old) and felt gladly the night breeze lift, ruffle his fell of ferns" (*U* 13.1177–1179).

This seems to turn Howth into a potential event, a Finemanian anecdote.[5] In Gerty McDowell's imaginary, Howth is a place of desire and shame; in the fiction

---

[5] For the classical definition of an "event" as "*the shifting of a persona across the borders of a semantic field,*" see Lotman (1977: 233; original italics); for a further elaboration of "event" and "eventfulness," see Mahler (2013: esp. 249–254). For an explicit link between the notion of the event and the anecdotal from a new historicist point of view, see Fineman (1989: 61). Lotman himself connects the two in his discussion of a cyclical plot type, which he calls "myth," and a linear plot type, which he calls "*sjuzhet*'" by pointing out that "myth" is bent on affirming the "world" as it is, whereas "*sjuzhets*" are instruments of suggesting, with the help of "events," how the "world" could be different: "Myth always speaks about me. 'News,' an anecdote, speaks

of Bloomsday, it is the symbol of a fateful, if not eventful, coming together, which forms a couple out of two individuals, uniting two divergent paths into a common life shared together. Coming back to the anecdote, this of course also applies to Nora and James, no matter whether it is true or not. The anecdote can be imagined as the beginning but also as a justification of their being together; and as the anecdote that it is, it is a kind of eventful starting point for the two spending their lives together: "singular" in contingently bringing together two individual human beings; "eternal" in binding them for life (and even after); "none at all" because it may after all be a fiction only, or a lie – once, none at all, always, never: *io*.

This kind of eventfulness is precarious. As a consequence, it is, as has already become transparent in the variations from the Nausicaa episode, in need of repetition.[6] Less perhaps as repetition in life than as repetition in writing, in the text. This would explain the dense frequency of the passage in *Ulysses*; it would also explain its marked reprise in *Finnegans Wake* (1939). The very first sentence of *Finnegans Wake*, if sentence it is, takes up all the familiar elements again:

> riverrun, past Eve and Adam's, from swerve to shore to bend of bay, brings us by a commodius vicus of recirculation back to Howth Castle and Environs.
> Sir Tristram, violer d'amores, fr'over the short sea, had passencore rearrived from North Armorica to wielderfight his peninsolate war (*FW* 3.1–6)

Following the "run" of the "river," passing again "Adam" and "Eve," moving along in the forms of a "bay" or a "vicus" apt to "recirculate" things – and words as things – the textual trajectory follows a track that "brings us," again, "back to Howth Castle" and even further back to its "peninsular" "Armorican" ancestors, thus starting a new cycle at its most linear beginning.[7] The very first lines of *Finnegans Wake* demonstrate again the Joycean program of a repetitive reworking of the anecdotal in the text.

---

about somebody else. The first organizes the hearer's world, the second adds interesting details to his knowledge of this world" (1979: 163).
6 For the suggestion that repetition should be seen as "sameness with a difference," see Rimmon-Kenan (1980).
7 This structure of a systematic self-encirclement of the Joycean narrative in *Finnegans Wake* is imbued by Joyce's reception of the ideas of Giambattista Vico's *La Scienza Nuova* (1725); for a brief summary, see Füger (1994: 267–268) as well as, in some more detail, Zimmerlich (2016: 42–45). The classical reference to Vico's influence on Joyce is Hart (1962).

Joyce's writing, his prose, is based on this kind of programmatic repetitiveness.[8] It is, as I have tried to show (cf. Mahler 2013), indicative of the modernist shift from topographical world-making to topological text-making. Obsessively, Joyce's prose repeats and reworks the same situations – Howth Hill, Phoenix Park, Chapelizod *alias* Chappelle d'Iseult – and goes through them again and again in ever new verbal realizations, and imaginations, of the same: "once, none at all, always, never." Accordingly, the narrating act is no longer, as in the classical novel, organized syntagmatically towards a representational ending or a solution; rather, it is organized paradigmatically as a series of variations linguistically and aesthetically re-presenting the same in ever new forms.

This shift can be seen as a shift from mimesis to performance.[9] What is at stake is no longer the representation of something seemingly extratextual but a repetitive presentation of the textual itself, of the textual artist's material, of a virtuoso handling of their medial instrument. The traces of eventfulness thus turn into traces of writing, which means that the anecdote, its "point,"[10] is no longer the aim of the narrative act – its end – but its beginning – its "starting point": it is the basis of interminable paradigmatic reconfigurations, of an infinite series of singularities, of "writing without an end."[11] In a way, the Joycean narrative seems to lead the anecdotal straight to its faultline.

---

8 For "repetition" as the ground of our appropriation of "reality," see the reflections in Deleuze (1995: esp. 90): "We produce something new only on condition that we repeat – once in the mode which constitutes the past, and once more in the present of metamorphosis. Moreover, what is produced, the absolutely new itself, is in turn nothing but repetition: the third repetition, this time by excess, the repetition of the future as eternal return. [...] It is repetition by excess which leaves intact nothing of the default or the becoming-equal. It is itself the new, complete novelty." In this book, he also establishes the distinction between a "naked" repetition (adhering to the illusion of sameness) and a "clothed" one (acknowledging the necessity of difference); cf. also, along similar lines, Derrida (2001). For an elaboration of the mechanisms of repetitiveness with regard to (modernist/postmodern) narrative, see the important essay by Warning (2001).
9 For this shift from (referential and, hence, "imitating") mimesis to (textual and "symbolizing") performance, see Iser (1993: 247–303).
10 This refers to the idea that a story is tellable only when it has a point; see classically Pratt (1977: 132–151). For a more thorough discussion of the concept of "tellability" from a systematic as well as a historical point of view, see Mahler (2017).
11 For the concept of "endless writing," see Frey (1990); for a highly suggestive development of a poetics of what he calls "paradigmatic narration," see Warning (2001).

3

Joyce's fellow countryman Samuel Beckett came, still very young, to Paris in 1928, and extremely soon, got under Joyce's spell. Despite his age starting as a teacher of English literature at the École normale supérieure, Beckett's initial ambition was to write academically about the work of contemporary authors, such as, e.g., Proust, unaware that at the time in academic circles this was in no way considered to be the done thing.[12] Joyce knew how to take this up: in all hubristic modesty, he made Beckett (along with others) write about him, Joyce, eulogistically with a view to his own *Work in Progress*, later to turn into *Finnegans Wake*. Beckett thanked him with the much-quoted sentence that Joyce's prose should not be seen as being "*about* something" but that "*it is that something itself*" (Beckett 1961, 14; original italics): not easily referenceable mimesis but nothing but "thick" performance throughout, not *re*presentation or (self-)representation but self-*pre*sentation.[13]

One can see this as the (meta-)beginning of the Beckettian project. But the project soon took another course. In short time, Beckett turned away from writing academically "about something" and became a prose author himself: a writer presenting nothing but writing, someone who produces, "com-poses" and paradigmatically "syntagmatizes" text – without, however, having in view the Joycean mania for plethora, universality, encyclopedic lust but instead going for emptiness, absence, gaps, nothingness. So instead of the "something itself," what is at the center of Beckettian prose is an invalidated, a-semantic "nothing."

This decisive shift shows itself programmatically in Beckett's famous letter to Axel Kaun, dated July 9th, 1937, which Beckett wrote in German. It can be seen as indicating a shift from a metapoetic something to an autopoetic nothing. Beckett writes:[14]

> Es wird mir tatsächlich immer schwieriger, ja sinnloser, ein offizielles Englisch zu schreiben. Und immer mehr wie ein Schleier kommt mir meine Sprache vor, den man zerreissen muss, um an die hinterliegenden Dinge (oder das hinterliegende Nichts) zu kommen.

---

12 For further biographical detail, see Knowlson (1997).
13 I (obliquely) borrow the idea of "thickness" for a somehow integral approach in describing cultural (or textual) phenomena from Geertz (1993: 3–30).
14 All quotes are Beckett (2009: 512–521); for the sake of better reading, I add the English translation by Viola Westbrook from the same volume, based on the (at times arguably more correct) one made by Martin Ensslin in Beckett (1983: 170–173). I have kept the original indentation of the paragraphs.

> Grammatik und Stil! Mir scheinen sie ebenso hinfällig geworden zu sein wie ein Biedermeier Badeanzug oder die Unerschüttlichkeit [sic] eines Gentlemans. Eine Larve. Hoffentlich kommt die Zeit, sie ist ja Gott sei Dank in gewissen Kreisen schon da, wo die Sprache da am besten gebraucht wird, wo sie am tüchtigsten missgebraucht [sic] wird. Da wir sie so mit einem Male nicht ausschalten können, wollen wir wenigstens nichts versäumen, was zu deren Verruf beitragen mag. Ein Loch nach dem andern in ihr [sic] zu bohren, bis das Dahinterkauernde, sei es etwas oder nichts, durchzusickern anfängt – ich kann mir für den heutigen Schriftsteller kein höheres Ziel vorstellen. (513–514)

> It is indeed getting more and more difficult, even pointless, to write for me in formal English. And more and more my language appears to me like a veil which one has to tear apart in order to get to those things (or the nothingness) lying behind it. Grammar and style! To me they seem to have become as irrelevant as a Biedermeier bathing suit or the imperturbability of a gentleman. A mask. It is to be hoped the time will come, thank God, in some circles it already has, when language is best used where it is most efficiently abused. Since we cannot dismiss it all at once, at least we do not want to leave anything undone that may contribute to its disrepute. To drill one hole after another into it until that which lurks behind, be it something or nothing, starts seeping through – I cannot imagine a higher goal for today's writer. (518)

Language at that time appears to Beckett as a "veil" that has to be "torn apart," or as a "mask," or as a mere surface one has to "drill holes into" in order to be able to "abusively" liberate "that which lurks," which "lies behind it," making it, whatever it is, come to the fore, or "seep through," as a "something," as a "thing," or in more likelihood, as a "no-thing."

Only in doing so, the letter continues, would there be a chance for verbal art, especially for prose, to keep up the *paragone*-like contemporary competition with the other arts:

> Oder soll die Literatur auf jenem alten faulen von Musik und Malerei längst verlassenen Wege allein hinterbleiben? Steckt etwas lähmend heiliges in der Unnatur des Wortes, was zu den Elementen der anderen Künste nicht gehört? Gibt es irgendeinen Grund, warum jene fürchterlich willkürliche Materialität der Wortfläche nicht aufgelöst werden sollte, wie z. B. die von grossen schwarzen Pausen gefressene Tonfläche in der siebten Symphonie von Beethoven, so dass wir sie ganze Seiten durch nicht anders wahrnehmen können als etwa einen schwindelnden unergründliche Schlünde von Stillschweigen verknüpfenden Pfad von Lauten? Um Antwort wird gebeten. (514)

> Or is literature alone to be left behind on that old, foul road long ago abandoned by music and painting? Is there something paralysingly sacred contained within the unnature of the word that does not belong to the elements of the other arts? Is there any reason why that terrifyingly arbitrary materiality of the word surface should not be dissolved, as for example the sound surface of Beethoven's Seventh Symphony is devoured by huge black pauses, so that for pages on end we cannot perceive it as other than a dizzying path of sounds connecting unfathomable chasms of silence? An answer is requested. (518–519)

And the letter goes on:

> Ich weiss, es gibt Leute, empfindsame und intelligente Leute, für die es an Stillschweigen gar nicht fehlt. Ich kann nicht umhin, anzunehmen, dass sie schwerhörig sind. Denn im Walde der Symbole, die keine sind, schweigen die Vögelein der Deutung, die keine ist, nie.
> Selbstverständlich muss man sich vorläufig mit Wenigem begnügen. Zuerst kann es nur darauf ankommen, irgenwie eine Methode zu erfinden, um diese höhnische Haltung dem Worte gegenüber wörtlich darzustellen. In dieser Dissonanz von Mitteln und Gebrauch wird man schon vielleicht ein Geflüster der Endmusik oder des Allem zu Grunde liegenden Schweigens spüren können. (514–515)
>
> I know there are people, sensitive and intelligent people, for whom there is no lack of silence. I cannot help but assume that they are hard of hearing. For in the forest of symbols that are no symbols, the birds of interpretation, that is no interpretation, are never silent.
> Of course, for the time being, one makes do with little. At first, it can only be a matter of somehow inventing a method of verbally demonstrating this scornful attitude vis-a-vis the word. In this dissonance of instrument and usage perhaps one will already be able to sense a whispering of the end-music or of the silence underlying it all. (519)

So what is at stake is the emptying out of all symbols, the annulment of all interpretation, with the aim of finally achieving a "dissonant," "abusive" language use, apt to counteract the cynicism of our everyday discursive use of language by developing a "method" of "verbally demonstrating" its "scornfulness vis-à-vis the word" so as to reach the "silence underlying it all."

This path, however, no longer leads via Joyce but, perhaps, *paragone*-bound and anecdotally, via Gertrude Stein:[15]

> Mit einem solchen Programme hat meiner Ansicht nach die allerletzte Arbeit von Joyce gar nichts zu tun. Dort scheint es sich vielmehr um eine Apotheose des Wortes zu handeln. Es sei denn, Himmelfahrt und Höllensturz sind eins und dasselbe. Wie schön es wäre, glauben zu können, es sei in der Tat so! Wir wollen uns aber vorläufing [sic] auf die Absicht beschränken.
> Vielleicht liegen die Logographen von Gertrude Stein dem näher, was ich im Sinne habe. Das Sprachgewebe ist wenigstens porös geworden, wenn nur leider ganz zufälligerweise, und zwar als Folge eines etwa der Technik von Feininger ähnlichen Vorfahrens. Die unglückliche Dame (lebt sie noch?) ist ja ohne Zweifel immer noch in ihr Vehikel verliebt, wenn freilich nur wie in seine Ziffern ein Mathematiker, für den die Lösung des Problems

---

[15] Beckett's relation to Stein ("lebt sie noch?") would in itself again suggest an anecdote. For the Steinian project as one of a repetition-based seriality as (above all) developed in dialogue with the art of painting, in particular with the works of Cézanne and Picasso, see Haselstein (2010); for Stein's experimental, intermedial blending of her textuality with cubist techniques of portrait painting in a discussion of her representation of "things" see Haselstein (2002), as well as Haselstein (2019).

von ganz sekundärem Interesse ist, ja ihm als Tod der Ziffern direkt schrecklich vorschweben muss. (515)

In my opinion, the most recent work of Joyce had nothing at all to do with such a programme. There it seems much more a matter of an apotheosis of the word. Unless Ascent into Heaven and Descent into Hell are one and the same. How nice it would be to be able to believe that in fact it were so. For the moment, however, we will limit ourselves to the intention.

Perhaps Gertrude Stein's Logographs come closer to what I mean. The fabric of the language has at least become porous, if regrettably only quite by accident and, as it were, as a consequence of a procedure somewhat akin to the technique of Feininger. The unhappy lady (is she still alive?) is undoubtedly still in love with her vehicle, if only, however, as a mathematician is with his numbers; for him the solution of the problem is of secondary interest, yes, as the death of numbers it must seem to him indeed dreadful. (519)

The method chosen looks more adequate because it abstracts from both sides of the coin, both from the signified and from the signifier:

Diese Methode mit der von Joyce in Zusammenhang zu bringen, wie es die Mode ist, kommt mir genau so sinnlos vor wie der mir noch nicht bekannte Versuch den Nominalismus (im Sinne der Scholastiker) mit dem Realismus zu vergleichen. Auf dem Wege nach dieser für mich sehr wünschenswerten Literatur des Unworts hin, kann freilich irgendeine Form der nominalistischen Ironie ein notwendiges Stadium sein. Es genügt aber nicht, wenn das Spiel etwas von seinem heiligen Ernst verliert. Aufhören soll es. Machen wir also wie jener verrückte (?) Mathematiker, der auf jeder einzelnen Stufe des Kalküls ein neues Messprinzip anzuwenden pflegte. Eine Wörterstürmerei im Namen der Schönheit. (515)

To connect this method with that of Joyce, as is fashionable, appears to me as ludicrous as the attempt, as yet unknown to me, to compare Nominalism (in the sense of the Scholastics) with Realism. On the road towards this, for me, very desirable literature of the non-word, some form of nominalistic irony can of course be a necessary phase. However, it does not suffice if the game loses some of its sacred solemnity. Let it cease altogether! Let's do as that crazy mathematician who used to apply a new principle of measurement at each individual step of the calculation. Word-storming in the name of beauty. (519–520)

This iconoclastic "word-storming" is what "unwords" the word, what turns it into a "non-word," what frees it from the "shackles" of its relations and disentangles it from the humdrum everyday game of communication.[16] The word is no longer fettered to a "something" like meaning or sense. The tyranny of meaning

---

[16] For the (carnivalesque) idea of "releasing" words "from the shackles of sense, to enjoy a play period of complete freedom and establish unusual relationships among themselves," see Bakhtin (1984: 423); for a classical reminder not to "forget that, even though a poem is composed in the language of information, it is not used in the language game of giving information," see Wittgenstein (1967: 28e).

is broken, and the game is finally over: "Let it cease altogether."¹⁷ What in Beckett's view ideally remains is nothing but the "beauty" of silence and nothingness.

What does such a constructive reduction look like in textual practice? In the first of his programmatic *Texts for Nothing* from the early 1950s, Beckett makes his prose composition begin like this:

> Suddenly, no, at last, long last, I couldn't any more, I couldn't go on. Someone said, You can't stay here. I couldn't stay there and I couldn't go on. I'll describe the place, that's unimportant. The top, very flat, of a mountain, no, a hill, but so wild, so wild, enough. Quag, heath up to the knees, faint sheep-tracks, troughs scooped deep by the rains. It was far down in one of these I was lying; out of the wind. Glorious prospect, but for the mist that blotted out everything, valleys, loughs, plain and sea. How can I go on, I shouldn't have begun, no, I had to begin. Someone said, perhaps the same, What possessed you to come? I could have stayed in my den, snug and dry, I couldn't. My den, I'll describe it, no, I can't. It's simple, I can do nothing any more, that's what you think. I say to the body, Up with you now, and I can feel it struggling, like an old hack foundered in the street, struggling no more, struggling again, till it gives up. I say to the head, Leave it alone, stay quiet, it stops breathing, then pants on worse than ever. I am far from all that wrangle, I shouldn't bother with it, I need nothing, neither to go on nor to stay where I am, it's truly all one to me, I should turn away from it all, away from the body, away from the head, let them work it out between them, let them cease, I can't, it's I would have to cease. (1995: 100)¹⁸

Again, we are on a textual mountain. Right from the start, the prose piece takes us – couldn't it be Howth? – on top a hill: "The top, very flat, of a mountain, no, a hill, but so wild, so wild, enough." But instead of fullness, it stages emptiness; instead of an "apotheosis" what we really and truly get is a "descent to hell"; instead of a cornucopian plenitude, nothing.¹⁹ No rhododendrons anywhere, not even a nannygoat, but: "Quag, heath up to the knees, faint sheep-tracks, troughs scooped deep by the rains." The piece starts with an event, only to annihilate its trace: "Suddenly, no, at last, long last, I couldn't any more, I couldn't go on." According to the Beckettian pattern of "emergence" and "residue," it begins with an (if not *the*) adverbial of eventfulness ("suddenly") only to be

---

17 For the notion of a "tyranny of meaning," characterizing above all the age of Enlightenment and linguistic transparency and influencing us up until today, see Barthes (1977: 185).
18 For a more thorough discussion of this, see Mahler (2018: 30–34).
19 With the idea of the "cornucopian text," I refer to the classical study by Cave (1979); for an attempt to read *Finnegans Wake* as cornucopian text, see Zimmerlich (2016). In contradistinction to Joyce, one could describe the Beckettian project in his *Texts for Nothing* as a kind of "cornucopian emptiness" or "negative cornucopia."

immediately hollowed out again into nothingness. This is probably even more evident in the French version with its much more marked abrupt beginning and its awkwardly pronounced "narrative" *passé simple:* "Brusquement, non, à force, à force, je n'en pus plus, je ne pus continuer" (Beckett 1981: 115).

The Beckettian text thus posits something only to negate it. From an anecdotal point of view, this looks like a literary mountain tour – be it Howth or, as for that, the Mont Ventoux – but what the tour eventually shows is nothing but a – nevertheless increasing – series of eventless failures.[20] As soon as there is a something, it is gone; and what remains is at best some kind of virtual eventfulness only, nothing but a trace.[21] What the textuality produces is not, as still with Joyce, the potential of an anecdote but only the faultline itself – a syntagm of remains flickeringly appealing to the imaginary: a trace of "residue(s)" fighting, and resisting to, language's accustomized immediate reduction to "meaning."[22] What we get is not so much the underlying "point" of the (oral) anecdote but the mere (written) surface of its ongoing erosion. In this way, Beckett looks like a negated Joyce.

So again, what is "always" repeated, at the same time looks as if it were posited just "once," only to be syntagmatically annihilated again into a "nothing at all" – "once, always, never": *ío* (Köbler be thanked).[23]

Works Cited

Bakhtin, Mikhail. 1984 [1965]. *Rabelais and His World.* Trans. Hélène Iswolsky. Bloomington: Indiana University Press.
Barthes, Roland. 1977. "The Grain of the Voice." In: Roland Barthes. *Image – Text – Music.* Ed. and trans. Stephen Heath. Glasgow: Fontana/Collins. 179–189.
Baugh, Albert C. and Thomas Cable. 1978. *A History of the English Language.* 3rd ed. London: Routledge & Kegan Paul.

---

20 In a way, this takes up the notorious dictum "Try again. Fail again. Fail better" from Beckett (1995a: 105); for the programmatic staging of ever-improving failures in Beckett, see Mahler (2018: 19–22).
21 For a discussion of the Beckettian reduction of whatever there is into mere "virtualities," see Iser (2013: esp. 265).
22 For recent readings along the lines of an active production of textual "residues" in Beckett, see, e.g., Bell (2011) and Boxall (2015).
23 For fairness's sake, it should be noted that the secret behind this apparent Köblerian nonsense (and the Donhauserian gift) lies in the fact that the entry somewhat infelicitously lumps together the uses of one and the same word, which in Modern High German would be *je* ("ever"), in its affirmative as well as in its negative contexts, so that a *nicht je* would indeed be a "never," but the *nicht* ("not") would of course have to be indicated.

Beckett, Samuel. 2009. *The Letters of Samuel Beckett*. Vol. 1. Eds. Martha Dow Fehsenfeld and Lois More Overbeck. Cambridge: Cambridge University Press.

Beckett, Samuel. 1995a. [1984]. *Nohow On. Company. Ill Seen Ill Said. Worstward Ho*. New York: Grove Press.

Beckett, Samuel. 1995. *The Complete Short Prose. 1929–1989*. Ed. S. E. Gontarski. New York: Grove Press.

Beckett, Samuel. 1983. *Disjecta. Miscellaneous Writings and a Dramatic Fragment*. Ed. Ruby Cohn. London: John Calder.

Beckett, Samuel. 1981 [1958]. *Nouvelles et Textes sur Rien*. Paris: Éditions de Minuit.

Beckett, Samuel. 1961 [1929]. "Dante...Bruno.Vico..Joyce." In: Samuel Beckett et al. *Our Exagmination Round His Factification For Incamination of Work in Progress*. London: Faber and Faber. 1–22.

Bell, L. A. J. 2011. "Between Ethics and Aesthetics. The Residual in Samuel Beckett's Minimalism." *Journal of Beckett Studies* 20: 32–53.

Boxall, Peter. 2015. "Still Stirrings. Beckett's Prose from *Texts for Nothing* to *Stirrings Still*." In: Dirk Van Hulle (ed.). *The New Cambridge Companion to Samuel Beckett*. Cambridge: Cambridge University Press. 33–47.

Cave, Terence. 1979. *The Cornucopian Text. Problems of Writing in the French Renaissance*. Oxford: Clarendon.

Cuddon, J. A. 1992. *The Penguin Dictionary of Literary Terms and Literary Theory*. 3rd ed. London: Penguin.

Deleuze, Gilles. 1995. *Difference and Repetition*. Trans. Paul Patton. New York: Columbia University Press.

Derrida, Jacques. 2001. *Writing and Difference*. Trans. Alan Bass. New York: Routledge.

Ellmann, Richard. 1982. *James Joyce*. New and revised ed. New York: Oxford University Press.

Fineman, Joel. 1989. "The History of the Anecdote. Fiction and Fiction." In: Aram Veeser (ed.). *The New Historicism*. New York: Routledge. 49–76.

Frey, Hans-Jost. 1990. *Der unendliche Text*. Frankfurt am Main: Suhrkamp.

Füger, Wilhelm. 1994. *James Joyce. Epoche – Werk – Wirkung*. München: C. H. Beck.

Geertz, Clifford. 1993 [1973]. *The Interpretation of Cultures. Selected Essays*. London: Fontana.

Gifford, Don. 1982. *Joyce Annotated. Notes for* Dubliners *and* A Portrait of the Artist as a Young Man. 2nd ed. Berkeley: University of California Press.

Gifford, Don and Robert J. Seidman. 1989. Ulysses *Annotated. Notes for James Joyce's* Ulysses. 2nd ed. Berkeley: University of California Press.

Hart, Clive. 1962. *Structure and Motif in Finnegans Wake*. London: Faber and Faber.

Haselstein, Ulla. 2019. *Gertrude Steins literarische Porträts*. Konstanz: Konstanz University Press.

Haselstein, Ulla. 2010. "Gertrude Stein and Seriality." In: David Seed (ed.). *A Companion to Twentieth-Century United States Fiction*. Chichester: Wiley-Blackwell. 229–239.

Haselstein, Ulla. 2002. "Gertrude Steins Porträts von Dingen." In: Gisela Ecker et al. (eds.). *Dinge. Medien der Aneignung, Grenzen der Verfügung*. Königstein: Ulrike Helmer. 197–217.

Iser, Wolfgang. 2013 [2006]. "Erasing Narration. Samuel Beckett's *Malone Dies* and *Texts for Nothing*." In: Wolfgang Iser. *Emergenz. Nachgelassene und verstreut publizierte Essays*. Ed. Alexander Schmitz. Konstanz: Konstanz University Press. 265–282.

Iser, Wolfgang. 1993. *The Fictive and the Imaginary. Charting Literary Anthropology*. Trans. David Henry Wilson. Baltimore: Johns Hopkins University Press.

Joyce, James. 1993 [1914]. *Dubliners*. Eds. Hans Walter Gabler and Walter Hettche. New York: Vintage.

Joyce, James. 1986 [1922]. *Ulysses*. Eds. Hans Walter Gabler, Wolfhard Steppe, and Claus Melchior. London: The Bodley Head.

Joyce, James. 1980 [1939]. *Finnegans Wake*. London: Faber and Faber.

Knowlson, James. 1997. *Damned to Fame. The Life of Samuel Beckett*. London: Bloomsbury.

Köbler, Gerhard. 1994. *Taschenwörterbuch des althochdeutschen Sprachschatzes*. 6th ed. Paderborn: Schöningh.

Lotman, Jurij M. 1979. "The Origin of Plot in the Light of Typology." Trans. Julian Graffy. *Poetics Today* 1.1/2: 161–184.

Lotman, Jurij M. 1977. *The Structure of the Artistic Text*. Michigan Slavic Contributions. Trans. Ronald Vroon. Ann Arbor: Michigan University Press.

Mahler, Andreas. 2018. "From Nothing to Nothing. Emergence(s) and Residue(s) in Beckett's Prose." *Comparatio* 10: 19–38.

Mahler, Andreas. 2017. "Tellabilities – Diatopic/Diachronic. Where and When a Story Is Worth Telling and Where and When It Is Not." *Zeitschrift für Anglistik und Amerikanistik* 65: 357–375.

Mahler, Andreas. 2013. "Joyce's Bovarysm. Paradigmatic Disenchantment into Syntagmatic Progression." *Comparatio* 5: 249–295.

McHugh, Roland. 1980. *Annotations to* Finnegans Wake. London and Henley: Routledge & Kegan Paul.

Pratt, Mary Louise. 1977. *Toward a Speech Act Theory of Literary Discourse*. Bloomington: Indiana University Press.

Rimmon-Kenan, Shlomith. 1980. "The Paradoxical Status of Repetition." *Poetics Today* 1.4: 151–159.

Schlaffer, Heinz. 1997. Art. "Anekdote". In: Klaus Weimar, Harald Fricke, Klaus Grubmüller, and Jan-Dirk Müller (eds.). *Reallexikon der deutschen Literaturwissenschaft*. Vol. 1. Berlin: Walter de Gruyter. 87–89.

Warning, Rainer. 2001. "Erzählen im Paradigma. Kontingenzbewältigung und Kontingenzexposition." *Romanistisches Jahrbuch* 52: 176–209.

Wittgenstein, Ludwig. 1967. *Zettel*. Eds. G. E. M. Anscombe and G. H. von Wright. Berkeley: University of California Press.

Zimmerlich, Antonia. 2016. "Joyce's *Finnegans Wake* as a Cornucopian Text." *Arbeiten aus Anglistik und Amerikanistik* 41: 39–56.

Gabriele Schwab
The Politics of Splitting: Gertrude Stein's "Reflection on the Atomic Bomb"

Abstract: This essay explores the rhetorical strategies and non-referential aesthetics of Gertrude Stein's posthumously published "Reflection on the Atomic Bomb," as they relate to a politics of splitting, formulated by Christa Wolf after Chernobyl, and the production of nuclear subjectivities in testimonials and critical theory. Provocatively remaking the monumental historical event of the atomic bomb in the aftermath of Hiroshima and Nagasaki as a casual and marginal anecdote, Stein breaks with the prevalent politics of fear that conceives the nuclear threat as a fissure in human history. Rather, she frames the Bomb as a rhetorical condition that both carries and exposes the symptoms of modernist discourse including schizophrenia and emotional detachment. Stein's performative indifference toward the nuclear age thus draws attention to the conditions of a critique of nuclear reason, which this essay, in closing, retrieves in a confrontation with Georges Bataille's sovereign sensibility.

Keywords: Apocalypse, Atom Bomb, Politics of Splitting, Radioactive Emotions, Sovereign Sensibility.

> "They asked me what I thought of the atomic bomb. I said I had not been able to take any interest in it." (Stein 1973: 161)

In 1946, in the wake of World War II and during the last year of her life, Gertrude Stein wrote her allegedly final piece, "Reflection on the Atomic Bomb." It was only published posthumously in 1947 in *Yale Poetry Review*. Stein's curious short piece resonates with the anecdote in a double sense. Not only is it anecdotal in the sense of the Greek origin of the term since it remained "unpublished" or "not given out" in her lifetime; it is also anecdotal in the provocatively brief story that relegates the atomic bomb to a marginal, uninteresting phenomenon not worthy of much attention. The very political event, which at the time generated the ontological and epistemological fissure that inaugurated the nuclear age, is, in Stein's quasi-anecdote, reduced to an object of the contemptuous disregard she likes to display toward overt politics more generally. In this vein, the short piece performs a blatantly ironic counterhistory and counter-politics.

Before I look at the latter in more detail, let me provide a larger context for the onto-epistemological fissure in question. The term "fissure" itself interestingly resonates with nuclear fission, that is, the splitting of the nucleus of an

https://doi.org/10.1515/9783110668490-010

atom into smaller nuclei. It is the latter that forms the basis of the atomic bomb. As is well known, atomic bombs get their explosive energy from the splitting of atoms in materials like uranium or plutonium. Since atoms are supposed to be indivisible, this splitting or fission entails an act of violence, one that was initially designed to harness the energies generated for building a weapon of hitherto unparalleled mass destruction. "How strange that a-tom in Greek means the same as in-dividuum in Latin: unsplittable. The inventors of these words knew neither nuclear fission nor schizophrenia" (2001: 29), writes Christa Wolf in *Accident: A Day's News* (1989),[1] her literary memoir about the Chernobyl accident. As Wolf suggests in this passage, there is a family likeness between nuclear fission and schizophrenia: they both divide something that should be indivisible: a rock or a self, an atom or an individual. Both nuclear fission and schizophrenia, according to Wolf, thus belong to a violent politics of splitting. We might even wonder if Stein chose the generic affinity to the anecdote as an indivisible singular tale in order to create her own fission with a world-wide consensus at the time, namely that the atomic bomb is the most consequential invention in human history because of its potential to destroy planetary life. In other words, Stein creates a "fission" at the very heart of the prevalent story of the Bomb.

From a psychodynamic perspective, however, splitting constitutes, at least initially, an attempt to adapt to an intolerable experience, an attempt to ward off trauma and protect the self from falling apart. In the aftermath of disasters such as Hiroshima or Chernobyl, the psychopolitics of splitting may be a precondition of psychic survival. At its extreme, however, it may also, as Wolf maintains, result in a schizoid division of the self. Svetlana Alexievich's interviews in *Voices from Chernobyl* (1997), for example, reveal that the Chernobyl nuclear disaster created a new form of what I call "nuclear subjectivity," one that Wolf links to a collective "compulsion to split" (2001: 29). The latter manifests in a fission at the core of the self, a nuclear schizophrenia of sorts that affects not only survivors but also humans living in the aftermath of Chernobyl's nuclear disaster. The historical rupture caused by this disaster – "Once again," Wolf writes, "our age had created a Before and After for itself" (36) – resonates with this fissure within the self that Wolf links to the isolation and encapsulation of toxic emotions. She proposes that unbearable "radioactive feelings" (89) need to be split off and stored like nuclear waste in an isolated waste disposal vault within the self. This image of a crypt of sorts that harbors the radioactive ghosts of nuclear subjectivities is suggestive of the haunting quality of this divided self.

---

[1] Originally published in German as *Störfall: Nachrichten eines Tages* (1987).

Nuclear fission, Wolf further argues, also causes an explosion within literary language. Old poetic metaphors like the "radiating sky" (30), or the "white cloud" (55) become, as she states, unusable because they now resonate with toxic meaning. Recalling the line "*Marvellous Nature Shining on Me!*" she cannot but wonder "what to do with the libraries full of nature poems" (37; original italics). Radioactive contamination is contagious, affecting not only the material world and its organisms but also the ecology of mind and nature, generating both a linguistic and psychic toxicity that transforms our being in the world. Language itself has been affected by nuclear fallout, and survivors are at a loss of words to describe this radically new experience. Nuclear psychopolitics thus becomes inevitably entangled with the politics of representation. In "No Apocalypse, Not Now" (1984), Jacques Derrida insisted on the fact that the ultimate threat of the atomic bomb, namely an all-out nuclear war, can only be apprehended as a rhetorical condition. In what follows, I will read Stein's piece as a performative enactment of this condition.

First of all, I would like to emphasize that both nuclear representational and psycho-politics are marked by irreducible ambivalence. In the wake of Chernobyl, for example, people cannot but oscillate between two modes of being. On the one hand, they live under traumatic shock and a haunting from the future. Fears of another nuclear disaster, if not war, augment fears of the slow radioactive violence that causes deadly illnesses after a period of latency. On the other hand, people are forced to continue living in a mode of "as if" – as if the disaster had not happened – a temporary denial in the service of adapting to the necessities of everyday survival. Splitting is thus a painfully ambivalent mode of defense that protects the self from traumatic assault while also tearing it apart.

I opened this essay, however, with a canonical pronouncement on the atomic bomb made by Gertrude Stein, written at the very dawn of the nuclear age in the wake of Hiroshima, that is, more than forty years before *Accident*. In an astounding *tour de force*, Stein introduces a specific queering of perspectives on nuclear world politics at this crucial time in history. Allegedly Gertrude Stein's last published piece, "Reflection on the Atomic Bomb" (1946), develops a unique, yet highly symptomatic expression of nuclear war as a psychological condition. Stein opens her argument with the statement I used as an epigraph: "They asked me what I thought of the atomic bomb. I said I had not been able to take any interest in it." She then adds, "if they [atomic bombs] are really as destructive as all that, there is nothing left and if there is nothing there is nobody to be interested and nothing to be interested about" (1973: 161). The very idea of what Jacques Derrida called "remainderless destruction" (1984: 24) becomes, for Stein, a barrier to an engaged affective response: "what is the use of bothering to be scared, and if you are not scared the atomic bomb is not interesting" (1973: 161).

Stein's piece is symptomatic in many respects. First of all, it exhibits, in her characteristically formulaic and formalist way, a form of denial as the most basic psychological defense against the fear of the atomic bomb. Since, according to Stein, any possible nuclear destruction is out of our control, the only viable reaction is to ignore the Bomb. This willful denial exhibits the remarkably detached psychological pragmatism, a familiar signature of Stein's: "really nobody else can do anything about it and so you have to just live along like always, so you see the atomic [bomb] is not at all interesting" (ibid.). Stein's disinterest constitutes a profound rhetorical provocation because of the casualness with which it exposes, in Hiroshima's immediate aftermath, what is in fact the inevitable politics of splitting Christa Wolf makes the explicit center of her memoir forty years later. Stein embraces splitting rhetorically as the only possible condition of living with the atomic bomb.

Psychological splitting is, according to Melanie Klein's theory of psychological development, a primitive defense mechanism developed in early infancy during the so-called paranoid-schizoid position. What is intolerable or unfathomable becomes split off from psychic awareness and consciously felt emotions. But splitting is arguably also the most basic adaptive psychic mechanism in a dangerous, destructive and persecutory world. Today one may wonder whether a pervasive politics of splitting is not an inevitable aspect of living in the Nuclear Age. In this respect, I think, Stein's piece contains an implicit diagnostic statement about the inauguration of the nuclear world order. Exhibiting the core symptom of living with the Bomb, the piece implicitly provokes a critique of nuclear reason.

At the level of Stein's politics of emotion, saying one has not been able to take any interest in the atomic bomb during the very year after it destroyed Hiroshima and Nagasaki – and, within four months, killed between 129,000 and 226,000 people – seems like the most callous dismissal of this monumental event that most claim had changed the world forever. If one tries to read Stein's statement as a queering of the atomic discourses at the time, and perhaps even the nuclear discourses today, one needs to look more closely at the provocation it might present.

Short of dismissing the piece out of hand, what, we may ask, are Stein's rhetorical moves? To begin with, her style bears the familiar Steinian signature, such as bending of grammar, use of minor function words without inflection, characteristic rhetorical repetitions, and familiar rhythms. Critics have largely ignored the piece, perhaps because they did not know what to do with it. They might also have avoided it because of its truly shocking rhetorical ruse. In "The Politics of

Politics; or How the Atomic Bomb Didn't Interest Gertrude Stein and Emily Dickinson" (2006), Brenda Wineapple argues that, given Stein's exclusive concern with literary form and her systematic undermining of referentiality, her self-contained pieces mark aesthetic objects in and of themselves and treat everything else, like the atomic bomb, as extrinsic. However, she also argues that the piece is an invitation to reconceive the place of moral questions in art and aesthetics. What then could be a greater provocation to do so than claiming in 1946 that one was not able to take any interest in the atomic bomb? As Wineapple puts it: "not to be interested in the atomic bomb in 1946 is an inimitable, annoying, and clever rhetorical device drawing attention to itself [...]" (2006: 43). What then is it that the piece is precisely drawing attention to and how is its in-your-face aesthetics designed to provoke a particular response, not to say resistance, in its readers?

Stein opens with a quasi-confessional statement: despite the fact that she likes detective and mystery stories, she could never read any that dealt with "death rays and atomic bombs" (1973: 161). (We may even assume that she knew of H. G. Wells's *The World Set Free* [1914], the first science fiction novel that dealt with death rays and atomic bombs, or, more precisely, invented them, only to inspire the scientists involved with the Manhattan Project.) Once we take Stein's reluctance to read atomic fiction as a possible resistance against closer confrontation with the nuclear work of death, we realize that her entire intervention is, in fact, less a "reflection on the atomic bomb," as the title suggests, than a reflection on the resistance against reflecting on the atomic bomb. The systematic purging of affect from reflection, a trademark of Stein's writing, only enhances this resistance.

The aesthetic strategy of purging affect from nuclear discourse showcases, I think, an important insight into the "politics of splitting" by driving it to its extreme internal logics.[2] Implicitly, Stein argues that nuclear war would only be interesting if it were an all-out nuclear war in which case there would be nobody left to be interested. She thus targets the immediate postwar warnings against nuclear annihilation, only to conclude that if "in spite of all destruction there are always lots left on this earth" (1973: 161) then why even care about the issue? While this statement certainly doesn't attenuate the shock of her provocation, Stein then recommends to leave the issue of the atomic bomb to those who are inventing it or starting it off, because "really nobody else can do anything about it so you have to just live along like always" (ibid.). This may appear

---

[2] See Melanie Klein on the "concept of splitting" and Bob Meister on its political use in *After Evil* (2011).

like a formulaic shorthand rationalization for the very politics of splitting that leads to a completely willful strategic depoliticization of the nuclear threat.

If splitting is usually designed to ward off intolerable affect, one could perhaps say of Stein that her entire writing is designed to ward off affect. However, her short piece nonetheless indirectly addresses the politics of fear at the center of nuclear necropolitics. Questioning the very motivation of those who reveal interest in the atomic bomb, she writes:

> Sure it will destroy and kill a lot, but it's the living that are interesting not the way of killing them [...]. They think they are interested about the atomic bomb but they really are not any more than I am. Really not. They may be a little scared, I am not so scared, there is so much to be scared of so what is the use of bothering to be scared, and if you are not scared the atomic bomb is not interesting. (ibid.)

Intriguingly, in its pseudo-logical abstraction, this passage goes to the core of how the politics of fear inevitably shapes nuclear subjectivities: we cannot but succumb to a certain amount of adaptive splitting if we want to continue leading our everyday lives. At the same time, in totalizing the politics of splitting by dismissing the interest in (or concern with) the split-off fearful (extrinsic) reality altogether, Stein displays an embrace of the very core of depoliticization. The effect of this rhetorical ruse is, almost paradoxically, that of a reverse psychology. The *pseudo-logical* reflection generates a *psycho-logical* one, designed to provoke resistance and, again paradoxically, enhance the interest in the atomic bomb.

We note, of course, that Stein's reflections position her at the opposite end of philosophers like Derrida who insists that every aspect of life, whether we know it or not, is marked by the atomic bomb or Michel Serres who stated in a conversation with Bruno Latour "Hiroshima remains the sole object of my philosophy" (1995: 15). While Derrida focuses on analyzing the rhetorical condition of apprehending the nuclear threat of annihilation, Stein performs a rhetorical play designed to hollow out its psychological condition. Moreover, to the extent that splitting is successful, the fear of nuclear destruction is relegated to the nuclear unconscious. While we "just live along like always" (1973: 161), as Stein says, our fears migrate to the unconscious, including the textual unconscious. In this vein, I am tempted to read Stein's assertion that she could never read detective or mystery stories about "death rays and atomic bombs" (ibid.) as a manifestation not only of her lack of interest but also of a split-off unconscious fear of what she calls (after Wells) the "death rays" of atomic bombs. At the very least, her rhetorical choice seems to point in this direction. Why, for example, did she say, "I never could read them" (ibid.) rather than "I was not interested in reading them"?

Stein's rhetorical strategy belongs to a more general "politics of queering" at the heart of her use of language and rhetoric. Writing against the grain of familiar discourses, not only of the time but also of discourse in general, Stein works within the larger modernist genealogy of an anti-referential experimental aesthetics. This also entails a particular queering of politics, namely one that looks at the central issues of global politics, including gender politics, through the lens of aesthetic abstraction. As I mentioned earlier, "Reflection on the Atomic Bomb" is most likely Stein's last piece. Written at the very inception of the so-called nuclear age, it also introduces a queering in the politics of modernism that, I would argue, presents itself as a resistance against the early formation of nuclear subjectivities. While everybody else seems to say that after the invention of the Bomb the world will not be the same, and that the knowledge that we have acquired the power to destroy our planet will change us as a species, Stein defiantly asserts, that since we cannot do anything about this, we "have to just live along like always" (ibid.).

But then Stein adds a crucial last sentence that has not caught much attention: "This is a nice story" (ibid.). With this sentence, I submit, she mocks any form of literalism or any attempt to read her story in referential terms. The atomic bomb, then, is removed from the monumental historical event that created a fissure in human history, ontology and epistemology. Its reduction to an anecdote – "a nice story" – marks an incendiary break with the harrowing narratives of Hiroshima that haunt her time. Written at the very end of her last word on the atomic bomb, this too is a queering of (aesthetic) nuclear politics. One of the most interesting aspects of this queering is that Stein's resistance to the shaping of nuclear subjectivities through a politics of fear comes at the very beginning of their earliest formation. To this day, Stein's piece remains unique and, as Brenda Wineapple says, an inimitable and annoying rhetorical device (2006: 43). Her attempt to think nuclear politics in non-referential and non-representational terms, however, presents a challenge that has remained with nuclear aesthetics ever since. Embracing the understanding of the Bomb as a rhetorical condition, the attempt to move beyond a merely representational aesthetics generated an entire range of experimental works, including – to name just a few examples – Samuel Beckett's *Happy Days* (1961), Isao Takahata's highly acclaimed *anime* film *Grave of the Fireflies* (1988), Roberto Favelo's hybrid human-insect sculptures, or Michael Madsen's use of a science fiction speculation in his documentary *Into Eternity* (2010).

As both Gertrude Stein and Christa Wolf seem to intimate, fear is harder to bear than indifference, or, we may add, hope. While there are undoubtedly certain symptomatic historical and cultural differences, nuclear subjectivities continue to be marked by a pervasive warding off of fear and the emotional numbing, psychic toxicity, and, most prominently, the splitting and denial that come with it. In the testimonies of survivors from Hiroshima, Chernobyl and other sites of nuclear disasters, we witness the clinging to hope against all odds or the psychic numbing that may easily turn into indifference. Anything seems better than living in the throes of quotidian fear or free-floating anxieties about the effects of a nuclear catastrophe. Gertrude Stein exposes the symptom of this nuclear condition, if not this nuclear reason, in a performative abstraction.

In terms of what we could call "A Critique of Nuclear Reason,"[3] it is interesting to juxtapose Stein's piece with another provocative intervention regarding the atomic bomb, namely Georges Bataille's "Concerning the Accounts Given By the Residents of Hiroshima" (1991). Written a year after Stein's, Bataille's piece develops a concept of "sovereign sensibility" based on the refusal to accept the limits imposed by the fear of death. Framed as a response to John Hersey's *Hiroshima* (1946), Bataille's intervention raises fundamental questions about nuclear sovereignty and subjectivity. Asserting the "primacy of the instant" (1991: 511) over against being ruled by a concern for the future and a fear of atomic annihilation, Bataille proclaims categorically: "the man of sovereign sensibility is not unrelated to the birth of the atomic bomb" (509). The "man of sovereign sensibility" emphatically embraces the only way to escape nuclear terror: becoming he who is as if nuclear death were not. Trying to escape the limits imposed by the fear of nuclear death by performing a radical psychic splitting, he becomes, paradoxically, the supreme embodiment of nuclear subjectivity. The primary goal and indeed ethics of Bataille's nuclear philosophy is "freeing the world from fear" (497). "[A movement that carries me beyond limits is more helpful than an oppressive worry and a fear of the future," he states. "The powerlessness of this world, established by the primacy of action, and by the atomic bomb, the latest expression of this powerlessness, is obviously detestable" (511).

Ultimately, Bataille's sovereign refusal to accept the limits imposed by the fear of death is grounded in a relinquishing of any hope for a better future. This is of course also the end of political action. As he asserts, the sensibility that "enters the path of politics is always of cheap quality" (506). First and foremost a rejection of the ecology of fear generated by the atomic bomb, Bataille's resistance embraces a paradoxical morality of inhabiting the horror: "Let us lift, in the instant, a form of life to the level of the worst" (511). In the last instance

---

[3] With a nod to a genealogy that extends from Immanuel Kant to Klaus Theweleit, Gayatri Spivak, and Achille Mbembe.

Bataille must embrace, paradoxically, "the level of the worst," that is, nuclear annihilation, if only to escape the regime of terror it imposes on the here and now.

Stein's and Bataille's voices remain unique among the writers and philosophers who have addressed what Bataille calls the "atomic effect" (1991: 498). If the renunciation of the limits imposed by the fear of death is indeed the hallmark of sovereignty, both Bataille's concept of sovereign sensibility and Stein's performative indifference displace sovereignty from politics to psychic life. Yet, "he who is, as if death were not" is, I have argued, a sovereign in a position of radical psychic splitting, one who lives in denial of death, including his own work of death.[4] Ultimately, Bataille's and Stein's performative sovereign sensibilities are designed to master nuclear terror by refuting fear. We may wonder if, as a precondition, the sovereign refutation or fear would not also require relinquishing the concern for the future altogether? Embracing a fearless "morality of the instant," Bataille asserts: "I am. In this instant I am. And I do not want to subordinate this instant to anything" (1991: 513). Yet, regarding their politics of emotion, Bataille and Stein are at opposite ends. While Bataille seeks to protect the most extreme emotional intensity, Stein embraces indifference, asserting, almost laconically, "if you are not scared the atomic bomb is not interesting." For Bataille, sovereign sensibility is a "Buddhist meditation on the boneheap" (1991: 509); for Stein, "this is a nice story."

Works Cited

Alexievich, Svetlana. 2005 [1997]. *Voices from Chernobyl: The Oral History of a Nuclear Disaster.* Trans. Keith Gessen. New York: Picador.
Bataille, Georges. 1993. *The Accursed Share.* Vol. 2 & 3. Trans. Robert Hurley. New York: Zone Books.
Bataille, Georges. 1991 [1947]. "Concerning the Accounts Given by the Residents of Hiroshima." Trans. Alan Keenan. *American Imago* 48.4: 497–514.
Beckett, Samuel. 1961. *Happy Days: A Play in Two Acts.* New York: Grove Press.
Derrida, Jaques. 1984. "No Apocalypse, Not Now: Full Speed Ahead, Seven Missiles, Seven Missive." Trans. Catherine Porter and Philip Lewis. *Diacritics* 14.2: 20–31.
Grave of the Fireflies. 1988. Dir. Isao Takahata. Studio Ghibli. DVD.
Hersey, John. 1946. *Hiroshima.* New York: Alfred A. Knopf.
Into Eternity. 2010. Dir. Michael Madsen. Magic Hour Films. DVD.

---

4 See Bataille (1993: 222); I am deliberately using the male pronoun here because the project of nuclear necropolitics is a deeply masculinist project fueled by male fantasies of sublime destruction.

Klein, Melanie. 1986. "Notes on some Schizoid Mechanisms." In: Juliet Mitchell (ed.). *The Selected Melanie Klein*. New York: The Free Press. 176–200.
Meister, Bob. 2011. *After Evil: A Politics of Human Rights*. New York: Columbia University Press.
Serres, Michel and Bruno Latour. 1995. *Michel Serres with Bruno Latour: Conversations on Science, Culture and Time*. Trans. Roxanne Lapidus. Ann Arbor: The University of Michigan Press.
Stein, Gertrude. 1973. "Reflection on the Atomic Bomb." In: Robert Bartlett Haas (ed.). *Reflection on the Atomic Bomb: Volume I of the Previously Uncollected Writings of Gertrude Stein*. Los Angeles: Black Sparrow Press. 161.
Wells, H.G. 1988 [1914]. *The World Set Free*. London: Hogarth.
Wineapple, Brenda. 2006. "The Politics of Politics; or, How the Atomic Bomb Didn't Interest Gertrude Stein and Emily Dickinson." *South Central Review* 23.3: 37–45.
Wolf, Christa. 1989. *Accident: A Day's News*. Trans. Heike Schwarzbauer and Nick Takvorian. Chicago: University of Chicago Press.

STORY

Heinz Ickstadt
Plot and Anecdote in Henry James and Julian Barnes

Abstract: The essay discusses two different ways the anecdote was made use of in early modernist and in postmodernist storytelling. For Henry James an anecdote, overheard at a social occasion, often becomes the germ of an "organically" developed plot (as, e.g., in *What Maisie Knew*); or it functions within the yet unfolding plot as revelatory image, event, or scene illuminating character or giving the story a new turn. With James, the anecdote – as "germ" or structural element – is thus always an organic part of the overall composition. This is not the case with Julian Barnes's novel about Dmitri Shostakovich, *The Noise of Time*. Although here, too, the anecdote is central to the novel's structural design, it has no "organic" function. Shostakovich's inner life – randomly connected by a network of anecdotal memories – is increasingly constrained by the plot imposed on him by State Power (Stalin, The Party), its terrifying reign maintained through rumor and a quasi-official use of anecdote. Apart from its structural function, the anecdote is thus an element both in a public story of repressive plotting and a contrapuntal narrative of withdrawal to a private inner sanctum, increasingly identified with the "temple" of art.

Keywords: Concept of Art, Dmitri Shostakovich, Henry James, Julian Barnes, Public/Private.

The anecdote is usually defined as a short narrative with a pointed ending revealing the character of a known personality, or the nature of a specific social or historical situation. As such it can be considered a genre in itself. Yet it can also be seen as a story *in nuce*, synecdochally or sequentially related to a larger narrative (or to narrative in general), its illustrative function used as part of a strategy of characterization, plot development, or composition. In what follows, I shall discuss two ways the anecdote was used as a structural element by two writers at the beginning and end of the modernist period. Both apply distinct (if related) concepts of narrative form to the representation of historically diverse moments and modes of social corruption.

https://doi.org/10.1515/9783110668490-011

1

In "The Art of Fiction" (1884), Henry James tells the story of an English novelist, "a woman of genius," who was able to imagine, on the basis of an intense visual impression (a scene she observed while going up a staircase), the life of protestant youth in Paris. For James, this was proof of the writer's imaginative power "to guess the unseen from the seen," to convert image into idea and idea back into "concrete image" (James 1984: 52). His novels abound with such impressions, pictures, anecdotal moments: the agonizing conclusions Isabel draws from a glimpse of intimacy between Gilbert Osmond and Madame Merle in *The Portrait of a Lady* (1881), for instance; or Strether's sudden recognition of the true nature of Mme de Vionnet's and Chad's relationship when he sees them together in a boat gliding down the river toward his point of observation in *The Ambassadors* (1903). It is images like these that tell a story and then give the story told another turn. James's plots develop from such moments of revelation that destroy prevalent assumptions or enforce another reading of persons and their relation by a character who – like Maggie Verver in *The Golden Bowl* (1904) – is also one of the novel's centers of consciousness and thus reader *and* maker of the text of which she is a part.

However, the anecdotal is not only a pivotal structural element in Jamesian narrative but also, in many cases, its origin. The *données* of his novels sometimes issue from an idea evoked during conversation (an idea subsequently converted into image), more frequently from an anecdote told to him during one of the many dinners he enjoyed attending. This then would be the "germ" – an anecdote told to him, then visualized as dramatic scene, and then further developed into a complex scenario ("intensely structural, intensely hinged and jointed" [James 1961: 257]) – out of which he would patiently and "organically" unfold the "tree" of his plot.[1] James uses this metaphor in his preface to *What Maisie*

---

[1] See his preface to *The Spoils of Poynton* (1897): "The germ, wherever gathered, has ever been for me the germ of a 'story,' and most of the stories straining to shape under my hand have sprung from a single small seed, a seed as minute and wind-blown as that casual hint for 'The Spoils of Poynton' dropped unwittingly by my neighbor, a mere floating particle in the stream of talk" (James 1934: 119). Most famous is the "anecdote," as James himself calls it (1961: 375), that not only became the "germ" of a central scene in *The Ambassadors*, but of the novel itself: the story his friend Jonathan Sturges told him about William Dean Howells when Sturges met him in Paris. Howells, moved by the sensuous ambience of Paris to regret the life he did (or could) not live, exhorted the much younger Sturges: "Oh, you are young, you are young – be glad of it and live. Live all you can [...]" (226). In Gloriani's garden, Strether addresses Little Bilham in a similar fashion.

Knew (1897) in order to describe "the growth" of what he calls "the 'great oak' from the little acorn" – "a tree that spreads beyond any provision its small germ might on a first handling have appeared likely to make for it" (1985: 23). The "germ" is in this case the "accidental mention" made to him about the situation of some "luckless child" whose divorced parents remarry: "The wretched infant," he notes, "was thus to find itself practically disowned, rebounding from racquet to racquet like a tennis-ball or shuttlecock" (ibid.). His *Notebooks* (1947) give evidence of how James, after having heard of the child's "situation" for the first time in November 1892, went back again and again to "the subject of the *partagé* child" (1961: 134). In several lengthy entrees during the next four years he added to the symmetries and complexities of a pattern of constantly shifting relations that not only document the growth of the tree (i.e. the slowly developing plot) but also the growth of the child's consciousness, so that the unfolding of the one is enacted in the development of the other, the end of the tree's growth coinciding with the end of Maisie's childhood.

James imagines the child of the anecdote as a little girl who is six at the beginning of his tale and subsequently bounced for several years between an ever changing configuration of twos, threes, and fours, first consisting of her parents and their lovers, who then become to her another set of parents, who then have new lovers, who become another set of would-be parents in a complex choreography of shifting marital and extra-marital relationships. This fictional social field – in which all players use Maisie to protect their precarious social respectability or as a cover for establishing a new round of profitable cohabitation – is one of general corruption, a collapse of private and collective *mores* from which only the child remains exempt; her "undestroyed freshness" allowing her to "live with all intensity and perplexity and felicity in [her] terribly mixed little world" (1985: 25). She reacts to the actions of those who constitute a kaleidoscopically changing environment of persons and places by adjusting to each new social and geographic constellation. As when she enacts, with the help of her French doll Lisette, the strange conduct of grown-ups and rehearses symbolically, in her conversations with Lisette, new strategies and patterns of her own behavior (55). For Maisie, the novel's slowly unfolding "center of consciousness," the ability to adjust (issuing from her desperate need to be loved), together with her ability to "wonder," is the condition of her gradually growing self- and world-awareness since it allows her innocence to "convert" whatever she observes into self-determined agency. Maisie's "small consciousness" thus expands with her eagerness to know and the growing "sense of freedom to make out things for herself" (96). She is, to the end, the object of the game of others – a cruel game of love and jealousy, of money and of sexuality – but she increasingly participates in it as an active player, as "a wonder-working agent" – thus James in his Preface (25) – intuitively grasping its rules without understanding them, yet able to shift the balance and the symmetry of the relations; until she sets herself free at last by stepping out of them. Whether her new freedom is safe with the highly moral but by no means unselfish Mrs. Wix, however, may be doubted.

From "dim discernment" (212) at the beginning, her knowledge slowly unfolds in several stages of awareness: there is, first, her keen but often clueless observation. By interacting with the other players, she then – "receptive and profound" (80) – gains the ability to feel her way through the games they play with her. Later, her sophistication grows from her aesthetic and sensuous appreciation of French culture in Boulogne ("to thrill with enjoyment of the picture" [181]); until, finally, she acquires what Mrs. Wix calls (but grossly misconceives as) "a moral sense" (211, 260). "Oh I know," Maisie keeps insisting till the very end. Although the reader can never be certain of what Maisie really knows, or merely *thinks* she knows, or only *pretends* to know, or eventually *comes* to know in a game where knowledge is inextricably mixed up with concealment, pretension, deception, and self-deception, yet is also advanced through intuition, metaphor, and a vague awareness of the complexity of human relations, of the emotional as much as the strategic function they may have.[2]

James's anecdotal "germ" surely provides the impulse to a wonderfully imaginative narrative, to a tightly structured and logically (or as he might say: organically) unfolding plot that has yet larger allegorical implications. In this novel, published in 1897, as in several others of the 1890s, he enacts, almost to the point of satire, his contempt for a society whose corruption becomes most evident in its selfish schemes against the "little unspotted soul" (37) of the innocent. Maisie is its victim, yet also something of an antidote – this, in fact, may be the reason for James's intense fascination with a story he was only "casually" told. For it gives evidence of his ultimate faith in the incorruptibility of innocence, "[t]he active, contributive close-circling wonder [...] in which the child's identity is guarded and preserved" (31). This trust in a regenerative "germ" ("the seed of the moral life," as he writes in his prefaces) has not only become the anecdotal basis of *this* novel but also, as in much of his late fiction, the idealistic basis of his work "on behalf of the something better [...] that

---

[2] In this game of shifting symmetries and readjusted balances, *What Maisie Knew* anticipates structurally, if not thematically, James's last published novel, *The Golden Bowl*.

blessedly [...] might be" (James 1934: 222)³ – even, perhaps, against the realist's better knowledge.

2

To go from here to Julian Barnes's *The Noise of Time* (2016), his fictional account of the life of Dmitri Dmitrievich Shostakovich, is not quite as far-fetched, absurd even, as it may appear at first. True, the corruption of Soviet society under the terror of the Stalin years and after is of a different kind and caliber than the moral decay of late-Victorian England. Yet although Shostakovich is not like Maisie, he is nevertheless childlike: the young musical genius (a Russian Mozart) as an innocent in a social world whose revolutionary fervor has given way to power games that may end not only with the loss of artistic freedom and personal integrity but also with the loss of life. What I found intriguing in comparing the two novels is the different use Barnes makes of the anecdote as an essential element of his narrative:

> Shostakovich was a multiple narrator of his own life [Barnes writes in his "Author's Note" at the end of the book]. Some stories come in many versions, worked up and "improved" over the years. Others [...] exist only in a single version, told many years after the composer's death [in 1975], by a single source. More broadly, truth was a hard thing to find, let alone maintain in Stalin's Russia. Even the names mutate uncertainly [...]. All this is highly frustrating to any biographer, but most welcome to any novelist. (2017: 184)

The anecdotal at first appears as a narrative counter-strategy to the massive plotting of Stalin's system of relentless suppression.⁴ Yet it is also perceived as a tool of control that the System exerts over the consciousness of those who need as much as they defy "order" in their individual lives. Barnes thus composes his biographical narrative as a sequence of anecdotal encounters with

---

3 See his preface to "The Lesson of the Master" (1888) where he speaks of his use of "operative irony" as part of a "campaign, of a sort, on behalf of the something better (better than the obnoxious, the provoking object) that blessedly, as is assumed, might be [...]. It implies and projects the possibly other case, the case rich and edifying where the actuality is pretentious and vain." He then continues: "What better example than this of the high and helpful public and, as it were, civic use of the imagination?" (1934: 222–223).

4 In the tales of Jorge Luis Borges – to refer to a related but inverse example – the anecdotal is, in fact, a form of narrative that amounts to a dominant "Historia de la Infamia," undermining any higher "plot" of perfection, i.e. of God's planning; in the end, not only undermining but usurping it.

"Power" – anecdotes told differently from different perspectives, according to the protagonist's wavering between resistance and compliance. At the same time the monolithic system asserts itself to him anecdotally in fearful and persuasive revelations of its almighty and omniscient presence. It progressively erodes resistance merely built on the anecdotal particular.

There is therefore a mimetic aspect to the anecdotal that is not evident in Henry James: Shostakovich was not only himself a man of many stories, anecdotes, and aphorisms (the latter being the title of one of his early compositions), but also a person about whom many stories and anecdotes were told.[5] In addition, he lived in a society that was permeated with gossip – with stories, rumors, and whisperings against an ever present "Power" (be they focused on Stalin himself or on the many stooges representing him) as much as with rumors, jokes, anecdotes, or tales of fear and terror planted by that very Power to take root in, and thus control of, the collective mind.[6]

From Elizabeth Wilson's voluminous biography, *Shostakovich: A Life Remembered* (1994), Barnes took an anecdote that he then turned into the structural

---

[5] Elizabeth Wilson's portrait of Shostakovich and his work is an over five hundred-page collage of Shostakovich's letters in addition to the stories, remembrances, and voices of the composer's relatives and friends as well as of his numerous colleagues and acquaintances. In Solomon Volkov's 1979 *Testimony: The Memoirs of Dmitri Shostakovich* (next to Wilson, Barnes's second most important source), the composer tells his own life and that of others in a string of stories and anecdotes, so that, together, they constitute something like a composite intellectual history of the Stalin period (as mediated through the memories of Shostakovich as mediated through the notes and memories of Volkov). Interesting examples of Volkov's anecdotal method are Chapters 2 and 5 (on Alexander Glazunov, Shostakovich's teacher at the Leningrad Conservatory who emigrated to Paris) and Chapter 3 (on Vsevolod Meyerhold, the influential avant-garde theater director whom Stalin had killed). One of several definitions of the anecdote James gives in his prefaces to the New York edition may also be applicable here: "The anecdote consists, ever, of something that has oddly happened to some one, and the first of its duties is to point directly to the person whom it so distinguishes. He may be you or I or any one else, but a condition of our interest – perhaps the principal one – is that the anecdote shall know him, and shall accordingly speak of him, as its subject" (preface to "The Reverberator" (1888) [1934: 181]).

[6] One of the many stories Barnes mentions is that of the feared cultural ideologue Zhdanov playing the piano to show decadent Russian composers what "real" music was: "[T]he story gained authority with each retelling, until some of those allegedly present had confirmed that, yes, it had happened exactly like that. [...] [I]t swiftly joined the songbook of believable myths circulating at this time. What mattered was not so much whether a particular story was factually true, but rather, what it signified. Though it was also the case that the more a story circulated, the truer it became" (2017: 104). Another is the story of Tikhon Khrennikov, leader of the Union of Soviet Composers, who is said to have shat into his pants when Stalin ignored him while Khrennikov presented to "the leader and teacher" his candidates for the next Stalin Prize (143–144; see also Volkov 1979: 196).

frame of his novel. As Wilson tells it via the memory of Flora Litvinova, Shostakovich and a friend travelled through Russia during the war (1994: 193). The train stopped at an Eastern station and a beggar who had lost both legs in the war approached the travelers singing a lewd song. Instead of money, the friends shared their vodka with him. Clinking the three unequally filled glasses in the usual salute produced a sound that Shostakovich, always an acute listener, defined, in a casual aside, as "triad" (ibid.)

What in Litvinova's text was mentioned only in passing as an example of the importance sound had in Shostakovich's "musical memory" becomes a pivotal event in the novel. Barnes begins and ends it with this anecdote which he expands to an introductory as well as a concluding scene, both focused on the theme of survival. (Well into the second part, the episode is also, if only vaguely, remembered by Shostakovich himself [Barnes 2017: 69–70]). Yet Barnes reserves disclosure of the name of its protagonist and what he actually murmured for his (untitled) epilogue (set in cursive print). The triad Shostakovich presumably hears also makes for the triadic structure of the book. Its three-line motto preceding the opening episode – the book's prologue, like the ending, untitled and set apart from the main text by cursive print – is a traditional piece of folk wisdom: "One to hear, / One to remember, / And one to drink." The "one to hear," no doubt, is Shostakovich; the "one to remember" possibly his introverted and self-reflective alter ego, or the narrator remembering the story he is telling through the mind of its protagonist; the "one to drink" would then be another alter ego, a Shostakovich in his degraded state, a heavy drinker, psychologically damaged by "Stalin's Terror."

If the three lines of the motto echo the triad of the anecdote, they also inform the structure of the novel. Each of its three parts is focused on an anecdotal encounter Shostakovich had with what is simply called "Power," dramatizing the different phases of Shostakovich's elevation and subjection by that Power: the first one, in 1936, comes in the wake of a critique, probably written by Stalin himself, of Shostakovich's acclaimed avant-garde opera "Lady Macbeth of Mtsensk" in a *Pravda* editorial headlined "Muddle instead of Music." It made Shostakovich an "enemy of the People" and put a temporary end to his promising career. It also made him fear for his life from then on. Accordingly, this first part of the novel, "On the Landing," shows the composer waiting for the emissaries of "Power" in front of an elevator, with a packed suitcase, so that his family might be spared the "spectacle" of his deportation.[7] And while he is waiting,

---

[7] Barnes places this scene in the immediate context of Shostakovich's first "conversation with Power" in 1937, although, according to Wilson, it happened in 1948 after Zhdanov's infamous

like thousands of others all over Moscow, his mind begins to drift, reflecting on his present situation and his past life, remembering in fragmentary flashbacks (he cannot "control his mind's rememberings" [Barnes 2017: 172]) impressions of smell, sight, or loving touch, love affairs, the "gypsy romances" (21) his father sang, episodes and anecdotes, told or experienced, that echo as *leitmotifs* throughout the text. Yet after ten nights of terrified waiting, "Power" still has not come for him – either because Stalin protects the nation's most gifted, if ideologically unreliable, composer after all, or because, in a bureaucracy gone wild, his interrogator had himself become a victim of deportation.[8]

In the second part, "On the Plane," set twelve years later in 1948, Shostakovich once again appears to be professionally ruined, this time by Zhdanov's attack on "Formalism in Music": his compositions can no longer be performed and he is fired from all teaching jobs, because, like Prokofiev, he is now regarded as one of "[t]he enemies of Russian music" (Wilson 2006: 235). At this lowest point of his career, he receives a telephone call from Stalin himself – a fact that immediately became anecdote – persuading him, in no uncertain terms, to become a member of a delegation of Soviet artists at an International Peace Conference in New York. Although he is thus nationally vindicated and

---

decree when the composer lost all his teaching positions and, expecting the worst, was ready to sign anything "even if they hand it to me upside down. All I want is to be left alone" (Wilson 2006: 211–212).

8 "Why had he been spared when so many around him had been arrested, exiled, murdered, or had disappeared into a fate which might become clear only decades later? One answer would fit all those questions: 'Stalin says he is not to be touched'" (Barnes 2017: 123). In *Testimony*, Solomon Volkov identifies the role Shostakovich played in Stalin's world of terror and oppression as that of the *yurodivye* – part of a long Russian tradition of "playing the idiot": "The origins of *yurodstvo* go back to the fifteenth century and even earlier; it existed as a noticeable phenomenon until the eighteenth century. During all that time, the *yurodivye* could expose injustice and remain in relative safety. The authorities recognized the right of the *yurodivye* to criticize and be eccentric – within limits. Their influence was immense. [...] A number of educated men became *yurodivye* as a form of intellectual criticism, of protest" (1979: xxi). If this evokes the function of the Shakespearian clown or court jester, in the context of Stalin's reign, it meant assuming the dangerous role of critic by hiding criticism behind a mask of assent, or in Shostakovich's case, by using music – his only form of "truthful" expression – as mask for a criticism he could not express in words. The mask protected him to some extent, but not completely. He speaks of the fear of persecution throughout his life. Wilson calls him "a master of subtext" and quotes one of Shostakovich's friends: "He felt that we were all participants in the farce. And having agreed to be a clown, one might as well play that role to the final curtain. [...] His only real life was his art, and into it he admitted no one. It was his temple: when he entered it, he threw off his mask and was what he was" (Galina Vishnevskaya qtd. in Wilson 1994: 487).

internationally acknowledged as the most prominent composer of the Soviet Union, he also feels deeply humiliated by having to give speeches he never wrote, thus making himself the mouthpiece of political and aesthetic doctrines he deeply despised, no matter how listlessly he delivered them. (He was especially ashamed to have to publicly condemn Stravinsky whom he in fact admired as one of the century's greatest composers). On the other hand, his own music, blacklisted before by Zhdanov, can now be performed again.

In the novel's third part, "In the Car," again twelve years later, in 1960, Shostakovich has his third and "most ruinous" (Barnes 2017: 148) encounter with "Power" – this time in its softer, post-Stalin incarnation as Nikita Khrushchev, the "Corncob." This third emissary of Power is smooth and flexible, yet insistent in his effort to persuade Shostakovich to join the Party, refusing to take the composer's initial "no" for a final answer. Although "Power" is not life-threatening any longer (he is even given a car – if only a Russian and not, as he had hoped, an American car – as sign of his now elevated status), this is yet the most thoroughly corrupting of his three encounters, since he is offered high honors for the price of acting against his deepest convictions by eventually becoming a Party member. ("He swam in honours like a shrimp in shrimp-cocktail sauce" is a recurring metaphor of self-deprecation [64, 118, 135]). When he finally does what he, until then, had refused to do, he renounces everything he had considered part of his personal integrity – except his music. He continues to produce obsessively and feverishly, sometimes openly defying the official demand for heroic optimism (as in his "pessimistic" Fourth Symphony in C minor); sometimes undermining it ironically (as in the last movement of his seemingly "optimistic" Fifth Symphony in D minor, which was officially accepted as "[a] Soviet artist's reply to just criticism" and called "an optimistic tragedy" [57, 58]); sometimes cynically giving in to it (as perhaps most obviously in his "Song of the Forest" whose "thunderous banality [...] had helped him win his fourth Stalin Prize: 100.000 roubles, and a dacha" [117]).

Especially the first part of Barnes's book is composed of remembered fragments of Shostakovich's early life when he – as Yevtushenko wrote in his poem on "Babi Jar" that Shostakovich later set to music in his Thirteenth Symphony – was pursuing a career "by trying not to pursue one" (Barnes 2017: 150). In the novel's second and third parts, the fragmentary and anecdotal elements of Shostakovich's personal life are increasingly set in counterpoint[9] to his Party-

---

9 I am tempted to compare this to James's *The Ambassadors*. That novel also projects an anecdotal counterplot to the "plot" of the morality play conceived in Woollett. It is this counterplot that slowly opens Strether's plotting mind (his framing imagination) anecdotally – via episodes of revelation – until, in the end, the Woollett-plot has been at once confirmed and dissolved

approved public career – a "destiny" he submits to with despair, shame, and self-loathing. The hero of subversive irony had, in his own eyes, turned into a self-hating and self-castigating coward. "Instead of killing him, they had allowed him to live, and by allowing him to live, they had killed him" (177).

Always under the suspicion of "formalist" elitism, he was never safe but forced to maneuver between two opposite dictates: the one issuing from his inner need to give expression to the agonies of war and persecution; the other from an ignorant bureaucracy's insistence on the heroic, the melodic, the hopeful, and the popular ("Our job is to rejoice!" [Wilson 2006: 206]).[10] While his public life was increasingly taking shape within an official mold, his private life slowly fell apart under incessant political and bureaucratic coercion. So that to pursue "truth" in music ("for the ears that could hear" [Barnes 2017: 92]), he had to retreat to a secluded inner realm, his "temple" (Wilson 2006: 487) of artistic work and aesthetic self-reflection ("some innermost shrine," as James had phrased it in his preface to *What Maisie Knew* [1985: 24]). Thus, Shostakovich's intensely personal "Eighth Quartet" was written at the very time when he felt forced to join the Party in 1960 – an act he had desperately tried to avoid.[11] (In this sense, the "Eighth Quartet" can also be understood as lamenting the loss of his artistic integrity):

> He told his friends that in his mind the work was dedicated "to the memory of the composer." Which would clearly have been regarded by the musical authorities as unacceptably egotistical and pessimistic. And so the dedication on the published score eventually read: "To the Victims of Fascism and War." This would no doubt have been viewed as a great improvement. But all he had really done was turn a singular into a plural. (Barnes 2017: 174)

His awareness of having allowed the System to corrupt him coincided with the need to protect whatever was left of his sense of personal dignity by turning the

---

(since it is true and yet totally wrong), leaving Strether disillusioned (plotless) and yet experientially enriched with nuance and appreciation of the sensuous particular.

10 In that respect Shostakovich asserts (via Barnes, Volkov, and Wilson) that the war proved to be the best time for the arts since during the terrifying period of German aggression patriotic and aesthetic commitments tended to overlap. The aggressor "outside" became the common enemy. As soon as that enemy was vanquished, however, the old antagonisms between politics and art reappeared and the suppression of elitist formalism was resumed with even greater vehemence.

11 Shostakovich finished the Eighth Quartet while in Dresden (then still a city heavily destroyed). Its main theme – DEsCH [DSCH] – is based on his initials. Although by no means a sentimentalist, he was greatly moved by the world of ruins that surrounded him and seemed to echo his own ruined state.

ironic distance to his "benevolent" oppressors into cynicism. At the same time, he became conscious of his slowly progressing physical decay. (He suffered from a rare neuro-muscular disease.)

In this context, the novel's central anecdote reveals its allegorical dimension. The "triad" that only Shostakovich hears *in* and *through* the noise of time (the horrors of war and of personal degradation) marks that enclave of art or music in which Shostakovich hopes to survive: "What could be put up against the noise of time? Only that music which is inside ourselves – the music of our being – which is transformed by some into real music. [...] This was what he held to" (125).[12]

It is here that James and Barnes meet, even if Maisie and Shostakovich do not: their belief in the vulnerability, yet also the indestructability of the imagination, the music heard *in* and *above* the noise of time; or, as James phrased it in his *Notebooks:* "Oh art [...], [w]ithout you the world, for me, would be, indeed, a howling desert" (1961: 68). But neither James, nor Shostakovich, nor Barnes conceive of "art" (*or* music *or* writing) as *removed* from world or history – rather as, inescapably, involved *in* it, beset *by* it, and *yet* beyond it.[13]

However, in James's early modernist aesthetics, the anecdotal "seed" is turned into "organic" plot according to an idea of wholeness, "where every word and every punctuation point contribute directly to the expression," as he wrote in "The Art of Fiction" (1984: 60) – no matter how processual, relational, or open-ended that "wholeness" may be conceived. But for Shostakovich's late modernism and Julian Barnes's postmodernism *all* plot, *all* concept of organic order, is *imposed* on music, on writing, or on life's singular moments of experience by the unity-enforcing "Power" to which they are exposed. These moments stay alive only when they are remembered and evoked by the medium of art as particular events of consciousness. *There* (and *then*) life can still be felt as private, and music can be formed by the inner rhythm of "our being."

---

12 Barnes may have taken the title of his novel from the account Mikhail Druskin, a fellow musician, gave of Shostakovich's early phase as composer: "For only a few creators of spiritual values knew how to listen to the true voice of history, the 'Noise of Time,' to use Alexander Blok's expression. One way or another the [revolutionary, H.I.] times held sway over people, and left their imprint on them, the impressionable Shostakovich included" (qtd. in Wilson 2006: 48).
13 To be sure, James's and Shostakovich's concepts of art's social function were entirely different – Shostakovich feeling himself connected to the "people" in a way James was never able or willing to. But even James talks of the "civic use of the imagination" (1934: 223), and both were called "elitist" since both refused – in their different ways – to betray art's "sacred office" (1984: 46) to commercial or political pressures.

And yet, there is no safety even in this retreat – if such retreat even continues to matter. For private life may always be further transformed into public life by whatever "Power" exerts pressure on it; and the discordant "muddle" of art may always be translated into more accommodating forms of aesthetic expression. In fact, so Barnes's novel seems to suggest, the softer the power, the harder to resist its all-pervasive persuasiveness.

Works Cited

Barnes, Julian. 2017 [2016]. *The Noise of Time*. London: Vintage.
Borges, Jorge Luis. 1999. *Collected Fictions*. Trans. Andrew Hurley. London: Penguin Books.
James, Henry. 2009 [1904]. *The Golden Bowl*. London: Penguin Classics.
James, Henry. 2008 [1903]. *The Ambassadors*. London: Penguin Classics.
James, Henry. 2003 [1881]. *The Portrait of a Lady*. London: Penguin Classics.
James, Henry. 1985 [1897]. *What Maisie Knew*. London: Penguin Books.
James, Henry. 1984 [1884]. "The Art of Fiction." In: *Henry James: Literary Criticism*. Vol. 1: *Essays on Literature, American and English Writers*. Ed. Leon Edel. New York: Library of America. 44–65.
James, Henry. 1961 [1947]. *The Notebooks of Henry James*. Eds. F. O. Matthiessen and Kenneth B. Murdock. New York: Galaxy Books.
James, Henry. 1948 [1910]. "Is There A Life After Death?" In: F. O. Matthiessen (ed.). *The James Family*. New York: Alfred Knopf. 602–614.
James, Henry. 1934. *The Art of the Novel: Critical Prefaces by Henry James*. Ed. Richard P. Blackmur. New York: Scribner's.
Volkov, Solomon. 1979. *Testimony: The Memoirs of Dmitri Shostakovich*. London: Faber & Faber.
Wilson, Elizabeth. 2006 [1994]. *Shostakovich: A Life Remembered*. London: Faber & Faber.

Thomas Claviez
The Relevance of the Irrelevant: Wisdom and/of Contingency

Abstract: The anecdote has, for quite some time, enjoyed a rather singular position within literary studies. When perusing the growing corpus of academic essays and books on the subject of the anecdote, one cannot fail to notice that hardly a single contribution exists that does not refer, one way or another, ex- or implicitly, to the thoroughly contingent nature of this phenomenon. In what follows, I will put this quality at the center of my investigation in order to inquire into the anecdote's epistemico-ontological status. And I will do so by reading it in connection with Walter Benjamin's famous essay on "The Storyteller," as this text provides us with a context that allows us to put its status – as something "irrelevantly relevant" – into perspective.

Keywords: Contingency, History, Storytelling, Unity, Walter Benjamin.

1 Anecdote and Contingency

In his thorough analysis of the role and significance of the anecdote in the romantic movement, David Simpson locates the anecdote in the context of what he terms the latter's "ethic of incompleteness";[1] and he concludes his analysis as follows:

> By making no claim for itself as other than anecdotal, as contingent and verging on the insignificant, it perhaps aspires to diminish (though it can never avoid) the anxieties that go with trying to construct anything called history from within the predicament of modernity, a predicament that has as one of its constitutive principles the impossibility of an unsituated knowledge. (1995: 53–54)

Simpson here aligns the anecdote's contingency with modernism's insistence that all knowledge is situated, and, as such, historical. It is one of the main characteristics of the anecdote, in his view, to be "convincing enough to come

---

[1] Simpson writes: "Since at least Friedrich Schlegel and Kierkegaard, we have had in place an ethic of incompleteness, a prioritizing of active interpretation and world making as the proper responsibility of romantic and Protestant personalities. This has often received positive codings, so that the knowledge thus produced becomes *authentic* for the self (and for its prospects of redemption) even as it necessarily strains consensus" (1995: 51; original italics).

across as real at the same time as it dramatizes the act of telling and requires an act of interpretation or application" (59). That is, it interrupts the flow and totalizing character of a dialectical regime that subordinates, in Hegelian fashion, everything to its main narrative. As Joel Fineman puts it succinctly:

> [...] the anecdote is the literary form that uniquely *lets history happen* by virtue of the way it introduces an opening into the teleological, and therefore timeless, narration of beginning, middle and end. The anecdote produces the effect of the real, the occurrence of contingency, by establishing an event as an event within and yet without the framing context of historical successivity, i.e., it does so only in as far as its narration both comprises and refracts the narration it reports. [...] [Hence] the seductive opening of the anecdotal form. (1989: 61; original italics)

That is, on a formal level, in retaining a remnant of history as contingent in the sense of non-totalizable, the anecdote introduces, by its sheer existence, a gap into the flow of narrative that invites readers to fill it, according to Wolfgang Iser's theory of "reader response."[2] On the level of content, it points out that things historically not only *could have been* different – which is the classical definition of contingency as non-necessary truth – but that they might indeed *have been* different. This is at least what Lionel Gossman suggests when, referring to the anecdote's inception in Procopius of Cesarea, he defines anecdotes as "a ragbag of stories of depravity and abuse of power" (2003: 152) that defy representations in official historiography. Gossman, too, emphasizes their contingent quality of "pris[ing] closed dramatic structures open by perforating them with holes of novelistic contingency" (145). This contingency manifests itself by the anecdote's "ostensible refusal of systematization, totalization, and ideological interpretation and by [its] reporting of only particular, relatively isolated episodes, often enough *in simple chronological order*" (150; my italics). What is so interesting about this quote is that Gossman here connects the anecdote's contingency with the fact that it follows "simple chronological order," which is to say that it escapes or defies the very selection and ordering principles of official historiography – which, as Hayden White has shown, itself very often follows literary models.

In the light of what has been said so far, I would now like to draw an arc from Aristotle's distinction between poetry and historiography, as he draws it in his *Poetics* (c. 335 B.C.), to Walter Benjamin's famous essay on "The

---

2 Simpson (1995) himself emphasizes the aspect of reader participation as part and parcel of the romantic project: "The whole romantic enterprise of aggressively stimulating a reader's response may be understood as a larger version of the anecdotal moment" (56).

Storyteller" (1936), in order to contextualize the contingent nature of the anecdote – which Gossman also and very tellingly describes "as fragments of some undecipherable whole, [which] as instances that resist neat interpretation, far from consolidating what we think we know, may cause us to question it and provoke inquiry into it" (161).

However, can we possibly consider an anecdote to be a fragment of a whole if this whole is, as Gossman says, indecipherable?[3] If said whole is indeed indecipherable, the fragment would not only enjoy the status of a contingency toward this whole, but the whole, as indecipherable, would in itself constitute an instance of contingency *qua* contiguity. Now, such a contradictory assessment is by no means an isolated phenomenon as regards the definition of the anecdote; an uncertainty as to the theoretical status of its nature seems to almost reflect its own qualities, as the anecdote's contingency seems to prove contagious to attempts to define it. Here are a few instances:

- It is allegedly (as yet) unpublished, which is what the word anecdote etymologically refers to;[4] a published anecdote would thus be an impossibility, and a *contradictio in adjecto*.
- It is about a real event, but can be fictive.[5]
- It is, by some, defined as a "story with a point" (Epstein 1989: xix) – which seems to imply that other stories do not have one.
- It has also been defined as a "truth more general than the story itself" (Neureuter 1973: 472; my translation), though, as we have seen, it cannot be generalized. But would not any story worth telling feature a truth larger than itself? What could the status of a non-generalizable truth possibly be?
- As such, it is both contingent (metonymic) upon the truth, and contingent upon the larger story it is embedded in.
- If the anecdote constitutes a digression, what is literature if it, too, offers informal evidence as compared to scientific evidence? Why can an anecdote *not* be "investigated" using the scientific method?
- If, as anecdotal evidence, it is juxtaposed to statistical evidence, does truth as "typical" in the case of the latter mean that statistical probability is the same as truth philosophically speaking?
- However, what would be the point of inserting an anecdote if it were not typical of, or relevant for, something?

---

[3] This question, if a little differently, is also addressed in Stefanovska (2009).
[4] Cf. Schäfer (1982: 9–10).
[5] Thus, Gossman claims that "even when its factual veracity was in doubt it still might be thought of as in some way illuminating historical reality" (2003: 159).

– Moreover, what are we going to do about the fact that it is usually defined as resistance both to political and philosophical authority (defying both the integrity of the emperors and politicians, and the integrity of their respective truth protocols) – but also, if contingent to the literary text it is imbedded in, even resistant to literary authority?

I will, needless to say, not be able to address – let alone answer – all these questions in the space allotted here; that is why I want to turn first to Aristotle, and then, as mentioned, to Benjamin to at least tackle a few of them.

As is well known, Aristotle distinguished between historiography and poetry in his *Poetics* in the following way: while historiography is preoccupied with rendering what very often seems a mass of utterly contingent facts, it is the task of poetry – through the *muthos* – to bring some kind of coherence, meaning, unity, and probability into this mess.[6] Now, we know not only since Hayden White's *Metahistory* (1973) that such a categorical distinction cannot be drawn, and that – specifically since Romanticism, but also before – what one could consider aesthetic or narrative elements have been and are being included in historiographic works as well. The conclusion to be drawn from Aristotle's original juxtaposition is that the truth of historic facts *is* their contingency, and that to introduce meaning into this entangled mess of facts thus means taking *a step away* from the very truth which *is* the contingency of the factual.[7]

Sneaking mythic aspects into historiography – that is, selection, ordering, and narrative meaning-making – is, as we all know, also in the interest of those in whose name histories have been and are very often written. These are histories that focus upon the achievements of heroes, kings, and generals; histories that prefer not to include the messiness of the lives of presumably less important human beings and even less the suffering that they have to go through as subalterns to those who define history's plots. That is why – and this is just an aside – the anecdote, having its *raison d'être* as counterhistory – would seem to be of enormous interest for any postcolonial project to provide such alternative and potentially subversive histories (not, mind you, alternative facts!). The problem here would be, however, to withstand the temptation to force the fragments provided by such an inquiry together into a story – or a decipherable whole – again. A temptation that is almost impossible, it seems to me, to avoid, but a

---

6 Cf. Aristotle (1996: 9.1451a38–b7; 23.1459a17–30).
7 Joel Fineman seems to agree when he connects, in the quote above, "the effect of the real" with "the occurrence of contingency."

successful instance of which is offered in Gloria Anzaldua's *Borderland/La Frontera* (1987).[8]

What this means is that what we are called upon to take into account is not so much the information (historical, statistical, or otherwise) that history (not historiography) provides, and whose contingency historiography is trying to exorcize out of it, but the *experience* of just these facts that otherwise either remain contingent, empty shells, or fall prey to the ideological regimes of official historiography. And this distinction is what provides me with a transition to the work of Walter Benjamin, and, more specifically, to his famous essay "The Storyteller: Reflections on the Works of Nikolai Leskov."

2 Walter Benjamin's "The Storyteller"

It is needless to say that I will not be able to gauge the depths of this multi-layered and dense text within the limits of this essay. But as others who have written about the anecdote have also referred to this text – if mostly in a cursory manner – it might provide us with some leverage as regards our topic. One of those critics is David Simpson, who examines what he considers the tendency – most obvious in new historicism, but for him typical for postmodern academia in general – to resort to conversation and anecdotes. In so doing, he argues, we seem to "embrace once again what Benjamin thought had gone forever" (that is, our capability to tell stories), and, in so doing, lift "'the burden of demonstrable explanation' from the teller" to make "space for interpretation" (1995: 64–65).[9]

According to Benjamin, an age of information has replaced the story and its attempt to transmit experience. What has changed is that information – provided by an army of experts that gather and present this information in a predigested way, thus relieving us from the task of finding out what it means – does not have to be interpreted anymore by its recipients. In contrast, according to Benjamin, the experience provided by the story requires just that. If we, however, now go further in drawing parallels between Benjamin's story and the anecdote, this would imply that the experience transported in such a story would also not be generalizable. This, in turn, would throw a rather strange light on the notorious moral of the story that we are usually so keen to extract from it. What

---

[8] In this work, whose generic borders traverse the autobiographical, the historical, the mythopoetic, and the lyric, Anzaldua manages to unfold a counterhistory that defies being unified into a "whole" as much as the author herself.
[9] Schäfer (1982) also draws a connection between the anecdote and Benjamin's "The Storyteller" (33).

kind of moral can possibly be drawn from a story that would prove nongeneralizable? What would it look like? And what does Benjamin have to say about it?

Right from the start, Benjamin locates this experience (and not just experience, but "moral experience") – and here we seem to encounter the first parallel to the anecdote – in contrast to those in power: "For never has experience been contradicted more thoroughly than strategic experience by tactical warfare, economic experience by inflation, bodily experience by mechanical warfare, moral experience by those in power" (2007: 84). And he specifies "moral experience" – or the connection between morality and power – as follows:

> All this points to the nature of every real story. It contains, openly or covertly, something useful. The usefulness may, in one case, consist in a moral; in another, in some practical advice; in a third, in a proverb or maxim. In every case the storyteller is a man who has counsel for his readers. But if today "having counsel" is beginning to have an old-fashioned ring, this is because *the communicability of experience is decreasing. In consequence, we have no counsel either for ourselves or for others.* After all, counsel is less an answer to a question than a proposal concerning the continuation of a story which is just unfolding. [...] Counsel woven into the fabric of real life is wisdom. The art of storytelling is reaching its end because the epic side of truth, wisdom, is dying out. (86–87; my italics)

It is important to note that the moral of the story, or the counsel that it offers, is intricately connected to the story itself, and thus cannot claim universal relevance. That is, it does not provide any truisms that would transcend the specific context of the story itself. And the story's wisdom might actually be ascribed to this very modesty that, in the face of the contingency of the world that surrounds us (and that it embodies itself), in fact abstains from providing eternal moral-philosophical maxims.[10]

What, however, does he mean by the decrease of "the communicability of experience"? This is not, I venture to say, Benjamin's prophetic foray into the consequences of the linguistic turn that throw into doubt the communicability of virtually anything; after all, why would postmoderns resort to the anecdote as story, as Simpson argues? Benjamin's answer to this is rather surprising, as he holds the rise of the novel partly responsible for this demise. And it is surprising because the novel does not seem to *reduce* the experience of contingency that the story seems to embody, but to *increase* it:

---

[10] On this, cf. also White (2017).

> What differentiates the novel from all other forms of prose literature – the fairy tale, the legend, even the novella – is that it neither comes from oral tradition nor goes into it. This distinguishes it from storytelling in particular. The storyteller takes what he tells from experience – his own or that reported by others. And he in turn makes it the experience of those who are listening to his tale. The novelist has isolated himself. The birthplace of the novel is the solitary individual, who is no longer able to express himself by giving examples of his most important concerns, is himself uncounseled, and cannot counsel others. To write a novel means *to carry the incommensurable to extremes* in the representation of human life. In the midst of life's fullness, and through the representation of this fullness, the novel gives evidence of the profound *perplexity* of the living. (87; my italics)

The isolation of novelists – their separation from the public nature and the performative character of storytelling – cuts them off from experiencing themselves (and from further transmitting this experience, in turn), thus giving "evidence of the profound perplexity of the living."

Thus, perplexity itself is nothing new; what distinguishes the novelist from the storyteller, however, is that they cannot give counsel or advice, having not been exposed to such counselling themselves. The nature of that counselling, however, would still be closely connected to the "perplexity of the living" (which might be the same as that of the "angel of history"); it would thus have to take into account, and to account for, the perplexity in the face of the contingency that surrounds us. Viewed this way, the oral and reproductive character of the story – in contrast to the novel – allows not only for this perplexity to be expressed in a social context, but also to be modified according to the moment and the context. In this regard, it might be important to point out the following paradox: that, while we have tended to tell the story of human development (at least since the Enlightenment) as ever more successful strategies of overcoming contingency – usually along the lines of myth/monotheism/reason – we are strangely enough describing our contemporary world as ever more contingent. Thus, the contingency of history that Aristotle presupposed seems to be with us still. There might, then, be something wrong with the story we tell ourselves about it; or, to be more precise, the *muthos* we inscribe into in.

What distinguishes both novel and story from information, however, is that, while the latter seems to be – or is at least made to seem this way – completely self-explanatory (or the explanation is provided by experts), the explanation of the story has to be actively created by the listener, in that "the psychological connection of the events is not forced on the reader. It is left up to him to interpret things the way he understands them, and thus the narrative achieves an amplitude that information lacks" (Benjamin 2007: 89).[11]

---

[11] Benjamin claims that the turn to information constitutes a larger threat to storytelling than

As far as any fable or moral of the story is concerned, then, it would automatically also fall prey to multiple and different interpretations. Thus, every listener can potentially carry a different moral message from the encounter with the story; a scenario that many scholars have also emphasized in the case of the anecdote[12] – one, however, that in light of what has been said about the story's wisdom confirms that this wisdom cannot possibly deal in timeless moral universals.

One additional connection between the anecdote and storytelling might be provided by Benjamin's distinction between the "chronicler" and the "historian";[13] and it is here that I would part ways with him, because he defines both the anecdote and historiography in ways that refer to a time before the break that Fineman so convincingly traces; the break that instituted a historiography that follows, if not a divine plan (which Benjamin attributes to the chroniclers) then at least the *muthos* of a telos (or the telos of *muthos*), and a more recent form of the anecdote which, if it ever implied such a divine plan, now emphasizes even more the latter's "inscrutability."[14] However, Benjamin notes that in the storyteller the chronicler is being "preserved in changed form, secularized, as it were" (96), which means that the former cannot assume any divine plan – inscrutable or not – to provide the explanatory frame for the particular instances and incidences that the story tells. This larger, explanatory

---

the novel itself: "it turns out that it [information] confronts storytelling as no less of a stranger than did the novel, but in a more menacing way, and that it also brings about a crisis in the novel" (2007: 88).

12 This quality is further emphasized in a passage in the essay where Benjamin comes closest to dealing with a genuine anecdote. It is the story provided by Herodotus in his *Histories* (c. 440 B.C.), in which he describes the reaction of the Egyptian king Psammenitus who, unmoved by the fate of his kin, reacts strongly to the suffering of an old servant of his. Here Benjamin draws a direct connection between the story's longevity and the fact that it can be interpreted in many different ways (2007: 89–90).

13 As Benjamin writes: "The chronicler is the historyteller. If we think back to the passage from Hebel, which has the tone of a chronicle throughout, it will take no effort to gauge the difference between the writer of history, the historian, and the teller of it, the chronicler. The historian is bound to explain in one way or another the happenings with which he deals; under no circumstances can he content himself with displaying them as models of the course of the world. But this is precisely what the chronicler does, especially in his classical representatives, the chroniclers of the Middle Ages, the precursors of the historians of today. By basing their historical tales on a divine plan of salvation – an inscrutable one – they have from the very start lifted the burden of demonstrable explanation from their own shoulders. Its place is taken by interpretation, which is not concerned with an accurate concatenation of definite events, but with the way these are embedded in the great inscrutable course of the world" (2007: 96).

14 Note how close this comes to the "indecipherable whole" that Gossman refers to.

frame is not needed because, according to Benjamin, the storyteller depends on "short-lived reminiscences," while the novelist relies upon "perpetuating remembrance" (98); a quality that she inherits from the epic.

Thus, the aspect – or rather, various aspects – of time plays a central role for distinguishing between the story and the novel. And it is only in this context that the role of death achieves the strange significance that it has in "The Storyteller." Quoting Georg Lukács's *Theory of the Novel* (1920), Benjamin introduces another categorical difference between the novel and the story:

> "The insight which grasps this unity [in the novel, T.C.] [...] becomes the divinatory-intuitive grasping of the unattained and therefore inexpressible meaning of life."
>
> The "meaning of life" is really the center about which the novel moves. But the quest for it is no more than *the initial expression of perplexity* with which its reader sees himself living this written life. Here "meaning of life" – there "moral of the story": with these slogans novel and story confront each other, and from them the totally different historical coordinates of these art forms may be discerned. (99; my italics)

Again, we encounter the perplexity that actually underlies both the novel and the story. But while the novel tries to achieve unity (according to a long moral philosophical tradition starting with Aristotle and leading via Rousseau and Hegel to Heidegger and Charles Taylor) in line with either a telos or an authentic core, the story defies such unity, and consequently defies an unequivocal answer to the question, "What should I do?" In fact, neither Leskov, nor some of the mythopoetic stories of earlier tribes, assume the authority to do so, as I have tried to show elsewhere.[15] This, in turn, has to be seen in light of the social and reproductive nature of storytelling itself, where the unity of the lived life – which, as Benjamin remarks, can only be assured by, and seen through, death – is replaced by the open-endedness of the story being listened to, and reproduced, without laying claim (in fact, actively denying any claim) to the closure that death implies. This pertains, as Benjamin remarks, not only to the author, but also the reader of the novel:

> [...] the reader of a novel actually does look for human beings from whom he derives the "meaning of life." Therefore he must, no matter what, know in advance that he will share their experience of death; if need be their figurative death – the end of the novel – but preferably their actual one. (101)[16]

---

15 Cf. Claviez (2000).
16 This is in line with Paul Ricoeur's definition of the novel as "apprenticeship of dying" – and his claim that "a fruitful exchange can be established between literature and being-toward-death" (1983: 162).

This constitutes a difference between the storytellers and the novelists, as the former

> [...] have in common the freedom with which they move up and down the rungs of their experience as on a ladder. A ladder extending downward to the interior of the earth and disappearing into the clouds is the image for a collective experience to which even the deepest shock of every individual experience, death, constitutes no impediment or barrier. (102)

If, however, we remind ourselves about what Benjamin writes as regards the "shortlivedness" of the incidents that the story narrates, we have to become aware that it distinguishes itself from both the entire life of a human being (and the alleged unity that the novel tries to impose on it), as well as the larger unity that history – if seen through the lenses of a divine or philosophical dialectic – achieves. The anecdote of Psammenitus, although it might shed light on the "indecipherable whole" that constitutes his life, and may be recorded under the shadows of an ending life, does not stand for this whole. Thus, in a paradoxical manner, the "shortlivedness" of the instances collected in anecdotes ensure the longevity of their relevance that Benjamin notes.

The "different historical coordinates" that Benjamin refers to in the quote above might then actually point back to Aristotle's implicit admission that history, after all, is but a heap of contingent facts that can only violently – that is, through political, philosophical, or poetic authority – be forced into a unified whole. The wisdom that comes with the acknowledgment of such different historical coordinates – which even go so far as to acknowledge that there might be no such coordinates – might be the wisdom that, to use a Heideggerian term, "lets contingency be." This is why Hebel, the anecdote-teller, is a point of reference for Benjamin: "[Hebel] will not for anything take a stand with any principle, but he does not reject it either, for any principle can at some time become the instrument of the righteous man" (106).

If, thus, the storyteller's wisdom turns her into the figure "in which the righteous man encounters himself" (109) – that is, encounters herself as contingent – the wisdom of the anecdotal character of storytelling might lie in the fact that it acknowledges the necessarily contingent character of experience as well as the fact that no closure can ever be provided to heal its effects. The healing effects that many commentators – especially on Native American stories – have alluded to might be ascribed to the fact that a story – more so than the novel and information – admits to the very fact that we can neither entirely control the contingency of our own life stories nor the contingency of that strange thing called history. As Nicolas Chamfort, one of the commentators on the anecdote, put it so succinctly: "Things are miscellanies [...]; men are patchworks. Ethics and physics are concerned with mixtures. Nothing is simple, nothing is pure" (qtd. in Gossman: 146). Nor, for that matter, is the anecdote.

Works Cited

Anzaldúa, Gloria. 1999 [1987]. *Borderlands/La Frontera: The New Mestiza*. 2nd ed. New York: Aunte Lute Books.
Aristotle. 1996 [c. 335 B.C.]. *Poetics*. Trans. Malcolm Heath. London: Penguin.
Benjamin, Walter. 2007 [1936]. "The Storyteller: Reflections on the Works of Nikolai Leskov." In: *Illuminations: Essays and Reflections*. Trans. Harry Zohn. New York: Schocken Books. 83–110.
Claviez, Thomas. 2000. "Narrating Environmental Ethics." In: Thomas Claviez and Maria Moss (eds.). *Mirror Writing: (Re-) Constructions of Native American Identity*. Glienicke: Galda + Wilch. 171–192.
Epstein, Lawrence. 1989. *A Treasury of Jewish Anecdotes*. Northvale: Jason Aronson.
Fineman, Joel. 1989. "The History of the Anecdote: Fiction and Fiction." In: H. Aram Veeser (ed.). *The New Historicism*. New York: Routledge. 49–76.
Gossman, Lionel. 2003. "Anecdote and History." *History and Theory* 42.2: 143–168.
Herodotus. 2003 [c. 440 B.C.]. *The Histories*. Trans. Aubrey de Sélincourt. London: Penguin Classics.
Lukács, Georg. 1971 [1920]. *The Theory of the Novel: A Historico-Philosophical Essay on the Forms of Great Epic Literature*. Trans. Anna Bostock. Cambridge: MIT Press.
Neureuter, Hans Peter. 1973. "Zur Theorie der Anekdote." In: Detlev Lüders (ed.). *Jahrbuch des freien deutschen Hochstifts*. Tübingen: Niemeyer. 458–480.
Ricoeur, Paul. 1983. *Oneself as Another*. Chicago: University of Chicago Press.
Schäfer, Rudolf. 1982. *Die Anekdote: Theorie – Analyse – Didaktik*. München: Oldenbourg.
Simpson, David. 1995. *The Academic Postmodern and the Rule of Literature*. Chicago: University of Chicago Press.
Stefanovska, Malina. 2009. "Exemplary or Singular? The Anecdote in Historical Narrative." *SubStance* 38.1: 16–30.
White, Hayden. 1973. *Metahistory: The Historical Imagination in Nineteenth Century Europe*. Baltimore: Johns Hopkins University Press.
White, Richard. 2017. "Walter Benjamin: 'The Storyteller' and the Possibility of Wisdom." *The Journal of Aesthetic Education* 51.1: 1–14.

Winfried Siemerling
Accumulated Time, the Anecdote, and the Vertical Imagination

Abstract: Exploring the critical relationship that the anecdote can entertain with the *grand récits* of history, this essay relates aspects of the anecdotal to the field of black Atlantic critical memory culture. Anecdotal strategies often support forms of critical witnessing by staging small historical details or fragments that invite further contextualization and narrative completion from potentially disruptive perspectives. The essay analyses three textual examples in order to demonstrate this potentiality of the anecdotal. A poem by black Nova Scotian filmmaker, educator, and author Sylvia Hamilton, a chapter from Bajan Canadian writer Austin Clarke's memoir '*Membering*, and a theoretical reflection by Trinidadian Canadian poet and novelist Dionne Brand serve to illustrate the use of anecdotal registers in the work of these authors. Their evocation of historical fragments, of seemingly mundane details as entrance points for reflection, and of notions of the unpublished and unrevealed, enables them to theorize and practice anecdotal disruptions of hegemonic narratives, offering black diasporic versions of a vertical imagination that reveals the ubiquitous presence of otherwise forgotten aspects of the past.

Keywords: Austin Clarke, Counterhistory, Critical Memory Culture, Dionne Brand, Sylvia Hamilton.

"but the ocean kept turning blank pages / looking for History." (Walcott 1979: 26)

Facets of the anecdotal help to illuminate salient aspects of a critical memory culture that my title associates with the "vertical imagination."[1] By this I mean an imagination that relates to the past as a continued presence, a reality that is not vanishing but accumulating. Past events accrue different meanings over time for this imagination also, however, and time has to be navigated in always new and often complex ways. The anecdotal dimension would appear to offer privileged access to such shifting territory, concentrating as it does on what seems small and inconsequential, and thus less circumscribed by the contextual constraints of larger narratives.

---

[1] I would like to acknowledge the support of an Insight Development Grant by the Social Sciences and Humanities Research Council of Canada (SSHRC) in the preparation of this essay.

https://doi.org/10.1515/9783110668490-013

I will pay particular attention here to the ambivalent relation of the anecdotal to the opposed impulses of disruption and connection (or completion), and examine the relationship between the anecdote and what surrounds it – that is, between the short form of the anecdote and the larger story it somehow seems to evoke or disrupt. I also find related points of interest, however, in the anecdote's relationship with the notion of the "unpublished," the hidden and the secret, and the unknown in the past but also in the future – and thus in its more general rapport with knowledge and time. Finally, the potentially disruptive or destabilizing aspect of the anecdote raises the question of its relation to recognizability from the perspective of the reader or listener.

I will try to put these aspects of the anecdotal in conversation with the vertical imagination of a memory culture that often finds the openings for nonsynchronous, accumulative, and recuperative notions and deployments of time in small quotidian details. My corpus here will come from a few black texts located, in the words of Christine Sharpe, "in the wake" of black Atlantic slavery and its historical consequences.[2]

1 History and Gleaning

Reflecting on the value of anecdote in his account of Louis XIV, Voltaire likened the form to a small field where one comes to "glean" after the large harvest of history has been completed. He nonetheless attributed a certain revelatory power to this form that picks up small things that history seems to have left behind. The philosopher and historian thus claimed that "anecdotes are small details that have been hidden for a long time" ("Les anecdotes [...] sont de petits détails longtemps caches" [Voltaire 1930: 348; my translation]). His formulation allows us to infer more than just careless neglect, since it is history's act of harvesting that has failed to choose, and that has by its different choices eventually hidden what was lying openly in the field. The potentially subversive force of gleaning, not unlike the small-scale tactical interventions Michel de Certeau understands to operate from positions of lesser control,[3] and Voltaire's implicit

---

2 See her volume *In the Wake: On Blackness and Being* (2016).
3 In the "General Introduction" to *The Practice of Everyday Life* (1984), Michel de Certeau offered a distinction between "tactics" and "strategies." While the latter presupposes a certain amount of control over a given field, the former "insinuates itself into the other's place, fragmentarily, without taking it over in its entirety" (xix). In addition, a tactic "depends on time – it is always on the watch for opportunities that must be seized 'on the wing'" (ibid.). An

hermeneutics of suspicion, are corroborated by standard dictionary glosses of the anecdote as "historical detail, small curious fact whose story can illuminate the underside of things" ("particularité historique, petit fait curieux dont le récit peut éclairer le dessous des choses" ["Anecdote" 2010: 94; my translation]).

Voltaire further suggested that the anecdote's name derives from this hiddenness (which the gleaner feasts on). It finds its etymological source in the Greek *anekdota* ("not published" or "not given out") and is rendered in French as "choses inédites" ("Anecdote" 2010: 94). The connection of the anecdote to the *inédit*, which in French refers to the not-edited or unpublished but also to what is unknown or what is entirely new, invites associations of the anecdotal not only with the unrevealed, secrecy, and rumors but in addition with the temporal dimension of the "not-yet" of discovery and publication; that is, with a "procrastination" that makes for the incompletion or as-yet hiddenness of not-yet revealed knowledge, as that which (in Latin) is *pro crastinus* – for tomorrow, the next day, and the future.

In the perspective of critical memory cultures that seek to uncover, collect, and (re)connect meaning in the wake of black Atlantic dispersal and diaspora (which I will turn to in a moment), the power of the anecdote to glean what has not been "published" by history and what is seemingly lost and scattered, can also help to remind us of the relationship and proximity between the collection of small pieces, debris, and fragments, with the spatial and temporal acts of re-membering the body and knowledge of dispersed communities.

2 Disruption and Completion

A certain ambivalence of the anecdotal, which carries within itself elements of disruption but also seems to call for forms of extension or completion, offers evocative connections with diasporic perspectives since the anecdotal seems to orchestrate related counterpoints. On the one hand, it opens up a register of temporality that is distinct from a larger flow of events, a contrapuntal temporality that can be associated with the disrupted historicity caused by diasporic dispersal but also with the disruption of dominant history by which aggrieved communities seek to undo hegemonic teleological narratives. On the other hand, there is a sense that the anecdotal detail, like the recovered shard of diasporic knowledge, needs to be complemented, in turn, by narrative on a larger

---

apposite relationship, it seems to me, can be perceived between the strategic deployment of historical (meta)narratives and the tactical investments of the anecdote.

scale that allows for an appropriate recontextualization of what otherwise appears fragmentary.

In the coauthored volume *Practicing New Historicism* (1997), for instance, Stephen Greenblatt thus emphasized the latter aspect by electing to pay particular attention to the potential completion called forth by the anecdote. As David Simpson put it in a review, Greenblatt evoked "Erich Auerbach's idea of the part as leading to a felt sense of the existential whole" (2001: 25). Greenblatt's coauthor Catherine Gallagher, however, rather associated the anecdote with the more disruptive term "counterhistory"; a term which served her "to name a spectrum of assaults on the *grands récits*" (Gallagher and Greenblatt 2000: 52).

The ambivalent contrast between the disruptive aspect of counterhistory and its implicit drive for new completion turns out to be highly productive, opening new spaces and narrative possibilities that are operative also in the functioning of the anecdote. While the anecdote as a sign of counterhistory disrupts the syntagmatic progress of the *grand récit* with a paradigmatic verticality that throws narrative time into disarray, the fragmentary aspect of the anecdote seems to call for a wider syntagmatic horizontality that can provide context and recognizability in a new larger whole. In addition to this generative duality it seems to share with counterhistory, the anecdotal impulse therefore also reinforces the previously noted association with that which is *pro crastinus*, uncovering a past moment that could help to illuminate a different, hopefully better tomorrow.

3 Witnessing and the Fragment

Ian Baucom's *Specters of the Atlantic* (2005) provides an example of how factors at work in the anecdote can also operate in a critical exploration of modernity. Baucom's investigation locates modernity squarely in the wake of the transatlantic slave trade. It pays particular attention to the fragment, exploring its potential within chains of transmission by way of its anecdotal force of gleaning, of making visible what was hidden. The fragment serves here in processes of witnessing that relate the past to the present and the future, creating in the process an ethically charged new connectivity through a critical temporality that unsettles such temporal distinctions. In this perspective, then, instead of passing, "time accumulates" (Baucom 2005: 24).

The larger context of Baucom's enterprise is constituted by emergent forms of finance capital that, together with the slave trade they underwrite, come to condition newly abstract forms of subjectivity in modernity. In this context, Baucom concentrates on the "counterhistory" (173) found in a few documents submitted by the abolitionist Granville Sharp to the British Lord Commissioners of the Admiralty in 1783. Alerted by Olaudah Equiano, Sharp intervenes after a judgment awarding insurance money to the owners of the slave ship Zong. Two years earlier, its captain and crew had murdered over one hundred and thirty slaves by throwing them overboard, purportedly discarding "cargo" in order to save the ship in a storm. Sharp's request for a murder prosecution will remain unsuccessful; and although during a hearing at which Sharp is present Lord Chief Justice Mansfield orders a new trial of what is exclusively framed as an insurance case, no record of such a trial seems to have survived (Austen 2011: 13). The Zong massacre, however, will come to play a considerable role in the development of British abolitionism.

Baucom understands Sharp's submission "as occupying a hinge between times" (2005: 174), an act of witnessing that recalls events in the year 1781 but ultimately extends its reach to us as readers and witnesses in the present. Drawing on reflections by Jacques Derrida on witnessing and testimony, he cites being present and surviving as meanings associated with witnessing but also insists on a third aspect, that of the "witness who calls into being a body of executers charged with the task of assuming and transmitting the property she has taken in the event as its observer/survivor" (176). In this perspective, the "witness exists for the nonwitness" (176–177); in addition, in Derrida's words, "the judge, the arbiter, or the addressee do have to be *also* witnesses; they do have to be able to testify, in their turn, before their consciences or before others, to what they have attended, to what they have been present at, to what they happened to be in the presence of, the testimony of the witness in the witness box" (qtd. in Baucom 2005: 177). As Baucom points out, the consequence of this perspective is "to serialize the event and its affect and also to elongate its temporality to stretch its time along the line of an unfolding series of moments of bearing witness" (177). In the last instance, it also implicates the reader in a newly created connection and ethically understood "whole" requiring, in turn, a further act of testimony that maintains the reality of what is witnessed as an event in the present.

This is how, in Baucom's perspective, an act of gleaning, the documents submitted by Sharp to the British Lord Commissioners of the Admiralty, can be part of a process with implications in the present, and for us as readers and witnesses within it. Baucom, in an overt allusion to the convolutes of Benjamin's *Arcades Project* (1999), refers to these papers as a "bundle" of documents;[4] in

---

[4] The submission consisted of Sharp's letter of July 2nd, 1783, in which he asked for a murder investigation, accounts of the first trial held on March 6th, 1783, a letter by the underwriters in

addition, he understands them in the light of a Benjaminian fragment, citing a passage in which Benjamin discusses montage in ways that very much resemble the new historicist understandings of the anecdote. Benjamin speaks here of his aim "to assemble large-scale constructions out of the smallest and most precisely cut components. Indeed, to discover in the analysis of the small individual moment the crystal of the total event" (1999: 461). This is in fact how Baucom, quoting Benjamin, reads Grenville Sharp's bundle of papers: as a fragment, "'a precisely cut component' that 'assemble[s] [a] large-scale construction' within itself" (2005: 173–174); and thus as a small but telling detail and *mise en abyme* that illuminates modernity and, as his (not exactly modest) subtitle states, the nexus between "Finance Capital, Slavery, and the Philosophy of History." The fragment of Grenville Sharp's witnessing, however, also calls for an ongoing completion on the part of later recipients and new witnesses.

4 Recognizability and Reading

Baucom's reading thus recognizes Sharp's "bundle" and submission – his call for murder charges in a case reducing humans to dispensable "cargo" for insurance purposes – as a "precisely cut" fragment that can "illuminate the underside of things"; like a tissue sample, it illuminates the degree of abstraction that governs modernity under the conditions of finance capital. Such a re-cognition, the capability and motivation of reading a small historical incident and discovering in this act of gleaning a larger connection to the present and the future, requires a specific situatedness on the part of the observer, and the conjunction of a particular constellation in the present with specific moments in the past: it is the result of a sudden insight that reveals and illuminates a crucial connection.

This issue of its readability in time ties Sharp's bundle (and Baucom's act of gleaning and narrativizing it) to an important aspect of anecdotal knowledge and transmission. As a form of witnessing that constitutes an act of gleaning and relies on a fragment or detail, the anecdote raises the question of its relationship to knowledge and recognizability for both the original gleaner and the subsequent listener or reader who is located in a later frame of understanding. In "Convolute N" of *The Arcades Project*, entitled "On the Theory of Knowledge, Theory of Progress," Benjamin reflects on such issues through the

---

which they voice their protest against the first judgment and ask for an appeal, and a transcription of the hearing before Chief Justice Mansfield and two other judges that resulted in the order for a new trial (Baucom 2005: 335n1).

notion of the dialectical image. Benjamin notes that an "image is that wherein what has been comes together in a flash with the now to form a constellation. In other words, image is dialectics at a standstill" (1999: 462). He also observes that the dialectical image "is an image that emerges suddenly, in a flash. What has been is to be held fast – as an image flashing up in the now of its recognizability" (473). As opposed to archaic images, dialectical images are for Benjamin "genuinely historical" because they are made possible and co-constituted by the moment of reading: "The image that is read – which is to say, the image in the now of its recognizability – bears to the highest degree the imprint of the perilous critical moment on which all reading is founded" (463).

One can thus make the case that anecdotal perception and selection, with ist unexpected attention to a small detail in the past in which some larger significance in the present might be recognized, partakes of the connective energy of a dialectical image. Benjamin's formulation also raises the question, however, whether in this act of connection a previous moment is simply *recognized* as such. Benjamin's condemnation of the "'once upon a time' of classical historiography" suggests otherwise, as does his dictum that "[t]he history that showed things 'as they really were' was the strongest narcotic of the century" (ibid.). Instead of such recognition, dialectical images as understood by Benjamin – and I would argue many forms of the anecdote – produce an act of mutual *re-cognition* that perceives the evoked incident or event from a new angle *and also* redefines the moment of its perception in the present, creating a new constellation.[5] Moments of disruption and recontextualization (or reconfirmation) pertain here to both sides, while the anecdotal image itself creates a new temporal and conceptual space that is not reducible to either.

Such issues of readability and re-cognizability are particularly at stake, I would argue, in forms of a critical memory culture in which time is not perceived as passing but as accumulating; that is, in a perspective in which notions of unfinished business and alternative possibilities and futures takes precedence over ideas of historical resolution and progress. Forms of this perspective are at work in three texts I will now use to concretize these frames of theoretical reference, texts that deploy frames of accumulated time to situate themselves in the wake of the transatlantic slave trade and use anecdotal forms of memory as critical tools for the future.

---

[5] I have developed elsewhere the shorthand double sign of "re/cognition" to signal the differential between simple "recognition" and the more complex act of "re-cognition," that is, the often simultaneous presence and conflict between assimilative incorporation into normative frames of understanding and the emergence of a genuinely new frame of reference (cf. Siemerling 2005).

5 Three Texts "In the Wake"

The first two of the texts I want to turn to for this purpose are by the Nova Scotian filmmaker and poet Sylvia Hamilton and the late Bajan Canadian writer Austin Clarke, who was also one of the early practitioners of black studies in the U.S. and Canada (teaching at Yale 1968–1970 and Duke 1971–1972). Bearing witness to being "in the wake," both of these texts work with small, anecdotal fragments in their recuperative deployments of accumulated time. The third text is Dionne Brand's "An Ars Poetica from the Blue Clerk" (2017), which served as teaser for her *The Blue Clerk: Ars Poetica in 59 Versos* (2018) and outlines a segment of her poetic itinerary, reflecting in particular on the disruptive side of "anecdota" as that which is unpublished.

Sylvia Hamilton's poem "Potato Lady" appears in her 2014 volume *And I Alone Escaped to Tell You*.[6] It consists only of a few lines:

> dusty brown potato
> white eyes protruding
> she turns it in
> her hand, knife poised
> and thinks of Mary Postell
> sold for a bushel of potatoes. (85)

The "dusty brown potato," ordinarily nothing but a humble purveyor of nourishment (and incidentally the subject animating one of Catherine Gallagher's chapters in *Practicing New Historicism*), stares back here at the narrator, who is poised to peel – or potentially take more violent action in line four. In this poem, a quotidian, seemingly insignificant moment evokes the gaze of history and solicits also our reaction as readers.

To contextualize the brief and somewhat enigmatic evocation of a historical personage at the end of the poem, it is helpful to know that the historian Harvey Amani Whitfield calls the 1791 case that followed Mary Postell's abduction and subsequent sale in exchange for potatoes "the most famous, or infamous, re-enslavement case of the Maritimes" (2016: 99–100).[7] It is also discussed by

---

[6] It was first published in a slightly different version in George Elliott Clarke's anthology *Fire on the Water* (1992: 93).

[7] George Elliott Clarke glosses the historical incident in the original publication of Hamilton's poem in his anthology *Fire on the Water* (1992: 93, 97).

Hamilton herself in an article ("Naming Names"), and for instance in Simon Schama's account of the black Loyalists, *Rough Crossings* (2008: 247–249).[8]

With the sudden, fragmentary, and initially enigmatic evocation of black Nova Scotian history, Hamilton demonstrates how the force of memory and the vertical imagination can be called forth by a seemingly insignificant object. In this case, a small daily detail is not only metonymically associated with a specific historical episode but, beyond that, with an entire regime of human relations under the conditions of slavery in Nova Scotia and the British empire in the late eighteenth century. The unintroduced appearance of a single name and incident at the end of the poem, anecdotal as it emerges as a vertical vector in our reading present, may cause a sudden flash of recognition for readers aware of the historical episode; or its recognizability may be minimal at first for other – and perhaps most – readers. In either case, the poem appeals to our response-ability by placing us in a position of witnesses to an act of witnessing.

The poem thus serves indeed "to serialize the event and its affect and also to elongate its temporality" to involve the reader in a "series of moments of bearing witness" (Baucom 2005: 177). The anecdotal evocation of historical incident, in addition, either creates an effective and memorable flash of recognition or asks us to engage further with the poem. And if we therefore complete this fragment, filling in some of the context (as in this discussion), chances are that when we prepare our next meal, peeling a potato perhaps, we may experience a mnemonic charge and moment of recognition strong enough to activate history in the midst of the present and our kitchen. Such a flash of re/cognition can extend its force to a suddenly renewed awareness of the various forms of financial abstraction that Baucom analyzes in an incipient form in the eighteenth century but which to this day reduces human lives in the equations of finance capital and political calculus.

Austin Clarke's memoir *'Membering*, published in 2015 shortly before his death, offers a larger and recursive version of such an extrapolation from a small individual moment by which the vertical imagination often annihilates the distance between past and present in a new configuration that liberates synergetic possibilities. Its apostrophized title, *'Membering*, signals not only a discursive irruption of the vernacular but also the reconstitution of the dispersed and dis(re)membered diasporic body through memory and witnessing.

In a chapter recounting some of his travels, Clarke evokes moments when a certain light on the houses of a number of important water-connected trading

---

[8] For a detailed essay about Postell, see Troxler (2008).

cities – Havana, Venice, Bordeaux, and his own Barbados's Bridgetown – leads him to "membering" the fragments of a counterhistory of empire.[9] Here are, for instance, his *anecdota* – the unpublished underside – of the beautiful canals of Amsterdam:

> But in this canal where we are now, traveling in a boat that looks like a launch [...] this sightseeing takes me back to the Wharf in Bridgetown, in the island; to the Venetian gondoliers; to the ships entering the Malecón in Havana; to the ocean-going, floating apartments [...] along the river (was it a sea?) in Bordeaux. All this history and history of architecture here in the Netherlands is bound up in slavery. "Bound up" is the ironical, intransitive verb. My history touches all of them: buildings in which I was tied up and flogged, but in which my spirits lived on. (2015: 260–261)

Clarke's use of the pronoun "I" functions in a metonymic sense that also nourishes the perspective of Langston Hughes's speaker in "The Negro Speaks of Rivers" (1990: 4), creating an all-encompassing "I" that has witnessed waterways and civilizations from a black perspective, and that has retained, accumulated, and remembered the significance of that presence and experience.

In Clarke's case, however, the small fragment – the short anecdote of how his memory works to glean and reveal the *anekdota* otherwise left in the dark, while his Dutch translator shows him Amsterdam – is characterized by an ambivalence that is narratively productive as it moves in two opposing directions. It is disruptive because it offers another account of modernity, a counterhistory, or an "assault on the *grands récits*," in Gallagher's words, that disturbs a placid scene of sightseeing; it is also an act of "'membering," however, that requires and creates "the felt sense of the existential whole" (in Simpson's comment on Greenblatt). Clarke manages indeed to read, in the narrative break he has created, the perspective of such a re-formed wholeness, claiming in the end his own symbolic co-ownership of the wealth resulting from slavery (2015: 278–9). Clarke thus uses the small anecdotal moment here to disrupt a general perception of Amsterdam's beauty, but also to scaffold a much more extensive act of personal (and by extension communal) "'membering."

This re-cognizing logic of anecdotal disruption and re-completion can be supplemented with another perspective on the relationship between a critical memory culture of the vertical imagination and things that are *an-ekdota*, or not published. I want to finish my discussion with this different vector in a text by Dionne Brand, a writer who tends to read the consequences of slavery as a still powerful "tear in the world" (2001: 4); and thus in a way that puts

---

[9] A more extensive discussion of this chapter appears in Siemerling (2019).

emphasis on the ongoing disruption and incompletion that continues to make itself felt "in the wake."[10] Things "unpublished," in this perspective, can certainly be thought of as the missing links of knowledge that have been disrupted and repressed as a consequence of slavery; they can also appear, however, as a reservoir of meanings that maintain a disruptive potential with regard to hegemonic knowledge, thus harboring signposts for the future. They can have such a potential, in this perspective, precisely *because* they have not been inserted in a type of "published" (publicly known or accepted) discourse that is corrupted or easily corruptible in a regime of possible meanings that are indebted to the powers that be.

Brand sets the scene of "An *Ars Poetica* from the Blue Clerk" (2017) on a wharf where a ship is expected, evoking a recurrent image familiar from other writers of the black Atlantic (such as Austin Clarke, Christina Sharpe, or Paul Gilroy in *The Black Atlantic* [1993]). In this case, however, the vessel is expected to carry away not the bodies of the enslaved but a stowage of words and writing. The blue clerk, in an "inky garment" (Brand 2017: 58), constantly monitoring the bales of paper on the wharf, is "finding the horizon, seeking the transfiguration of the ship" (ibid.). Brand's text is very much interested in the transformative power of words; it also raises the question, however, of which ones will be published.

Brand stages an editorial drama between two aspects of writing that she associates with the left and the right page. The blue clerk is responsible for the "cubic meters of senses, perceptions, and resistant facts" of the "left-handed pages," as we learn in a section entitled "Verso 1.1." Brand glosses "Verso" as "[a] left-hand page of an open book; the reverse of something; the underside of a leaf" (77n2). The blue clerk is thus in charge of pages that are unpublished and unrevealed: "no one need be aware of these, no one is likely to understand, some of these are quite dangerous and some of them are too delicate and beautiful for the present world" (58). The blue clerk, it turns out, works in the service of the author, who "record[s] the right-hand page" and chooses "the presentable things, the beautiful things" (59), transforming some of the left-page *anecdota* into the right-hand page that is ready for publication and the audience.[11]

---

10 In *A Map to the Door of No Return* (2001), Brand emphasizes such an unsettled state of black subjectivities, for instance in a section entitled "Ruttier for the Marooned in the Diaspora," referring to the "[m]arooned, tenantless, deserted. [...] All unavailable to themselves [...]" (213).
11 In a 2018 interview with Winston Smith, Brand has also commented on her figure of the blue clerk as the one who collects the "surplus," "detritus," and what is "too much for the author" – and thus also for the published page and the audience. The blue clerk, Brand has further commented, is "trying to work herself into a new language."

This editorial drama, then, is overdetermined by a politics of reading. More specifically, Brand seeks to connect reading processes and habits in particular with issues related to genre – or to understand genre as facilitating, encouraging, or enabling certain kinds of reading. As her title suggests, this endeavor results in an apology for poetry. Her text, in fact, accuses the reader of narrative to exercise a policing power that tends to repress what she refers to as the diacritical capacities of poetry.[12] Brand perceives these capacities as a critical potential that can help to overwrite what Christina Sharpe has called the "dysgraphia" caused by the black Atlantic slave trade (2017: 59). Brand pithily posits: "If we think about the reading practices that attend those two shapes, Poetry and Narrative, I suggest that the reader interrogates Narrative but Poetry interrogates the reader. [...] Poetry requires a deciphering of meaning whereas narrative enjoins, hails the known world" (ibid.). In addition, and more specifically, Brand claims that

> [c]haracter in narrative [...] and landscape [...] are weighted with whiteness as a fundamental/originary category. The Black body in narrative is always spectacular, always spectacularized, marked. The dysgraphia, of dominant and of dominating narratives, unwrites, and makes incoherent, Black presence as presence. (60)

Brand therefore heralds not forms of knowing but forms of "unkowning" (62); and a kind of "being who might be unavailable to the rules of character" and refuses the efforts to renovate narratives of coloniality and imperialism. Importantly, this being owes nothing to "spectatorship" (63) or the interrogative gaze of the reader (64).[13]

Brand suggests that the reader of prose especially seems to expect and then request a coherence that is recognizable in a given regime of meaning,[14] and that this reader is thus all too ready to fill in bits and pieces that are in sync with the status quo and a degraded present. Such a tendency that "hails the known world" – a tendency that can make itself felt as a limiting force in the act of

---

12 Brand explains: "Much in the way that diacritical marks supplement certain alphabets changing the sound, tone, or meaning of certain words, Poetry, in my formulation, changes what I see as the racist alphabets of narratives – the prevalent modes of speech and key impediments to Black being" (2017: 59).
13 With reference to a section from her earlier *Map to the Door of No Return* entitled "Ruttier for the Marooned in the Diaspora," Brand observes: "The citizen of the Ruttier is inattentive to the gaze of the reader" (2017: 64).
14 While for Brand prose may be located "on the continuum between what is written and what is withheld [...] perhaps, somewhere in the middle," poetry would perhaps reveal only half of that (2017: 73).

writing itself – seems inimical to the reservoir and potential that is offered by the left-hand page, the unpublished or the *an-ekdota*.[15]

Brand reports having considered "silence as the radical project" (2017: 61) in this context and references other registers of syntagmatic de-sedimentation (such as certain varieties of jazz). She also cites here her 2010 collection of poetry *Ossuaries*, however, which tends towards the enigmatic, fragmentary, and unresolved. Racial characteristics, for instance, are mostly withheld in this text,[16] in which an enigmatic character pursues an underground existence. In addition – as if to emphasize the refusal of making connections available to the reader – one poem (which she cites in "An *Ars Poetica* from the Blue Clerk") announces the cancellation of verbs:

> After consideration you will discover, as I,
> That verbs are a tragedy, a bleeding cliffside, explosions,
> I'm better off without [...]. (2010: 14; qtd. in 2017: 65)

After these lines the poem continues indeed for four pages without any verbs. Instead, it offers an inventory of qualities and perceptions in the life of the speaker. Using catalogues, juxtaposition, and montage, the poem produces an ongoing anecdotal incompletion that leaves it up to the reader to try to compose a narrative, but refuses to do so itself.

Such techniques – the withholding of verbs and certain kinds of specificity – are important registers of non-configuration and fragmentation in this text. Brand thus often withdraws narrative comfort and disappoints readerly expectations, challenges the mandate of immediate recognizability, and forces the audience into uncertain positionalities. While this is not the place for a discussion of Brand's varied writing strategies elsewhere, her pursuit of "passports to unknowing everything" (2017: 62) here can be said to partake of a fugitive poetics (instantiated in *Ossuaries* also by the fugitive movement of a character), or what Fred Moten has called a "fugitive movement in and out of the frame" (2008: 179). In Brand's poem, such a poetics pushes towards the suspension of recognition in favor of a de-sedimentation that paradoxically seeks to render – or maybe

---

15 These concerns are evidently related to issues raised by a number of reader-response theorists. From a psychoanalytic perspective, for instance, Norman Holland has educed an "identity theme" (1980: 127) and a particular style of "coping" through which readers deal with literary texts similar to how they deal with life experience, using characteristic patterns of defense; Wolfgang Iser, to name but one other theorist, has drawn attention to the virtuality of literary works as "halfway" between the text and its realization by the reader (1980: 50).
16 See Toni Morrison's essay "The Color Fetish" in her *The Origin of Others* (2017) for a discussion of related strategies in her own work.

better, simulate – *an-ekdota,* the unpublished and perhaps unpublishable things of the left-hand page, which refuse insertion into a compromised discourse and which thus defer narrative fullness *pro crastinus,* for another day and another future.

This avoidance of spectactularity, of attempting to renovate "narratives of coloniality and imperialism" (63), and of owing "something to the reader" (2017: 73), configures here an anecdotal impulse that differs from the one we have encountered in Clarke's memoir and from the more elliptical one in Hamilton's poem. Brand's attention to the "transfiguration of the ship," and thus to the available means of conveyance, emphasizes in particular the continued investigation of the effects of hegemonic language and perspective on black diasporic thought and expression, an investigation undertaken by so many other black and diasporic thinkers before her.[17] In the case of all three texts, however, an anecdotal dimension functions as a placeholder and translational gateway of a vertical imagination that is in conversation with the historical and present dimensions of the black Atlantic. This gateway remains nonetheless full of uncertainties in the space between disruptive fragment and narrative completion, and thus hardly appears to fulfill the promise of precision that Benjamin seemed to espy in the relation between fragment and "large-scale construction" (1999: 461).

The anecdotal dimension, and Brand's problematic or poetic of "what is said and what is withheld" (2018), are thus also part of a complicated ethics of representation that raises difficult questions with regard to slavery and its historical consequences. With reference to the extensive corpus of black Canadian writing, for instance, one can think here of the contrast between a text like Marlene NourbeSe Philip's poem *Zong!* (2008; a response to the same events that preoccupy Baucom) – which presents the reader mostly with sentence fragments and sparse words on the page – and the narrative exuberance and fullness of Lawrence Hill's *The Book of Negroes* (2007), which complements the fragments of a 1783 ledger into what seems closer to an "existential whole."[18] Such a contrast raises further questions with regard to the different strategies pursued by the writers I have discussed in dealing with the "unpublished" and unrevealed "underside of things"; it also underlines, however, the usefulness of investigating the disruptive and connective aspects of the anecdote and of its relation to accumulated time, the fragment, and recognizability for

---

17 W.E.B. Du Bois's notion of double consciousness, Frantz Fanon's concerns in *Black Skin, White Masks* (1967), or Stuart Hall's reflection on these concerns in "Cultural Identity and Diaspora" (1990) are a few of the examples that come to mind.

18 See Siemerling (2015: 170–185, 232–239).

the study of the vertical imagination of the black Atlantic. By implication, and as a corollary, the study of what I have called the "vertical imagination" and its operation in the specific context of the black Atlantic may thus also contribute to the examination – and perhaps expansion – of the spectrum of possible meanings that the field of the "anecdotal" might be productively thought to include.

Works Cited

"Anecdote." 2010. *Le Nouveau Petit Robert: Dictionnaire de la Langue Française*. 94.
Austen, Veronica. 2011. "*Zong!*'s 'Should We?': Questioning the Ethical Representation of Trauma." *English Studies in Canada* 37.3–4: 61–81.
Baucom, Ian. 2005. *Specters of the Atlantic: Finance Capital, Slavery, and the Philosophy of History*. Durham: Duke University Press.
Benjamin, Walter. 1999. *The Arcades Project*. Trans. Howard Eiland and Kevin McLaughlin. Cambridge: Harvard University Press.
Brand, Dionne. 2018. Interview by Winston Smith, Guelph Jazz Festival. University of Guelph.
Brand, Dionne. 2017. "An *Ars Poetica* from the Blue Clerk." *The Black Scholar* 47.1: 58–77.
Brand, Dionne. 2010. *Ossuaries*. Toronto: McClelland & Stewart.
Brand, Dionne. 2001. *A Map to the Door of No Return: Notes to Belonging*. Toronto: Doubleday Canada.
Clarke, Austin. 2015. *'Membering*. Toronto: Dundurn.
Clarke, George Elliott. 1992. *Fire on the Water: An Anthology of Black Nova Scotian Writing*. Vol. 2. Lawrencetown Beach: Pottersfield Press.
de Certeau, Michel. 1988 [1984]. *The Practice of Everyday Life*. Trans. Steven Rendall. Berkeley: University of California Press.
Derrida, Jacques. 2000. "'A Self-Unsealing Poetic Text': Poetics and the Politics of Witnessing." Trans. Rachel Bowlby. In: Michael P. Clark (ed.). *Revenge of the Aesthetic: The Place of Literature in Theory Today*. Berkeley: University of California Press. 180–207.
Du Bois, W. E. B. 1986 [1903]. *The Souls of Black Folk*. In: Nathan Irwin Huggins (ed.). *Writings*. New York: Library of America. 357–548.
Fanon, Frantz. 1967 [1952]. *Black Skin, White Masks*. Trans. Charles Lam Markmann. New York: Grove.
Gallagher, Catherine and Stephen Greenblatt. 2000. *Practicing New Historicism*. Chicago: University of Chicago Press.
Gilroy, Paul. 1993. *The Black Atlantic: Modernity and Double Consciousness*. London: Verso.
Hall, Stuart. 1990. "Cultural Identity and Diaspora." In: Jonathan Rutherford (ed.). *Identity: Community, Culture, Difference*. London: Lawrence & Wisehart. 222–237.
Hamilton, Sylvia. 2014. *And I Alone Escaped to Tell You*. Kentville: Gaspereau Press.
Hamilton, Sylvia. 1994. "Naming Names, Naming Ourselves: A Survey of Early Black Women in Nova Scotia." In: Peggy Bristow (ed.). *"We're Rooted Here and They Can't Pull Us Up": Essays in Canadian Women's History*. Toronto: University of Toronto Press. 13–40.

Hamilton, Sylvia. 1992. "Potato Lady." In: George Elliott Clarke (ed.). *Fire on the Water: An Anthology of Black Nova Scotian Writing*. Vol. 2. Lawrencetown Beach: Pottersfield Press. 93.

Hill, Lawrence. 2007. *The Book of Negroes*. Toronto: HarperCollins.

Holland, Norman N. 1980. "Unity Identity Text Self." In: Jane P. Tompkins (ed.). *Reader-Response Criticism: From Formalism to Post-Structuralism*. Baltimore: Johns Hopkins University Press. 118–133.

Hughes, Langston. 1990. "The Negro Speaks of Rivers." In: *Selected Poems of Langston Hughes*. New York: Vintage Classics.

Iser, Wolfgang. 1980. "The Reading Process: A Phenomenological Approach." In: Jane P. Tompkins (ed.). *Reader-Response Criticism: From Formalism to Post-Structuralism*. Baltimore: Johns Hopkins University Press. 50–69.

Morrison, Toni. 2017. *The Origin of Others*. Cambridge: Harvard University Press. 41–53.

Moten, Fred. 2008. "The Case of Blackness." *Criticism* 50.2: 177–218.

Philip, Marlene NourbeSe. 2008. *Zong!: As Told to the Author by Setaey Adamu Boateng*. Toronto: Mercury Press.

Schama, Simon. 2008 [2005]. *Rough Crossings: Britain, the Slaves, and the American Revolution*. Toronto: Penguin.

Sharpe, Christina. 2016. *In the Wake: On Blackness and Being*. Durham: Duke University Press.

Siemerling, Winfried. 2019. "Austin Clarke: 'Membering Home and the Black Atlantic." *Revista Canaria de Estudios Ingleses* 77 (January): 75–81.

Siemerling, Winfried. 2015. *The Black Atlantic Reconsidered: Black Canadian Writing, Cultural History, and the Presence of the Past*. Montreal: McGill-Queen's University Press.

Siemerling, Winfried. 2005. *The New North American Studies: Culture, Writing, and the Politics of Re/Cognition*. New York: Routledge.

Simpson, David. 2001. "Touches of the Real." *London Review of Books* 23.10 (May 24th): 25–26.

Troxler, Carole Watterson. 2008. "Re-Enslavement of Black Loyalists: Mary Postell in South Carolina, East Florida, and Nova Scotia." *Acadiensis* 37.2: 70–85.

Voltaire. 1930 [1751]. *Le Siècle de Louis XIV*. Préface et notes par René Gros. Paris: Classiques Garnier.

Walcott, Derek. 1979. *The Star-Apple Kingdom*. New York: Farrar, Straus and Giroux

Whitfield, Harvey Amani. 2016. *North to Bondage: Loyalist Slavery in the Maritimes*. Vancouver: University of British Columbia Press.

RUMOR

Fig. 1. Unidentified Artist. *Unidentified Woman (Formerly Edward Hyde, Lord Viscount Cornbury).* Early 18th century. Oil on canvas, 124.8 x 98.7 cm. New-York Historical Society, New York. © New-York Historical Society.

Ralph J. Poole
The Fun of Deep Gossip: Lord Cornbury as Queen in Drag

Abstract: In 1990, the New-York Historical Society decided to end an enigma that had caused (art) historians to ponder the origins of a portrait depicting a lady in a blue dress and a beard shadow. The portrait for the longest time was believed to represent Viscount Cornbury, royal governor of New York and New Jersey in the early 1700s, who was rumored to have appeared in public in lady's clothes to better represent his cousin, Queen Anne. This essay explores the anecdote of the cross-dressing Cornbury, tracing three hundred years of debate about evidence of such improper behavior. Known as "worst British governor," Cornbury asserted his despotic rule in many ways, one of which may well have been his use of cross-dressing to distress his most fervid political opponents. While some critics claim that the factual evidence of his cross-dressing was but an effort of his enemies to slander his reputation, others take this habit as mark of eccentricity associated with aristocratic self-fashioning. The continuous debate about whether Cornbury appeared and acted as representative of the queen in drag is proof to the lasting power of deep gossip. After all, *what if* Cornbury, royal governor in colonial America, really was a *drag queen?*

Keywords: Colonial America, Cross-dressing, Deep Gossip, Drag, Lord Cornbury.

> "an act of revanchist revisionist history, inspired by a portrait of His Lordship in drag, which hangs in the New York Historical Society" (Hoffman 1979: xxxviii)
>
> "*funny emotions* should be genuinely valued, and *deep gossip* genuinely shared" (Abelove 2003: xviii)

1 The Anecdote

The anecdote I chose for my essay leads us back to the first decade of eighteenth-century colonial America. The focal point of the anecdote is a painting of a woman in a blue dress, exhibited in the hallway of the New-York Historical Society (fig. 1). The description informs us that this is an "Oil on canvas" portrait of an "Unidentified woman, ca. 1700–1725" by an "Unidentified artist." However, only a few years ago, the painting was exhibited with this caption: "Portrait, said to be of Edward Hyde, Viscount Cornbury." Who was this Edward

https://doi.org/10.1515/9783110668490-014

Hyde, formerly thought to be posing in women's clothes? And what happened that the portrait is now believed to be of a properly dressed, if plain-looking woman instead of an improperly cross-dressing viscount? My first entryway into the anecdote of the cross-dressing Viscount Cornbury is through a history of scandals in American politics, which includes Cornbury as one of its first major players. I will then discuss the evidence of Cornbury's cross-dressing, as well as the efforts to invalidate both the historical evidence and the claim that the portrait depicts Cornbury. Finally, arguing in favor of the possibility of Cornbury as early American cross-dresser, I step into the traces of deep gossip that leads me to the contemporary celebration of this historical personage as *drag queen*.

2 The Legend

Edward Hyde (1661–1723) was the Third Earl of Clarendon and most notably the cousin of Queen Anne. He was better known by his father's secondary title Lord Cornbury, and after having served in the Royal Regiment of Dragoons and being elected as a Tory MP for Wiltshire, his family's home, he became one of the first commanders to desert his uncle King James II in 1688. As a reward for his desertion, which arguably helped trigger the Glorious Revolution, he was appointed governor-in-chief of New York and New Jersey in 1701, a position he held until 1708. He is generally acknowledged as "being the worst governor ever appointed to the colony" (Ripley and Dana 1874: 360).[1] After his return and until his death in 1723, he continued his career of being in Queen Anne's favor, even being made Privy Councillor and Envoy Extraordinary to Hanover.[2]

In 1848, the British historian Thomas Macaulay in his *History of England* described Cornbury in his early career stage prior to his American post as "a young man of slender abilities, loose principles, and violent temper" (Macaulay 2008: Chapter 9). Since "[h]e had been early taught to consider his relationship to the Princess Anne as the groundwork of his fortunes, and had been exhorted to pay her assiduous court" (ibid.), Cornbury became easy prey for being manipulated and exploited. Macaulay therefore found it "extraordinary that [...] the army on which every thing depended should have been left, even for a moment, under command of a young colonel who had neither abilities

---

1 This verdict can be followed through history, up to the present; see, e.g., Leonard (1910: 161); Horne (1916: 152); Greene (1931: 427); Cunningham (1976: 53); Van Tuyl and Groenendijk (1996: 128); Englund-Krieger (2015: 17).
2 For Cornbury's life, see Cody (1982); "Edward Hyde, Earl of Clarendon" (2003).

nor experience" (ibid.). Similarly disavowing Cornbury's aptness of leadership, William Russell, who was professor of elocution at the Brooklyn Female Academy, included a chapter on Cornbury in his *Harper's New-York Class Book* of 1847. He calls Cornbury an unfortunate choice as governor, because "he was needy and avaricious," merely keen on securing "his personal and pecuniary interests" (1847: 133). About the latest stage of his governorship, Russell writes:

> The illegal and oppressive conduct of the governor [...] and his habitual misapplications of the public funds, together with his inveterate spirit of enmity, on religious grounds, towards the Dutch and New-England population, at last reached such a height as to attract the royal notice [...] and he was dismissed from office, with expressions of indignation, on the part of the queen. (135)

First divested of his office, then thrown into prison, he was only released due to his father's death, "which put him in possession of the earldom of Clarendon" (ibid.).

Both the British historian and the American educator stress Cornbury's professional and personal flaws. They do not, however, mention his legendary cross-dressing, which nevertheless caused a debate early on and still triggers fascination today. Already in 1914, an American historian from Princeton, Charles Worthen Spencer, writing for the New York State Historical Association, critically assesses what he calls "The Cornbury Legend." He writes: "The vehemence with which these hostile opinions are expressed might easily prompt the stirrings of doubt. Was he so black as he is painted? [...] May not a legend of exceeding villainy have been built upon a comparatively limited foundation of actual guilt?" (1914: 309). Looking into the claims against Cornbury for being a spendthrift, and into his mismanagement of ecclesiastical and factional-political rifts, Spencer concludes that Cornbury's "utter failure" (319) is substantiated by an abundance of facts. As for the alleged cross-dressing, Spencer finds the charge "fully sustained," listing testimonies by "powerful figures in the province" (310). Writing in 1935, American church historian William Wilson Manross calls Cornbury "a degenerate and pervert, who is said to have spent half of his time dressed in women's clothes, [and who] was one of the most despicable of the colonial governors" (117). In 1976, *American Heritage* published a story about Cornbury entitled "His Most Detestable High Mightiness," denouncing him as "a fog and a wastrel," who "had some peculiar fetishes" such as dressing as a woman and then delighting in "lurking behind trees to pounce, shrieking with laughter, on his victims" (De Kay 1976). Even the recent 2010 book by British writer Tony Grumley-Grennan, which collects *Eccentrics, Fraudster, Cheats and Other Disparate Characters* in English history, includes Cornbury – once more reprinting the legendary portrait – right at the beginning of his first chapter,

"Lords & Ladies," and calls his colonial governance the "worst" in American colonial history. But referring to his assumed cross-dressing, Grumley-Grennan in contrast to other accounts such as Spencer's concedes that "I have been unable to discover any contemporary evidence of such behaviour and it is possible his enemies, both in America and England, did their best to blacken his name" (2010: 13).[3]

3 The Scandal

Most, though not all, accounts on the atrociousness of Cornbury's governorship culminate in his infamous habit of cross-dressing. Politically, his financial mismanagement and – being a staunch High Church Anglican – his determination to secure the Church of England as the state religion in the colonies had dire consequences, leading to his arrest for outstanding debts and his eventual recall to England. It is, however, his public appearance in women's clothes that seems to outshine his overall scandalous personage. Reportedly, he opened the New York Assembly in women's clothes and upon complaints as to the impropriety of such an appearance, he is said to have answered that as Queen Anne's relative and representative, he should emulate her as literarily as possible: "You are very stupid not to see the propriety of it. In this place and particularly in this occasion I represent a woman (Queen Anne) and ought in all respects to represent her as faithfully as I can." This widely circulating quote was most prominently told as an anecdote by Horace Walpole in a conservation with his friends George James Williams and Sylvester Douglas, Lord Glenbervie, in 1796. The latter recorded the incidence in his diary, adding that Walpole's anecdote reminded Williams that his father

> told him that he has done business with him [Cornbury] in woman's clothes. He used to sit at the open window so dressed, to the great amusement of the neighbours. He employed always the most fashionable milliner, shoemaker, staymaker, etc. Mr. Williams has seen a picture of him at Sir Herbert Packington's in Worcestershire, in a gown, stays, tucker, long ruffles, cap, etc. (Glenbervie 1928: 76–77)

While all "three gentlemen were well-known gossips" (Bonomi 1998: 15), the portrait mentioned by Williams indeed refers to the one exhibited at the New-York Historical Society. In fact, this is the very first traceable occasion of Cornbury

---

[3] For more accounts, including pedagogical websites, with special focus on Cornbury's cross-dressing, see Pierce (1965); Benson (2012); Troy (2015); Paulino.

being associated with the painting (12). Walpole's anecdote and Douglas's diary entry along with other such accounts are used as *evidence* for Cornbury's cross-dressing scandal. Explicitly referring to the reproduction of said portrait, Shelley Ross picks Cornbury as the inaugural example for her study of what she calls America's *Fall from Grace: Sex, Scandal, and Corruption in American Politics from 1702 to the Present* (1988).[4] Ross argues that Cornbury was the main actor in one of the most notorious and bizarre tales about colonial American leadership. Cornbury's legacy certainly encompasses all three attributes – sex, scandal, and corruption – that Ross highlights for her historical samples. While first being welcomed as colonial governor by the local aristocrats, he was later spurned by them and the larger public for being "a thief, a bigot, a grafter, a drunk, and strange as it was, a transvestite" (Ross 1988: 3). Allegedly, the "combination of public and private wrongdoings was so outrageous that Lord Cornbury fanned the fires of revolution and later served as an inspiration for the articles of impeachment in the United States Constitution" (ibid.). These quotes from the very first page of Ross's book – as well as the earlier ones mentioned in Douglas's diary – point to two crucial issues when dealing with Cornbury: the myth-making surrounding this *monstrous* politician, and the strangeness of his transvestism.

4 The Evidence

Besides the often-mentioned Walpole anecdote, amongst other alleged proofs documenting Cornbury's clothing style, there is, interestingly enough, a theater play. This closet drama and "crude theatrical polemic" (Davis 2015: xix) is considered by many to be the first play written and printed in America.[5] The play, *Androboros: A Biographical Farce*, features the character Lord Oinabaros. *Oinabaros* (Greek for "wine drinker") is based on Cornbury and is the only character in the play who does not appear on stage but is only spoken of (149). The play was written in 1714 (or 1715 as Davis suggests, given some historical incidences in the play [55–56]) by Governor Robert Hunter, one of the successors of Cornbury as colonial governor of New York, reigning from 1710 to 1719. Of this character it is said he is "a Devotee to Long Robes of Both Genders."[6] This

---

[4] Ross discusses political scandals up to the one concerning Bush and Dukakis during the 1988 presidential campaign.
[5] See Bordman (1992: 29); Shaffer (2008: 458).
[6] The quote is taken from Lawrence Leder's edition of Hunter's play (1964: 174). Commenting on the character of Lord Oinabaros aka Edward Hyde, Leder writes: "Hunter despised him for his

seems to be "the first, and so far as is known the only, contemporary *printed* reference to Cornbury's alleged cross dressing" (Bonomi 1998: 238n51; my italics).

Further indications are several letters written by contemporaries of Cornbury between 1707 and 1709, all of them by political opponents and all of them referring to Cornbury's public appearances in women's clothes. Robert Livingston, Lewis Morris, and Elias Neau wrote a total of four letters to England recounting amongst other complaints that Cornbury cross-dressed in the Assembly on a daily basis, and especially also on Sunday, i.e. on sacrament or holy days. Livingston, a member of the New York Assembly, sent a letter to William Lowndes, Secretary to the Treasury under Queen Anne, in June, 1707: "Tis said he [i.e. Cornbury] is wholly addicted to his pleasure ... his dressing himself in womens Cloths common[ly every] morning is so unaccountable that if hundreds of Spectators did not dayly see him it would be incredible" (qtd. in Leder 1961: 202). The second letter-writer Morris, a member of both the New Jersey Provincial Council and the New Jersey General Assembly, wrote to Robert Harley, the Secretary of State under Queen Anne, on February 8th, 1708, about Cornbury, "of whom I must say something which perhaps no boddy will think worth their while to tell, and that is, his dressing publicly in woman's cloaths every day, and putting a stop to all publique business while he is pleaseing himselfe with [that] peculiar but detestable magot" (qtd. in Brodhead 1855: 38). In an earlier letter, probably from late 1707 and also addressed to Harley, Morris wrote of Cornbury that:

> the Scandal of his life is [...] he rarely fails of being drest in Womens Cloaths every day and almost half his time is spent that way and seldom misses it on a Sacrament day was in that Garb when his dead Lady was carried out of the fort and this not privately but in face of the Sun and sight of the Town; But I'll not enter into his privacies, his public vices are scandalous enough. (qtd. in Hills 1876: 81)

And Neau, a French Huguenot turned Anglican catechist, wrote on February 27th, 1709, to Harley:

> My Lord Cornbury has and does still make use of an unfortunate Custom of dressing himself in womens Clothes and of exposing himself in that Garb upon the Ramparts to the view of the public; in that dress he draws a world of spectators about him and consequently as many censures especially for exposing himself in such a manner all the great Holidays and even in an hour or two after going to the Communion. (qtd. in Hills 1876: 87)

---

venality, and his evaluation of Cornbury in the play follows the generally accepted interpretation of this official who publicly paraded on the ramparts of the fort in New York dressed in women's clothes and who was known for running up exorbitant liquor bills" (1964: 160).

Besides these letters by presumable eyewitnesses, there remains another letter, written June 16th, 1714, by the German diplomat Baron von Bothmer to Hanover. It denigrated Cornbury "as a selfish and presumptuous fool, and a fool to such a degree, that being appointed governor by the Queen [...], he thought that it was necessary for him, in order to represent her Majesty, to dress himself as a woman, which he actually did" (qtd. in Macpherson 1775: 626). As can be seen from these references, the Cornbury anecdote surfaced at the time of his governance or shortly after, with ostensibly sufficient people actually having witnessed the occurrence or being acquainted with people who had. The question is whether we can believe these accounts and accountants, or whether we need to doubt their verity and credibility. But then, of course, there is the portrait.

5 The Portrait

Today on its website, the New-York Historical Society gives a lengthy explanation about "this rather curious portrait of a woman" that had long been identified as Edward Hyde. Referring to the rumors of his cross-dressing, it mentions that "[r]ecent scholarship has [...] removed some of the blemishes added to Cornbury's gubernatorial abilities by nineteenth century detractors" ("Portrait of an Unidentified Woman"), and although the sitter's identity remains a mystery, the portrait is now officially believed to be of a female. The scholarship mentioned refers to Patricia Bonomi, professor emerita of history at New York University, who since 1990, in several instances such as her article "Lord Cornbury Redressed" (1994) and finally in a book-length study *The Lord Cornbury Scandal* (1998), claims to have put a stop to any further discussion. Some of the anecdotal evidence that Bonomi ascertains as falsified is that Cornbury's name was attached to the portrait as late as 1867 (1998: 17), and that the portrait was then exhibited at London's South Kensington Museum with a label affixed to the frame which refers to Cornbury's wearing women's clothes as "truly" representing the queen:

> Among other apish tricks, Lord Cornbury half-witted son of Henry Earl of Clarendon, is said to have held his state levees at New York, and received the principal Colonists dressed up in complete female court costume, because, truly, he represented the person of a female Sovereign, his cousin German queen Anne.

The same note is still attached to the painting displayed at the New-York Historical Society today, who bought the painting at an auction in 1952. The quote is attributed to British historian Agnes Strickland's *Lives of the Queens of England* (1840–1848), who in turn relies for the rumor about the cross-dressing Cornbury on Horace Walpole's rendering of the anecdote.[7]

Before its display in London in 1867, which made the news through a report in the *New-York Daily Tribune*, no one in America knew of this painting; no American artist of the early eighteenth century was skilled enough for such a painting; an English artist would have chosen an engraving or drawing for a caricature of Cornbury; and Cornbury himself sitting for the portrait seems unlikely and would have been known, Bonomi concludes her list of disavowals (1998: 18–19). She supports her revision with various art consultants such as Robin Gibson of the National Portrait Gallery in London, who "feel[s] certain that the so-called portrait of Lord Cornbury is a perfectly straightforward British provincial portrait of a rather plain woman c. 1710" (qtd. in 1998: 19). Bonomi's basic claim is that if there had been a cross-dressing governor, this fact would have caused a much greater stir, and that all the existing allegations – way too few – were solely made to slander Cornbury's reputation and lacked any solid evidence.

6 Deep Gossip

Not all experts and historians agree wholeheartedly though. Senior curator at the New-York Historical Society, Annette Blaugrund, for instance, refers to the beard shadow on the portrait and concedes that "a lot of these paintings have both women and men seemingly with five o'clock shadows. That's a matter of painting technique, the undercoats coming through" (qtd. in Armstrong 1990).

---

7 Strickland's comment on Cornbury actually reads as follows: "Henry, earl of Clarendon, the queen's elder uncle, was, as previously shown, a self-banished exile from her presence, and his half-witted son, lord Cornbury, whose merits in being the proto-deserter from her father required some gratitude, was sent to play his imbecile pranks as the *governor* of the invaluable colonies James II. had founded in North America. Among other apish tricks, lord Cornbury is said to have held his state levees at New York, and received the principal colonists dressed up in complete female court costume, because, truly, he represented the person of a female sovereign, his cousin-german, queen Anne! It is said, and with great probability, that the follies of this ruler laid the foundation of that system of evil colonial government which deprived Great Britain finally of one of the brightest gems in her crown" (1848: 132; original italics). In a footnote to the anecdote, Strickland refers to "Horace Walpole, who hates the Hyde family with as much rancour, if possible, as he did that of Stuart, gives two or three editions of this strange anecdote" (ibid.). Bonomi falsely claims that Strickland's "only one specific source" (1998: 17) was Bothmer's letter of 1714.

And yet she continues that in this case and although "there were some pretty hefty women in their day, [i]t's pretty clearly a man ... He has a man's facial features: a bigger nose, more jowly" (ibid.).[8] And what are we to make of yet another portrait, exhibited at the Dallas Museum of Art, tagged as "Portrait of a Lady, Possibly Edward Hyde, Lord Cornbury in a Dress. Artist Unknown. c. 1705–1750" ("Portrait of a Lady")? There have been other detested colonial governors, but none was represented in quite the same manner as Cornbury. On the other hand, we do have later eighteenth-century examples of self-declared cross-dressers, such as Chevalier d'Éon as portrayed by Thomas Stewart in 1792 ("The Chevalier d'Eon").

While many historians laud Bonomi for her reappraisal and indeed vindication of Cornbury, Alan Taylor, in an essay suggestively entitled "Devil in a Blue Dress" and written in response to Bonomi's book, not only derides Bonomi for "depriving us of a wonderful scandal" (2005: 121), but charges her of advancing "a scholarly trend known as the 'new imperial history' [...] by taking more seriously, and treating more sympathetically, the administrators of the colonial empire" (125). Taylor situates Bonomi's argument within a historiographical discourse of colonial partisanship that for long has chosen to favor the Whig side over the Tories. The Whig tradition in both American and English history-writing

> tells a liberal story of progress from the bad old days of aristocratic privilege and monarchical power onward and upward toward enlightenment, egalitarianism, and democracy. This progressive story offers a moral polarity that divides historical figures into visionary heroes who advanced the democratic future, and reactionary villains who retarded it. (ibid.)

In vindicating Cornbury, a staunch Tory, Bonomi according to Taylor inverts this Whig account of colonial America to reinvent Cornbury as "one of the best of a good breed" (126). As part of her exoneration, she might have demonstrated that there is no hard evidence of Cornbury's cross-dressing, but she also cannot prove that he did *not* publicly don women's clothes. Contrary to Bonomi's intentions, this continues to offer a conspicuous arena for speculation, imagination, and gossip.

---

8 Another scholar arguing against Bonomi's claim is British historian Richard Davenport-Hines, who asserts that Cornbury "was undeniably a man who felt false when he dressed and behaved as men were expected to do" (qtd. in Pace 1990). Commenting on the dispute between Bonomi and Davenport-Hines, Philip Gwyn Jones, who is editor at Collins Publishers, where Davenport-Hines's book was put out, says: "It seems a very English exchange. It's funny to see an American coming to the defense of such a distant and rather peculiar historical figure – with such dispatch and in the grand British manner" (qtd. in ibid.).

Although so far I have been following the factual traces of, and critical debates about Cornbury's cross-dressing, I am ultimately not interested in assessing its validity like Bonomi has done. My interest arose from the productivity of the anecdote, from the cultural work that has been invested in keeping the legend alive and thriving. After all, Bonomi's conclusion renders the portrait itself rather insignificant and uninteresting. To believe that the painting merely depicts some ordinary, unknown woman robs it of its surplus mystery. Trying to decode its veiled meanings is no longer of any relevance and all that remains is a historical anecdote of misidentifying a painting. It tells us something about mishaps in exhibition practices of a historical celebrity, but nothing about the actual portrayed person. And yet, and against (some) evidence to the contrary, the portrait for me retains the lure of the possible, the *what if* that I hope to evoke in my anecdotal chronicle.

In thus wishing to take pleasure in the possibility of this portrait being Cornbury after all, I am following the logic of deep gossip that Henry Abelove draws from "curator[s] of funny emotions," who have a "common ear for our deep gossip" (2003: xi). Abelove takes his notion of "deep gossip" from Allen Ginsberg's elegy on Frank O'Hara, titled "City Midnight Junk Strains," in which Ginsberg describes O'Hara as such a "curator of funny emotions" (1968: 189). From Latin, *cura*, these curators "care for those who at times cannot even identify, but who more often cannot give voice to, their funny emotions for fear of reprisal in the corporate sphere or public square," explains Robert Dykstra (2009: 581), since attending to these funny emotions that defy conventions is to watch out for how such feelings find alternate outlets, for example via underground networks. In this O'Hara's common ear would be "a democratic ear, an unpretentious ear, a generous and empathic ear attuned to those marginalized by funny emotions" (ibid.). Besides the danger of overlooking and neglecting the rich potential that such funny emotions may bring forth, lending an ear to gossipy accounts might also alter our traditional understanding of archives. Expanding on Abelove's theorizing of deep gossip as "illicit speculation, information, knowledge [that] is deep whenever it circulates in subterranean ways and touches on matters hard to grasp and of crucial concern" (2003: xii), Pamela VanHaitsma makes a strong point for implementing deep gossip as a speculative methodology for queer historiographic practice. Treating gossip as illicit evidence gives scholars the chance to "treat speculation about the past, much like more traditional archival materials, as grounds on which to develop narratives about non-normative sexual, romantic, and/or erotic practices – while simultaneously underscoring the impossibilities and uncertainties inherent in attempts to know the 'truth' of sexuality, identity, and history" (2016: 139). Similarly, Gavin Butt urges to engage in the perhaps risky, but ultimately rewarding move to regard gossip as deviant evidence for tracing a crucial mode of communication in the dissemination of queer meanings:

> By adding in gossip to the category of evidence, by allowing it to supplement the "hard facts" of history, I offer a rethinking of the evidential which deconstructs the bases of authoritative constructs of truth. This I do by allowing the *dangerously* supplemental nature of gossip to displace so-called verifiable truths from their more positivistic frames of reference and to render them instead, like gossip's narratives, as projections of interpretive desire and curiosity. In this way I bring the sometimes racy narratives of gossip's "hard core" into play with the realm of "hard" facts in a bid to pay heed to (homo)sexuality's disruptive effects on evidential discourse. (2005: 7; original italics)

Deep gossip's potential for disrupting normative scholarship by listening to illicit resources and following covert traces in turn lead to a queerly illicit narrative which "might operate *as* history" (2005: 9; original italics). The historian lending an ear to deep gossip becomes the gossiper, partaking in the risky act of gossiping. While this "bad" behavior might not be in accordance with the "straight" rules of scholarship, it is indispensable to unearth stories that are believed to be non-existent or have been devalued in order not to be told. And it takes a suggestive openness, to return to Abelove's theory, to prevent closing down on opportunities when it comes to the question of belonging: "who are the 'we' that make up the antecedent of 'our' – the 'we' to whom the deep gossip belongs?" asks Abelove suggesting that "[n]o 'we' is defined or specified here. [...] So the antecedent of 'our' is left suggestively indefinite, unfixed, open" (2003: xii). Taking his cue from Ginsberg's terms of description for O'Hara, Abelove calls to follow in hearing "the intimation of an intellectual vocation" (ibid.). He is convinced "that *funny emotions* should be genuinely valued, and *deep gossip* genuinely shared" (xviii; original italics). Thus, while funny emotions can lean towards the evocation of pleasure as well as mockery, the gossiper's common ear is willing to listen "to all those high or low, extraordinary or ordinary, within one's own circle and kind, or outside of both, who experience and express funny emotions and with them make lives" (xii). Ultimately, such a curator who shares deep gossip to foster funny emotions is valuable in their intellectual vocation. By delving into deep gossip, the curator is providing illicit speculation as "an indispensable resource for those who are in any sense of measure disempowered" (ibid.). The deepness of gossip touches on matters of "crucial concern" (ibid.) oftentimes denounced, many of which deal with the history of sexuality – especially queer sexuality in relation to culture and politics.

While Cornbury in many ways was empowered and thus in charge of his own history in the making, I take the illicit speculations about Cornbury's own funny emotions to be such deep gossip, produced within and outside his own circles and finding its ways through channels of high and low culture to our present times. And I attest to contributing to the curating of such funny emotions, thus taking pleasure in leaning my own queerly inclined ear to such deep gossip.

7 Cross-Dress for Success

One such curator investing in deep gossip is Marjorie Garber who in her seminal study on cross-dressing, *Vested Interest* (1993), includes Cornbury in her chapter on transvestism and the power elite. Not convinced by Bonomi's conclusion but rather sensing that "nothing is proven" (1993: 53), she claims that cross-dressing may well be at "the very heart of public, institutional, and mainstream structures" as opposed to just a "marginalized and privatized expression of gender" (52).[9] In this sense, Cornbury's cross-dressing would be part of a technique of dressing for success, parading his elitist status as a marker of distinction.

This argument relates to other historical accounts that portray the early eighteenth century as a period where festivities such as masquerades boomed among the English aristocrats. Many of the masqueraders enjoyed dressing in clothes of the opposite sex for the occasion. While moral reform societies, concerned with the promiscuous disorder of English life, called for stricter rules of appropriate masculine and feminine behavior, the masquerades became even more frequent and lavish. As contemporaries observe, the by-then-proscribed erotic behavior including cross-dressing was even more celebrated at such festivities and became more inclusive as increasingly public events. Terry Castle calls this period an English "culture of travesty [that found] expression in a persistent popular urge toward disguise and metamorphosis" (1987: 156–157). The heightened sense of gender blurring that Castle depicts also included an overlap of sartorial extravagance such as cross-dressing with notions of sexual licentiousness such as sodomy (170).

While in England cross-dressing at masquerades gave participants the opportunity to cross boundaries of both gender and class, the situation in the

---

[9] Interestingly, similar to Ross's history of political scandals, Garber brings speculations about Cornbury's cross-dressing as possible slander of a politician's reputation to present times: "The portrayal of a man in a dress has, in fact, been a time-honored way of attempting to demean him in Western culture from Hercules (forced by the Lydian Queen Omphale to wear women's clothes and to spin) to Michael Dukakis. In today's largely homophobic mainstream America, to picture a heterosexual politician in full-scale drag is to accuse him of 'unmanliness,' and it often carries a tacit message of closet homosexuality" (1993: 53).

colonies was very different due to the stronghold of Protestant and especially Puritan and Quaker moral strictures regulating social life. Cornbury's extravagant aristocratic life-style, even without his claim of cross-dressing to *properly* represent his cousin Queen Anne, must have been seen as an affront by the local non-aristocrats. Even more so if we believe in his cross-dressing habits. Returning to the portrait possibly showing Cornbury, Garber plays with the idea of an actual commission by Cornbury: "If the Cornbury portrait is authentic, it represents the sitter's desire to be portrayed in this fashion" (1993: 53). Accordingly, Cornbury's self-assertion as cross-dresser refers to a culture in which such behavior could signify empowerment, regardless of whether contemporary critics would use this behavior to slander his reputation, to accuse him of unmanliness, and even to disgrace him as a sodomite.

8 Drag Queen Cornbury

And Cornbury as sodomite is just what contemporary gay subculture wants him to have been. My last example to enrich the unresolvable, yet highly productive Cornbury anecdote, is a play by William Hoffman and Anthony Holland of 1976, still being performed today: *Cornbury: The Queen's Governor*.[10] In my understanding, it follows a "perversely presentist model of historical analysis" (Halberstam 1998: 52). Through this model, Judith Halberstam acknowledges the need of contemporary theory to shed light on a historical case *and* be cautious not to project contemporary understandings onto such historical incidents. Halberstam suggests this perversely presentist model as a way to avoid "the trap of simply projecting contemporary understanding back in time, [...] one that can apply insights from the present to conundrums of the past" (52–53). Similarly, Hoffman and Holland, referring to the nation's early history, claim to have written their play "in reaction of the meaningless pieties of the Bicentennial celebrations. It was an act of revanchist revisionist history, inspired by a portrait of His Lordship in drag, which hangs in the New-York Historical Society" (Hoffman 1979: xxxviii). They deliberately want their comedy to be understood as "a conscious act of gay mythmaking. The authors do not know for certain if their transvestite hero was gay [...]. But they decided to make him definitely gay" (ibid.) Are they making up history *ad lib*? My claim is that they rely on further deep gossip and establish hitherto unclaimed connections, instead.

---

10 The Hudson Guild Theater staged Hoffman's and Holland's play in 2008 and 2009, and New York's Fraunces Tavern Museum performed a stage reading on February 18th, 2018.

In their play, they deflect the sole focus on Cornbury and shift it to encompass Queen Anne, who is part of any Cornbury discussion but never in actual close proximity. The playwrights conjure up anecdotes about Queen Anne's habit of forming passionate relationships with women and also voice suspicions of the close friendship between King William of Orange and Cornbury as being more than just a friendship. They rely on rumors of William's documented interest in beautiful young men, rumors already circulating during his lifetime and resurfacing through various channels and events to the present day.[11] From the start, the play repeatedly references the connection between the three, relating, for example, to Cornbury and Anne playing as children, to Cornbury pursuing a well-endowed footman, and to William wanting to "bugger" Cornbury instead of Johann Wilhelm Bentinck, the Duke of Portland, who actually was one of William's favorite male beauties:

> EDWARD [*Puts on jewels and arranges his wig and details of his gown.*]: We have all been vomited on this continent. [...] I was hurled across an angry ocean by my cousin royal, Anne, the Queen. As children we played together at Windsor [...]. Once while we were whispering together we saw one of the footmen playing with his big thing, his breeches down. Lady Frances laughed when Anne told her; I, silly boy, followed him around that palace until ... [*Mock embarrassment*] [...] Who would have thought there would be so many queens among us? Ah, me, Mary had William to guide her, lead her. She accepted his favorites, and even smiled when she stumbled on us romping together at the Old Palace. The Duke of Portland was furious because William wanted to bugger me and not him. Such a scene. And who should walk in but Mary, with some idea of founding a college. (Hoffman and Holland 1995)[12]

Of course, given the scheme to *make Cornbury gay*, indications of Cornbury in drag are prominently highlighted throughout the play. Drawing on the well-documented hearsay, Hoffman and Holland include quotes that resemble the ones by Livingston, Morris, and Neau mentioned above:

> PASTOR: – do hereby request of Her Royal Highness that the Governor be removed from office, the reasons being the following:

---

11 The playwrights state that "Queen Anne *did* form passionate relationships with women. King William, of William and Mary, *was* gay. Any good history book will let one know this, but not always with convenient labels" (Hoffman 1979: xxxviii; original italics). See Peter Ackroyd's *History of England* (2016), where he quotes a verse that was circulating during William's childless reign insinuating that he preferred sodomy: "Let's pray for the good of our State and his soul / That he's put his Roger in the right Hole" (4). See also Lacey (2008); Reid-Smith (2017).

12 Hoffman's and Holland's play is included in the *Gay Plays* anthology (1979), but I am quoting from the revised manuscript of 1995, kindly provided by William Hoffman.

That Edward Hyde, Lord Cornbury, has demeaned his office by the disgusting and unnatural practice of dressing in women's attire at public functions, not to mention even more ungodly behavior in private, his explanation being that since he represents the person of a female sovereign he must dress like one. (7)

Turning Cornbury gay is a willful act on behalf of the playwrights who insist, beyond gossip, that "gays have existed in America from its inception and the knowledge of them has been suppressed" (Hoffman 1979: xxxix). In view of today's politics, it is noteworthy that in the introduction to the revised 1995 version of the play, Hoffman draws a parallel between the uncertain path New York was taking at the time of Cornbury's rule and the political climate of the 1990s, which was characterized by a "rising reaction among people who feel themselves ruled by liberalism unconstrained" (Hoffman and Holland 1995). The play is about the "conflict of the baroque English court with Calvinist New York sobriety," and into the somber setting of "Dutch Colonial" style Cornbury enters as an "extravagant figure [who] represents a different sort of world, one of testing limits, of expansive emotions and desires, of embracing all kinds of people, no matter how unorthodox or 'different'" (ibid.). This is a different approach to Bonomi's. Her cleansing of Cornbury's spoiled reputation implicitly propagates a *new British imperial history* that "was, of necessity, more inclusive, cosmopolitan, and tolerant of ethnic, racial, and religious diversity than was the provincialism of white colonists" (Taylor 2005: 126). In contrast, Hoffman and Holland follow a different agenda when showing Cornbury as he surrounds himself with people of diverse ethnic backgrounds and sexual leanings. The two playwrights envision an "early template for an inclusive America" (Isherwood 2009), but one that is replete with outrageously politically incorrect jokes and characters in a deliberately anachronistic and spectacular plot and setting. Hence, while some historians in their revisionism try to clear Cornbury of false slander, morphing him into a rather bland politician, queerly inclined critics and artists – those "curators of funny emotions" – move beyond such constraints and attempt a revision of history through sharing their common ear for deep gossip. So, what if there could have been a drag queen such as Cornbury in early America? Isn't it fun to humor such illicit queer speculations?

Works Cited

Abelove, Henry. 2003. *Deep Gossip*. Minneapolis: University of Minnesota Press.
Ackroyd, Peter. 2016. *The History of England*. Vol. 6: *Revolution*. London: Macmillan.

Armstrong, Kiley. 1990. "Historical Society Ponders Man in Dress." *Associated Press News*, May 31; no pg. <www.apnews.com/43c9cc33a5f3adcc93191cfb70caa77e> [accessed October 28, 2018].

Benson, Eric. 2012. "English King Appoints Drag Queen." *New York Magazine News & Politics*, April 2; no pg. <nymag.com/news/features/scandals/edward-hyde-2012-4/> [accessed October 31, 2018].

Bonomi, Patricia U. 1998. *The Lord Cornbury Scandal: The Politics of Reputation in British America*. Chapel Hill: University of North Carolina Press.

Bonomi, Patricia U. 1994. "Lord Cornbury Redressed: The Governor and the Problem Portrait." *The William and Mary Quarterly* 51.1: 106–118.

Bordman, Gerald Martin. 1992. *The Oxford Companion to American Theatre*. Oxford: Oxford University Press.

Brodhead, John Romeyn. 1855. *Documents Relative to the Colonial History of the State of New York*. Vol. 5. Ed. E. B. O'Callaghan. Albany: Weed, Parsons and Co.

Butt, Gavin. 2005. *Queer Disclosures in the New York Art World, 1948–1963*. Durham: Duke University Press.

Castle, Terry. 1987. "The Culture of Travesty: Sexuality and Masquerade in Eighteenth-Century England." In: G. S. Rousseau and Roy Porter (eds.). *Sexual Underworlds of the Enlightenment*. Manchester: Manchester University Press. 156–180.

Cody, Edward J. 1982. "Edward Hyde, Viscount Cornbury." In: Paul A. Stellhorn and Michael J. Birkner (eds.). *The Governors of New Jersey 1664–1974: Biographical Essays*. Trenton: New Jersey Historical Commission. 36–38.

Cunningham, John T. 1976. *New Jersey, America's Main Road*. Garden City: Doubleday.

Davis, Peter A. 2015. *From Androboros to the First Amendment: A History of America's First Play*. Iowa City: University of Iowa Press.

De Kay, Ormonde, Jr. 1976. "His Most Detestable High Mightiness." *American Heritage* 27.3. <www.americanheritage.com/content/his-most-detestable-high-mightiness> [accessed October 28, 2018].

Dykstra, Robert C. 2009. "Subversive Friendship." *Pastoral Psychology* 55: 579–601.

"Edward Hyde, Earl of Clarendon (1661–1724)." *David Nash Ford's Royal Berkshire History*, 2003; no pg. <www.berkshirehistory.com/bios/ehyde_3eofc.html> [accessed October 24, 2018].

"Edward Hyde, Lord Cornbury (1661–1723)." outhistory.org, not dated; no pg. <www.outhistory.org/exhibits/show/the-age-of-sodomitical-sin/1700s/edward-hyde-lord-cornbury-1661> [accessed October 31, 2018].

Englund-Krieger, Mark J. 2015. *The Presbyterian Mission Enterprise: From Heathen to Partner*. Eugene: Wipf and Stock.

Garber, Marjorie. 1993. *Vested Interests: Cross-Dressing & Cultural Anxiety*. New York: Harper Perennial.

Ginsberg, Allen. 1968. "City Midnight Junk Strains." *The Paris Review* 42: 189.

Glenbervie, Sylvester Douglas. 1928. *The Diaries of Sylvester Douglas (Lord Glenbervie)*. Vol. 1. Ed. Francis Bickley. London: Constable & Co Ltd.

Greene, Nelson. 1931. *History of the Valley of the Hudson, 1609–1930*. Vol. 1. Chicago: S. J. Clarke Publishing Company.

Grumley-Grennan, Tony. 2010. *Tales of English Eccentrics, Fraudsters, Cheats and Other Disparate Characters*. Raleigh: Lulu.

Halberstam, Judith. 1998. *Female Masculinity*. Durham: Duke University Press.
Hills, George Morgan. 1876. *History of the Church in Burlington, New Jersey*. Trenton: William S. Sharp.
Hoffman, William M. 1979. "Introduction." In: William M. Hoffman (ed.). *Gay Plays: The First Collection*. New York: Avon. vii–xxxix.
Hoffman, William M. and Anthony Holland. 1995. *Cornbury: The Queen's Governor. A Comedy in Two Acts*. Manuscript.
Horne, Charles Francis. 2009 [1916]. *History of the State of New York*. Boston: D.C. Heath & Co.
Isherwood, Charles. 2009. "The Man Who Would Be Queen." *The New York Times*, January 30; no pg. <www.nytimes.com/2009/01/30/theater/reviews/30corn.html> [accessed November 1, 2018].
Lacey, Brian. 2008. "Billy's Boys, or an Orangeman's Dilemma." *History Ireland* 16.5: 18–19.
Leder, Lawrence H. 1964. "Robert Hunter's *Androboros*." *Bulletin of the New York Public Library* 68.3: 153–190.
Leder, Lawrence H. 1961. *Robert Livingston and the Politics of Colonial New York, 1654–1728*. Chapel Hill: The University of North Carolina Press.
Leonard, John William. 1910. *History of the City of New York, 1609–1909*. New York: Journal of Commerce & Commercial Bulletin.
Macaulay, Thomas Babington. 2008. *The History of England From the Accession of James II*. Vol. 2, not dated; no pg. <www.gutenberg.org/files/2439/2439-h/2439-h.htm> [accessed October 24, 2018].
Macpherson, James (ed.). 1775. *Original Papers: Containing the Secret History of Great Britain, from the Restoration, to the Accession of the House of Hannover*. London: W. Strahan and T. Cadell. Ann Arbor: University of Michigan Library, 2007.
Manross, William Wilson. 1935. *A History of the American Episcopal Church*. New York: Morehouse.
Pace, Eric. 1990. "A Tempest in a Portrait: Was That Lady a Lord?" *The New York Times*, May 30; no pg. <www.nytimes.com/1990/05/30/nyregion/a-tempest-in-a-portrait-was-that-lady-a-lord.html> [accessed October 28, 2018].
Paulino, Rubby Valentin. "The Lord Cornbury Scandal." *Quest: Queer UnitEd States Research Hub*, not dated; no pg. <sites.google.com/site/ushistorythroughglbteyes/research-help/our-research/the-lord-cornbury-scandal> [accessed October 31, 2018].
Pierce, Arthur D. 1965. "A Governor in Skirts." *Proceedings of the New Jersey Historical Society* 83: 1–9.
"Portrait of a Lady, Possibly Edward Hyde, Lord Cornbury in a Dress." *Dallas Museum of Art*, not dated; no pg. <collections.dma.org/artwork/4278319> [accessed October 28, 2018].
"Portrait of an Unidentified Woman." *New-York Historical Society*, not dated; no pg. <www.nyhistory.org/exhibit/portrait-unidentified-woman-2> [accessed October 28, 2018].
Reid-Smith, Tris. 2017. "The Secret History of the Gay Kings and Queens of England." *Gaystarnews*, 14 January; no pg. <www.gaystarnews.com/article/secret-history-gay-kings-queens-england/#gs.bfxa5vo> [accessed October 31, 2018].
Ripley, George and Charles A. Dana (eds.). 1874. *The American Cyclopaedia: A Popular Dictionary of General Knowledge*. Vol. 5. New York: D. Appleton and Co.
Ross, Shelley. 1988. *Fall from Grace: Sex, Scandal, and Corruption in American Politics from 1702 to the Present*. New York: Ballantine.

Russell, William. 1847. "Reading Lesson LX: Lord Cornbury." In: William Russell (ed.). *Harper's New-York Class Book. A Reading-Book for Schools*. New York: Harper & Brother. 133–135.

Shaffer, Jason. 2008. "Early American Drama." In: Kevin J. Hayes (ed.). *The Oxford Handbook of Early American Literature*. Oxford: Oxford University Press. 453–476.

Spencer, Charles Worthen. 1914. "The Cornbury Legend." *Proceedings of the New York State Historical Association* 13: 309–320.

Strickland, Agnes. 1848. *Lives of the Queens of England, from the Norman Conquest*. Vol. 12. London: Henry Colburn.

Taylor, Alan. 2005. "Devil in a Blue Dress." In: Alan Taylor (ed.). *Writing Early American History*. Philadelphia: University of Pennsylvania Press. 120–127.

"The Chevalier d'Eon." *National Portrait Gallery London*, not dated; no pg. <www.npg.org.uk/research/new-research-on-the-collection/the-chevalier-deon.php> [accessed October 28, 2018].

Troy, Michael. 2015. "The First Transgender Governor of New York." *Unlearned History*, not dated; no pg. <unlearnedhistory.blogspot.com/2015/10/the-first-transgender-governor-of-new.html> [accessed October 31, 2018].

VanHaitsma, Pamela. 2016. "Gossip as Rhetorical Methodology for Queer and Feminist Historiography." *Rhetoric Review* 35.2: 135–147.

Van Tuyl, Rory L. and Jan N. A. Groenendijk. 1996. *A Van Tuyl Chronicle: 650 Years in the History of a Dutch-American Family*. Decorah: Amundsen.

Hendrik Birus
An Anecdote Peddler from the Age of Goethe
Translated by Michael Thomas Taylor

Abstract: Among all of those whose conversations with Goethe entered into print – including Johann Peter Eckermann, Chancellor von Müller, Friedrich Wilhelm Riemer, Johannes Daniel Falk, and others – Karl August Böttiger had by far the worst reputation in Jena on account of his malicious gossip about Goethe's private life, the "Weimar period of genius," and the philosophy of German idealism. Yet Böttiger did not despise Goethe; he only meant to protest against what Blumenberg later called the "self-idealization of the Weimar world" (1999: 147). Far more than Eckermann's canonical collection of conversations with Goethe, it was Böttiger's indecent anecdotes that became the tacit starting point and model for positivist collections of Goethe's conversations and confidential letters, which remain indispensable tools of Goethe research to this day.

Keywords: Collections of Conversations, Goethe, Gossip, Secret Histories, Karl August Böttiger.

> An *anecdote:* the book printer *Schmieder* in Carlsruhe stopped the reprint of Oberon when he heard that the lawful publisher Hofmann had died, leaving behind a widow and children. Ex Büttneri ore, qui tum forte Caroliruhae degebat. (Böttiger 1998: 193; original italics)[1]

1

The leading German dictionary of Goethe's time, Johann Christoph Adelung's *Grammatisch-kritisches Wörterbuch der Hochdeutschen Mundart* (Grammatical-critical dictionary of the High German dialect [1793]), contains the following definition of the term "Anekdote": "a secret, unknown circumstance; likewise, a small, unimportant circumstance of private life. Hence the anecdote hunter, or anecdote catcher, who is always on the lookout, in an indecent or exaggerated

---

[1] Unless otherwise indicated, all translations are by Michael Thomas Taylor.

https://doi.org/10.1515/9783110668490-015

way, for such secret and small circumstances" (1970: 284). Joachim Heinrich Campe's *Wörterbuch zur Erklärung und Verdeutschung der unserer Sprache aufgedrungenen fremden Ausdrücke* (Dictionary to explain and germanize the foreign phrases that have been imposed upon our language [1813]) furthermore explains: "The word is apt; but only for those cases concerning derogatory, vicious anecdotes that belong to malicious gossip about a person (to their *histoire scandaleuse*)" (110). If one leafs through the brief text "Der Anekdotenkrämer: Eine ausgewählte Sammlung neuer, ächtkomischer Anekdoten, witziger und geistreicher Einfälle, überraschender Wortspiele und frappanter Characterzüge" (The anecdote peddler: a selected collection of new, truly comic anecdotes, funny and witty ideas, surprising puns, and striking character traits [1806]) expecting to be entertained, disappointment is bound to result. For the short texts collected here are mostly droll stories, jokes, or aphorisms rather than a "concise, pointed story about a real person" (Schlaffer 1997: 87). And even where such texts can be found – for example about French poets and philosophers like Rabelais, Marivaux, Pelisson, and Helvetius – they are mostly unspeakably dull. The following two anecdotes are among the most pointed:

> Moliere.
> "I've heard you have a personal physician," Ludwig XIV once said to Moliere. "How satisfied are you with him?" "Sire," Moliere answered, "we chat for a while, he prescribes me medicines, I do not take them – and I am soon healthy again." ([Anon] 1806: 13)

And –

> Voltaire.
> Voltaire once sinned against a certain nobleman by telling a joke. Once in the evening, as Voltaire was going home, the nobleman encountered him and gave him a thorough beating. Voltaire complained about this to the Duke of Orleans, who was the regent at the time, asking the duke to give him justice in the matter. It has already happened, the duke replied with a smile. (17)

But in Goethe's posthumously compiled *Maxims and Reflections* (1906), too[2] – in contrast to Nicolas Chamfort's *Maximes et pensées, caractères et anecdotes* (Maxims and thoughts, characters and anecdotes [1795]) and related witty sketches by representatives of the French aristocratic and literary society from the *ancien*

---

[2] These are systematically arranged in Harald Fricke's edition (the Frankfurt edition) like mikado sticks; see Goethe (1993). Cited hereafter with the abbreviation *FA* ("Frankfurter Ausgabe") followed by section, volume, and page number.

*régime*³ – the anecdotal plays only a minor role. This broadly significant absence of the anecdotal also applies to most of the publications of conversations with Goethe that began to appear immediately after his death.

Yet Goethe himself notes, in an aphorism from the collection *Eigenes und Angeeignetes* (On what is one's own and what is appropriated [1821]): "For the man of the world a collection of anecdotes and maxims is of the greatest value, if he knows how to intersperse the one in his conversation at fitting moments, and remember the other when a case arises for their application" (*FA:* 23; English: Goethe 1906: 93). Indeed, in a work as early as the *Unterhaltungen deutscher Ausgewanderten* (1795; published in English as *Conversations of German Refugees* [1989]), Goethe has the Abbé say:

> I have neither the strength nor the courage to review the history of the world at large, and isolated historical episodes confuse me. But of the many personal histories, true and false, that circulate in public or are whispered about in private, some have a greater, more genuine charm than mere novelty; some amuse us by an ingenious twist; some reveal for a moment the innermost secrets of human nature; and others delight us by their bizarre absurdities. Countless stories attract our attention and our malice in ordinary life, and are as ordinary as the people who tell or live them. Of these I have collected the ones that I felt had some special quality that touched and intrigued my judgement, or my heart, and whose recollection gave me a moment of sincere, calm pleasure.⁴ (*FA* I 9: 1013; English: 1989: 26–27)

It is therefore not surprising that Goethe ends his first two books of *Dichtung und Wahrheit* (Truth and poetry) with a characteristic anecdote (*FA* I 14: 15–52; 91–92)⁵ – or indeed, that anecdotes generally play an important role in his autobiographical writings.

Given the way Goethe prepared his legacy – with his autobiographical writings (beginning in 1812), the *Vollständige Ausgabe letzter Hand* of his works (a complete edition of his writings authorized by Goethe [1827–1842]), and the publication of the correspondence with Schiller (1828/1829) and Carl Friedrich Zelter (1833) – he must have been aware of and supported Johann Peter Eckermann's plans (which had already existed since the spring of 1825) to publish his *Gespräche mit Goethe* (Conversations with Goethe [1836]),⁶ despite not wishing for the

---

3 See Schlaffer (1997: 88–89).
4 On this point, see also Schäfer (1982: 58–61).
5 See Wellbery (2019).
6 See the entries in Goethe's diary: "[February 15th, 1824:] Drove out for a walk with Eckermann. Shared a meal with him. Returned with the first years of a chronicle and a written version of an earlier conversation" (1987 III 9: 179). "[May 24th, 1825:] Read through and checked Eckermann's

work to be printed before his correspondence with Schiller.[7] The conclusion of Eckermann's summary of Goethe's last days shows how little he intended for the reproduction of these conversations to end up as anecdotes. "Goethe was silent. But I cherished his great and good words in my heart" (*FA* II 12: 750; English: Goethe 1901: 386). This, not coincidentally, sounds like the conclusion of the New Testament account of Christ's birth: "But Mary treasured all these words and pondered them in her heart" (Luke 2.19).[8] After more than a century of disregard, Hans Blumenberg finally thanked Eckermann with the astounding praise:

> Access to Goethe is opened most readily by a work whose uniqueness was first recognized and articulated, with his propensity for provocation, by Nietzsche: namely, Eckermann's "Conversations." Nietzsche's predilection was also not independent of the finding that, in this text, the parts of the master and the reporter overlap, that admiration was due not only to the heights of the genius but also to the unique upsurge of mediocrity producing this flawless achievement of composition and, at times, well-polished mimesis. (1999: 221–222)[9]

In contrast to Eckermann, Chancellor von Müller's *Unterhaltungen mit Goethe* (Conversations with Goethe [dating back to 1812 and edited in 1835]), present their interlocutor "[June 6th, 1824:] in a shirt, with no jacket"(Kanzler 1959: 105) and give us "deep insight into the everyday life of the aged Goethe."[10] One need only recall the sketch from October 2nd, 1823:

> The heavier his tongue became, the more wittily and humorously his ideas pushed their way forth, too. [...] Then he hit upon Byron, offered praise for his Cain and, above all, for the deathblow scene. "Byron alone I consider my equal. Walter Scott is nothing compared to him."
> "In five centuries, the Persians recognized only seven poets, and among those rejected were several scoundrels better than me." When he noticed that Ulrike had become sleepy, he joked that his Persian literary history was wasted on her and the rest of the young people, and chased them all away with comic fervor. (76)

---

conversations" (III 10: 59); and "[June 5th, 1825:] Lunch Dr. Eckermann. About the conversations edited by him" (III 10: 64).
7 See Christoph Michel's commentary on Eckermann's *Gespräche mit Goethe in den letzten Jahren seines Lebens* (Eckermann 1999: 931–932).
8 Quoted from the New Standard Revised Version. See the comments by Heinz Schlaffer in Eckermann's *Gespräche mit Goethe in den letzten Jahren seines Lebens* (1986n19: 701–702) and by Christoph Michel (*FA* II 12: 917).
9 In the aphorism "The Treasure of German Prose" Nietzsche refers to Eckermann's *Unterhaltungen mit Goethe* as "the best German book in existence" (1913: 250).
10 This is Ernst Grumach's commentary (Kanzler 1959: 191).

No wonder that such "clattering cynicisms"[11] were not received well when delivered at a private reading for the Weimar court in the spring of 1836, or that the Grand Duchess Maria Paulowna was so ungracious that these *Unterhaltungen mit Goethe* could not be published until 1870, more than twenty years after Chancellor von Müller's death – although it must be noted that even such lively scenes as the one quoted above had only rarely been fashioned into a pointed anecdotal form.

This applies all the more to the third contemporaneous collection of Goethe's words published by the former private tutor of his son, and later professor at the Weimarer Gymnasium, Friedrich Wilhelm Riemer, whom Wilhelm von Humboldt dubbed – not without reason – in a letter to his wife, Caroline, dated January 9th, 1809: "the famulus of the great man" (1921: 65). In Eckermann's *Gespräche mit Goethe in den letzten Jahren seines Lebens*, it was the conclusion rather than the preface that shed light on the author's true intentions. But in Riemer's *Mitteilungen über Goethe* (1841), this happens in the very first sentence of the preface:

> The many-sided relationships in which I, over thirty years, enjoyed the fortune, indeed the distinction, of standing with Goethe not only permit me, but also demand (since the whole world is writing and talking about him, whether they be authorized to do so or not), that I, too, as someone who is informed about the matter, bear a true witness of him – if only in order to satisfy, to the best of my ability, the piety and gratitude I have for him, first as patron, then in his official capacity as my superior, but certainly as a gracious and benevolent benefactor. (1921: 25)

In immediately distinguishing himself from the testimonies of those who are "not authorized" to speak or write about Goethe, Riemer first mentions Johannes Daniel Falk's book *Goethe aus näherm persönlichen Umgange dargestellt* (A depiction of Goethe from a close personal relationship [1832]), published six years after his death, and Bettina von Arnim's *Goethes Briefwechsel mit einem Kinde* (Goethe's correspondence with a child [1835]), which Riemer rejects with the argument that "here the main matter is fiction, around which something true has been hung here and there. In a word, the whole thing is a novel that borrows its time, place, and circumstances from reality" (1921: 47). And, as Wilhelm Grimm observes: "There is hardly a famous man about whom no anecdotes exist, told in the most graceful and witty manner, because language has

---

11 This is Schlaffer's apt commentary (Eckermann 1986n19: 724).

tremendous power (qtd. in Arnim 1986: 696).¹² But for Falk, too, according to Riemer,

> the credibility of his relations suffers already from multiple doubts, both concerning the content and the manner of its expression; not to mention that he was both initially in a position too removed from Goethe and, in the end, on account of the change of mind that had taken place within himself, too little capable of coming into closer contact with Goethe. (Riemer 1921: 38)

And this, the argument continues, made Falk even more dependent on informants:

> *Falk* first had dealings with *Wieland,* as well with *Herder* and *Böttiger,* and what flowed and continues to flow, especially from these latter sources, is already tinted, if not clouded. This is already shown by the assertion he cooked up with Böttiger on a journey they took together: that Goethe and Schiller would not remain friends for long, because two great men would not get along with each other. (40–41; original italics)

Riemer's later editor, Arthur Pollmer, writes even more clearly about him: "He regarded Böttiger's 'Literarische Zustände und Zeitgenossen' [Literary conditions and contemporaries] as a contemptible book of gossip" (19).¹³ In other words, namely those of Johann Christoph Adelung, this book made Böttiger, for his successor at the Weimar Gymnasium, nothing more than an "anecdote hunter, an anecdote catcher, who is always looking to seize on such secret and small circumstances in an unseemly, or exaggerated way" (Adelung 1970: 284).

2

Without a doubt Eckermann's "admiration and love" (*FA* II 12: 301) or Riemer's "piety and gratitude" (1921: 25) were not the guiding stars of Karl August Böttiger's *Begegnungen und Gespräche im klassischen Weimar* (Encounters and conversations in classical Weimar),¹⁴ with which he succeeded in annoying

---

12 Wilhelm Grimm to Anna von Arnswaldt, October 29th, 1834.
13 In Grothe's "Typengeschichte der Anekdote" (Typological history of the anecdote), they belonged to the first category of the "Klatschanekdote" ("gossip anecdote" [1971: 86]).
14 This is the subtitle chosen by the editors for the new edition, exactly reproducing the original with commentary, published by Karl August Böttiger for the first time in 1838: *Literarische Zustände und Zeitgenossen* (1998).

a number of his contemporaries – including Johann Wolfgang von Goethe, Friedrich Schiller, Johann Gottfried Herder, the brothers August Wilhelm and Friedrich Schlegel, Ludwig Tieck, Georg Wilhelm Friedrich Hegel and Friedrich Wilhelm Schelling – to such a degree that they publicly denigrated him as an "asshole," "ragamuffin," "liar" or "blow-fly." (Sternke 1998: 5)

Yet Böttiger gave informative and impartial reports about the meetings of the Weimar Society of Scholars ("Weimarer Gelehrtenverein") or Madame de Staël's stay in Weimar.[15] And even the material that he himself presented, drawing on Goethe's report, as "several anecdotes acquired through Murr's diligent work" offered no more reason for aggressive defense than did "several most interesting anecdotes" of the "very learned and kind" Prince August of Saxony-Gotha (59).

But Böttiger's malicious gossip, such as that in the story about Goethe's private life found in Böttiger's first Weimar sketches from October 1791, is true:

> People still think that he will, one day, marry his mistress, the Dem[oiselle] Vulpius. Some time ago, when a young Göthe was born of this liaison, he asked the duke to be the boy's godfather, and to the great annoyance of all the honest citizens of Weimar, the duke was happy to oblige. This Vulpius is, by the way, a small, unsightly person, presenting no small contrast to the well-built, masculine Göthe (look, for instance, at the extremely well-done painting done by Lips). (34)

Or five years later, in an even more pointed anecdote:

> Par depit [for spite] against Madame von Stein (who in fact morally sucked him dry, and was the source of the distrust that spoiled humanity for him), he reached for the lady Vulpia. It is ridiculous & tramples upon all ideas of prosperity that, after sitting at home with her seven-year-old little Göthe, she goes about in public at the theater & elsewhere as a mademoiselle. *Wieland* once put it like this: all this happens on account of absolute Goethean power. Göthe certainly has poetic moments when he considers himself to be the Holy Spirit, the Vulpia to be the blessed Virgin Mother, and his boy to be the Christ Child. (77; original italics).[16]

Böttiger is no less an important source on the "doings of the Weimar genius" (35–46), for instance with the following anecdote:

---

15 See Böttiger (1998: 47–66; 347–396).
16 The fact that Riemer deliberately refrained from such anecdotal material in his *Mitteilungen über Goethe* is shown by a note in his diary from August 3rd, 1809: "A closer look at the old copperplate etchings. Regarding a drawing in Michaelangelesque style, of Vulcan, Cupid, and Venus, forging arrows, Goethe remarked: 'A cuckold, a whore and a changeling always make a holy family'" (1921: 309).

> Once (at Bertuch's father-in-law's), someone put a sauce full of grated and blended gingerbread into the sheets beneath Einsiedel's bottom [specifically, Chamberlain Augustus v. E.] – a man who liked to lie in bed for a long time – and then they woke him up and shouted at him for defiling his bed. He jumped up, took off his soiled shirt, and teasingly ran after all the people in the house. *Göthe* meanwhile threw the sheet through a hole into the lower room, and roared: *Look at this pig!* (40; original italics)

Or about Goethe's relationship to Duke Carl August during the "Weimar period of genius, from 1775–[17]81" (71–80):

> The genius *Göthe* could not capture his *world spirit* (a fashionable expression at the time) in a narrow puddle of effluvium, vulgo, city. *Bertuch* had to give *Göthe* his garden at the park, and it was there that *Göthe* now established his enterprise of genius. Notes, as follows, were usually delivered every morning to the duke:
> "I'm still sitting here in the *shitter*, in the most hideous shitter. If you want to eat this lunch today at my place, my dear*, I have nothing to offer but a partridge who has been beaten to death and snatched from the hunt. You'll have to bring the rest yourself. – *Wolfgang*." (72–73; original italics)
> * This is how Göthe usually addressed the duke.

On the other hand, there is a whole positive chapter with the title "Göthe liest mir seinen Hermann und Dorothea" (Goethe Reads Me His Hermann and Dorothea [80–89]), which closes with the admiring sentences:

> Everything is developing. The last hundred verses a splendid reverberation and soothing.
> O, there is such unnamable art in the entire composition. One might boldly try to accept any case, any knot of entanglement, differently. Nowhere would *this* effect be the result. The ancients said precisely this of the *Odyssey:* in the whole poem there are only two similes, and the invocation of the muses does not occur until the last song.
> The glorious verses that end in a full spondee. (88–89; original italics)

Hence Böttiger was no despiser of Goethe (as were Adolf Müllner, Ludwig Börne, or Wolfgang Menzel, later on) blind to his poetic qualities. Rather, it is important to him to undermine Goethe's increasing dominance in and far beyond Weimar by publishing targeted provocations and thus demonstrating his own intellectual independence.

3

Such resistance is, of course, already characteristic of the earliest surviving text with the title *Anekdota:* the *Historia arcana* by Procopius of Caesarea.[17] For in contrast to his *Bella* and the *Aedificia* that pay homage to the emperor Justinian, these *anekdota* written in 550 A.D. are

> a pamphlet of the vicious kind against Belisar and Antonina, but especially against Justinian and Theodora. P[rocopius] feels himself to be the spokesman for a group that, out of hatred for the government, had placed all its hopes in Belisar and is now venting its disappointment at his failure in vile invective. Whereas the anecdote recognizes the general's overall achievement and reserves criticism for his private life, it presents a thoroughgoingly devastating portrait of Antonina and the imperial couple. (Folkert 1979: 1167)

Hence, even if these *anekdota* that circulated since the tenth century cannot claim "objective" historical truth for themselves, they enable, as the flipside of Procopius's "official" writings, a balanced judgment about the reign of Justinian (527–565 A.D.) and the campaigns of Belisar. Despite the temporal remove of more than a millennium and the very different dimensions of Constantinople and Weimar, we can observe a comparable counter-striving between, on the one hand, Goethe's *Dichtung und Wahrheit* and Eckermann's *Gespräche mit Goethe* and, on the other, the anecdotes of Böttiger and other opponents protesting against the "self-idealization of the Weimar world" (Blumenberg 1999: 147).

Indeed, in literary studies over the past several decades, we see a fundamental revaluation of historical anecdotes, which were, for a long time, disdained as merely "no-account items: tolerable, perhaps, as rhetorical embellishments, illustrations, or moments of relief from analytical generalization, but methodologically nugatory" (Gallagher and Greenblatt 2000: 49). Hans Blumenberg, for example, develops a "protohistory of theory"[18] in reading the metamorphoses of the anecdote about the philosopher Thales, who was laughed at by a Thracian servant maid after he fell into a well while looking up at the heavens; and most chapters of his book on Goethe, which remained fragmentary, begin with an anecdote as a crystallizing nucleus – unlike in any other philosophical representations of Goethe before it. Yet here, too, as in Blumenberg's *Work on Myth* (1979), Böttiger plays a role as an intimate reporter, which we should not

---

17 This title (Greek for "unpublished") was given to this sixth-century text in the Suda, the most comprehensive surviving Byzantine lexicon of the tenth century.
18 See Blumenberg (1987).

underestimate.[19] Yet it is in new historicism that we find a fundamental revaluation of the anecdote and its subversive potential vis-à-vis established hierarchies: "The turn to the historical anecdote in literary study promised both an escape from conventional canonicity and a revival of the canon, both a transgression against the domestic and a safe return to it" (Gallagher and Greenblatt 2000: 47).

Böttiger had fallen into disrepute during his lifetime and for a long time thereafter on account of his gossiping and pedantry. Nevertheless, together with Chancellor von Müller's *Unterhaltungen mit Goethe*, and to a much greater degree than the canonized collections of conversations published by Eckermann and Riemer, which aimed to convey a polished façade, Böttiger's indiscreet and disparate *Literarische Zustände und Zeitgenossen* were the starting point and model for Flodoard Freiherr von Biedermann's positivist collection of *Goethes Gespräche* (Goethe's conversations). This collection has grown since 1889 to encompass more than six thousand testimonies. Böttiger's work was also the basis for the anthology *Goethe in vertraulichen Briefen* (Goethe in confidential letters) first published by Wilhelm Bode in 1918–23. Yet both of these editions have been surpassed – and not only quantitatively – by the collection *Goethe: Begegnungen und Gespräche* (Goethe: encounters and conversations) that has been published since 1965 by Ernst and Renate Grumach, and yet remains far from complete: "Have you never read in the scriptures: 'The stone that the builders rejected has become the cornerstone'?"[20]

Works Cited

Adelung, Johann Christoph. 1970 [1793]. *Grammatisch-kritisches Wörterbuch der Hochdeutschen Mundart, mit beständiger Vergleichung der übrigen Mundarten, besonders aber der Oberdeutschen.* Vol. 1. 2nd ed. Hildesheim: Olms.

[Anon.] 1806. *Der Anekdotenkrämer: Eine ausgewählte Sammlung neuer, ächtkomischer Anekdoten, witziger und geistreicher Einfälle, überraschender Wortspiele und frappanter Charakterzüge.* Wien: Doll.

Arnim, Bettina von. 1986 [1835]. *Goethes Briefwechsel mit einem Kinde.* Ed. Heinz Härtl. Berlin: Aufbau-Verlag.

Blumenberg, Hans. 1999. *Goethe zum Beispiel.* Eds. Manfred Sommer and Hans Blumenberg-Archiv. Frankfurt am Main: Insel.

Blumenberg, Hans. 1985 [1979]. *Work on Myth.* Trans. Robert M. Wallace. Cambridge: MIT Press.

---

19 See also Blumenberg (1999: 218–219).
20 Matthew 21.42; the reference in the verse is to Psalm 118.22–23.

Blumenberg, Hans. 1987. *Das Lachen der Thrakerin. Eine Urgeschichte der Theorie.* Frankfurt am Main: Suhrkamp.
Bode, Wilhelm (ed.). 1979 [1918]. *Goethe in vertraulichen Briefen seiner Zeitgenossen.* 3 vols. Eds. Regine Otto and Paul-Gerhard Wenzlaff. Berlin: Aufbau-Verlag.
Böttiger, Karl August. 1998 [1838]. *Literarische Zustände und Zeitgenossen: Begegnungen und Gespräche im klassischen Weimar.* Eds. Klaus Gerlach and René Sternke. 3rd ed. Berlin: Aufbau-Verlag.
Campe, Joachim Heinrich. 1813. *Wörterbuch zur Erklärung und Verdeutschung der unserer Sprache aufgedrungenen fremden Ausdrücke: ein Ergänzungsband zu Adelung's und Campe's Wörterbüchern.* New and rev. ed. Braunschweig: Schulbuchhandlung.
Chamfort, Nicolas. 1795. *Produits de la Civilisation perfectionnèe. Maximes et pensées, caractères et anecdotes.* In: *Œuvres complètes.* Paris: Ginguené.
Eckermann, Johann Peter. 1999 [1836]. *Gespräche mit Goethe in den letzten Jahren seines Lebens.* Eds. Christoph Michel and Hans Grüters. Frankfurt am Main: Deutscher Klassiker Verlag.
Eckermann, Johann Peter. 1986 [1836]. *Gespräche mit Goethe in den letzten Jahren seines Lebens.* Ed. Heinz Schlaffer. München: Hanser.
Falk, Johann Daniel. 1832. *Goethe aus näherm persönlichen Umgange dargestellt: ein nachgelassenes Werk.* Leipzig: F. A. Brockhaus.
Folkert, Menso. 1979. "Prokopios 3." In: Konrat Ziegler and Walther Sontheimer (eds.). *Der Kleine Pauli. Lexikon der Antike.* Vol. 4. München: Deutscher Taschenbuch Verlag. 1165–1169.
Gallagher, Catherine and Stephen Greenblatt. 2000. *Practicing New Historicism.* Chicago: University of Chicago Press.
Goethe, Johann Wolfgang. 1993. *Sprüche in Prosa. Sämtliche Maximen und Reflexionen.* In: Harald Fricke (ed.). *Sämtliche Werke. Briefe, Tagebücher und Gespräche.* [Frankfurter Ausgabe] Vol. 13. Frankfurt am Main: Deutscher Klassiker Verlag.
Goethe, Johann Wolgang von. 1989. *Conversations of German Refugees. Wilhelm Meister's Journeyman Years or the Renunciants.* Ed. Jane K. Brown. Trans. Jan van Heurck, Jane K. Brown, and Krishna Winston. *Goethe's Collected Works 10.* New York: Suhrkamp.
Goethe, Johann Wolfgang. 1987 [1887–1919]. *Werke. Hg. im Auftrage der Großherzogin Sophie von Sachsen.* [Weimarer Ausgabe]. Weimar: Böhlau; Repr. München: Deutscher Taschenbuch Verlag.
Goethe, Johann Wolfgang. 1965–. *Begegnungen und Gespräche.* Eds. Ernst and Renate Grumach. Berlin: De Gruyter.
Goethe, Johann Wolfgang. 1906. *The Maxims and Reflections of Goethe.* Trans. Bailey Saunders. New York: Macmillan & Co., LTD.
Goethe, Johann Wolfgang. 1901 [1836]. *Conversations with Eckermann: Being Appreciations and Criticisms on Many Subjects.* Eds. Frédéric Jacob Soret and John Oxenford. New York: M. Walter Dunne Publisher.
Grothe, Heinz. 1971. *Anekdote.* Stuttgart: Metzler.
Herwig, Wolfgang (ed.). 1965–1987. *Goethes Gespräche. Eine Sammlung zeitgenössischer Berichte aus seinem Umgang.* 5 vols. Zürich: Artemis.
Holy Bible: New Revised Standard Edition with Apocrypha. 1989. New York: Oxford University Press.

Humboldt, Wilhelm. 1909. *Wilhelm und Caroline von Humboldt in ihren Briefen.* Vol. 3: *Weltbürgertum und preußischer Staatsdienst. Briefe aus Rom und Berlin-Königsberg 1808–1810.* Ed. Anna von Sydow. Berlin: Mittler.

Kanzler, Friedrich von Müller. 1959. *Unterhaltungen mit Goethe. Kleine Ausgabe.* Ed. Ernst Grumach. Weimar: Böhlau.

Nietzsche, Friedrich. 1913 [1878]. *Human, All-Too-Human: A Book for Free Spirits, Part II.* Trans. Paul V. Cohn. In: Oscar Levy (ed.). *The Complete Works of Friedrich Nietzsche.* Vol. 7. New York: The Macmillan Company.

Riemer, Friedrich Wilhelm. 1921 [1841]. *Mitteilungen über Goethe.* Ed. Arthur Pollmer. Leipzig: Insel.

Schäfer, Rudolf. 1982. *Die Anekdote: Theorie – Analyse – Didaktik.* München: Oldenbourg.

Schlaffer, Heinz. 1997. "Anekdote." In: Klaus Weimar, Harald Fricke, Klaus Grubmüller, and Jan-Dirk Müller (eds.). *Reallexikon der deutschen Literaturwissenschaft. Neubearbeitung des Reallexikons der deutschen Literaturgeschichte.* Vol. 1. Berlin: De Gruyter. 87–89.

Sternke, René. 1998. "Vorwort." In: Karl August Böttiger. *Literarische Zustände und Zeitgenossen: Begegnungen und Gespräche im klassischen Weimar.* Eds. Klaus Gerlach and René Sternke. 3rd ed. Berlin: Aufbau-Verlag. 5–24.

Wellbery, David E. 2019. "Anekdoten." At the conference *Dichtung und Wahrheit: Goethe's (Auto-)Biographica*, 17th April, Goethe- und Schiller-Archiv/Klassik Stiftung Weimar, Petersen-Bibliothek. Unpublished lecture.

Frank Kelleter
Anecdotal Manifestations of the Evangelical Here and Now: Four Conversions in Jonathan Edwards's Northampton

Abstract: This essay discusses the close affinity between religious rhetoric and anecdotal storytelling, focusing on evangelical notions of mediated immediacy during the Great Awakening (1730s to 1740s). In particular, it deals with four conversion accounts contained in Jonathan Edwards's writings on the religious revival in Northampton, Massachusetts. The essay argues that the ideological and soteriological work of these and other evangelical anecdotes is dependent, most of all, on their communicative velocity (rather than their formal brevity).

Keywords: American Enlightenment, Early Modern Media, Evangelicalism, Great Awakening, Jonathan Edwards.

The etymology of the word *anecdote* (Greek for "unpublished") obscures more than it reveals. Associations of orality, privacy, provisionality, and even secrecy are common when one speaks of anecdotes, but such terms indicate no clear distinction between what is published and what is not. Rather, they raise questions about the scale and scope of different modes of sharing a story. A rumor circulated among family members, a joke told to a select group of partygoers, a note written to myself for later use: All these communications are kept away from larger audiences, but their resulting privacy, exclusivity, or secrecy in every case expresses a special degree of publicity rather than a state of non-disclosure. Since the public is not a place – not a physical area that autonomous individuals can choose to visit or stay away from – but a temporary gathering of communicative practices, there are many ways (and many media, including the human voice) in which things can be published or put on a path for wider distribution. We do well to consider that words such as "publication," "writing," "fiction," and, yes, "anecdote" do not refer to ideal forms or organic objects in the world, but to historically configured actions, that is, matters of self-description.

Genres, too, exist and develop as consolidated practice. This is of some relevance whenever we speak of anecdotes in generic terms. I take my departure from one such definition, which describes anecdotes as short but exemplary stories about relatively insignificant events happening to relatively significant

https://doi.org/10.1515/9783110668490-016

historical figures.¹ Understood and reproduced in this fashion, anecdotal stories are often situated in specific times and places, and they show fictionalized versions of real human beings in singular everyday incidents. These stories are concentrated and revealing at the same time. They bring together unique lives and general insights. Their evolving art consists in connecting concrete moments and localities to universal patterns of perceptions. This is why anecdotes have proven highly attractive to systems of thought that understand the empirical world as an expression of *something else*, something both immanent in and yet fundamentally separate from the quotidian experience of "here and now."

Religious rhetoric, for example, abounds with anecdotes. At the same time, religious rhetoric typically claims to have transcended this particular mode of storytelling. And true, when religious anecdotes are strung together into larger units, like beads on a chain, they can form gospels, scriptures, holy books. My essay will address this literary alchemy, focusing on the 1730s and 1740s, when evangelical movements in North America, as part of a larger spiritual shift within the Atlantic West, coalesced into what would later be called the "Great Awakening."² Three decades before the American Revolution, this series of evangelical revivals transformed the colonial public sphere, not only because the Great Awakening diversified North America's religious landscape, undermining the hegemony of orthodox Puritanism in New England and Anglicanism in the Southern colonies, but also because evangelical communication effectively modernized many of the available modes and media of public storytelling in British America.³

It is no coincidence that this turning point in the history of American publicity can also be portrayed as a key episode in the American history of anecdotal storytelling. After all, the very word "evangelical" suggests a type of revelation that represents events in this world as bringing "good news" about another world, which is infinitely more meaningful.⁴ While I will not be able to do justice to all the theological intricacies of the four conversions mentioned in my essay's subtitle, I will nevertheless employ these narratives to make two larger points about anecdotes and their history. The first of these points, building on Joel Fineman's (1980; 1989) landmark discussions of the anecdotal, holds that anecdotes

---

1 Cf. Wilpert (1979: 27) and Cuddon (1991: 42).
2 This essay relies on my previous discussion of the Great Awakening in the context of the American Enlightenment (Kelleter 2002; esp. 242–310).
3 For a more detailed discussion of this aspect of the Great Awakening, see Lambert (1999).
4 On the role of Puritan typology in this regard, sidelined in the present essay but of central importance to the issues discussed here, see Brumm (1963); Bercovitch (1972); Miner (1977); Kelleter (2002: 248–252).

are usually not the opposite of so-called grand narratives. Rather, anecdotes regularly serve as functional elements within larger rhetorical and ideological frameworks. Therefore, the cultural work performed by anecdotes has less to do with the much-quoted size of these stories – that is, their brevity or compactness – than with their rapid connectivity. Put more abstractly, a history of communicative practices will be more interested in the effective temporality of these seemingly minor and often incidental narratives than in their formal definition. Accordingly, my second point holds that anecdotes are best understood and studied not as *small forms*, as if they were isolated textual structures, but as *fast forms*, because they exist as highly connective structures with a special capacity for speeding up acts of storytelling.

To approach anecdotes in this manner, as techniques of larger narratives and larger narrative acts, means to ask which communities are (intended to be) constituted – and for how long – by such speedy communications.[5] This question is important because anecdotal storytelling is often defined as we have seen by its limited address. The notion of universal reach seems to run counter to the literary self-understanding of anecdotes. However, Christianity and the Enlightenment – two frameworks of rhetoric and ideology that are indeed huge but no less real for their bewildering diversity – have turned anecdotal stories into key components of emphatically universal narratives: divine love for humanity on the one hand, enabling forms of address no longer circumscribed by hereditary concerns or local necessities, and the sensual commonality of human beings on the other hand, allowing for the revolutionary concept of an all-inclusive public sphere, which claims to be capable of absorbing, potentially, every individual interest and experience. In the evangelical movements of the early eighteenth century, these two universalisms came together.[6] New methods of linking up singularity and truth were the result. The scientific case study, for instance, even and especially in its medical versions concerned with deviation, owes much to Enlightenment concepts of common sense and empirical reason. For Christian storytellers, in turn, the sublime model of narrative transcendence is the New Testament itself, or more precisely: the Gospels and their massive canon of learned hermeneutic expansion. Thus, evangelical rhetoric of the 1730s comes equipped with a highly complex, almost absurdly elaborate, theory of anecdotal storytelling.

---

5 Cf. "Temporal Communities" (2018). Relying on Fineman (1989), a first hypothesis addressing this question might propose that in anecdotes, "literary" and "historiographic" communities meet each other and constitute themselves.
6 See Fiering (1981).

In colonial New England, the most sophisticated scholar of religious narrative was Jonathan Edwards, the minister of Northampton, Massachusetts, who walked a fine line between theologically legitimizing the Great Awakening and pragmatically controlling what he regarded as its enthusiastic and antinomian excesses. As an almost orthodox Puritan strongly drawn to the unorthodoxies of contemporary thought and expression, Edwards was a somewhat reluctant apologist of the colonial revival. He was also its most subtle theorist, especially concerning the role played by storytelling in the event of divine grace. It does not come as a surprise, therefore, that Edwards's own writings about the awakening of his hometown, Northampton, contain a number of stories that can reasonably be called anecdotal. By documenting local details, these stories are meant to exemplify the authenticity of the mass conversions happening simultaneously on a much larger scale throughout the colonies. Thus, in *A Faithful Narrative of the Surprising Work of God in the Conversion of Many Hundred Souls in Northampton* (1737), Edwards inserts into the larger trajectory of his theological argument a number of individual conversion accounts, among them the stories of Abigail Hutchinson, a single young woman, and Phebe Bartlett, a four-year-old child. Five years later, in *Some Thoughts Concerning the Present Revival in New England and the Ways It Ought to Be Acknowledged and Promoted* (1742), Edwards gives another short account of a powerful conversion, but this time withholding information about the name, age, and gender of the person in question. A fourth, quite different type of conversion is depicted in one of Edwards's letters at the time and then again anonymously in *A Faithful Narrative:* this is the tragic story of Edwards's Uncle Hawley.

In formal terms, the conversion tales of Abigail Hutchinson and Phebe Bartlett are interesting because they constitute anecdotes in which the spiritual function of anecdotal storytelling is explicitly addressed and theorized. We can almost call them meta-anecdotes – and as such, these narratives, in turn, are embedded in a larger theory of evangelical storytelling that ultimately refers back to the Gospels. Thus, the story of Abigail Hutchinson's conversion begins with Hutchinson hearing the story of another woman, a neighbor, who is little respected in town, but then, because of her conversion, becomes a public figure of sorts. Edwards writes:

> This news wrought much upon [Hutchinson], and stirred up a spirit of envy in her towards this young woman, whom she thought very unworthy of being distinguished from others by

such a mercy; but withal it engaged her in a firm resolution to do her utmost to obtain the same blessing. (4: 192)[7]

Edwards thus admits, and even stresses, that Hutchinson's wish to be converted was mediated by previous narratives, or more precisely: by rumors. Nevertheless, *A Faithful Narrative* insists that the resulting conversion was authentic. In other words, Edwards holds that narrative arbitration and even the un-Christian disposition of "envy" can foster genuine salvation. This is an important point for Edwards, because his own telling of Hutchinson's story is supposed to do more than merely authenticate this conversion and others like it: it is supposed to mediate them, in the sense of actively preparing and provoking further "surprising works of God." And so it did, probably on a massive scale, if we regard Edwards's books, published in the authoritative voice of a theological storyteller, as crucial contributors to the Great Awakening rather than mere depictions of it.

Evangelical anecdotes have a twofold function here, a rhetorical and a soteriological one, or put differently: one having to do with strategic *mediation*, one with *immediate* salvation. Abigail Hutchinson, for example, gains a twofold distinction through storytelling. According to her minister's theory of narrative revelation, Hutchinson receives God's authentic grace despite the fact that she merely tried to imitate another person's rumored actions. Although her individual case is shown to spring from questionable ambitions, this shaky source is instantly transformed – by divine grace, which is said to be working through the "faithful" publication of a theological narrator – into "good news," that is, into an exemplary story that becomes a model, in turn, for "the conversion of many hundred souls."

A similar communicative structure is attributed to the conversion of Phebe Bartlett. At first glance, it seems as if Edwards selected this particular case for inclusion in *A Faithful Narrative* because the conversion of a four-year-old is difficult to trace back to previous theological knowledge. This was a central point of critique against the Great Awakening at the time: the idea that it was driven, not by grace, but by theological topoi. The conversion of a child would have been particularly attractive for defenders of the revival in this regard. Edwards, however, concedes that Phebe's conversion was, again, prepared by conversation: "[S]he was greatly affected by the talk of her brother, who had been hopefully converted a little before, at about eleven years of age, and then seriously talked to her about the great things of religion." Phebe also pays close attention to what

---

[7] *The Works of Jonathan Edwards* (1957–2008) are quoted here by volume number rather than year.

her minister has to say (as does Abigail Hutchinson): "I love to hear them talk," she tells her mother about her spiritual teachers (4: 202). In this fashion, the young listener soon turns into a lecturer; the pupil becomes an instructor herself, and a stern one:

> [T]he child took her opportunities to talk to the other children about the great concern of their souls, sometimes so as much to affect them and set them into tears. [...] "I have been talking to Nabby and Eunice." Her mother asked her what she had said to 'em. "Why," said she, "I told 'em they must pray, and prepare to die, that they had but a little while to live in this world, and they must be always ready." (4: 204)

This sounds terrifying. Phebe's childish lectures read like oddly concentrated versions of Edwards's own celebrated revival sermons with their fire and brimstone rhetoric, such as "Sinners in the Hands of an Angry God" (more about this below). But what makes Phebe's talks with her friends even more terrifying is that Edwards seems unaware of this similarity. Or why did he include Phebe's telling statements in his apology of the Great Awakening? After all, eighteenth-century theological discourse already understood the precarious status of child conversions. As William Rand wrote in *The Late Religious Commotions in New-England Considered* (1743):

> *Imitation* is *natural* to Children, especially in Language; and when such Imitation is *taken notice of* with *apparent* Pleasure and Applause, it is nothing *marvellous* if it encreases, and the pious Expressions they hear are caught, and repeated by them. – Whilst at the same Time they understand not what they say, and speak *only by Rote*. (10; original italics)

It can be assumed that Jonathan Edwards, one of the most discerning readers of contemporary philosophy in colonial America, was familiar with this line of argument. Why, then, did he include Phebe's imitative speeches in his book? I suggest he did so because Phebe's story and Phebe's language fit a pattern of selection that determines all four anecdotes discussed here. This brings me back to the complex double function of evangelical anecdotes. As stories that fulfill both a rhetorical and a soteriological purpose, these religious narratives, situated at the threshold of the literary and the historiographic, serve to *mediate immediacy*. This is the ultimate and paradoxical goal of their "good news," according to Edwards's own biblical theory of storytelling: "There is no one thing that I know of, that God has made such a means of promoting his work amongst us, as the news of others' conversion" (4: 176).

If this is so, the evangelical storyteller needs to acknowledge the agency of narratives and media in the conversion process, but at the same time he also needs to dispel any suspicion that the reception of grace is a fantasy that merely reproduces previous conversations. In order to achieve this – in order to mark divine communication as irresistible but nevertheless allow for human influence and storytelling – evangelical theology relies on the metaphysical concept of *preparation*, which defines the linguistic activities of competent speakers, such as ministers, missionaries, or theologians, as inviting the event of grace, but not causing it. That this construction shaped the selection of converts in Edwards's writings on Northampton becomes evident in the case of the unnamed person in *Some Thoughts Concerning the Revival*, because this unspecified convert – "unpublished" and yet made public – was none other than Edwards's wife Sarah Pierrepont. Notably, by withholding this information, Edwards changed the story. For when the narrator of the conversion tale subtracts himself and his own evangelical actions from the narrative, this distinguishes the experience of grace as all the more immediate in a literal sense of the term.

However, converts are converted into discourse as much as faith. In fact, claiming the priority of the latter over the former – claiming that affect precedes social interaction – is a defining discursive feature of faith itself. Already in *A Faithful Narrative*, one has to read between the lines to notice how much Phebe truly yearned to be acknowledged by the adult world and, in particular, by her spiritual mentor Jonathan Edwards, to gain rhetorical authority herself. In fact, even Abigail Hutchinson's conversion obliquely partakes of this pattern, because when *A Faithful Narrative* was published in 1737, Hutchinson was already dead. For the overall logic of evangelical story distribution, this fact is significant for two reasons. First, the model convert's physical demise takes care of one of the chief public arguments against the revival, which concerned the transient nature of many contemporary conversions. Critics repeatedly described the Great Awakening as a dramatic but short-lived religious epidemic, highly dependent on passing moments of crisis such as earthquakes or the arrival of charismatic itinerant preachers like George Whitefield.[8] In this situation, Hutchinson's conversion must have been particularly welcome to Edwards, because with the convert already dead, there could be no spiritual backsliding. This fact conveniently removed Hutchinson's life story from further social actions, turning her case into a singular one indeed.

But Hutchinson's singularity is instructive for a second reason as well, again connected to her death, or rather: her sense of mortality. If we read carefully, we

---

8 On Whitefield's role in the Great Awakening, see Stout (1991); Lambert (1994). For epidemiological accounts of the Great Awakening, see the writings of Charles Chauncy, such as *Enthusiasm Described and Caution'd Against* (1742), *Seasonable Thoughts on the State of Religion in New-England* (1743), and *A Letter to the Reverend Mr. George Whitefield* (1745).

notice that Hutchinson's desire for salvation was closely linked to her wish to commit suicide. At the time of her conversion, Hutchinson was suffering from a painful and visibly fatal throat disease. Edwards tells us about her "great longings to die, that she might be with Christ; which increased till she thought she did not know how to be patient to wait till God's time should come" (4: 196). Naturally, Edwards convinced her that this was a theological mistake and that she had to let God decide. This she did – and resigned herself to her fate. "After this," Edwards innocently declares, "her illness increased upon her" (4: 196). However we want to interpret the relationship between Hutchinson's orthodox resignation and the contrary reaction of her body, her re-evaluation of suicide fully accords with a typical doctrine of her spiritual teacher. For already in his early years as a minister, Edwards had preached on the topic of "Dying to Gain." In a sermon of this title, delivered in 1722, he described death as "a perfect freedom from temptation." But although the "gain of dying" is thus said to consist in the end of all "worthless, miserable, wretched, dull, earthly vanities" (10: 587), no human being has power over life and death, so that the beauty of a Christian death, according to Edwards, resides in its divine dispensation, its foreign sovereignty: "[Y]et let it come when, how, and where it will, it will be your unspeakable gain" (10: 590). The same scenario of renouncing suicide while affirming death organizes Hutchinson's narrative and, apparently, life. (Hutchinson eventually died of malnutrition; she might have refused food or was unable to swallow and starved to death.)

In this light, Edwards's anecdotes about the Northampton revival appear highly selective. Moreover, their selection appears to be strategic. It is firmly based in Edwards's theory of evangelical storytelling, which stresses the legitimacy of narrative influence on the event of grace, while the storyteller himself works hard to qualify (or even conceal) obvious signs of influencing. This explains why Edwards's conversion accounts deal with a dying woman, a child, and his own wife: people who have a vested interest in bringing themselves in accordance with Edwards's evangelical discourse. All three converts are dependent, in one sense or another, on Edwards's attention and approval, but in every case, their special dependence is de-emphasized, covered up, or denied in the act of storytelling. In this fashion, the evangelical doctrine of preparation serves to obscure the fact that certain effects are, if not directly caused, then strongly co-determined by the techniques and authorities of evangelical narration itself.

Evidently, gender plays a vital role in the generic allocation of these three stories; they are anecdotal because they touch on female lives. By contrast, when Edwards presents an ideal male convert, he opts for a mixture of curatorial and hagiographic modes, as in *An Account of the Life of the Late Reverend*

Mr. David Brainerd (1749), his most frequently reprinted book, a five hundred-page tome much closer to the analytical ambitions of the modern-day case study than the conversion narratives of *A Faithful Narrative* and *Some Thoughts Concerning the Revival*. In any case, Edwards's method of mediating immediacy – turning the here and now of individual moments into an evangelical truth – did not always work out as expected. The act of storytelling itself puts strong limitations on authorial control. Thus, a fourth conversion narrative in Edwards's writings on the Northampton revival takes a different turn: the story of Uncle Hawley, who suffered a death wish quite similar to Hutchinson's. In this case, however, Hawley's minister (Jonathan Edwards again) failed to theologically curb his subject's desire for suicide.

In terms of communicative structure, Hawley's story, despite its male protagonist, is virtually identical to the other three cases of evangelical exemplarity. This adds to Edwards's distress about his uncle's fate, because Hawley's story is not supposed to become another model tale – and yet it does. In the summer of 1735, Edwards reports in a letter to Benjamin Colman that Uncle Hawley, who had been converted under Edwards's guidance, cut his throat last Sunday:

> He had been for a considerable time concerned about the condition of his soul; till, by the ordering of a divine providence he was suffered to fall into deep melancholy, a distemper that the family are very prone to; he was much overpowered by it; the devil took the advantage and drove him into despairing thoughts. (4: 109)

Evidently, satanic power has to be invoked when evangelical communication develops an unpredictable momentum of its own. Without the devil, how can faith address its own involuntary effects? Sensing the power of "suggestion" but unwilling to trace it to the worldly instruments of transcendence, Edwards requires a divine antagonist, both a nonhuman person and a subject without subjectivity, to explain why Hawley's desperate act soon inspired others in *quite the same manner* that the evangelist's own storytelling prepared the event of grace for many souls now saved. In *A Faithful Narrative* Edwards writes about Hawley:

> After this, multitudes in this and other towns seemed to have it strongly suggested to 'em, and pressed upon 'em, to do as this person has done. And many that seemed to be under no melancholy, some pious persons that had no special darkness, or doubts about the goodness of their state, nor were under any special trouble or concern of mind about anything spiritual or temporal, yet had it urged upon 'em, as if somebody had spoke to 'em, "Cut your own throat, now is good opportunity: *now, NOW!*" (4: 207; original italics)

The temporality of this final suggestion with its fierce sense of urgency, its contagious conjuring of a sudden opening, an auspicious moment in time that would pass instantly, never to return perhaps, if that singular chance was missed – such imperative demands on a living body's here and now illustrate what fast narratives can do. What they are capable of. Satanic whispers are forceful not because they are short and succinct but because they act quickly. It is no coincidence that the pivotal word Hawley hears spoken to him by the devil is "opportunity." To understand the full force of this special temptation, we need to remember that the massive success of the colonial revivals in the 1730s and 1740s did not come out of the blue nor from hell but that it was the result of intense publicity measures and innovative media technologies. In this context, it bears repeating that Edwards's own revival sermons consisted of more than drastic warnings and threats. Despite what is suggested by the canonized example of "Sinners in the Hands of an Angry God" (1741) and its curious reception history, Edwards's sermons during the Great Awakening emphatically encouraged the positive self-reproduction of evangelical communication by insistently promoting exemplary conversion cases. In this fashion, Edwards and other eighteenth-century evangelicals developed techniques of spiritual peer pressure that in more than one way anticipated the language of modern advertising.

Hence, besides Satan, it was the Great Awakening's own itinerant preachers and keen local ministers who constantly stressed the unique "opportunity" that prospective converts needed to exploit while the divine offer still stood. Or in Edwards's own words (from "Sinners in the Hands of an Angry God"): "*now* you have an extraordinary *opportunity*," "*many* are *daily* coming from the east, west, north and south; *many* that were very *lately* in the same miserable condition that you are in, are in *now* an happy state," "[h]ow awful is it to be left behind at such a day!" (22: 416–417; my italics).[9] In this state of self-reproducing emergency, the rhetorical and ideological work of evangelical anecdotes resided less in their formal structure – their smallness, which has tempted post-1960s

---

[9] Like a good marketing strategist, Edwards focuses especially on adolescents, the consumer group most susceptible to peer pressure: "And you that are *young men*, and *young women*, will you neglect this precious season that you now enjoy, when so many others of your age are renouncing all youthful vanities, and flocking to Christ? You especially have now an extraordinary opportunity; but if you neglect it, it will soon be with you as it is with those persons that spent away all the precious days of youth in sin." While adolescents are offered a chance to feel trendy and popular, children are addressed in a more authoritarian tone: "And you *children* that are unconverted, don't you know that you are going down to hell, to bear the dreadful wrath of that God that is now angry with you every day, and every night?" (22: 417; original italics). Given such statements, it is not surprising that *Some Thoughts Concerning the Revival* declares: "The work has been chiefly amongst those that are young" (4: 504).

scholars to contrast anecdotes favorably with grand narratives – than in what is afforded, indeed mobilized, by such small forms: large and growing numbers of stories traveling at high speed from place to place.

In the 1730s, Edwards was well aware of the spiritual capacities of space-transcending communication technologies (from itinerancy to transatlantic print circuits) and he methodically translated this awareness into a revivalist media strategy. To name just one example, early on in "Sinners in the Hands of an Angry God" we find a sentence directly addressed to Edwards's audience in the town of Enfield, Connecticut. "Are not your souls as precious as the souls of the people at Suffield" (22: 418), Edwards asks the good people of Enfield, encouraging them to follow the example of their neighbors. In Edwards's original manuscript, there is a revealing note written in the text's margins at this point. Referring to the word "Suffield," Edwards jots down, "[t]he next neighboring town." If we assume that Edwards knew where Suffield was (and did not need to remind himself in a note), it appears that this sermon was written for repeated usage, in different localities, all with their own "next neighboring towns," the names of which could be inserted upon delivery in place of "Suffield" to evoke evangelical competition in the service of trans-local salvation. Something similar can be said about the anecdotes in Edwards's writings on the Great Awakening. The tales of individual salvation that we find in *A Faithful Narrative* and *Some Thoughts Concerning the Revival* are no longer classical Puritan conversion narratives. Rather, these are functional elements within a new and wide-ranging genre of religious storytelling that Michael Crawford (1991) has termed "revival narratives." Crucially, this storytelling genre is a *publication genre:* a genre, that is, which has fully grasped and embraced the soteriological affordances of print culture.

In sum, Edwards's short conversion stories function as print-cultural preparations of ongoing mass events, speedy technologies of salvation. Much like the public sphere of the European Enlightenment, from which Edwards takes his cue for his Protestant media theory, the evangelical public sphere of the early eighteenth century is driven by exemplary narratives so quick that they constantly regenerate their own communicative conditions. Or as Edwards put it in *Some Thoughts Concerning the Revival:*

> A history should be published once a month, or once a fortnight, of the progress of [this work of God], by one of the ministers of Boston, who are near the press and are most conveniently situated to receive accounts from all parts. It has been found by experience that the tidings of remarkable effects of the power and grace of God in any place, tend greatly to awaken and engage the minds of persons in other places. 'Tis great pity therefore, but that some means should be used for the most speedy, most extensive and certain giving

information of such things, and that the country ben't left only to slow, partial and doubtful information and false representations of common report. (4: 529)

We are at the beginning of a modern media history here. Anecdotes – in a wider, praxeological sense of the term – are crucial players in this process. Therefore, whenever we study narratives that link the concision of individual moments to overarching truths and their demands, we are well advised to dispense with analytical models that treat these stories as if they were isolated formal structures. Instead, it pays to look at their specific temporalities and their technological connectivities, that is, their speeds and reaches. In fact, this perspective may be appropriate for all kinds of literary brevities, from pre-evangelical note-taking, as Meredith Neuman (2013) has shown in her study of early New England print culture, to Twitter, which is not understood adequately by studies focusing on individual tweets and their formal constraints of one hundred and forty or two hundred and eighty characters. For cultural historians it seems more fruitful to attend to the increasingly large and fast systems of interaction that generate, and are generated by, such seemingly small communications.

Works Cited

Bercovitch, Sacvan. 1972. *Typology and Early American Literature*. Amherst: University of Massachusetts Press.
Brumm, Ursula. 1963. *Die religiöse Typologie im amerikanischen Denken: Ihre Bedeutung für die amerikanische Literatur- und Geistesgeschichte*. Leiden: Brill.
Chauncy, Charles. 1745. *A Letter to the Reverend Mr. George Whitefield*. Boston: Rogers & Fowle for Eliot.
Chauncy, Charles. 1743. *Seasonable Thoughts on the State of Religion in New-England*. Boston: Rogers & Fowle for Eliot.
Chauncy, Charles. 1742. *Enthusiasm Described and Caution'd Against*. Boston: Draper for Eliot and Blanchard.
Crawford, Michael J. 1991. *Seasons of Grace: Colonial New England's Revival Tradition and Its British Context*. New York: Oxford University Press.
Cuddon, J. A. 1991. *The Penguin Dictionary of Literary Terms and Literary Theory*. London: Penguin.
Edwards, Jonathan. 1957–2008. *The Works of Jonathan Edwards*. 26 vols. Eds. Perry Miller, John E. Smith and Harry S. Stout. New Haven: Yale University Press.
Fiering, Norman. 1981. *Jonathan Edwards's Moral Thought and Its British Context*. Chapel Hill: University of North Carolina Press.
Fineman, Joel. 1989. "The History of the Anecdote: Fiction and Fiction." In: H. Aram Veeser (ed.). *The New Historicism*. Abingdon: Routledge. 49–76.
Fineman, Joel. 1980. "The Structure of Allegorical Desire." *October* 12: 46–66.

Kelleter, Frank. 2002. *Amerikanische Aufklärung: Sprachen der Rationalität im Zeitalter der Revolution*. Paderborn: Schöningh.
Lambert, Frank. 1999. *Inventing the Great Awakening*. Princeton: Princeton University Press.
Lambert, Frank. 1994. *"Pedlar in Divinity": George Whitefield and the Transatlantic Revivals, 1737–1770*. Princeton: Princeton University Press.
Miner, Earl (ed.). 1977. *Literary Uses of Typology from the Late Middle Ages to the Present*. Princeton: Princeton University Press.
Neuman, Meredith Marie. 2013. *Jeremiah's Scribes: Creating Sermon Literature in Puritan New England*. Philadelphia: University of Pennsylvania Press.
Rand, William. 1743. *The Late Religious Commotions in New-England Considered; An Answer to Jonathan Edwards "Distinguishing Marks."* Boston: Green, Bushell & Allen for Fleet.
Stout, Harry S. 1991. *The Divine Dramatist: George Whitefield and the Rise of Modern Evangelicalism*. Grand Rapids: William B. Eerdmans.
"Temporal Communities." Research Cluster. Freie Universität Berlin, 2018. <www.fu-berlin.de/en/sites/inu/excellence-strategy/proposals/temporal-communities/index.html> [accessed 17 September 2018].
Wilpert, Gero von. 1979. *Sachwörterbuch der Literatur*. 6th ed. Stuttgart: Kröner.

DETAIL

Fig. 1. Francesco del Cossa. *Annunciation*. 1470–1472. Tempera on poplar, 139 x 113 cm (54 3/4 x 44 1/2 in.). Staatliche Kunstsammlungen, Dresden/Hans-Peter Klut. © bpk-Bildagentur.

Friedrich Teja Bach
The Cage of the Image and the Trace of the Snail: On the Language of Pictorial Detail
Translated by Michael Thomas Taylor

Abstract: The essay explores potential affinities between the literary genre of the anecdote, on the one hand, and the detail in the visual arts, on the other, by following the trail of the humble snail in a Renaissance painting of the quattrocento. Analyzing the function of the snail motif in Francesco del Cossa's *Annunciation* (1470–1472) in particular, it shows that this detail has the power to reconfigure and yet more powerfully consolidate the fundamental event and implications of incarnation.

Keywords: Anecdote in Art History, Pictorial Detail, Renaissance Painting, Snails in Art.

For an art historian who is asked to contribute to a volume of essays on the anecdote, the most obvious material to turn to are legends of artists. Fascinating as these legends and their abundance of anecdotes may be, I am more interested in the relationship between anecdotes and images. Can pictures be anecdotal? Can we conceive of a pictorial equivalent to the narrative genre of the anecdote? Addressing the latter question, the following essay will explore the affinity between the anecdote and the detail – in the hope of being led from a detail to questions that also may prove productive for the anecdote.

One such detail is the snail found on the *Annunciation* by Francesco del Cossa (fig. 1), painted from 1470 to 1472 in tempera on poplar wood. The snail is located in the extreme foreground of the painting, at Mary's side and right above the picture frame. Daniel Arasse has read the disturbance of the image and the perspectival order that results from this snail as an indication of the incommensurability of God's infinity with the perspectival construction of an infinite space (cf. 2003: 88). I will not follow this interpretation here. Instead, I will pursue a different trace, by focusing on the resonances of the motif and its function in the pictorial narrative of the panel.

As we will see, the motif of the snail is an element in a double narrative, since the snail is both inside and outside the narrative frame of the painting. It is located "within" the frame inasmuch as it is part of the pictorial orchestration, that is, an element of the painting's Christian iconography. Originally a

https://doi.org/10.1515/9783110668490-017

symbol of listlessness, *accedia*, and of cowardice, the meaning of the snail in a Christian context shifted to acquire a positive valence around 1400. The snail became a symbol of wise caution, a sign of birth and rebirth, and a symbol of the resurrection; after all, the animal covers up the entrance to its shell in the fall and then breaks it open in the spring. Most importantly, however, snails and slugs came to symbolize Mary's virginity. This meaning was supported by the popular belief that lower animals such as worms, beetles, mosquitoes, and snails originate from clay without procreation. This idea of spontaneous generation, of a *genesis autómatos* of the lower forms of life, goes back to Aristotle and persisted into the eighteenth century (see Leonhard 2013: 47–56).

As pictorial signs and erudite reminders of Mary's virginity, snails are therefore rather frequently found in the decorative accessories to paintings of the birth of Christ and in depictions of Mary. The central panel of the winged altar in the so-called *Pearl of Brabant* (c. 1465, oil on oak panel, 62.7 x 62.6 cm [c. 24 7/10 x 24 3/5 in.], Alte Pinakothek, München), which was created at the same time as Cossa's *Annunciation* and is usually attributed to Dieric Bouts, can serve as an example. A snail or, in this case more precisely a slug, has been placed on a low brick retaining wall in the lower right-hand corner of the painting.

In a certain sense, the snail in Cossa's *Annunciation* is located "outside" the frame of the pictorial narrative sheerly on account of its size. Nearly as long as Gabriel's hand, it does not appear to be within the pictorial world but rather to crawl along the lower edge of the wooden frame of the main panel, as a *trompe-l'oeil* reproduction of a living snail. Like the beholder of the altarpiece, the snail appears to be located in real space – similar, in a certain sense, to its counterpart, the tip of Gabriel's right wing, which protrudes outward from the plane of representation.

In crossing the border between these worlds, this snail functions as part of a symbolic referential system, while at the same time opening this system up to a reality other than the one depicted by the painting. The snail is part of a double narrative – or should we say a triple narrative? For it is likely that the historical-theological context of the altarpiece is also inscribed into this painting. Cossa's *Annunciation* was originally installed in the church of the monastery complex of the Minori Osservanti in Bologna, which housed the first general chapter of this reform movement in 1431. It was precisely these Franciscan observers from Bologna who, around 1470, commissioned Francesco del Cossa to make this representation of the *Annunciation to Mary* as an altarpiece for their church. The aim of this reform movement, the popular devotions of which placed particular importance upon the veneration of the incarnation of Christ and the immaculate conception of Mary, was observance: adherence to the strict *Regula* or Rule of

St. Francis, and not least of all to his command to live in poverty. It therefore seems logical to also read the snail in Cossa's altarpiece as a sign of *humilitas*, an emblem, as it were, of the humility and simplicity preached by the reformed Franciscans – similar to the snail at the feet of St. Francis on the altarpiece *The Virgin and Child with Saints Francis and Sebastian*, painted in 1491 by Carlo Crivelli, another great master of the school of Ferrara (egg and oil on poplar, 175.3 x 151.1 cm [69 x 59 1/2 inch.], National Gallery, London).

Cossa's snail is thus not only both a pictorial detail that designates something that escapes pictorial representation – namely, the virginity of the Mother of God – and a *trompe-l'oeil* representation of a real, living snail that has crawled onto the panel. It is also a pictorial emblem that refers, in the context of a political church conflict, to the client who commissioned this altarpiece.

And finally: where is this snail really located? Is it on the lower edge of the wooden frame, as has been claimed so far? Or isn't it rather a part of the panel itself, a large, fully grown animal, placed at the outermost and barely visible edge of the marble floor in the vestibule of Mary's chamber, into which the angel has just entered? The master of the *Pearl of Brabant* clearly placed his snail within the painted pictorial world; in Cossa's painting, it is not only the animal's size but also its location that is vexing. The snail is a pictorial symbol on the border, on the threshold between real space and pictorial space, just as that which it signifies, Mary, is reproduced on a threshold, namely the threshold between her chamber and the space in which the angel appears. As a border-crosser between the worlds, the snail in Cossa's *Annunciation* functions as part of a topically closed action; and at the same time, it opens this action up to ambivalences, to different perspectives and unforeseeable questions.

Summing up, Joel Fineman writes in "The History of the Anecdote: Fiction and Fiction" (1989):

> In formal terms, my thesis is the following: that the anecdote is the literary form that uniquely *lets history happen* by virtue of the way it introduces an opening into the teleological, and therefore timeless, narration of beginning, middle, and end. The anecdote produces the effect of the real, the occurrence of contingency, by establishing an event as an event within and yet without the framing context of historical successivity. (61; original italics)

If one takes these often-quoted sentences as a guide, the affinity between the anecdote and our "strong" detail is obvious. But that is not all that can be deduced from our detail with regard to its half-sister, the anecdote. Seen more precisely, this detail not only opens the symbolic reference system for the framing narrative of the altarpiece panel but also manifests a constitutive power: it creates its own semantic field by suggesting an additional meaning for elements of the picture as a whole, shifting, as it were, this meaning into an additional perspective. Cossa's main panel and predella are closely related to each other: the vertical central axis of the panel runs through the central column of the architecture in the *Annunciation*, through the small flower rosette in the middle of its base; and on this central axis, in the predella, one finds the annunciation's counterpart in the future, the star in the stable of Bethlehem and the Christ Child (fig. 2). The snail at Mary's feet is placed exactly above the ox and donkey standing next to the crib. In early representations of the birth of Christ – for example, on the narrow side of the Sarcophagus of Stilicho in the Basilica of Sant'Ambrogio in Milan, from around 385 – one still finds just the ox and donkey alone, without Joseph and Mary worshiping the baby Jesus; the animals stand in for the creaturely creation and perhaps also for the ancient gods. The ox, for instance, reminds us – as if from a distance – that in ancient Egyptian mythology (as reported by Herodotus) the divine bull of Apis is conceived in its mother by a ray of light, and that this mother is a manifestation of the goddess Isis and also functions, in many ways, as a prefiguration of the Christian mother of God, Mary, just as the stable in Bethlehem appears in many ways to be a literal translation of the image of the late Egyptian birthplace of Mammisi. And is the arcade in the background of the left half of the painting not odd? The arcade in which we find a dog where we would expect Gabriel's left hand? Though what is most rewarding here is to take an even closer look at the figuration of the act of procreation; for in Cossa's *Annunciation*, the ray of light emanating from God the Father, the trajectory of the dove of the Holy Spirit, does not strike Mary's breast, or her heart, as is often the case in depictions of the annunciation. This ray of light of the Holy Spirit is aimed rather at a salient formation of folds in her robe (cf. fig. 1).

The life-size snail in Cossa's *Annunciation* constitutes an autonomous network of references that also includes the formation of folds in Mary's robe and the animals around the stall. This is a semantic field of the physical, the creaturely, the other side of incarnation, of becoming flesh: it is a field representing precisely that aspect of the theme of annunciation and procreation that falls between the "before" of the main panel and the "after" of the predella and that the narrative of the altarpiece omits or shifts elsewhere, as it were. This field of the creaturely has the function of supplementing and providing a countervoice to the voice of the narrative frame; and it is not least of all this network of references that lends the detail of the snail painted over the lower picture frame a narrative character, making the snail an almost anecdotal hint of a counternarrative.

Certainly, describing the position of the dog on the left side of the picture as "odd" is a matter of taste and subject to debate. The Egyptian "background" of

Fig. 2. Francesco del Cossa. *Annunciation*. Detail from fig. 1.

crib with ox and donkey is perhaps somewhat far-fetched; at the very least, it is an association outside the artist's intention. But does a "strong" detail, such as the snail in Cossa's *Annunciation*, not almost inevitably begin to develop a life of its own, an independent effective power, in addition to its intended function – to become an element whose meaning eludes definition, whose semantic implications resonate in ways that cannot ever be entirely foreseen? And which then – as an agent of other possible narratives – retrospectively has an effect on its own frame of meaning?

The strict symmetry of the stone architecture constructed according to the law of central perspective is disrupted by the out-of-place creature of the snail. This snail not only contrasts the events of the *Annunciation*, the space for this salvation history, with the lifeworld of lower creatures, or even – as a *trompe l'oeil* – the fictional pictorial space of a remembrance of this salvation event with the space of reality itself. It also contrasts the events of the altarpiece with another time: against the time of the unchangeable reality of salvation history, it sets real time; against the planning time of providence, it sets the time of chance and contingency; against the frightening suddenness of the appearance of the angel, it sets the banal length of time that the animal must have required in order to crawl to its present place; against the fulfilled time of a complex history, it sets the empty time of a mere event that leaves only a shapeless trace of slime. The snail in Cossa's *Annunciation* is like a worm in the woodwork of the building of salvation history; it is a relative of the snake in the Garden of Eden. And yet it is also a picture of the Mother of God herself.

In the school of Ferrara of the quattrocento, specifically in works by painters such as Francesco del Cossa, Cosimo Tura, or Carlo Crivelli, one frequently encounters small animals, or fruits and vegetables, such as apples, grapes, and cucumbers – and we also especially encounter them in representations of the Mother of God with her child.[1] Art history has interpreted these as signs of fertility and abundance, as signs of vitality. This may be the case on the level of motifs or iconography. What is striking, however, is how much this abundance of life contrasts with the often petrified, crystalline-ornamental quality of the worlds depicted in this kind of painting. In short: what is striking is the discrepancy between this petrification and the liveliness apostrophized by these objects as emblems. In our context, this means that the specific relationship between the narrative whole and detail itself is more meaningful than the narrative detail taken by itself.

---

[1] See, for example, Crivelli's *Madonna and Child* (c. 1480, tempera and gold on wood, 37.8 x 25.4 cm [14 7/8 x 10 in.], Metropolitan Museum of Art).

A "strong" detail prompts the question of the extent to which this detail is, as a condensed and displaced aspect, an essential part of the whole; and of what, in the constitution of this whole, favors or compels the emergence of one of its central dimensions as an independent element that is, at the same time, located both inside and outside the framework of this whole.

In Cossa's *Annunciation*, the snail crawling on the lower frame of the panel is the organizing center of the signs of natural creatureliness, which as such represents a countervoice to the salvation history of immaculate conception. At the same time, however, it is the most artificial element of the picture, the one that most clearly exhibits the conceptual dimension of this painting. The slow duration associated with a snail creates what its form promises: a vortex of levels of representation and reality.

It is premature, however, to determine the motif of the snail and the semantic field it opens up as a mere countervoice in Cossa's painting. One is tempted to say that the snail – in its resonance with the snail-like fold in front of Mary's womb that is struck by the Holy Spirit's ray of light – does not contradict the event of the great narrative of the altarpiece. Rather, it transforms it and repeats it in a different code. And that, together with the larger narrative of the altarpiece, it thus forms a figure for the twofold nature of the incarnation, tracing, as it were, the floor plan of the building of a myth in which virginity and fertility, providence and coincidence, time and eternity, come to stand together.

Works Cited

Arasse, Daniel. 2003. "Gott im Detail: Über einige italienische Verkündigungsszenen." Trans. Gustav Rößler. In: Wolfgang Schäffner, Sigrid Weigel, and Thomas Macho (eds.). *"Der liebe Gott steckt im Detail": Mikrostrukturen des Wissens*. München: Wilhelm Fink Verlag. 73–90.

Fineman, Joel. 1989. "The History of the Anecdote: Fiction and Fiction." In: H. Aram Veeser (ed.). *The New Historicism*. New York: Routledge. 49–76.

Leonhard, Karin. 2013. *Bildfelder: Stilleben und Naturstücke des 17. Jahrhunderts*. Berlin: Akademie Verlag.

Susanne von Falkenhausen
Anecdote vs. History: Jeff Wall's *Dead Troops Talk*

Translated by Michael Thomas Taylor

Abstract: This essay is an experiment, testing the use of the term "anecdote" for the analysis of images. In the general understanding of the term, "anecdote" designates a format that simply does not exist in the discipline of art history. The narrative focus of the anecdotal narrows its use for painting and other media of art to the figurative element. Therefore, my analysis takes a pictorial genre as its starting point which for centuries has represented the pinnacle of narration in the visual arts: history painting. Jeff Wall's *Dead Troops Talk*, a transparency with the gigantic measurements of 229 x 417 cm (90 x 164 in.), takes up history painting in the medium of photography. *Dead Troops Talk* is compared with large-scale history painting, large-scale abstract painting (Jackson Pollock), and with the small-scale history genre and a painting of contemporary history as seen and lived by the painter Ernest Meissonier.

Keywords: Anecdote in Art History, History Painting, Jeff Wall, Photography.

The anecdote from the lives of famous artists is well established as a genre of text in art history. Giorgio Vasari's *The Lives of the Artists* (1550–1568) is one prominent example. Yet, unlike literary studies, art history does not recognize the anecdote as a specific genre of painting. The anecdote as a genre also does not appear in the classical hierarchy of genres that was cultivated by art academies up to the nineteenth century. On the contrary, when the descriptive adjective *anekdotisch* ("anecdotal"), does appear – which is not often – in order to describe a visual narrative, it usually has a pejorative tone. Its use in these cases is thus descriptive. It transports a textual category into the visual and thus mainly relies on the contrast between a small form or history – such as genre painting, which was the second lowest in the hierarchy of genres of painting, just one place up from the still life – and the large form or history that is found in history painting, the highest genre in this hierarchy (although it must be said that the concern of history painting is not a single story but rather history as such in the sense of the collective singular described by

Reinhart Koselleck).[1] It is in this descriptive-evaluative, rather than classificatory, function that the anecdotal is linked to the formal-aesthetic and genre-specific problems that arise when paintings tell stories. In history painting, the problem of telling a story under the force of history is doubled, as it were, which is why the following considerations focus on this genre.[2]

In art history, comparison is a proven means of illuminating questions of visual analysis. An essential requirement for such a procedure is the *tertium comparationis* common to the objects being compared, which provides the anchoring without which the comparison would appear arbitrary. Hence, the comparison I propose making between Jackson Pollock's *One (No. 31)* (1950, oil and enamel on canvas, 269.5 x 530.8 cm [ca. 106 x 208 in.], The Museum of Modern Art) and Jeff Wall's *Dead Troops Talk (a vision after an ambush of a Red Army patrol, near Moqor, Afghanistan, winter 1986)* (1992, transparency in a lightbox, 229 x 417 cm [90 x 164 in.] [fig. 1]) might seem both historically and formally surprising.[3] At first glance, nothing connects the images. One image is representational, the other abstract; the representational image is photographed, the abstract image painted. So why am I making this juxtaposition – which (I have to admit) possesses considerable rhetorical allure? Despite the enormous differences between the images, there are certain similarities here that serve as *tertia comparationis:* the wide-screen format and a limited tonality of colors between black, brown, and just a bit of white. The format is something both images have in common with the great battle scenes from the nineteenth century; it is associated with the hunger for images that, beginning in the late eighteenth century, gave rise to the panorama[4] and, during the last century, the CinemaScope film. As history painting, the large format connotes great history. It is only in being contrasted with great history and its pictorial equivalent that the anecdote becomes pejoratively tinged. So why am I making this juxtaposition of two images, which share a format with classic history painting, if my topic here is the anecdote? And why have I turned to a so-called abstract image, without narrative or figures, without the accentuated center of the image that creates a space for the hero in history painting?

According to Clement Greenberg, Pollock's work gives rise to pure painting, without the production of a mimetic appearance, without referentiality, and thus without representation.[5] Pure painting would thus be pure presence, pure

---

1 See Koselleck (1975).
2 On historical painting, see von Falkenhausen (1997; 2011).
3 For further details, see Wall (1993).
4 Cf. Plessen (1993).
5 Cf. Greenberg (1955).

Fig. 1. Jeff Wall. *Dead Troops Talk (a vision after an ambush of a Red Army Patrol, near Moqor, Afghanistan, winter 1986)*. 1992. Transparency in a light box, 229 x 417 cm (90 x 164 in.). © Courtesy of the artist and the Broad Art Foundation, Los Angeles.

self-reference. The misery of representation would be overcome, making painting an act without denotations – which, however, cannot be "seen" in its act but only in its product. The often-lamented break between the presence of the creative act and the representation in the image nourishes a pictorial desire documenting this act – a desire catered to by the well-known photographs that Hans Namuth took of Pollock in the act of painting, which we could also regard as a version, in images, of the artist's anecdote that testifies to the creative act (printed in Goodnough 1951). And now, forty years later, we have Wall's large-scale transparency. Is it a battle image equivalent to history painting? A return to everything that already appears to have been vanquished – to remain with the metaphor of war – by painting as practiced by someone like Pollock: representation, figure, narration, naturalism, heroes? The slide shows an ascending hollow in stony terrain, crossed by beaten paths and bullet holes. Across the lower half of the image, groups of soldiers are spread out in twos and threes, with one group of four. The soldiers are all wounded, deathly pale; the wounds are in part so grave that upon studying the details one concludes the soldiers must be dead. Yet some of the figures are quite active. At the upper right edge of the image, we can see the legs of Afghan Mujahideen fighters, cut off by the top of the photo; a small wall of loose stones and oil barrels delineate the upper pictorial space. There is a piece of battered corrugated metal on the left, and other war rubbish is scattered all over the area. After looking for a while, one can pick out another Mujahideen figure, almost invisible between the boulders in his earth-toned garments. He is squatting above the group of soldiers on the left and rummaging in a backpack. As with Pollock's painterly all-over structure, here, too, there is no obvious pictorial center. The distribution of the figures and details creates an equivalence of the entire surface of the image, and this contradicts the conventional modes of pictorial narration. This is considerably different from classic history painting: there is no single hero in this narrative placed in a compositionally accentuated pictorial center; what we have is, so to speak, an all-over narrative.

The exact title and the hyperprecise reproduction of the scene suggest a factuality of the event. But is this image a "real" war photo? The very qualities that make the image appear to belong to the genre of history painting are evidence that it is not: the huge landscape format can hardly be achieved with a reporter's small-format camera; the depth of field in the entire image – none of the movements are blurred – is unusual in the genre of photo reportage simply because motion blur is considered to be proof of the authenticity of having been there. The careful placement of the groups in the pictorial space or on the surface of the image is also evidence that it did not originate in a war situation; this placement could hardly have been managed by an embedded war photographer.

However, the seven groups of (un)dead caught up in activities that look quite absurd can only be distinguished if the pictorial surface is carefully scanned with the eye, which in turn contradicts the narrative strategy of history painting, which is focused on the individual hero. The facial expressions and gestures of these dead figures are reminiscent of slapstick cinema. Their multiple activities contrast strangely with the calm after the storm emanating from the figure of the young Mujahid immersed in his activity.

These characteristics reveal that we are not dealing with a snapshot, but with so-called staged photography (as we would expect from Wall, incidentally). *Dead Troops Talk* can certainly be described in terms of the image-making machineries of the nineteenth century: every detail was carefully planned; the image's individual parts were developed separately and only assembled in the final version, similar to the way the history painters worked in their studios. The technology used is nevertheless significantly different: computers, photography, and the computer-controlled make-up artistry of horror and war films. The production conditions corresponded to those of film – except that here, they were employed with the aim of creating a *still* image. However, both forms of production – history painting and Wall's large-scale photos – share a structural feature: they produce something that functions only in fetishizing the imitation of reality down to the last detail. But the new image technologies are not simply contemporary substitutes for the outdated mimetic techniques of painting, because these technologies have also changed the prerequisites for the genres of images bound to mimesis – their generic boundaries, their apparatus (also in the ideological sense), their rhetorical laws and codes, their reception, and their embeddedness in the history or histories of discourse. This difference of technologies is why *Dead Troops Talk* looks like a history painting at first glance and thus seems to confirm this genre. Yet Wall also situates the image as an anachronism, because at the time of its creation in the 1990s neither history paintings nor large-format war photography were current genres. Even the wide-screen war film, with its affordance of perceptual immersion, is not a suitable media-specific equivalent.

A further break with the narrative style of history painting is the negation of the image's narrative center mentioned above. In its place, Wall offers the viewer seven small groups, which could perhaps be described in a stylistic sense as a small form, as "anecdotal." However, one thing I learned from a brief foray into the attempts that literary scholars have made to define the term is that the anecdote is "told *like* a fact" (Niehaus 2013: 196; original italics).[6] Given

---

6 Unless otherwise indicated, all translations are by Michael Thomas Taylor.

the accuracy of the details, one might be able to agree here on this "like" as a stylistic device. "This means that signals of fictionality cannot occur in the anecdote" (ibid.). And this specifically proves not to be the case when we more closely examine the highly active undead figures. Ultimately, however, it is possible here to work only with the category of the "anecdotal," meaning that the criteria for the ascription of this term can be relaxed.

A further comparison is now intended to illustrate the problem of the formal conditions of pictorial narrative in relation to the genre of history painting. In the middle of the nineteenth century, contemporaneous with the crisis of large-format history painting (and its clientele, the princely houses), the genre of small-format history painting emerged. The genre was not, however, devoted to the great events or heroes of history. Rather, it realized a historical turn in genre painting in the form of decoration for bourgeois homes, specialized in scenes of rural, domestic idylls. Because of the genre's small form, we could describe it as anecdotal. To conclude my argument, I now offer a comparative juxtaposition between such a small-format image of history, a large-format history painting, and a picture of an event that in turn breaks down these generic boundaries – all of which were executed by the same painter, Ernest Meissonier (who is thus another *tertium comparationis*). I employ this juxtaposition to make a cross comparison with *Dead Troops Talk* that sharpens the contours of the anecdotal within images.

A battle scene, *Friedland*, painted by Ernest Meissonier between 1861 and 1875 in the monumental format of 135 x 242 cm (ca. 33 x 95 in.) shows the French troops jubilantly parading in front of Napoleon after their victory over the Prussian army in 1807 at Friedland (oil on canvas, The Metropolitan Museum of Art, New York). Meissonier created a thrilling rotational movement that combines a wealth of detail with an almost cinematic overall effect. The collective heroism of the soldiers is combined with the staging of the hero who holds this collective together.[7] This is quite different from Meissonier's *Un jeu de piquet* (1861), a so-called historical genre painting only slightly larger than DIN A4 that shows soldiers in seventeenth-century garb playing chess (oil on canvas, 29.3 x 36.7 cm [ca. 11 1/2 x 14 in.], National Museum Cardiff). Here, the painting tells a scene from the soldier's daily life, both formally and thematically, as an idyll, or anecdote, that is further distanced from its cruel realities by the historicizing clothing. Yet there is a painting by Meissonier that violates this generic convention, even though it has the same format: *Souvenir de guerre civile* (1849, oil on canvas, 29 x 22 cm [11 x 8 1/2 in.], Louvre), shows a barricade during

---

7 On the relation between collective and individual heroism, see von Falkenhausen (1996).

the June Days uprising of 1848 in the Rue de la Mortellerie, near the Hotel de Ville in Paris, after it was stormed by the National Guard.[8] It is too small for a history painting – no larger than a DIN A4 sheet. Moreover, the painting is not about a historical event, but rather a contemporary one. For the historical genre painting, by contrast, the format fits but not the theme, which calls to mind for the viewers the traumatic consequences of a very present, civil-war-like conflict. Théophile Gautier spoke of "this veritable truth that no one wants to say" ("*cette vérité vraie que personne ne veut dire*" [qtd. in Durey et al. 1993: 166]). The first sketches were made shortly after the battles in which Meissonier took part, fighting on the side of the National Guard. When it comes to contemporary but historically significant events, art historical scholarship speaks not of history painting, *Historienbild*, but of an event image, *Ereignisbild*. Yet as a rule, contemporary events were only regarded as historically significant and thus worthy of representation if they featured heroes. *Souvenir de guerre civil*, however, depicts no heroes from either side; it exclusively shows corpses; it is more of a (literal) *nature morte* (French for still life) than an event, and contemporary critics did in fact give it the label of still life. In view of the gruesome sight that Meissonier pictured, this classification strikes today's beholders as cynical. Unimpressed by the subject matter, the Parisian critics at the painting's exhibition in the Paris Salon of 1851 viewed it as connoisseurs and judged it according to the laws of genres and craftsmanship. Can we therefore call Meissonier's image of the barricade, on account of its small size, anecdotal? In any case, it is "told *like* a fact" (Niehaus 2013: 196; original italics). However, likely due to its comparably small format, it was exhibited in the Salon alongside historical genre paintings that mostly showed imaginary, popular scenes in a historical setting and together with the picture of the soldiers playing chess. Nevertheless, Meissonier operates here as an eyewitness: he had seen what was being recounted, and in this sense, it indeed was a fact. He expels the idyll from the small format and produces a kind of war photography *avant le lettre*.

Beyond the question of scale, one can compare a detail from one of the groups of figures in *Dead Troops Talk* to this painting. It becomes clear that the factual quality suggested by photography as a recording medium is frustrated by the grotesquely busy undead figures, whom, however, one can filter out only upon studying this picture, which is teeming with details up close.

---

8 The small-scale oil painting is based on a watercolor completed in the immediate aftermath of the battle. For further details regarding the painting, see Durey et al. (1993: 162–166); regarding the watercolor and sketches, see Durey et al. (1993: 181–183); see also Hungerford (1979).

They make *the anecdotal* all too visible as a *remainder,* a detritus of the historical when, as here, this quality appears in the large format of history painting itself. Wall himself says that his work is concerned with the grotesque (1997: 44–45). Seen from the medium's point of view, the grotesque could already emerge via the anachronism of a "history" painting perfectly staged with the technical means of the 1990s. Without the historical tradition of the visual codes of history painting, this image would not exist. But this image would not exist either without a nonpainterly technology for its production. It is photography that makes this updating possible in the first place. And this is a consequence of the break with representation that I sketched with the example of Pollock. A return to the codes of history painting in the tradition of the nineteenth century, therefore, is no longer possible within the system of art, no matter in which medium. *Dead Troops Talk* operates with the visual signifiers of an obsolete genre that have lost the syntax formed by the conventions of the genre. The referential system of the battle scene, which had already begun to waver with Meissonier's small, heroic painting of the corpses on the barricades, is gone. But that is not enough for Wall, who – with this update of the genre – not only demonstrates its obsolescence: he wants to say something beyond a purely formal critique of the genre system of art. He needs the small, anecdotal form in a large format to communicate what he understands to be grotesque: "a rather dramatic state, the state of not yet being completed and suffering from deformities due to social, political, psychological circumstances" (Wall 1997: 44–45). Into this image, which appears so seamless in its mimesis and spatial organization, the small form of the anecdotal within this large historical format thus introduces, in the first place, the disturbance of perception enabling Wall's artistic critique of the deformities of the present.

Works Cited

Durey, Philippe et al. 1993. [Exhibition Catalogue] *Ernest Meissonier: rétrospective.* Lyon: Musée des Beaux-Arts de Lyon.
Goodnough, Robert. 1951. "Pollock Paints a Picture." *Art News* 50.3: 38–41, 60–61.
Greenberg, Clement. 1993 [1955]. "'American-Type' Painting." In: John O'Brian (ed.). *The Collected Essays and Criticism.* Vol. 3: *Affirmations and Refusals 1950–1956.* Chicago: Chicago University Press.
Hungerford, Constance Cain. 1979. "Meissonier's *Souvenir de guerre civil.*" *The Art Bulletin* 61.2: 277–288.
Koselleck, Reinhart. 1975. "Geschichte." In: Otto Brunner, Werner Conze, and Reinhart Koselleck (eds.). *Geschichtliche Grundbegriffe: Historisches Lexikon zur politisch-sozialen Sprache in Deutschland.* Vol. 2. Stuttgart: Klett-Cotta. 593–718.

Niehaus, Michael. 2013. "Die sprechende und die stumme Anekdote." *Zeitschrift für deutsche Philologie* 132.2: 183–200.
Plessen, Marie-Luise (ed.). 1993. *Sehnsucht: Das Panorama als Massenunterhaltung des 19. Jahrhunderts*. Basel: Strömfeld.
Vasari, Giorgio. *The Lives of the Artists*. 1998 [1550–1568]. Trans. Julia Conaway Bondanella and Peter Bondanella. New York: Oxford University Press.
von Falkenhausen, Susanne. 2011. "Wie die Gewalt aus der Kunst 'spricht': Über visuelle Codierung von Gewalt." In: Ilaria Hoppe, Bettina Uppenkamp, and Elena Zanichelli (eds.). *Praktiken des Sehens im Felde der Macht: Gesammelte Schriften*. Hamburg: Fundus. 53–78.
von Falkenhausen, Susanne. 1997. "1880–1945: Wie kommt Geschichte ins Bild? Warum verschwindet sie daraus? Und taucht sie wieder auf? Eine Skizze." In: Wolfgang Küttler, Jörn Rüsen, and Ernst Schuling (eds.). *Geschichtsdiskurs*. Vol. 4: *Krisenbewußtsein, Katastrophenerfahrungen und Innovationen 1880–1945*. Frankfurt am Main: Fischer Wissenschaft. 247–275.
von Falkenhausen, Susanne. 1996. "Vom Ballhausschwur zum Duce: Visuelle Repräsentation von Volkssouveränität zwischen Demokratie und Autokratie." In: Annette Graczyk (ed.). *Das Volk: Abbild, Konstruktion, Phantasma*. Berlin: Akademie Verlag. 3–17.
Wall, Jeff (with Anne-Marie Bonnet and Rainer Metzger). 1997. "Eine demokratische, eine bourgeoise Tradition der Kunst. Ein Gespräch mit Jeff Wall (1994)." In: Gregor Stemmrich (ed.). *Szenarien im Bildraum der Wirklichkeit: Essays und Interviews*. Amsterdam: Philo Fine Arts. 33–45.
Wall, Jeff. 1993. *Dead Troops Talk*. [Exhibition Catalogue Kunstmuseum Luzern, The Irish Museum of Modern Art Dublin, and Deichtorhallen Hamburg] Luzern: Kunstmuseum Luzern.

Fig. 1. Ben Shahn. *The Lucky Dragon*. 1960. Tempera on board, 215 x 122 cm (84 1/2 x 48 in.). Fukushima Prefectural Museum of Art, Japan. © VG Bild-Kunst, Bonn 2020.

Christof Decker
A Unique Universalism: Ben Shahn and the Rhetoric of Visual Anecdotes

Abstract: Anecdotes have often been discussed as textual forms shaped by means of language and narrativity. Yet various traditions in visual culture have explored the representation of anecdotal scenes in paintings, drawings, or other media. While some scholars link the notion of visual anecdotes to specific traditions such as genre paintings, this article argues for an anecdotal style that emerged in the period of American modernism and featured unique combinations of image and text. Looking at the work of Ben Shahn, one of the most prolific American artists in the first half of the twentieth century, I contend that the interplay, in his art, of textual fragments with images of the human body established an intricate visual rhetoric. Produced in the 1950s against the historical backdrop of the Atomic Age, these hybrid forms aimed for historical specificity and served as a critique of acts of injustice, ultimately supporting Shahn's conviction that art could be used for the purposes of communication. Yet I argue that his work also explores, at both a textual and visual level, the challenge of art in general and anecdotes in particular to relate the peculiar to the universal without becoming merely more abstract or losing the connection with human experience.

Keywords: Ben Shahn, Cold War Culture, Political Art, Sacco and Vanzetti, Visual Anecdote.

1 Ben Shahn and American Visual Culture in the 1950s

In the mid-1950s, the painter and photographer Ben Shahn gave a series of lectures at Harvard University later published as *The Shape of Content* (1957) in which he reflected on the development of his art and career.[1] A contemporary of artists such as Stuart Davis, Raphael Soyer, William Gropper, and Walker Evans, Shahn had produced a substantial body of work in painting, large-scale murals, lithographs, and illustrations as well as photographs for the

---

[1] I would like to thank the Terra Foundation for American Art, which supported research for this article through a Senior Scholar Travel Grant.

https://doi.org/10.1515/9783110668490-019

Farm Security Administration and posters for the Office of War Information (OWI). After working as a modernist in the 1920s and turning to social realism during the Great Depression, the war years had seen him moving away from the depiction of topical issues, instead attempting to express a universal experience of humankind. Yet, as an artist suspicious of modern science and statistical thinking, Shahn wanted to avoid abstract generalities and formulated a notion of universal experience that was grounded in uniqueness and peculiarity. While to him the sociology of the 1950s propagated averages devoid of individual qualities, Shahn suggested that "the universal is that unique thing which affirms the unique qualities of all things." He went on to explain: "The universal experience is that private experience which illuminates the private and personal world in which each of us lives the major part of his life" (1957: 47). This seemingly paradoxical idea of a unique universalism, which regarded the specificity of experience – its singularity and peculiarities – as universally relatable, is an apt shorthand description for the special quality of Shahn's work from the 1950s that I wish to focus on, in particular two series of images I will consider as visual anecdotes in this essay.

In the two series to be discussed here, Shahn references concrete historical incidents: on the one hand, the infamous 1920s trial of the two anarchists Nicola Sacco and Bartolomeo Vanzetti; on the other, the Cold War reality of atomic tests, in particular the so-called *"Lucky Dragon* incident." While the case of Sacco and Vanzetti culminated in their execution in 1927, the *Lucky Dragon* incident concerned the contamination of Japanese fishermen after the testing of an American atomic bomb in 1954 and the subsequent death of one of the crewmen, Aikichi Kuboyama. Both series include images of human beings, combining textual and visual elements and embedding them in a historically specific scene with a place, a time, and a powerful storyline. Semiotically, then, the visual objects to be considered as visual anecdotes in this essay create multiple meanings at both a pictorial and a language-based level as well as through their combination and juxtaposition. Shahn, who was trained as a lithographer, meticulously worked on the typeface of his written material, making it unique and highly individual. The lettering had "a place in and around pictures both as communication and as design," as he stated in a 1949 reflection on "If I Had to Begin My Art Career Today" (1972: 97). But by laying out exemplary situations and experiences, he ultimately shifted the emphasis from an individual to a systemic level – from the trial of two Italian immigrants to the U.S. American justice system and from Japanese fishermen to the specter of atomic war.

In this sense, Shahn's images are different from other types of visual anecdotes which, understood as a distinct category, need careful consideration. By incorporating textual inscriptions Shahn's work explores the dialectic of singularity and exemplariness, a crucial element of anecdotes according to Malina Stefanovska (2009), at different semiotic levels. Following art scholar John Fagg (2004) and his discussion of early American modernism, anecdotal paintings may depict self-contained scenes, or they may represent genre paintings featuring small, anecdotal details. Shahn's visual anecdotes share the quality of presenting brief, self-contained incidents and, furthermore, incorporate what Fagg calls "a reality claim as well as the potential to puncture and disrupt" (2004: 475). However, the inherent tension between text and image also makes them different. They combine representations of the human body with stories of its dissolution in ways that highlight vernacular language and individualized images but also aim for general insights and meanings. In other words, Shahn's anecdotes establish the dialectic of singularity and exemplariness through their peculiar combination of text and image.

Shahn developed this form of text-image combinations during the 1930s, in part working against then prevalent notions of (French) avant-gardism but also shaping his style from within a New York-based immigrant culture enmeshed as much in political activism as in popular and mass culture. While producing a series of watercolors dedicated to the Dreyfus Affair – dating back to 1890s France and dealing with injustice and antisemitism – Shahn discovered his predilection for expressive directness and communicability. He recalls that he began to see a new form of expression, "a means by which I could unfold a great deal of my most personal thinking and feeling without loss of simplicity. I felt that the very directness of statement of these pictures was a great virtue in itself" (1957: 36–37). According to Susan Chevlowe, this moment of linking politics and aesthetics in the Dreyfus series was typical for Shahn's generation of Jewish artists for whom left-wing politics had become a "secular religion" and who "were shaped by the immigrant experience, by labor struggles, and by the Great Depression" (1998: 25). After the historical rupture of the First World War with images serving as propagandistic elements of warfare, American visual culture increasingly faced the artistic challenge of using actual and individualized incidents – narrative fragments or anecdotes – to signify a generalizable and common experience. For Shahn and other socially conscious artists, this challenge revolved around the question of how the modern, increasingly devastating experience of destruction and injustice could be represented through pictorial forms that were at the same time highly symbolic *and* based on individual experience.

Viewed through the lens of American cultural history, the underlying question of how individual anecdotes may be related to more comprehensive narratives of injustice, has been a pressing issue for artists and authors since the early republic. One of the bestsellers of American short fiction, Washington Irving's

The Sketchbook of Geoffrey Crayon from 1820, featured an essay on "Traits of Indian Character," which criticizes American society for its lack of understanding of Native Americans and which includes an anecdote about the violation and plundering of the Sachem mother's tomb by the planters of Plymouth. The function of this anecdote was to show how Native Americans had been mistreated and to explain why this mistreatment justified their frequent outbursts of violence and cruelty. In Irving's essay, therefore, the anecdote serves metonymically to reference an experience that illustrates the larger narrative of injury, presenting an individual scene as a typical instance of atrocities perpetrated by white men and thereby using it to put forward a general and comprehensive argument – a pattern which would resurface in later decades. Authors such as Richard Wright or Ralph Ellison invoked the exemplary status of cruel anecdotes for a vision of racial and racist hierarchies inherited from slavery, while Bernard Malamud, writing about the Holocaust in the 1960s, spotlighted the random quality of murderous acts in "The German Refugee" (1964) and suggested in the concluding section that they were presented most forcefully through the matter-of-factness and understated quality of their plain description. In literary history, then, anecdotal evidence of cruel or atrocious acts survives most forcefully in the genre of the short story.

In Shahn's case, numerous of his paintings and illustrations combine text and image in ways that create meanings at the textual level of micro-narratives as well as at the pictorial level of figurative representations. As a social realist and a member of the left-leaning intellectual milieu and Jewish community of New York City, Shahn aimed to link the topicality of journalism with the universality of symbolic or allegorical depictions (cf. Pohl 1998). Bringing together a journalistic and an art discourse, he focused on specific, individual groups of victims, but also on the more general and abstract conditions of victimization. Likewise, he depicted the random and contingent scene – the incident – but also included references to its enormous historical and moral significance. Thus combining textual material with corporeal gestures, Shahn's images were readable, first, as historically specific scenes and, second, as reflections on their meaning and moral implications. In this way, the often shocking and unfathomable quality of acts of injustice throughout the twentieth century, which was present in all discourses ranging from journalism to art, was framed by a meditation on their representability with artistic means.

In Shahn's development as an artist, the shift from topical issues of the Great Depression to a broader notion of universal experience took place during the years of the Second World War. One reason for this changing outlook was the enormity of war-related events, including acts of persecution and destruction taking place in Europe and Asia, another the need to address a broader audience while working for government projects and institutions. A crucial case in point is the war poster "This is Nazi Brutality" (1943), which Shahn created at the Office of War Information after the assassination of Reinhard Heydrich in Prague and subsequent German revenge killings at Lidice (then Czechoslovakia) in 1942. It shows the hooded, shackled figure of a man to be executed and the official Nazi statement announcing the destruction of Lidice. In his design, Shahn uses the statement as both a detached *and* a personal narrative, signifying something that had happened to an individual subject – represented by the shackled figure – as well as to abstract categories of victims. However, by not showing the victim's face, Shahn blocks the viewer's access to common markers of suffering and interiority, thus withholding crucial aspects of individual experience (cf. Decker 2019).

In this case, then, Shahn's poster design and the tensions between its textual and graphic elements suggest an ambiguous stance on the ability of art to bring together individual experience and its general, or even universal, significance in meaningful ways. The horrific experience of total warfare with its millions of dead or displaced persons cried out for less local and topical forms of expression, but these forms always seemed to come at a price. Shahn put the dilemma succinctly in one of his Harvard lectures: "How can one actually achieve a universality in painting without becoming merely more generalized and abstract?" (1957: 45). While his individual style had evolved from a desire for directness and simplicity, the transition that a global war seemed to be calling for posed new challenges. Looking back on this period, Shahn noted the wish to broaden his outlook. Earlier in his career he had believed that the incidental and the topical could evoke life as a whole; now his view had changed: "I wanted to reach farther, to tap some sort of universal experience, to create symbols that would have some such universal quality" (ibid.). However, since becoming more universal should not mean merely becoming more general, Shahn pursued the aspiration of a unique universalism, or, as art historian Cécile Whiting has suggested, a "pluralistic universalism" in his art of the 1950s (2016: 13) – a universalism that avoids the naive humanism critics noted in the 1950s about ambitious and seminal shows such as *The Family of Man* exhibition at the Museum of Modern Art in 1955.[2]

---

[2] See Winfried Fluck for an instructive reconsideration of *The Family of Man* exhibition. Following his analysis, traditional references to the common humanity of the show or, alternatively, to its lack of difference, no longer do justice to its legacy. He suggests a new "narrative of poetic self-recognition" to describe the complex aesthetic and social dimensions of the exhibition and concludes that it was "not simply a naïve liberal confirmation of a universal humanity narrative, but an inventory of imaginary possibilities of the self at a particular time" (2018: 129).

On the one hand, Shahn's search for this new symbolism produced a series of paintings titled "allegory," which includes condensed, emblematic images of intense feelings or states of mind, most importantly a lion-like head surrounded by a wreath of flames (cf. Shahn 1957: 129). This allegorical image evolved from a commercial assignment for an article on a tenement fire which had killed four children of a black man named John Hickman (cf. Shahn 1957: 25–52; Pohl 1989: 66–72). On the other hand, the wish to capture a universal experience without, however, abandoning the unique and peculiar quality of that experience also found expression in text-image combinations that belonged less to the transhistorical trajectory of allegories and more to the historically grounded character of visual anecdotes. Thus, during the course of the 1950s, Shahn shifted his attention to the threat of nuclear warfare and he returned to the infamous trial and conviction of Nicola Sacco and Bartolomeo Vanzetti, which had been the topic of his breakthrough series of paintings in the early 1930s.

2 The Human Body in the Atomic Age

Shahn's series of paintings on the threat of nuclear weapons – eventually called the *Lucky Dragon* series – emerged from an assignment to create a number of drawings for an article about the *Lucky Dragon* incident in which a Japanese fishing vessel was accidentally exposed to atomic fallout near the Marshall Islands, causing the death of fisherman and radio operator Aikichi Kuboyama. Four years later, in 1958, *Harper's Magazine* commissioned Ralph Eugene Lapp, a physicist and scientific advisor on atomic energy during the Second World War, to write an essay on the 1954 testing of the H-Bomb and the fate of the *Lucky Dragon*. "The new Bikini bomb was of incredible destructiveness," Lapp conceded (1958: II, 54). Shahn provided numerous drawings for the essay and these drawings, in turn, became the basis for his independently produced *Lucky Dragon* series.

In one of these paintings Shahn combines a personal statement of the fisherman Kuboyama with an image of his sick and dying body at the Tokyo hospital. Kuboyama's body, which had been exposed to radioactive fallout, is placed at the center of the painting against an abstract background; he is seated on a thinly sketched and seemingly fragile hospital bed (fig. 1). Hardly wearing any clothes, Kuboyama's body is presented in a semi-transparent state that allows the viewer to see through his skin and gaze at the system of arteries and veins pumping blood through a body that had been poisoned as a result of the atomic tests. Indeed, although Kuboyama is sitting in an upright position, parts of his body are so transparent that they seem to lack any substance and appear as if they will soon collapse. In his right hand, he presents a written note.

The design of Shahn's painting combines elements of two drawings he created for the *Harper's* article. One drawing from a section of the article on the hospitalization of the boat's crew showed a half-naked fisherman sitting on a bed and looking to the left (cf. Lapp 1958: II, 55). Significantly, this body looks younger, stronger, and shielded by an impenetrable outer skin. The second drawing that Shahn incorporated into his later painting – a black patch to the left of the fisherman's head – had originally been included in the article's description of the atomic explosion in a section called "Sunrise in the West" (cf. Lapp 1957: I, 30). This drawing evokes the mushroom cloud following an atomic blast, but it also includes the signature allegorical element of Shahn's work: the image of a lion's head surrounded by flames and representing, as Shahn put it in one of the Harvard lectures, "some inner figure of primitive terror" (1957: 31). This motif had been used in earlier paintings as an allegorical representation of fire and destruction, and it was now related to the *Lucky Dragon* incident. As art historian Frances Pohl points out, in earlier paintings "the fire-wreath symbolized injustice and the destructive power of fire." In the 1950s, however, the motif had "come to symbolize the destructive power and unjust use of another cataclysmic 'fire' – nuclear weapons" (1998: 121).

Yet this allegorical reference recedes into the background, visible only upon close view. What the painting (fig. 1) displays in more prominent form is the textual note in Kuboyama's hand, meticulously crafted in a unique typeface. It presents in condensed, anecdotal form the incident:

> I am a fisherman Aikichi Kuboyama by name. On the first of March 1954 our fishing boat the Lucky Dragon wandered under an atomic cloud eighty miles from Bikini. I and my friends were burned. We did not know what happened to us. On September twenty third of that year I died of atomic burn.

Similar to the Lidice poster produced during the Second World War, Shahn focuses on the final moments in Kuboyama's life, putting his weakened body on display for the viewers as the corporeal gesture of the painting, while the textual inscription serves to reference the generalizable implications of his trip. In this case, however, the moral framing of the incident is less accusatory and specific, leaving out who was responsible for the "atomic cloud." Yet the text clearly addressed an American public, which would have understood the references, having learned, as *Life* magazine put it in 1954, that the fisherman's story "translated the awesomeness of the H-bomb into human terms all Americans can comprehend" (Martin 1954: 17). This understanding allows the visual anecdote to oscillate between the mundane world of a fishing trip and the horrific implications of atomic burn, between the lack of knowledge of the common people and the secrecy of a military superpower.

Thus, even though Shahn includes one of his typical allegorical motifs symbolizing fire and destruction, the painting aims for historical specificity. Against the powerful, but abstract scientific and military forces of destruction, looming like wild and evil beasts in the background, Shahn uses the fisherman's story to juxtapose the contingent scene of his crew's boating trip with the enormous historical and moral significance of its outcome. As Lapp stated in the conclusion of his essay for *Harper's Magazine:* "The true striking power of the atom was revealed on the decks of the *Lucky Dragon.* When men a hundred miles from an explosion can be killed by its silent touch, the world suddenly becomes too small a place for men to clutch such weapons" (1958: III, 79). The exposure to the blast and subsequent symptoms of atomic fever mentioned in the text and visible on Kuboyama's body demonstrate not only the frailty of human beings and the carelessness of the military, but also the lethal consequences of atomic weapons polluting the environment on an unprecedented scale. The universalism of this linkage was underscored by the fact that, in some of Shahn's other paintings from the *Lucky Dragon* series, Kuboyama's skin appeared to be significantly darker, almost black. Following Whiting's interpretation, the various ways of showing Kuboyama's body represented Shahn's attempt to elicit "empathy from the viewer, extending compassion across national, ethnic, and racial divides" (2016: 5). Just as the incident showed that military and economic relations had global repercussions, Shahn's pictorial variations implied that spotlighting one group of individuals affected by the explosion needed to be broadened to include other non-white minority groups.

Although testing nuclear weapons was not the same as atomic war and, thus, not an atrocious crime in the sense of the massacre at Lidice in 1942, Shahn's attempt to link Kuboyama's experience with the enormity of nuclear warfare points to similar challenges for his work. By combining figurative representations and textual inscriptions, Shahn's visual anecdotes create a unique hybrid form. At the figurative level, his corporeal gestures present the individual in intense moments of crisis and highly symbolic moments of truth. In this way, the body images establish the visceral, climactic intensity of the individual's final moments. At the level of textual inscription, on the other hand, Shahn's work establishes historical specificity and context but also introduces abstract linguistic categories. By combining the two levels, the recognizable human body in Shahn's visual anecdotes disrupts and freezes the flow of the textual narrative, while the textual inscription, in turn, legitimizes its claim as an exemplary image.

This unique combination in Shahn's work indicates that he attempted to face head-on the dilemma of how to negotiate the representation of the human body with the knowledge of its dissolution and death. By contrasting human figure and textual inscription, Shahn's visual anecdote produces a rift between the visual imprint of the body and the textual evidence of its eventual dissolution. This rift between corporeal presence and knowledge of its disappearance, between lifelike imprint and retrospective narrative of loss suggests that, multilayered as they were, Shahn's visual anecdotes about large-scale threats ultimately highlight the modernist dilemma of attempting to signify the unsignifiable: to present individuals as human beings with dignity and value, while also having to make sense of, and give meaning to, the contingency of their death.

3 Revisiting Sacco and Vanzetti

In the 1950s, Shahn revisited the trial of the two anarchists Nicola Sacco and Bartolomeo Vanzetti when, in order to mark the twenty-fifth anniversary of their execution, he was commissioned to draw the cover for the August 23rd, 1952 issue of *The Nation*. The trial, conviction, and execution of the two Italian-American men – a complex history sketched by Nunzio Pernicone (2001) – had been the subject of a series of paintings in the early 1930s. This series had helped Shahn to establish his style of personal involvement and directness, and to develop his topical interests. Now, following his gradual shift toward a unique universalism, he reinterpreted the iconography and meaning of their visual depiction. Among his earlier 1930s series, Shahn had produced the painting *Bartolomeo Vanzetti and Nicola Sacco* (1931–1932, Museum of Modern Art), which was based on a press photograph showing the two men handcuffed and sitting next to each other facing the reporters. The photograph from 1923 served as an inspiration for the overall scene, but Shahn carefully painted the men's facial expressions and clothes, brought out intense colors in the room, and shifted the viewers gaze to the handcuffs, shining and clearly visible against the black background. Even if their "somber expressions" were reinforced by the setting, as art scholar Laura Katzman contends (2001: 57–58), the men were clearly represented as dignified individuals facing the public with an element of calm resolve as well as subdued anger, their features highlighted by sharply drawn facial lines, but not exaggerated to the point of caricature.

The drawing from 1952 uses the same scene but reduces its graphic structure to the essential contours and outlines of the two men; it adds, in handwritten form, the famous personal statement by Bartolomeo Vanzetti made to a journalist before his execution (fig. 2; cf. Pernicone 2001: 37). The result of this process – of this different form of repurposing the press photograph – was an image with less topical detail and individual humanity, but with an intensified and timeless, universal appeal. The two men are no longer flesh-and-blood victims of injustice put on display for a sensation-hungry public; instead, the drawing from 1952 presents them as flat, two-dimensional, yet condensed symbols of injustice with massive, hollow-eyed heads resembling death-masks more than living human beings. As Alejandro Anreus suggests, the image gives up "the rumpled individuality of the earlier likenesses for a more formal visual language, presenting Sacco and Vanzetti as members of the pantheon of victims of American injustice" (2001: 120). At the height of the Cold War, this could be seen as a statement against McCarthyism, the revisiting of an earlier historical moment to bring into sharp relief "a time of even greater division," as Louis Joughin suggested about the 1950s in "25 Years Since Sacco and Vanzetti," his article for the same issue of *The Nation* that Shahn provided the cover for (1952: 152).

Below the drawing of the two men Shahn includes, in his own handwriting, Vanzetti's statement which, in the later serigraph *The Passion of Sacco and Vanzetti* from 1958 (New Jersey State Museum), was transformed into finely crafted capital letters similar to the *Lucky Dragon* painting. Both versions retained the stylized vernacular of Vanzetti's Italian-American speech patterns, giving voice to his simple, but effective assessment of their situation:

> If it had not been for these thing, I might have live out my life talking at street corners to scorning men. I might have die, unmarked, unknown a failure. Now we are not a failure. This is our career and our triumph. Never in our full life could we hope to do such work for tolerance, for joostice, for man's onderstanding of man as now we do by accident. Our words – our lives – our pains nothing! The taking of our lives – lives of a good shoemaker and a poor fish peddler – all! That last moment belongs to us – that agony is our triumph. [sic] (fig. 2)

In Shahn's design, Vanzetti's statement serves as a final plea to the public, at the same time expressing, just as in the representation of Kuboyama, incredulity at the men's involuntary fame and acceptance, even pride, regarding their significance for the causes of tolerance and justice, and provoking the heroic stance that "agony is triumph." Shahn shifts the setting from the courtroom to an empty space which, judging from Vanzetti's final words, is to be seen as the last step on their way to the electric chair. Again, the typeface of the statement emphasizes individually drawn letters and vernacular idiosyncrasies, but the two men and their curiously shrunken bodies seem to be speaking from their graves. As in the photograph, they look toward the viewers, but like ancient

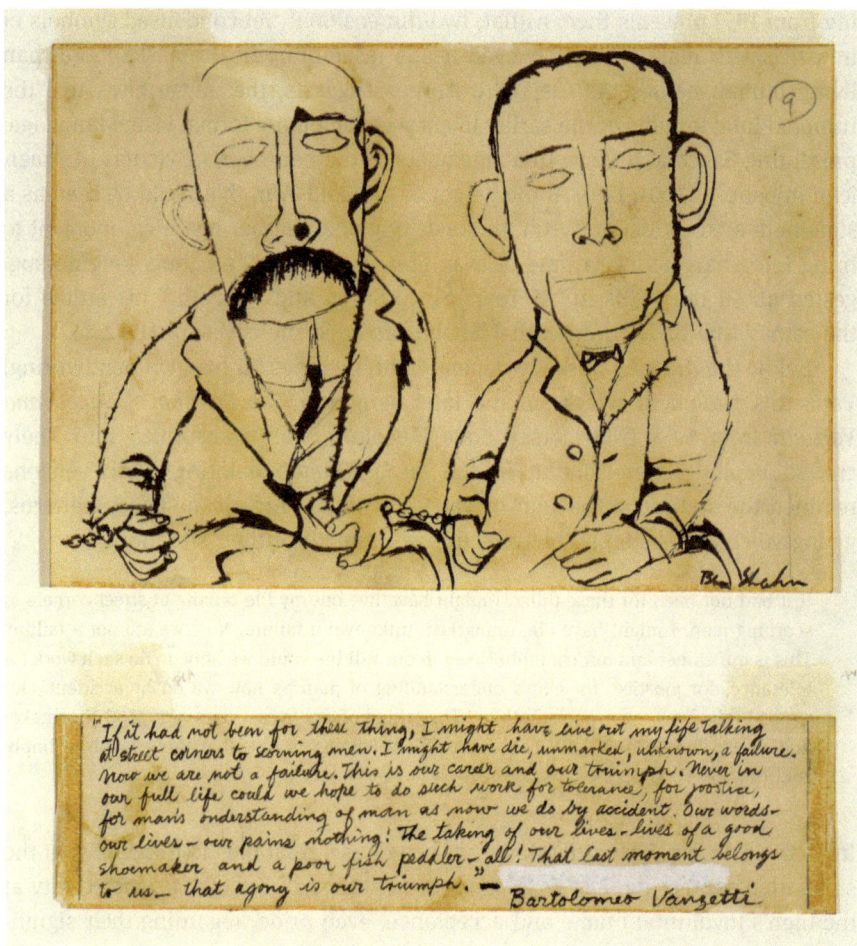

Fig. 2. Ben Shahn. *Sacco and Vanzetti: Caption*. 1952. Black ink on cream wove paper, 5.2 x 21.5 cm (2 1/16 x 8 7/16 in.). Photo: N/A. Harvard Art Museums/Fogg Museum, Gift of Meta and Paul J. Sachs. 1956.184.B. Artwork © Estate of Ben Shahn / © VG Bild-Kunst, Bonn 2020.

statues or, as Anreus writes, "ancient Greek theatrical masks" (2001: 120), the sockets of their eyes are empty, their bodies transparent.

Similar to the *Lucky Dragon* example, the combination of body image and textual inscription contrasts the anecdotal, informal tone of the brief narrative fragment with the disruptive force of a dying body put on display. Both visual anecdotes bring together the textual reference to a fateful historical incident – a secret test of atomic weapons and a politically motivated sentence of death – with an image of simple, ordinary people affected by it. Furthermore, both emphasize the act of making the anecdote's meaning public by showing the men facing the viewers and pointing their fingers, as in Kuboyama's case, directly to the message. Yet in the case of Sacco and Vanzetti, the text is longer, less descriptive than celebratory and, overall, clearly partisan. It shifts the meaning of the historical events from the trial to the execution, from the accidental circumstances of the men's lives to the universal significance of their death, ultimately helping the cause of tolerance and justice.

If, viewed from today, the vernacular style of Vanzetti's statement sounds overly stylized, it still serves as a good example of the unique universalism Shahn was aiming for. Just as he manages, in his drawing, to capture the individual features of the two men, while also showing them as timeless masks, Vanzetti's statement and his references to "man's onderstanding of man" [sic] indicate that language – and typography – establish individuality but, crucially, that their uniqueness is also relatable and translatable to others. Shahn's visual anecdotes, therefore, combine image and text in multi-layered ways. Yet in the end they postulate that individual peculiarities and their connection with universal qualities can be communicated by means of art. In this sense, revisiting the case of Sacco and Vanzetti in the early 1950s became an act of political resistance. While Joughin's text in the issue of *The Nation* from August 1952 focused on the changes in the legal system, hoping that they had improved the search for justice, Shahn's depiction on the cover memorializes Sacco and Vanzetti as martyrs in an ongoing struggle.

4 Art and Communication

Art historian Alejandro Anreus suggests that Shahn's message was not just aimed at the anticommunist crusades of the early 1950s, but equally at the "apoliticized formalism of the New York School" (2001: 120) dominating the art scene after the war. Although, as Stephen Polcari has shown, there was some overlap between Shahn's postwar work and the soon triumphant schools of abstract expressionism, Shahn made clear that he saw himself as an artist dedicated to the communicative function of art, not to what he called its expressive function dealing with subjectivity and the self (1972: 93). For the visual anecdotes discussed in this essay and their idea of a unique universalism, the communicative function was based on two premises. On the one hand, as Shahn explained in his Harvard lectures, he believed that "individual peculiarities" were the most interesting aspects about people. Since art audiences were made up of individuals, they could be addressed in ways that affirmed their uniqueness (Shahn 1957: 38–39). Universalism in Shahn's theory of reception, then, did not imply the notion of a homogenized audience; it posited that the individual peculiarities inscribed into art works were universally relatable by an audience equally made up of individuals.

On the other hand, the communicative function of Shahn's work was built on the belief in the "unifying power of art," to which he subscribed (Shahn 1957: 39). Again, as with his theory of reception, Shahn tried to establish a notion of the universal that was not based on generalities and abstract categories but included a sense of uniqueness. Although he claimed that the public was shaped and even unified by art works, his sense of unification retained, at its core, the idea of individual peculiarities and differences. As Shahn put it in his lecture: "One might say that a public may be so unified because the highly personal experience is held in common by the many individual members of the public" (ibid.). Both aspects of Shahn's aesthetic theory – an audience made up of, and responding as, individuals, on the one hand, and the power of art to unify, but also to retain the sense of the peculiar and the personal, on the other – informed his search for a unique universalism in the 1950s and shaped the combinations of text and image discussed as visual anecdotes in this essay.

At a basic level, Shahn's anecdotes express straightforward messages by putting individuals on display who had experienced accidental and contingent, but also symptomatic stories of injustice and death. Yet at the more intricate levels of their design, Shahn's visual anecdotes produce a rift between the historical temporality of their narrative fragments and the timeless quality of their figures' bodies, between the flow of the storylines and the hollow stasis of the figures' faces. With their unique combination of text and image they attest to the artistic challenge of trying to give form to the relation, or, rather, the relatability of the peculiar and the universal. If, from today's perspective, Shahn's political messages appear to be delimited by McCarthyism and the Cold War politics of the 1950s, his experimentation with image, text, and typography represents an important step in the development of visual anecdotes. Shahn's work not only confronted the paradox of giving meaning to the contingency of death, he also firmly placed his belief in the individual as irreducible object *and* subject of art, while also trying to transcend individualism for an inclusive social vision.

Shahn's idea of a unique universalism, then, may be seen as an attempt of dealing, politically and artistically, with the modern era of mass destruction by aiming for historically significant and individually grounded forms of visuality and by reinforcing, not in a naive way but rather in complex and critical terms, the hope of art as a communicative force in society.

Works Cited

Anreus, Alejandro. 2001. "Ben Shahn and The Passion of Sacco and Vanzetti." In: Alejandro Anreus (ed.). *Ben Shahn and the Passion of Sacco and Vanzetti*. Jersey City: Jersey City Museum. 110–123, 138.

Chevlowe, Susan. 1998. "A Bull in a China Shop: An Introduction to Ben Shahn." In: Susan Chevlowe (ed.). *Common Man Mythic Vision: The Paintings of Ben Shahn*. New York: Princeton University Press. 3–35.

Decker, Christof. 2019. "Fighting for a Free World: Ben Shahn and the Art of the War Poster." *American Art* 32.2: 84–105.

Fagg, John. 2004. "Anecdote and the Painting of George Bellows." *Journal of American Studies* 38.3: 473–488.

Fluck, Winfried. 2018. "Picture and Image: Another Look at *The Family of Man*." In: Gerd Hurm, Anke Reitz, and Shamoon Zamir (eds.). *The Family of Man Revisited: Photography in a Global Age*. London: Tauris. 117–131.

Irving, Washington. 1988 [1819/1820]. "Traits of Indian Character." In: *The Legend of Sleepy Hollow and Other Stories*. New York: Penguin. 225–233.

Joughin, Louis. 1952. "25 Years Since Sacco and Vanzetti." *The Nation* 23 (August): 152.

Katzman, Laura. 2001. "'Mechanical Vision': Photography and Mass Media Appropriation in Ben Shahn's Sacco and Vanzetti Series." In: Alejandro Anreus (ed.). *Ben Shahn and the Passion of Sacco and Vanzetti*. Jersey City: Jersey City Museum. 51–80, 126–135.

Lapp, Ralph E. 1958. "The Voyage of the Lucky Dragon [Part III]." *Harper's Magazine* 216 (February): 72–79.

Lapp, Ralph E. 1958. "The Voyage of the Lucky Dragon [Part II]." *Harper's Magazine* 216 (January): 48–55.

Lapp, Ralph E. 1957. "The Voyage of the Lucky Dragon [Part I]." *Harper's Magazine* 215 (December): 27–36.

Malamud, Bernard. 1999 [1964]. "The German Refugee." In: John Updike (ed.). *The Best American Short Stories of the Century*. Boston: Houghton Mifflin. 438–449.

Martin, Dwight. 1954. "First Casualties of the H-Bomb." *Life* 36.13: 17, 19, 20.

Pernicone, Nunzio. 2001. "The Sacco-Vanzetti Case: An Overview." In: Alejandro Anreus (ed.). *Ben Shahn and the Passion of Sacco and Vanzetti*. Jersey City: Jersey City Museum. 7–39, 124–125.

Pohl, Frances K. 1998. "Allegory in the Work of Ben Shahn." In: Susan Chevlowe (ed.). *Common Man Mythic Vision: The Paintings of Ben Shahn*. New York: Princeton University Press. 111–141.

Pohl, Frances K. 1989. *Ben Shahn: New Deal Artist in a Cold War Climate, 1947–1954*. Austin: University of Texas Press.

Polcari, Stephen. 1998. "Ben Shahn and Postwar American Art: Shared Visions." In: Susan Chevlowe (ed.). *Common Man Mythic Vision: The Paintings of Ben Shahn*. New York: Princeton University Press. 67–109.
Shahn, Ben. 1972 [1949]. "If I Had to Begin My Art Career Today." In: John D. Morse (ed.). *Ben Shahn*. New York: Praeger Publishers. 93–100.
Shahn, Ben. 1957. *The Shape of Content*. Cambridge: Harvard University Press.
Stefanovska, Malina. 2009. "Exemplary or Singular? The Anecdote in Historical Narrative." *SubStance* 38.1: 16–30.
Whiting, Cécile. 2016. "Ben Shahn: Aggrieved Men and Nuclear Fallout during the Cold War." *American Art* 30.3: 2–25.

Andrew S. Gross
Wallace Stevens: Anecdote and Lyric

Abstract: Wallace Stevens's "Anecdote of the Jar" tells a brief poetic story about a found object. Indeed, Stevens suggests that the found object is itself a kind of a story, providing a materialist account of art through his description of what is essentially the poetic equivalent of a ready-made. My essay holds up Stevens's materiality against standard accounts of his post-romantic sensibility in order to stress what I see as the characteristically modernist elements of his early verse. Stevens, like many modernists, is preoccupied with waste, which he collects rather than throws away. This curatorial approach to waste became difficult as Stevens grew older, both because he was faced with the challenge of curating his own discarded images and because the sheer amount of waste produced by a throw-away society was also on the rise. In this context, the anecdote appears to be a strategy for isolating images in a world overflowing with images and things, and exemplary singularity is the result of curation, rather than any uniqueness inherent in stories or objects themselves.

Keywords: Lyric, Modernism, Wallace Stevens.

1

"Anecdote of the Jar" is one of a batch of poems Wallace Stevens submitted to Harriet Monroe at *Poetry* in 1919. They appeared in the magazine under the title "Pecksniffianna" and would go on to win a five-hundred-dollar prize (Mariani 2016: 116). In his recent biography of Stevens, Paul Mariani points out that the "Pecksniffianna" reference is to "Dicken's [...] hypocritical character [Seth Pecksniff] in *Martin Chuzzlewit*": "Some people likened him to a direction-post [...] which is always telling the way to a place, and never goes there" (ibid.). With titles like "Fabliau of Florida," "Homunculus et la Belle Etoile," "The Weeping Burgher," "Exposition of the Contents of a Cab," and "Banal Sojourn," these poems, taken as a collection, suggest one of those mock signposts pointing towards several distant tourist attractions at once.

The location of "Anecdote of the Jar" at least seems clear:

> I placed a jar in Tennessee,
> And round it was, upon a hill.
> It made the slovenly wilderness
> Surround that hill.

> The wilderness rose up to it,
> And sprawled around, no longer wild.
> The jar was round upon the ground
> And tall and of a port in air.
>
> It took dominion everywhere.
> The jar was gray and bare.
> It did not give of bird or bush,
> Like nothing else in Tennessee. (Stevens 1990: 76)

Then again, the poem reveals very little about Tennessee beyond the usefulness of its three-syllable name for completing the iambic tetrameter of the opening and closing lines ("I placed a jar in Tennessee," "Like nothing else in Tennessee"). At first glance, this does not seem like much of an anecdote. The poem might offer a surreal parable of colonization, but it deliberately withholds details about place, person, and event in a way that seems to disqualify it as a source of information. Like the other poems in the batch, it points to a destination without ever seeming to go there.

In what follows, I will argue that this lack of specificity is a calculated part of Stevens's effort to transform objects, like the jar, into signposts. I will also argue that this is what Stevens means by anecdote, a term showing up repeatedly in his work, and especially in the early poems collected in *Harmonium* (1923). An anecdote, for Stevens, is a formal means of separating an object from its surroundings. Contrary to the common understanding, the Stevensian anecdote is not an informal story providing characteristic details about people, places, and events. It is also not a lyric, which typically places objects in relation to feelings through a poetic journey of self-discovery. (The "I" in the poem is as empty as the jar and the place.) The anecdote, in Stevens, is an anti-lyrical and abstract form that achieves exemplary singularity by separating objects from other objects. This perhaps counterintuitive definition of anecdote is useful for making sense of the material context of Stevens's poem, or the relation his jar has to other jars, to modernism, and ultimately, I will argue, to waste.

2

"Anecdote of the Jar" takes a deliberately humble object as its subject. Though the preceding poem in the "Pecksniffianna" sequence, "The Indigo Glass in the Grass," describes a similar container as litter, scholars have tended to emphasize the jar's relation to obsolete images over discarded objects. Helen Vendler, for instance, sees "Anecdote of the Jar" as a palinode – "a vow to stop imitating

Keats and seek a native American language that will not take the wild out of the wilderness" (1984: 46, see also 44). The jar, in this reading, is a stripped-down Grecian urn; Tennessee is a metaphor for any wild place. Unlike Keats's precious relic, the jar does not speak of truth and beauty, but organizes the American landscape in a manner at once pragmatic and banal (45). The poem thus offers a critique of romanticism by stripping a traditional image of its decoration in order to reinvest it with symbolic power. The plainness of the jar renders it personally authentic. The authenticity gives it dominion. In this lyrical account of self-expression, symbolic reduction clears the way for the poet to say something meaningful by putting him in direct relation to his provenance.

In its basic contours, this reading aligns with the interpretive framework proposed by Harold Bloom in *Wallace Stevens: The Poems of Our Climate* (1977). Though Bloom does not discuss "Anecdote of the Jar," he does place Stevens's work "in the romantic traditions – British and American – of the crisis-poem" (2). With the term "crisis," Bloom means to draw attention to the struggle between the poet and his predecessors. The emphasis is, once again, on establishing obsolescence within a poetic tradition – not on the materiality of objects. Bloom sees Stevens as one in a long line of writers (including Ralph Waldo Emerson and Walt Whitman) interested in "reducing" romantic tropes to render them adequate to real experience: "the quest for a reality principle, a moral, aesthetic, and psychological reductiveness willing to risk the ruin brought about by the destruction of illusions" (54). The risk of symbolic reduction is that if it goes too far, it leaves the poet with nothing to say. Nothing, however, turns out to be something in Stevens, as is suggested by the triple negative at the end of a poem Bloom does discuss at length, "The Snow Man" (1921): "And, nothing himself, he beholds / Nothing that is not there and the nothing that is" (Stevens 1990: 9). Bloom famously describes the ending of "The Snow Man" in this way: "The listener, reduced to nothing, remains human because he beholds something shagged and rough, barely figurative, yet still a figuration rather than a bareness. This 'nothing' is the most minimal or abstracted of fictions, and yet still it is a fiction" (1977: 63). The simple jar – empty of decoration and of content – might be read as another minimal fiction. Its plainness renders it an apt container of lyrical subjectivity.

Though the lyrical interpretation of Stevens, emphasizing subjectivity over the materiality of objects, is most strongly associated with Vendler and Bloom, it actually goes back to the earliest scholarship on Stevens. The first book-length study of Stevens's poetry, William Van O'Connor's *The Shaping Spirit*, published in 1950, also praises Stevens as a champion of the imagination who gets in touch with his world by rendering old images and forms obsolete: "In order to live really in a physical world we have to slough off the cliché forms, get rid of the habit of forcing all knowledge into neatly rational patterns and admit the transforming and ennobling power of the imagination" (30). This lyrical reading of Stevens is canonical; indeed, it is Emersonian. The transparent jar is the latest incarnation of the "transparent eye-ball," both absolutely original and a part and particle of the world around it (Emerson 1982: 39; Bloom 1977: 326). Nevertheless, when placed in a series, these celebrations of American originality do not seem original at all. They all celebrate the novelty of American poetry (the rejection of clichés) and the American scene (the wilderness) in the same, old derivative ways.

I argue that the lyrical approach to "Anecdote of the Jar" obscures the true novelty of Stevens's poetry, which is its materiality. Stevens struggled against poetic traditions, to be sure, but he was not always interested in finding a new language for authentic emotions, nor was he interested in describing what was new or authentic about Tennessee. He was traveling as a representative of the Hartford Insurance Agency when he wrote "Anecdote of the Jar" in the 1910s. He passed through Tennessee and found it dull (Mariani 2016: 94, 111). Stevens and his wife had recently moved to Hartford, which would remain their home as the poet would soon be promoted to vice president of the insurance company (95). Previously he had lived for over a decade in New York, forging connections with modernist writers like William Carlos Williams and visiting exhibitions like the Armory Show of 1913. At this stage in his career, and partly due to his experiences with modern art, Stevens was concerned with material objects – not merely with traditions and places (especially when they were dull). This is why he turns to the anecdote as a literary form, using its narrative structure to isolate objects from their surroundings. His anecdotes are "Pecksniffianna," putting up signposts rather than locating themselves in particular places. They are concerned less with lyrical authenticity or the American scene than with the materiality of things.

Edward Ragg has recognized the anecdotal quality of Stevens's earlier work, but he argues that Stevens abandoned the "spontaneous" or "unpublished quality" of the form to strive for a more permanent style based on poetic abstraction. "Anecdote was [...] the signature of Stevens' earlier poetic style," as Ragg puts it, a "quasi-impromptu aesthetic [...] an unrepeatable, 'one-off' performance" (2010: 31). According to this argument, Stevens did not want to clutter his first published book, *Harmonium* (1923), with the impromptu poems taken from magazines. He would eventually include "Anecdote of the Jar" in *Harmonium*, but in preparing the book he told Harriet Monroe that "to pick a crisp salad from the garbage of the past is no snap" (qtd. in Ragg 2010: 32). Ragg argues that eventually Stevens would achieve "crispness" by moving away from the anecdotal towards a more abstract style of writing, in effect rarifying his own images in the way Bloom and Vendler claim he purifies romantic tropes. However, it should be pointed out that Stevens continued to publish anecdotes, in *Harmonium* and later books, including "Earthly Anecdote," "The Anecdote of Canna," "Anecdote of the Prince of Peacocks," and "Anecdote of Men by the Thousand" (all in *Harmonium*). The accumulation of these poems suggests an ongoing fascination with the form, which persisted into Stevens's late phase. Anecdotes, it seems to me, are not merely spontaneous or unpublished utterances prone to wilting; they are curated objects, picked out from the trash, and isolated as representative examples. In other words, the anecdote, as a poetic form, does not render its predecessors obsolete, but signals their continued, material presence – and the presence of other forms of waste.

Stephen Greenblatt follows Clifford Geertz in calling an anecdote a "note in the bottle" (2005: 32). Unadorned and plain in style, its narrative structure is self-enclosed (like a bottle or a jar) and capable of preserving details over time.[1] This definition, more anthropological or historicist than Ragg's notion of "one-off performance," is useful for moving away from the lyrical understanding of Stevens to a notion of the poet as collector. Stevens is concerned with the message in the bottle, but also with the bottle (or jar). The result, as Robert Frost once told Stevens, is poetry full of bric-a-brac (Mariani: 210–211, 244). It is also poetry that uses bric-a-brac to think about poetry. Stated positively, we might say that the material object exerts a fascination for Stevens on par with what a carafe exercises for Gertrude Stein or a red wheelbarrow or a plate full of plums exerts for William Carlos Williams. It is telling that Williams's favorite anecdote about Stevens involves discarded objects. Once the young poet, contemplating suicide, went to the water's edge, but he was so distracted by the tidal debris that he put aside his depressing thoughts and began to write about garbage instead (O'Connor 1964: 14).

He never stopped. "Anecdote of the Jar" is a poem about materiality in a concrete sense. As Glen MacLeod, following Roy Harvey Pearce, has pointed out, the poem may describe an actual jar, the Dominion brand canning jar, which was widely distributed in the early part of the century. Initially Stevens worked in the livestock division at Hartford Insurance and dealt with farmers, so it is likely that he encountered such jars on his business trips (1993: 22–23). The Dominion jar was one of the first consumer products to display its brand name on the outside, perhaps because in a sense the product was *all* outside; consumers were supposed to fill it with contents themselves. Stevens literalizes the brand name by de-functionalizing the product, refusing to fill the

---

[1] See also von Wilpert (1989: 31).

jar with, say, preserved strawberries or stewed pears in order to make *dominion* an act of commercial imperialism that recalls the history of the "Old Dominion," a nickname for Virginia and by extension the South. (This in spite of the fact that the mason jars were and still are made in Canada.)

Another way to put this is that Stevens isolates a single jar from countless others in order to *jar* his readers with several different but overlapping stories, one about mass production, another about the history of Western expansion, and still another about avant-garde art. The strategy is similar to what Babette B. Tischleder calls "singularization" in her recent study of things in literature (2014: 25). Singularization makes the jar exemplary by transforming a mass-produced object into a readymade (MacLeod 1993: 19–20). Stevens places the jar in his poem in the same way Duchamp attempted to place his urinal in an exhibition to "critique the art-work as product and commodity" as well as the "cycle of production and consumption" (Armstrong 1998: 66). Duchamp was one of the artists Stevens knew in New York (Mariani 2016: 117; MacLeod 1993: 7–22). Glen MacLeod goes so far as to argue that Dada is a "fitting analogy for Stevens' *Harmonium* period" (1993: 24).

Emphasizing the materiality of objects in Stevens dislodges him from the romantic lyrical tradition, but places him more firmly in modernism. Tim Armstrong has demonstrated that modernists, living in the early heyday of mass production and consumption, were often preoccupied with waste. *The Waste Land* (1922) is more than a spiritual desert. It is literally full of trash, and was even more abject and cluttered before Ezra Pound edited T. S. Eliot's draft with Eliot's goal in mind: to ritually purify culture of pollution (Armstrong 1998: 69, 73). Stevens was not interested in purification, but in collecting garbage, as is suggested by the famous catalogue of discarded objects (including containers) in "The Man on the Dump" (1942). As MacLeod points out, Stevens also tended to view modern art from the perspective of a collector rather than an artist (1993: xxix). If lyricism expresses the struggles of the poet to express authentic feelings by rendering traditional images obsolete – as Vendler, Bloom, and O'Connor suggest – the anecdote is a way of curating objects in an age of abundance. In reading "Anecdote of the Jar," it is important to focus on the jar as a container of lyrical subjectivity, but also on the jar as a *container* in a world inundated with identical containers, and repurposed as art.

The remainder of my essay will analyze the link between the anecdote and the readymade in four ways. First, I will explore what the readymade has to say about the structure of the anecdote as well as the anecdote's relation to materiality. Second, I will explore what Stevens's use of anecdotes reveals about the lyricism or anti-lyricism of his poems. Third, I want to think about the role played by the anecdote in Stevens's critical reception at midcentury, when

O'Connor began to celebrate him as a lyricist and a late romantic. Finally, I will contextualize Stevens's anecdotal approach to bric-a-brac in the cultural history of garbage and think about the relation of the anecdote to waste. In focusing on the materiality of things, I do not claim that anecdotes are somehow more empirical than lyrical poetry. Anecdotes do not have to be factually true to be poetically or even historically significant. What is perhaps the most famous anecdote in American history, Parson Weems's tale about the young George Washington cutting down his father's cherry tree, is actually a lie meant to demonstrate the importance of the truth. Non-scholarly collections are quick to recognize the fabricated nature of anecdotal evidence: "So," as Philip Gooden puts it in his preface to *The Mammoth Book of Literary Anecdotes* (2002), "the criterion for selecting these anecdotes hasn't been their reliability but whether they make entertaining tales or scenes or whether they throw a bit of light on some literary figure" (x). Stevens also tells fabricated or entertaining tales through anecdotes: tales about objects that seem to take on a life of their own, just as the natural lifecycle of the commodity would condemn them to clutter.

3

First, Stevens's poem does not tell an anecdote *about* a jar, but it does transform the jar into an anecdote. The readymade is the anecdote of material culture, abstracting an object from a series to make it exemplary (MacLeod 1993: 19–20). As John Scanlan points out in his analysis of Duchamp, the readymade "reverse[s] the conventional trajectory of manufactured objects (value to garbage) by reconstituting them in disguise" (2005: 95). Scanlan sees the disguise (garbage masquerading as art) as a commentary on the art world and artistic creation as such (96–97). I would argue that the disguise is more of a multidirectional signpost. The readymade crosses an object firmly embedded in one symbolic system, in this case mass production, with another symbolic system such as poetry or art, in order to tell a story about both systems. This definition is reversible: an anecdote occurs when two symbolic systems cross at the level of an object, experience, or place. The empirical grounding, or point of intersection, is important, but it is more an occasion than a cause. My central claim is that anecdotes are often more about the message *of* the bottle than the message contained *in* it. Another way to put this is that anecdotes are signposts that do not go anywhere because they are so firmly embedded in the coordinate systems that make directions meaningful.

Stevens makes this point strongly in a poem that stages the confrontation between lyrical and anecdotal modes of representation without mentioning the word "anecdote." I am thinking of "The Idea of Order at Key West" (1936), which is often celebrated as a restatement of William Wordsworth's "The Solitary Reaper" (1807) in the same way "Anecdote of the Jar" is taken to be a palinode to John Keats's "Ode on a Grecian Urn" (1819). A solitary singer mimics the sound of the sea with her voice, but in doing so she becomes its source: "She was the single artificer of the world / In which she sang. And when she sang, the sea, / Whatever self it had, became the self / That was her song, for she was the maker" (Stevens 1990: 129). The strength of her song seems to testify to the power of lyrical imagination. However, her song is also a prelude to a different account of meaning elaborated in the final two stanzas. The speaker asks a third-party observer why the lights on fishing boats map the sea in a visual, rather than strictly song-like or lyrical, coordinate system: "tell why the glassy lights, / The lights in the fishing boats at anchor there, / [...] / Mastered the night and portioned out the sea, / Fixing emblazoned zones and fiery poles" (130). Each point of light is a boat, and each boat might as well be a jar, fixed in but also constituting the coordinates that give it meaning. In the end, the lyrical exploration of the power of song gives way to an anecdotal account of how objects embody structures of meaning that extend through and beyond them. The cartographic perspective, in this sense, is a more distant form of (data) collection, voiced by an observer too far away to distinguish individual objects, but cognizant of the way the objects make up a system.

Stevens celebrates the materiality of objects in much of his work, sometimes at the expense of interiority, sometimes by mapping the contents of consciousness onto its material containers, and always by approaching objects as directional signs or parts of coordinate systems. The lyrical self has to pick its way through an accumulation of things – and not always as a means of finding its way back to itself. In "Anecdote of Canna" (1923), the lyrical subject is reduced to the algebraic figure X, and his thoughts "cling" to the flowers on his terrace, which prove more powerful than his dreams (Stevens 1990: 55). "Anecdote of the Prince of Peacocks" (1923) follows a similar pattern by setting "traps / In the midst of dreams," and forcing the dreamer to recognize the materiality of objects populating the oneiric landscape: "the blue ground / Was full of blocks / and blocking steel" (58). Much more explicitly than in "The Idea of Order at Key West" (1936), these anecdotal poems reduce the lyrical subject in order to focus on the material object, which becomes a signpost of meanings that have little to do with the subject's dreams or goals.

The abstract quality of these anecdotes might seem strange or even untimely. Contemporary scholars seem to turn to the anecdote in the hopes of finding a fixed place to stand in an age of language games and post-factual fabrications. Earlier, I mentioned Greenblatt's analogy between an anecdote and a message in a bottle. It occurs in an essay called "The Touch of the Real" (1997), which attempts to explain the anecdote's "stronger claim to reference" (2005: 32). "Touch of the Real" was a touchstone essay for the new historicism. Originally published in *Representations* in 1997, a journal launched by Greenblatt and like-minded colleagues in 1983 and the principle platform for disseminating and consolidating new historical positions, the essay was then reprinted as the programmatic opening essay in *Practicing New Historicism*, which Greenblatt coauthored with Catherine Gallagher in 2000. Despite the essay's concern with reference, Greenblatt does not see the anecdote as factual in any simple way, but rather as offering a glimpse into a broader social world (35). He invokes many guides here, including Gilbert Ryle and Clifford Geertz, but he spends the most time with Erich Auerbach, whose book *Mimesis* (1946) in some ways sets a trap for the unwary in the same way Greenblatt's title does, seeming to promise empirical fidelity through resemblance. However, Auerbach, like Greenblatt, is less concerned with how stories imitate the world than with how fragments of stories – details or anecdotes – evoke culturally specific representational systems (36). The pattern for this is the *figura*, which encodes two representational structures – the temporal and the timeless – in one experience, object, or event (Auerbach 2015: 75). An anecdote is a secularized version of the *figura* insofar as it simultaneously encodes two historical temporalities, the antique and the contemporary, or the mass-produced and the poetic. Important enough to be recorded in former times and significant enough to be repeated now, the anecdote is occasioned by an object or event – say Stevens regarding the garbage at the water's edge – but it registers the intersection of two structures of meaning: the debris of yesteryear and the collectibles of today.

It is widely assumed that Stevens sought refuge in his imagination as he aged. This is another version of the lyrical struggle between inadequate objects and authentic emotions – perhaps its final, terminal stage. There are reasons given for his alleged flight from reality, though some of them – like his job at Hartford Insurance – seem unconvincing. I will return to that in a moment. What I want to point out here is that the poetry suggests a more complicated story. Stevens did not turn away from reality, but he did turn towards his own habitual objects and images; at times his massive collection threatened to overcome him with clutter.

I take as an example his late poem "An Ordinary Evening in New Haven" (1950), which Bloom sees as a victorious expression of the power of the imagination and Vendler sees as a resigned recognition of the inadequacy of objects (Bloom 1977: 324–25; Vendler 1984: 78–79). Stevens composed the poem during his walks to and from work in Hartford, but read it at an event in the city named in the title, about forty miles away. This was in 1950, the same year Stevens won the Bollingen Award (awarded for 1949) and the year that O'Connor's book-length study, *The Shaping Spirit*, was first published. A number of awards would follow in the next five years, which were also the last years of Stevens's life: two National Book Awards, the Frost Medal, a Pulitzer, and several honorary degrees, including an honorary doctorate at Yale. This is significant because one of the characters in this poem, Professor Eucalyptus, is a worshipper of the real who presumably teaches at Yale (Stevens 1990: 481). Stevens distinguishes his "ephebe" or poet from this professor and also frees him from the empiricism he calls the "journalism of subjects" (474). The ephebe seeks to compose "[t]he poem of pure reality," but to do so he has to describe "the metaphysical streets of the physical town" and focus on the "total double thing" (471, 472). The "double thing" in "The Idea of Order at Key West" (1936) is the woman who invents the sea by imitating it; in the more anecdotal poetry it is the isolated object or readymade. In "An Ordinary Evening in New Haven" (1950), the scenery is double because the poet encounters images from his own poems next to objects in the street. Thus, as he describes "the consolations of space" (482), he also alludes to "The Man with the Blue Guitar" (1937), "The Comedian as the Letter C" (1923), "Sunday Morning" (1923), and also "The Anecdote of the Jar" (published in *Poetry* 1919, in *Harmonium* 1923). By 1950, the jar has been broken to pieces: "A porcelain, as yet the bats thereof" (467).

As Mariani points out, Stevens shatters the jar – now made of porcelain like Duchamp's "Fountain" – in order to scatter its fragments throughout his poem (2016: 336). The result is a poem that is no longer about containers and no longer contains a material object, but *is* the material object, albeit in a fragmented form. The two temporalities or structures of meaning of the readymade/anecdote – often coded as the old and the new, but in this case coded as reality and imagination – no longer intersect in objects but run parallel to and entwine with each other throughout. The result is a peripatetic poem composed like a stream-of-consciousness narrative, blending images and objects into a sometimes indistinguishable blur. The poem, rather than the object or image, becomes its own occasion: "The poem is the cry of its occasion / part of the res itself and not about it" (Stevens 1990: 473). The effect is neither anecdotal nor lyrical. This poem resists interpretation, as Stevens said good poetry must do, almost successfully (Mariani 2016: 116; O'Connor 1964: 119). In a sense, Stevens has moved from the techniques of high modernism to the linguistic analogy of color fields in abstract expressionism (MacLeod 1993: 148–149, 157). Contrary to Bloom and Vendler, the poem does not side with or flee from either imagination or reality. It is cluttered with objects both mental and material, and searches for a method to impose a pattern on the overwhelming quantity of things. Stevens's work experience might have come into play here. Joseph Harrington suggests that the insurance actuarial table is a model for Stevens's mature work: "From the point of view of the insurance business, each instance can be abstracted into an actuarial table and a uniform premium affixed" (1995: 107–108). There are an extraordinary number of instances or "cases" in "An Ordinary Evening in New Haven" (1950), but they can no longer be separated from other instances or integrated into a lyrical account of personal growth.

The problem of clutter brings me to my third point. Stevens's poetry becomes cluttered with images and objects at the very moment he gains recognition as a poet. Insofar as his late technique is abstract, it is as much a part of the midcentury moment as, say, a Mark Rothko painting in a Bauhaus-inspired corporate headquarters. Nevertheless, the scholars and institutions who began to recognize him also *misrecognized* his mainstreaming in a fundamental way. O'Connor, for instance, argues that Stevens "[i]n his own person [...] dramatizes the opposition between the world of business and the alienated artist. In his poetry, the careful craftsmanship of the symbolists, who most strongly opposed the values of the bourgeois world, finds its best American expression" (1964: 21). It is astonishing that O'Connor could claim to find an anti-business orientation in the work of a poet who actually turned down an honorary poetry professorship at Harvard because he thought he might have to retire from the insurance company to accept it – and this while he was in his seventies! Nevertheless, there is a final lesson about the anecdote in this extremely powerful misreading of Stevens's lyrical significance. Stevens is turned into an anecdote for modernism just as the anecdote goes to pieces in his poetry. His contemporaries saw him as occupying the moment where the symbolic systems of business and poetry intersected, but only in order to be firmly segregated from each other. As I have already argued, the occasion of an anecdote does not have to be factual to reveal something real. Here Stevens, as anecdote, reveals the ideological position of modernist poetry at midcentury. As the Cold War elevated the lyric into a symbol of liberal freedom, poetry was meant to represent the superiority of the American way of life by being different from it (Gross 2015: 1–41). Stevens was honored for being singular, private, and lyrical while modernism was going mainstream (19–20).

The mainstreaming of modernism was linked in significant ways to the expansion of the consumer economy. It is no accident that the work of a poet obsessed with litter would become cluttered in 1950. This is the moment in the history of consumer culture when a lifestyle characterized by what Susan Strasser calls "the stewardship of objects" gave way to landfills overflowing with disposable commodities (1999: 21, 161). Stevens's "The Man on the Dump" (1942) is often seen as one of the first garbage poems; Christopher Todd Anderson argues that such poems "exist[...] on the border between the natural and the artificial and, by extension, between human culture and wild nature" (2010: 35). However, in terms of waste disposal, the catalogue of interesting objects in this early poem merely anticipates what was to come. Anderson points out that "several garbage poems appeared during the economic boom of postwar America, for the underside of that era's prosperity was the rampant wastefulness of an emerging throwaway society" (41). With this historical development in mind, I would point to "An Ordinary Evening in New Haven" (1950) as Stevens's quintessential garbage poem. Unlike "The Man on the Dump" (1942), it does not revel in bric-a-brac, but struggles against a flood of accumulating clutter.

Stevens turned to the anecdote to salvage debris from the rubbish heap. In doing so, he drew attention to intersecting structures of meaning, for instance the lifecycle of the commodity and the longevity of art, that make an object meaningful beyond its intended use. However, the transition from an economy of scarcity to an economy of abundance makes it difficult to pick out particular objects. When the anecdote shatters on sheer plenitude, it is hard to isolate the singular example from overproduction, and the anecdote loses its exemplary status and becomes a garbage poem. By this, I do not mean a worthless poem or an ecological poem or even a modernist poem in the sense of *The Waste Land* (1922). The garbage poem is a new literary form in which subjects and objects, imagination and reality, form a substratum where it is difficult to distinguish the usable from waste. This is the moment when scholars like O'Connor pick out Stevens himself as collectible object, or as an anecdote of individuality, stressing the lyrical aspects of his writing. Stevens the lyricist becomes an anecdote, but Stevens the anecdotalist provides insight into the material aspects of writing, its institutional context, and its relation to things.

Works Cited

Abrams, M.H. 1965. "The Greater Romantic Lyric." In: F. Hilles and H. Bloom (eds.). *From Sensibility to Romanticism*. New York: Oxford University Press. 76–108.
Anderson, Christopher Todd. 2010. "Sacred Waste: Ecology, Spirit, and the American Garbage Poem." *Interdisciplinary Studies in Literature and Environment* 17.1: 35–60.
Armstrong, Tim. 1998. *Modernism, Technology, and the Body*. Cambridge: Cambridge University Press.
Auerbach, Erich. 2015 [1946]. *Mimesis. Dargestellte Wirklichkeit in der abendländischen Literatur*. Tübingen: A. Francke Verlag.
Bloom, Harold. 1977. *Wallace Stevens: The Poems of Our Climate*. Ithaca: Cornell University Press.
Eliot, T.S. 2013 [1922]. *The Waste Land*. New York: Liveright.

Emerson, Ralph Waldo. 1982 [1836]. "Nature." In: Larzer Ziff (ed.). *Selected Essays*. New York: Penguin. 35–82.

Gooden, Philip. 2002. "Introduction." In: Philip Gooden (ed.). *The Mammoth Book of Literary Anecdotes*. New York: Carroll & Graff. ix–x.

Greenblatt, Stephen. 2005 [1997]. "The Touch of the Real." In: Michael Payne (ed.). *The Greenblatt Reader*. Malden: Blackwell. 30–50.

Gross, Andrew S. 2015. *The Pound Reaction: Liberalism and Lyricism in Midcentury American Literature*. Heidelberg: Universitätsverlag Winter.

Harrington, Joseph. 1995. "Wallace Stevens and the Poetics of National Insurance." *American Literature* 67.1: 95–114.

Keats, John. 2001. *Complete Poems and Selected Letters of John Keats*. New York: Modern Library.

MacLeod, Glen. 1993. *Wallace Stevens and Modern Art: From the Armory Show to Abstract Expressionism*. New Haven: Yale University Press.

Mariani, Paul. 2016. *The Whole Harmonium: The Life of Wallace Stevens*. New York: Simon & Schuster.

O'Connor, William Van. 1964 [1950]. *The Shaping Spirit: A Study of Wallace Stevens*. New York: Russell & Russell, Inc.

Ragg, Edward. 2010. *Wallace Stevens and the Aesthetics of Abstraction*. Cambridge: Cambridge University Press.

Scanlan, John. 2005. *On Garbage*. London: Reaktion Books.

Stevens, Wallace. 1990. *The Collected Poems*. New York: Vintage.

Strasser, Susan. 1999. *Waste and Want: A Social History of Trash*. New York: Metropolitan/Henry Holt and Co.

Tischleder, Babette Bärbel. 2014. *The Literary Life of Things*. Frankfurt am Main: Campus Verlag.

Vendler, Helen. 1984. *Wallace Stevens: Words Chosen Out of Desire*. Knoxville: University of Tennessee Press.

von Wilpert, Gero. 1989. *Sachwörterbuch der Literatur*. 7th ed. Stuttgart: Alfred Kröner Verlag.

Wordsworth, William. 1952 [1807]. *Poems in Two Volumes*. Ed. Helen Darbishire. Oxford: Clarendon Press.

CODA

Anselm Haverkamp
Philosophy and Anecdote: Hegel's "Lehrer Löffler"

Abstract: Hegel's school teacher bequeathed Shakespeare's works to the eight-year-old student and thus initiated the later philosopher's theory of history. Hegel's student Karl Rosenkranz in turn relates the origin of his teacher's theory as an anecdote of his teacher's teacher – philosophy as a matter of learning from learning (technically speaking, a Hegelian *reflective mechanism*).

Keywords: Biography, Hegel, Learning, Reading, Shakespeare.

Hegel's first biographer as well as one of his best-known students, Karl Rosenkranz, begins his portrait of the philosopher with an anecdote: Hegel's school teacher Löffler (no first name known) had given to his talented student, the eight-year-old Hegel, Wieland's (at the time) new translation of Shakespeare's works; he would not understand them yet, but learn to understand them soon ("Du verstehst sie jetzt noch nicht, aber du wirst sie bald verstehen lernen" [Rosenkranz 1844: 7]).[1] The prediction proved true and the recommendation valid: Hegel's philosophy did develop by learning how to read Shakespeare. Not only the conventional pillars of instruction, Greek tragedy and the Church fathers, were formative in Hegel's education (all of classical literature, Greek and Latin, in fact), but so was their modern antipode Shakespeare – a commonplace illustrated by *Wilhelm Meister's Apprenticeship* (1795), the educational novel par excellence and still part of the agenda in Joyce's portrait of a young man in *Ulysses* (1922).

Compared to Shakespeare's general notoriety, established by Herder and Wieland (in England by Pope, Young, and Dr. Johnson), Hegel's interest in Shakespeare seems unremarkable and remained in fact unremarked. Philosophers are less and less able to identify unmarked references and not interested in literary allusion. Philological Shakespeare studies, on the other hand, are even less capable to read a philosopher's use of their bard beyond the bard's natural talent to depict "the Human" (Harold Bloom's notorious subtitle of his

---

[1] Cited from Hegel's brief school diary 1785–1787. Looking back in 1785, after the beloved preceptor's untimely death, the young Hegel acknowledges and includes in his mourning remembrance the gift of "eight volumes Shakespeare already in 1778" (Rosenkranz 1844: 434; my translation); Löffler's verbatim recommendation is Rosenkranz's well-meaning interpretation.

book on Shakespeare). Philosophical reflections in American criticism are often coincidences of a generalized Hegelianism (or Hegelian Marxism). As far as Shakespeare is concerned, they have a *fundamentum in re:* Hegel writing with Shakespeare on the side. Hegel knew the Wieland translation early on, read (some) Shakespeare in the original, and later on also used the Schlegel-Tieck translation of the next generation together with Schlegel's, Solger's, and Tieck's essays on Shakespeare. The philological difficulty which remains is a question of method. The conceptual impact of literary texts on philosophy cannot be limited to explicit references, verbatim quotes, or statements, whose literary, in this case dramatic, *mise en scène* is at stake – philosophically at stake. Or, as Hegel would have put it: *in der Sache selbst.*

Anecdotes have a point, and since Rosenkranz's is closely tied to the literary pretexts of Hegel's philosophical development, the point seems of a limited reach. Rather than adding to Hegel's picture a curiously fashionable accent, the story is meant to compensate some flaws, which ask for an explanation in a genius like Hegel's career. Since this is indeed Rosenkranz's problem, the crux he has to master and does indeed master with the Shakespeare anecdote, revealing thereby an interesting aspect of Shakespeare after *Wilhelm Meister,* is the improbability of the modern philosopher as genius. It is not that Hegel had read Aristotle or Kant as an eight-year-old boy, or that he excelled in mathematics like Pascal or Leibniz. The celebrated philosopher of history had read Shakespeare for a start. Hegel was no prodigy in his profession, but an amiable young student and a friendly, unassuming professor later on, about whom the biographer had to confess that all who knew him in his younger years were utterly surprised to hear of the fame in his later years. The only consistency Rosenkranz elaborates in his presentation of the biographical sources, as if it was the cunning of reason itself, is the parallel development of Hegel as a philosopher and lover. Notoriously shy in his way with women – gifted with an unusual respect for the *fairer sex*, but without success in courting the admired ones – Hegel married late, as a surprise almost, and it was a *beau* marriage in the most substantial sense, which characterized his life and philosophy throughout. Thus, why and in what respect Shakespeare?

Rosenkranz states the case of his admired teacher with utmost care and cleverness; it is the case of the exemplary philosopher of enlightened times in a bourgeois society. As an institution of dialectical self-understanding, the theater provides – asks for and supports – the public consciousness of enlightened subjects. In *The Phenomenology of Mind* (1807), which has been also translated as one *of Spirit*, Shakespeare does not simply mirror the world-historical process of the Enlightenment. He does not just illustrate this process, but the stage is the medium of what came to happen through it. It is not easy, but philologically difficult, to prove this point of Rosenkranz's anecdote. And precisely this is the merit of an anecdote: to point out within the context of a life – a life's text – the vicissitudes that would otherwise escape, since they are beyond the biographer's means. Which does not mean that they would escape his mind. Ominously, Rosenkranz carried, and was certainly conscious of it, a name from *Hamlet* – an involvement of the author in his anecdote that would need an anecdote of his own.

Works Cited

Bloom, Harold. 1989. *Shakespeare: The Invention of the Human*. New York: Riverhead Books.

Hegel, Georg Wilhelm Friedrich. 2018 [1807]. *The Phenomenology of Spirit*. *Trans*. Terry Pinkard. Cambridge: Cambridge University Press.

Rosenkranz, Karl. 1844. *Georg Wilhelm Friedrich Hegels Leben: Supplement zu Hegels Werken*. Berlin: Duncker & Humblot.

Barbara Vinken
"Fleurs de Paris"

Abstract: The Eiffel Tower was first perceived as a monstrous Babylonian tower, which disfigured the incomparable beauty of Paris, city of cities. A lot of reinterpretation, and some serious work on myth, was needed to transform it into a new Notre Dame de Paris. The gothic cathedrals had, in their turn, been recast by the writers of the nineteenth century as Babylonian. Nowadays, thanks to this work of translation and rereading, the Eiffel Tower is a new protecting Notre Dame at whose feet the city gathers. She signifies a coming home, and a coming into her own once the Germans were driven out of the city and Paris was free again.

Keywords: Eiffel Tower, Guy de Maupassant, Paris, Roland Barthes, *translatio Babylonis*.

Guy de Maupassant, the story goes, used to lunch at a restaurant on the first platform of the Eiffel Tower – in spite of thoroughly disliking the cuisine. When asked why he did this, he answered that this was the only place in Paris from where one could not see the Eiffel Tower.

Maupassant was part of a group of artists, who were passionately in love with the beauty of Paris, the most beautiful city of the world, but protested vehemently against the construction of the Eiffel Tower: she was a disfiguring ink blotch, a monstrous erection in the very heart of an otherwise perfect city, a stain on a spotless beauty:

> We come, we writers, painters, sculptors, architects, lovers of the beauty of Paris which was until now intact, to protest with all our strength and all our indignation, in the name of the underestimated taste of the French, in the name of French art and history under threat, against the erection in the very heart of our capital, of the useless and monstrous Eiffel Tower which popular ill-feeling, so often an arbiter of good sense and justice, has already christened the Tower of Babel. ("Protest")

When realizing that the Eiffel Tower was not of the *maux passant*, but had become unavoidable and literally flooded the whole of Paris, an exasperated Maupassant left France:

> I left Paris, and France, too, on account of the Eiffel Tower. It could not only be seen everywhere, but it could be found everywhere, made of every kind of known material, exhibited in all the windows, an ever-present and racking nightmare. [...] I should like to know what

would be thought of our generation if some riot does not soon make this high and lanky pyramid of iron ladders crumble [...] But then I prefer the old idea of the ancient architects, of making again the naïve attempt of the Tower of Babel, just as those of the Campanile of Pisa did in the twelfth century. (1922: 1–2)

Babel was in the air when the Eiffel Tower, reaching with her peak 322 meters into the sky, was built. Paris, capital of the nineteenth century – to invoke Walter Benjamin – interpreted herself, city of art and letters, as a new Rome. The writers, realists and naturalists alike, condemned Paris as a Rome that turned out to be another Babel. In Gustave Flaubert's *Madame Bovary* (1856), Rouen is explicitly named a new Babel; his *L'Éducation sentimentale* (1869) depicts the Paris of the 1848 Revolution until the coup d'état of 1851 as a new Babel. Émile Zola presents the Paris of the Second Empire as a *translatio Romae* and reveals it as a *translatio Babylonis*. In these novels, the Paris of the second half of the nineteenth century, the Paris of high capitalism, industrialization, colonization, and financial speculation is denounced as a decadent city under a tyrannical, despotic rule, a city where everybody fights for themselves and God against all, a city of corruption where prostitution and idolatry are the background metaphors for the social bond. What should have stood against Babel, her very antitype, the Church and its most visible expression, the cathedrals with their gothic towers, were stigmatized as the reincarnation of Babel. The towers of Our Lady had turned into monuments of an unholy alliance of throne and altar, signs of the corrupted reign of Church and State.

It was Maupassant, who most pointedly recoded the cathedral tower as Babylonian. His *Bel-Ami*, the bestselling French novel of all times, was published in 1885, shortly before the construction of the Eiffel Tower. An iron tower of 151.5 meters was put on Notre Dame de l'Assomption in Maupassant's (and Flaubert's) home town, Rouen, in 1877. Until 1880, when the twin towers of Cologne's cathedral were finished, this was the highest of the world.

In the novel, the iron cast tower of the Rouen cathedral darts its pointed arrow in monstrous ugliness into the sky, despotically towering above everything around it. Maupassant condensates two Babylonian myths in one; he describes the contemporary Rouen lasciviously spread out in the Seine valley like the Whore of Babylon of the Apocalypse, and he alludes to the myth of Nimrod and his tower. In his description, industrial capital and church are united in their superb splendor, their excessive, monstrous, autocratic, brutally subjecting tyranny. In the Occident, the Orient triumphs with the tower of Babel and the Pyramids of Cheops. Again, the great hunter Nimrod, founder of Babel and builder of its tower, shoots his arrow into the sky in blasphemous revolt against the heavens, this time from the tower of Rouen.

Roland Barthes redeemed the Eiffel Tower from the Babylonian curse and turned her into a new Notre Dame de Paris who unites the city in protecting love. She, *la tour Eiffel*, unites the city by an *absolute sign* of a liberty that even the darkest chapters in the history of Paris could not take away. Barthes writes in 1964, twenty years after the liberation of Paris, at a time when the Eiffel Tower had become a symbol of resistance to the German occupation. The tower is like a woman, a mother who watches over Paris. The monstrosity of Babylon is explicitly refuted by Barthes. As the faithful gather under the coat of the Madonna, so the Parisians gather at the feet of the Eiffel Tower:

> The Tower is a human silhouette; it may be headless, except for a fine spire, and armless (though it is way beyond the monstrous), but it is still a long bust perched on two widely parted legs; what's more, it is this figure that gives it its tutelary function: the Tower is a woman watching over Paris, holding Paris gathered at her feet; both seated and standing, she inspects and protects, surveys and shields. (2012: 131)

For Barthes, the characteristic features of gothic architecture, as we find them in Notre Dame de Paris, but more so in the flamboyant gothic of Notre Dame de Rouen, are perfected in the iron construction of *la tour Eiffel*. The lofty tower elevates herself lightly into the sky. Her effortless airiness has nothing of the colossal, the gigantic, the oversized of the tower of Babel and its monstrous successors. Weightless, she seems to float, as if levitating, to the heavens that open up to her. In her magic ascension, she is the opposite of the monumental, sweaty, menacing force confronting the heavens. In Barthes's writing, the Eiffel Tower has shed all earthiness, the heavy, stony weight that characterizes the tower of Babel like the pyramids. This soaring tower seems to be made in heaven; there is no material bulkiness, she is but an elegant slim line uniting base and peak, heaven and earth, bound to finally get lost in the skies. She unites the Parisians looking at her and unites the city of Paris looked at from her. Eiffel had worked the iron as skillfully as the gothic masons had treated the stone, Barthes points out. The hardest, heaviest material is turned into lofty lace: "the Tower is a piece of iron lace – latticework – and this theme is reminiscent of the convoluted hollowing out of stone that has always been seen as the hallmark of the gothic: here, once again, the Tower takes over from the cathedral" (131).

The lacework overcomes material heaviness, turns light and air into her material, there to adorn. The open-worked stone, the open-worked iron is meant to show the air, to be flooded by light. This magical transformation from heavy, low iron into a deliciously wrought arabesque, this metamorphosis from tower to plant, iron to flower, transforms the whole building into an ornament. The cosmic order is not blown apart by this tower, but is prodigiously adorned. The tower turns into a blossoming flower: "we rise through it as if we were rising through a flower made of air and iron: in it are to be found the straightness of filaments, the arabesque of petals, the tight thrust of buds, the spreading of leaves and the very movement that pulls this complex and ordered matter upwards" (Barthes 2012: 131). This assurgent iron air-flower calls to mind the magnificent, glorious blossoming of the delicate gothic rosette of the Virgin. The Eiffel Tower is a translucent flower of the air, not a flower of evil, but a rose without thorns or, to put it with Maurice Chevalier in "Fleur de Paris" (1944): "Fleur de chez nous […] fleur du retour."

Works Cited

"An extract from the 'Protest against the Tower of Monsieur Eiffel,' 1887." *toureiffel.paris*, not dated; no pg. <www.toureiffel.paris/en/the-monument/history> [accessed February 3, 2019].

Barthes, Roland. 2012. "The Eiffel Tower." *AA Files* 64: 112–131.

Chevalier, Maurice. 1944. "Fleur de Paris." *paroles.net*, no pg. <www.paroles.net/maurice-chevalier/paroles-fleur-de-paris.> [accessed February 3, 2019].

Maupassant, Guy de. 1922 [1911]. *La Vie errante and other stories*. Trans. Albert M. C. McMaster et al. New York: J. H. Sears.

Maupassant, Guy de. 1885. *Bel-Ami*. Paris: Ollendorf.

List of Contributors

Friedrich Teja Bach is a Professor Emeritus at Universität Wien whose work focuses on modern and contemporary art, perspective studies, primitivism, and early Mediterranean civilizations. He has also taught at the Humboldt-Universität zu Berlin, Harvard University, and Princeton University. His publications include *Öffnungen: Zur Theorie und Geschichte der Zeichnung* (2009) and *Shaping the Beginning: Modern Artists and the Ancient Eastern Mediterranean* (2006) as well as monographs on the sculptures of Constantin Brancusi and the graphic art of Albrecht Dürer.

Hendrik Birus founded the Institute for General and Comparative Literature at Ludwig-Maximilians-Universität München in 1988 and has been vice-president of the Bavarian Academy of Science since 2017. He has served as dean of Jacobs University Bremen and taught as a visiting professor at several prestigious universities in Europe and the US; he was named a Fellow at the Wissenschaftskolleg (Institute for Advanced Study) of Berlin 1995–1996. A renowned Goethe scholar and editor, his most recent publications include *Goethes Zeitschrift* "Ueber Kunst und Alterthum". *Von den "Rhein- und Mayn-Gegenden" zur Weltliteratur* (2016) and *Aufgegebene Werke: Goethe:* "Wilhelm Meisters theatralische Sendung" – *Joyce:* "Stephen Hero" – *Proust:* "Jean Santeuil". *Ein komparatistischer Versuch* (2018).

Helmbrecht Breinig is Professor Emeritus of American Studies at Friedrich-Alexander-Universität Erlangen-Nürnberg and the founding director of the Bavarian American Academy in Munich. He has also taught at the Universities of Freiburg, Mannheim, Bamberg, Frankfurt am Main, and UC Berkeley. He has published widely in the fields of nineteenth- and twentieth-century American fiction and poetry, intercultural and inter-American studies, Native American literature, human-animal studies, and cultural theory. His latest monograph is *Hemispheric Imaginations: North American Fictions of Latin America* (2016). He is also a literary translator.

Thomas Claviez is Professor for Literary Theory at Universität Bern, Switzerland. He has previously taught at Universitetet i Stavanger, Norway as well as at the University of Bielefeld. He has written and edited studies on, among others, pragmatism, otherness, ecology, American literature, and American Studies. Most recently, he co-edited, with Kornelia Imesch and Britta Sweers, the collection *Critique of Authenticity* (2019). Currently, he is preparing the publication of two volumes: the monograph *The Metonymic Society: Toward a Poetics of Contingency* and the edition *Throwing the Moral Dice: Ethics and Contingency*.

Christof Decker is Professor of American Studies at Ludwig-Maximilians-Universität München whose research encompasses film, media, and visual culture studies, nineteenth- and twentieth-century American literature and culture, and media aesthetics. His most recent publication is *Transnational Mediations: Negotiating Popular Culture between Europe and the United States* (2015, co-edited with Astrid Böger). Recent essays have considered Ben Shahn and the art of the war poster as well as love and politics in the cinema of the 1930s and 1940s.

Susanne von Falkenhausen is an art historian, art critic, and Professor Emerita at Humboldt-Universität zu Berlin where she taught Recent Art History with a concentration on modern art and visual culture until 2016. Her prolific research work has addressed, among other topics, the relations between art, architecture, and power since the French Revolution; theories and practices of representation; and rhetoric and media encoding models in post-1945 art. *Beyond the Mirror: Seeing in Art History and Visual Culture Studies*, her latest monograph, was published in 2020.

Andrew Gross is Professor of American Literature at Georg-August-Universität Göttingen. Publications include a monograph entitled *The Pound Reaction: Liberalism and Lyricism in Midcentury American Literature* (2015), the coauthored *Comedy, Avant-Garde, Scandal: Remembering the Holocaust after the End of History* (with Susanne Rohr, 2010), the co-edited *Pathos of Authenticity* (with Ulla Haselstein and MaryAnn Snyder-Körber, 2010); and guest-edited issues of *Amerikastudien* and the *American Studies Journal*. A co-edited volume on *Surveillance/Society/Culture* (with Florian Zappe) was published in 2020. He is currently pursuing projects on Thomas Paine's relation to populism and Hannah Arendt's relationships with two poets in New York.

Anselm Haverkamp is Professor Emeritus at New York University and Europa-Universität Viadrina as well as Honorary Professor of Philosophy at Ludwig-Maximilians-Universität München. He is internationally renowned for his writings on aesthetics, rhetoric, and literary theory. His most recent books include *Shakespearean Genealogies of Power: A Whispering of Nothing in* Hamlet, Richard II, Julius Caesar, Macbeth, The Merchant of Venice, and The Winter's Tale (2011); *Productive Digression: Theorizing Practice* (2017); *Metapher – Mythos – Halbzeug. Metaphorologie nach Blumenberg* (2018); *Klopstock/Milton – Teleskopie der Moderne* (2018); *Fernahnend. Hölderlin und Keats* (2020); and *Latenz. Zur Genese des Ästhetischen* (2020).

Heinz Ickstadt is Professor Emeritus of American Literature at the John F. Kennedy Institute for North American Studies, Freie Universität Berlin. His research and publications have focused on the history of the twentieth-century American novel, late nineteenth-century US literature and culture, modernist and postmodernist American fiction and poetry, and American Studies theory and history. His most recent publication is the collection *Aesthetic Innovation and the Democratic Principle: Essays on Twentieth Century American Poetry and Fiction* (2016). He was president of the German Association of American Studies and of the European Association of American Studies.

Frank Kelleter is Chair of the Department of Culture and Einstein Professor of North American Cultural History at the John F. Kennedy Institute for North American Studies, Freie Universität Berlin. His main fields of interest include the American Enlightenment, and American media and popular culture since the nineteenth century. His most recent publications include *Projecting American Studies: Essays on Theory, Method, and Practice* (ed. with Alexander Starre, 2018); *Media of Serial Narrative* (ed., 2017); *David Bowie* (2016); *Serial Agencies:* The Wire *and Its Readers* (2014); and *Populäre Serialität. Narration – Evolution – Distinktion* (ed., 2012).

List of Contributors — **305**

Verena O. Lobsien is Professor of English Literature at Humboldt-Universität zu Berlin. Her research interests include early modern literature and culture, Shakespeare, the reception and transformation of antiquity, poetics and aesthetics, and the theory of the imagination. She is the author of *Subjektivität als Dialog. Philosophische Dimension der Fiktion* (1994); *Skeptische Phantasie. Eine andere Geschichte der frühneuzeitlichen Literatur* (1999); *Transparency and Dissimulation: Configurations of Neoplatonism in Early Modern Literature* (2010); *Jenseitsästhetik. Literarische Orte letzter Dinge* (2012); *Shakespeares Exzess. Sympathie und Ökonomie* (2015); and, with Eckhard Lobsien, *Die unsichtbare Imagination. Literarisches Denken im 16. Jahrhundert* (2003). At present she is writing a book on sympathy.

Andreas Mahler is Professor of English Literature at Freie Universität Berlin. His research focuses on early modern epistemology, plot-making on the early modern stage, Elizabethan satire, early modern genres, and London as an early modern center. His publications include the monograph *Moderne Satireforschung und elisabethanische Verssatire* (1992) as well as the edited collections *Komödie. Etappen ihrer Geschichte von der Antike bis heute* (2013), *Handbuch Literatur & Raum* (2015), and *Gangsterwelten. Faszination und Funktion des Gangsters im französischen Nachkriegskino* (2017).

Bettine Menke is Professor for General and Comparative Literature at Universität Erfurt and a renowned international Walter Benjamin scholar. She has also taught at Universität Konstanz, Europa-Universität Viadrina Frankfurt (Oder), Goethe-Universität Frankfurt (Main), and Philipps-Universität Marburg as well as at the University of California, Santa Barbara. Additionally, she has held fellowships at IKKM Bauhaus Universität Weimar, Kulturwissenschaftliches Kolleg Universität Konstanz, IFK Wien, and Alfried Krupp Wissenschaftskolleg Greifswald. Her recent publications include the co-edited volumes *Flucht und Szene. Perspektiven und Formen eines Theaters der Fliehenden* (2018) and *Experimentalanordnungen der Bildung. Exteriorität – Theatralität – Literarizität* (2014). Most recently, she has published essays on the importance of gesture and citability for a conception of theater as critical praxis as well as on the techniques and operations Jean Paul performs on excerpts.

Inka Mülder-Bach is Professor Emerita of German and Comparative Literature at Ludwig-Maximilians-Universität München. She has also taught at Freie Universität Berlin, Columbia University, Heinrich-Heine-Universität Düsseldorf, and New York University. In 2012 she became a Permanent Visiting Professor at Princeton University. She is chief editor of the *Werke* of Siegfried Kracauer and co-editor of the journal *POETICA*. Her most recent publications include the monograph *Der Mann ohne Eigenschaften. Ein Versuch über den Roman* (2013) and the co-edited volumes *Was der Fall ist. Casus und Lapsus* (with Michael Ott, 2015) and *Prosa schreiben. Literatur – Geschichte – Recht* (with Jens Kersten and Martin Zimmermann, 2019).

Ralph J. Poole is Professor of American Studies at Universität Salzburg. He has also taught at Ludwig-Maximilians-Universität München and at Fatih University in Istanbul. His publications include *US American Expressions of Utopian and Dystopian Visions* (ed. with Saskia Fürst and Yvonne Kaisinger, 2017) and *Austria and America: 20th-Century Cross-Cultural Encounters* (ed. with Joshua Parker, 2017). His research interests range from gender and feminist theory and LGBTIQ and masculinity studies to transnational and comparative American Studies. His current projects are "Remember the Ladies: Gender and Comedy in the Age of American Revolution" and "Rugged Rocks, Gentle Men: Hollywood's Influence on the Austrian *Heimatfilm*."

Gerhard Regn is Professor Emeritus of Italian Philology at Ludwig-Maximilians-Universität München. He has also taught at Freie Universität Berlin. Further, he has been a member of the Bavarian Academy of Science since 2005 and a Commander of the Italian Republic since 2007. His areas of expertise include late medieval and early modern Italian literature as well as the relations between life sciences and nineteenth- and twentieth-century French and Italian literature. He coauthored *Lyriktheorie(n) in der italienischen Renaissance* in 2012 (with Bernhard Huss and Florian Mehltretter) and has most recently published essays on ekphrastic tradition and Aristotelian mimesis in Tasso as well as on textual margins as an index of epochal change in Boccaccio's *Decameron*.

Gabriele M. Schwab is Distinguished Professor in Comparative Literature, Anthropology, English, and European Languages and Studies at the University of California, Irvine. Her key publications include *Subjects Without Selves: Transitional Texts in Modern Fiction* (1994); *The Mirror and the Killer-Queen: Otherness in Literary Language* (1996); *Haunting Legacies: Violent Histories and Transgenerational Trauma* (2010); and *Imaginary Ethnographies: Literature, Culture, Subjectivity* (2012). Her most recent monograph is *Radioactive Ghosts* (2020). She is currently preparing *Beckett in the End Times* for publication and is working on a new book on *Transspecies Imaginaries*.

Winfried Siemerling is University Research Chair and Professor of English at the University of Waterloo and Associate of the W. E. B. Du Bois Institute at Harvard University. He has also taught at the John F. Kennedy Institute, Freie Universität Berlin and at Université de Sherbrooke, Québec. His work addresses issues of recognition in North American and Hemispheric Studies, postcoloniality, and race. His books include the co-edited volume *Canada and Its Americas: Transnational Navigations* (with Sarah Phillips Casteel, 2010) and the award-winning monograph *The Black Atlantic Reconsidered: Black Canadian Writing, Cultural History, and the Presence of the Past* (2015). He was elected to the Royal Society of Canada in 2019.

Barbara Vinken is Professor of French Literature and Literary Theory at Ludwig-Maximilians-Universität München. She previously held the chairs of French and Comparative Literature in Hamburg and Zurich. As a visiting professor, she has taught at the École des Hautes Études en Sciences Sociales, Paris, at New York University, Humboldt-Universität zu Berlin, and Johns Hopkins University. Important publications include *Fashion Zeitgeist. Trends and Cycles in the Fashion System* (2005); *Flaubert Postsecular: Modernity Crossed Out* (2009); *Bestien. Kleist und die Deutschen* (2011); *Angezogen. Das Geheimnis der Mode* (2013); *Die Blumen der Mode – Klassische und neue Texte zur Philosophie der Mode* (2016); and *Gustave Flaubert*, Trois contes. Nouvelle édition critique avec trois essais (2020).